Rick Steves'
GERMANY, AUSTRIA & SWITZERLAND
2001

Other ATP travel guidebooks by Rick Steves
Rick Steves' Europe Through the Back Door
Rick Steves' Europe 101: History and Art for the Traveler
   (with Gene Openshaw)
Rick Steves' Mona Winks: Self-Guided Tours of Europe's Top Museums
   (with Gene Openshaw)
Rick Steves' Postcards from Europe
Rick Steves' Best of Europe
Rick Steves' France, Belgium & the Netherlands (with Steve Smith)
Rick Steves' Great Britain & Ireland
Rick Steves' Italy
Rick Steves' Scandinavia
Rick Steves' Spain & Portugal
Rick Steves' London (with Gene Openshaw)
Rick Steves' Paris (with Steve Smith and Gene Openshaw)
Rick Steves' Rome (with Gene Openshaw)
Rick Steves' Phrase Books: German, French, Italian, Spanish/Portuguese,
   and French/German/Italian

Thanks to my hardworking team at Europe Through the Back Door; the readers who shared experiences from their travels; the Europeans who make travel such a good living; and, most of all, to my wife, Anne, for her support.

Avalon Travel Publishing, 5855 Beaudry Street, Emeryville, CA 94608

For the latest on Rick's lectures, guidebooks, tours, and public television series, contact Europe Through the Back Door, Box 2009, Edmonds, WA 98020, tel. 425/771-8303, fax 425/771-0833, www.ricksteves.com, or e-mail: rick@ricksteves.com.

ISBN 1-56691-233-4
ISSN 1085-7222

Europe Through the Back Door Editors Risa Laib, Jacquie Maupin
Avalon Travel Publishing Editor Kate Willis
Copy Editor Donna Leverenz
Research Assistance Brent A. Hurd
Production & Typesetting Kathleen Sparkes, White Hart Design
Design Linda Braun
Cover Design Janine Lehmann
Maps David C. Hoerlein
Printer Publishers Press
Cover Photo Neuschwanstein Castle, Bavaria, Germany;
   copyright © Blaine Harrington III

Distributed to the book trade by
Publishers Group West
Berkeley, California

CONTENTS

Top Destinations in Germany, Austria, and Switzerland

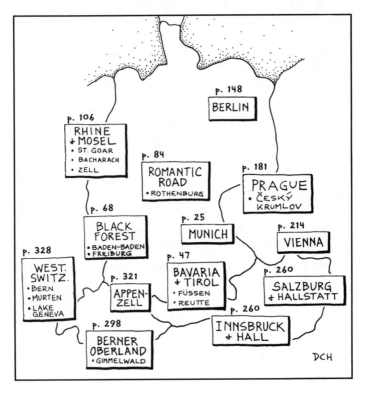

p. 148
BERLIN

p. 106
RHINE & MOSEL
• ST. GOAR
• BACHARACH
• ZELL

p. 84
ROMANTIC ROAD
• ROTHENBURG

p. 181
PRAGUE
• ČESKÝ KRUMLOV

p. 68
BLACK FOREST
• BADEN-BADEN
• FREIBURG

p. 25
MUNICH

p. 214
VIENNA

p. 328
WEST. SWITZ.
• BERN
• MURTEN
• LAKE GENEVA

p. 321
APPEN-ZELL

p. 47
BAVARIA & TIROL
• FÜSSEN
• REUTTE

p. 260
SALZBURG & HALLSTATT

p. 298
BERNER OBERLAND
• GIMMELWALD

p. 260
INNSBRUCK & HALL

DCH

INTRODUCTION

This book breaks Germany, Austria, and Switzerland into their top big-city, small-town, and rural destinations. It then gives you all the information and opinions necessary to wring the maximum value out of your limited time and money in each of these destinations. If you plan a month or less in this region, this lean and mean little book is all you need.

Experiencing this region's culture, people, and natural wonders economically and hassle free has been my goal for 25 years of traveling, tour guiding, and travel writing. With this book, I pass on to you the lessons I've learned, updated for 2001.

Rick Steves' Germany, Austria & Switzerland is your friendly Franconian, your German in a jam, a tour guide in your pocket. The book includes a balance of cities and villages, mountaintop hikes and forgotten Roman ruins, sleepy river cruises and sky-high gondola rides. It covers the predictable biggies and mixes in a healthy dose of Back Door intimacy. And to spice things up I've added Prague, the liveliest city in Eastern Europe, and the quaint little Czech town of Český Krumlov.

Along with visiting Rhine castles, Mozart's house, and the Vienna Opera, you'll ride a thrilling Austrian mountain luge, soak in a Black Forest mineral spa, share a beer with Bavarian monks, and ramble through traffic-free Swiss Alpine towns. I've been selective, including only the most exciting sights. For example, it's redundant to visit both the Matterhorn and the Jungfrau. I take you up and around the better of the two.

The best is, of course, only my opinion. But after more than two busy decades of travel writing, lecturing, and tour guiding, I've developed a sixth sense for what stokes the traveler's wanderlust. Just thinking about the places featured in this book makes me want to slap dance and yodel.

This Information Is Accurate and Up-to-Date

This book is updated every year. Most publishers of guidebooks that cover a country from top to bottom can afford an update only every two or three years (and even then, it's often by letter). Since this book is selective, covering only the top destinations in Germany, Austria, and Switzerland, I am able to personally update it each year. Even with an annual update, things change. But if you're traveling with the current edition of this book, I guarantee you're using the most up-to-date information available (for the latest see www.ricksteves.com/update). Use this year's edition. You'd be crazy to save a few bucks by traveling on old information. If you're packing an old book, you'll understand the gravity of your mistake...in Europe. Your trip costs about $10 per waking hour. Your time is valuable. This guidebook saves lots of time.

Planning Your Trip

This book is organized by destination. Each destination is covered as a mini-vacation on its own, filled with exciting sights and homey, affordable places to stay. In each chapter you'll find:

Planning Your Time, a suggested schedule with thoughts on how to best use your limited time.

Orientation, including tourist information, city transportation, and an easy-to-read map designed to make the text clear and your arrival smooth.

Sights with ratings: ▲▲▲—Worth getting up early and skipping breakfast for; ▲▲—Worth getting up early for; ▲—Worth seeing if it's convenient; No rating—Worth knowing about.

Sleeping and Eating, with addresses and phone numbers of my favorite budget hotels and restaurants.

Transportation Connections, including train information and route tips for drivers, with recommended roadside attractions along the way.

The **Appendix** is a traveler's tool kit, with a climate chart, telephone tips, rail routes, and German survival phrases.

Browse through this book, choose your favorite destinations, and link them up. Then have a great trip! You'll travel like a temporary local, getting the absolute most out of every mile, minute, and dollar. You won't waste time on mediocre sights because, unlike other guidebook authors, I cover only the best. Since lousy, expensive hotels are a major financial pitfall, I've worked hard to assemble the best accommodations values for each stop. As you travel the route I know and love, I'm happy you'll be meeting some of my favorite Europeans.

Trip Costs

Five components make up your trip cost: airfare, surface transportation, room and board, sightseeing/entertainment, and shopping/miscellany.

Airfare: Don't try to sort through the mess. Get and use a good travel agent. A basic round-trip United States-to-Frankfurt flight should cost $600 to $1,000, depending on where you fly from and when. Always consider saving time and money in Europe by flying "open jaw" (flying into one city and out of another).

Surface Transportation: For a three-week whirlwind trip of all my recommended destinations, allow $650 per person for public transportation (train pass and buses) or $600 per person (based on 2 people sharing the car) for a three-week car rental, parking, gas, and insurance. Car rental is cheapest when reserved from the United States. Train passes are normally available only outside of Europe. You may save money by simply buying tickets as you go (see "Transportation," below).

Room and Board: You can thrive in this region on $70 a

day per person for room and board. A $70-a-day budget per person allows $10 for lunch, $15 for dinner, and $45 for lodging (based on 2 people splitting the cost of a $90 double room that includes breakfast). That's doable. Students and tightwads do it on $40 a day ($20 per bed, $20 for meals and snacks). But budget sleeping and eating requires the skills and information covered later in this chapter (and in much more depth in my book *Rick Steves' Europe Through the Back Door*).

Sightseeing and Entertainment: In big cities, figure $5 to $10 per major sight, $3 for minor ones, $30 to $40 for bus tours and splurge experiences (e.g., concert tickets, Alpine lifts, conducting the beer-hall band). An overall average of $20 a day works for most. Don't skimp here. After all, this category directly powers most of the experiences all the other expenses are designed to make possible.

Shopping and Miscellany: Figure $1 per postcard and $2 per coffee, beer, and ice-cream cone. Shopping can vary in cost from nearly nothing to a small fortune. Good budget travelers find that this category has little to do with assembling a trip full of lifelong and wonderful memories.

Approximate Exchange Rates

I've priced things throughout this book in local currencies.

---

1 Deutsche Mark (DM) = 50 cents, and 2 DM = $1.
1 Austrian schilling (AS) = 7 cents, and 15 AS = $1.
1 Swiss franc (SF) = 60 cents, and 1.70 SF = $1.
1 Czech koruna (kč) = 3 cents, and 38 kč = $1.

To convert prices into dollars, divide prices in Deutsche Marks by half (e.g., 37 DM = about $18). To roughly convert prices in Swiss francs, divide by half (e.g., 60 SF = $30, actually $36) or, more precisely, multiply by six and drop the last digit (e.g., 60 SF: 60 x 6 = 360, or $36). For Austrian schillings, drop the last zero and subtract one-third (e.g., 300 AS = about $20, actually $21). Drop the last zero off Czech prices and divide by three. So, that 40-DM cuckoo clock is about $20, the 15-SF lunch is about $9, the 450-AS concert in Vienna is about $30, and the 2,000-kč taxi ride through Prague is . . . uh-oh.

Euro: The euro, adopted as a currency by 11 countries in Europe, won't concern you until 2002, when it materializes into actual bills and coins. For a preview, Germany and Austria will switch to euros. Switzerland and the Czech Republic, which aren't members of the European Union or Euroland, will hang on to their currencies.

Prices, Times, and Discounts

The prices in this book, as well as the hours and telephone numbers, are accurate as of late 2000. Europe is always changing, and I know you'll understand that this, like any other guidebook, starts to yellow even before it's printed.

In Europe—and throughout this book—you'll be using the 24-hour clock. After 12:00 noon, keep going—13:00, 14:00, etc. For anything over 12, subtract 12 and add p.m. (14:00 is 2:00 p.m.)

This book lists peak-season hours for sightseeing attractions. Off-season, roughly October through April, expect generally shorter hours, longer lunchtime breaks, and fewer activities. Confirm your sightseeing plans locally, especially when traveling between October and April.

While discounts for sightseeing and transportation are not listed in this book, seniors (60 and over), students (only with International Student Identity Cards), and youths (under 18) often get discounts—but only by asking.

When to Go

Summer (peak season) has its advantages: best weather, snow-free Alpine trails, very long days (light until after 21:00), and the busiest schedule of tourist fun.

In "shoulder season"—May, June, September, and early October—travelers enjoy fewer crowds, milder weather, plenty of harvest and wine festivals, and the ability to grab a room almost whenever and wherever they like.

Winter travelers find concert seasons in full swing, with absolutely no tourist crowds, but some accommodations and sights are either closed or run on a limited schedule. The weather can be cold and dreary, and nighttime will draw the shades on your sightseeing before dinnertime. You may find the climate chart in the appendix helpful. Pack warm clothing for the Alps no matter when you go.

Sightseeing Priorities

Depending on the length of your trip, here are my recommended priorities.

3 days:	Munich, Bavaria, Salzburg
5 days, add:	Romantic Road, Rhine castles
7 days, add:	Rothenburg, slow down
10 days, add:	Berner Oberland (Swiss Alps)
14 days, add:	Vienna, Hallstatt
17 days, add:	Bern, Danube Valley, Tirol (Reutte)
21 days, add:	West Switzerland, Baden-Baden, Mosel Valley, Köln
24 days, add:	Berlin, Appenzell
30 days, add:	Black Forest, Prague, and slow down

(The map on page 6 and the three-week itinerary on page 7 include everything in the top 30 days except Berlin and Prague.)

Prague: Prague is a major detour, both culturally (Slavic rather than Germanic) and geographically (about 6 hours one-way by train from Berlin, Frankfurt, Munich, or Vienna). But I have never met anyone fresh from a visit to Prague who didn't rave about the city. You have all the information you need for two or three days in Prague in this book. If you have the time, go.

Red Tape and Banking

Currently you need a passport, but no visa and no shots, to travel in Europe (including Prague). Even as borders fade, when you change countries, you still change money, telephone cards, postage stamps, and *Unterhosen.*

Bring your ATM, credit, or debit card, along with some traveler's checks in dollars as a backup. The best and easiest way to get cash is to use the omnipresent bank machines (always open, low fees, quick processing); you'll need a four-digit PIN (numbers only, no letters) with your Visa or MasterCard. Some ATM bankcards will work at some banks, though Visa and MasterCard are more reliable. Before you go, verify with your bank that your card will work. Bring two cards; demagnetization seems to be a common problem. The word for cash machine in German is *Bankomat.*

Regular banks have the best rates for cashing traveler's checks, but many German banks now charge 5 DM (about $3) per check cashed, so rather than cashing five $100 checks, cash one $500 check. For a large exchange, it pays to compare rates and fees. Post offices (business hours) and train stations (long hours) usually change money if you can't get to a bank.

Just like at home, credit (or debit) cards work easily at larger hotels, restaurants, and shops, but smaller businesses prefer payment in local currency.

Germany: Banks are generally open Monday through Friday from 8:00 to noon and from 14:00 to 16:00.

Austria: Bank hours are roughly Monday through Friday from 8:00 to 15:00 and until 17:30 on Thursday. Austrian banks charge exorbitant commissions to cash traveler's checks (about $8). Bring plastic. As a backup, carry American Express checks and cash them at American Express offices (no commission).

Switzerland: Bank hours are typically Monday through Friday from 8:00 to 17:00.

Czech Republic: Banks are open every day except Saturday and Sunday from 9:00 to 17:00.

Travel Smart

Upon arrival in a new town, lay the groundwork for a smooth departure. Reread this book as you travel, and visit local tourist

Germany, Austria, and Switzerland Best Three-Week Trip

Day	Plan	Sleep in
1	Arrive in Frankfurt	Rothenburg
2	Rothenburg	Rothenburg
3	Romantic Road to the Tirol	Reutte
4	Bavaria and castle day	Reutte
5	Reutte to Munich	Munich
6	Munich	Munich
7	Salzburg	Salzburg
8	Salzkammergut Lakes District	Hallstatt
9	Mauthausen, Danube to Vienna	Vienna
10	Vienna	Vienna
11	Vienna to the Tirol	Hall
12	Tirol to Swiss Appenzell	Ebenalp
13	Appenzell to Berner Oberland	Gimmelwald
14	Free day in the Alps, hike	Gimmelwald
15	Bern, west to French Switzerland	Murten
16	French Switzerland	Murten
17	Murten to Black Forest	Staufen
18	Black Forest	Baden-Baden
19	Baden-Baden, relax, soak	Baden-Baden
20	Drive to the Rhine, castles	Bacharach
21	The Mosel Valley, Burg Eltz	Bacharach/Zell
22	Köln and Bonn, night train to Berlin, or fly home	

Note: While this itinerary is designed to be done by car, with minor modifications it works by train. For the best three weeks by train, sleep in Füssen rather than Reutte, sleep on the train from Vienna to the Swiss Alps (skipping Hall and Appenzell), skip French Switzerland, skip the Black Forest, and add two days in Berlin, connecting it by night trains.

information offices. Buy a phone card and use it for reservations and confirmations. Enjoy the hospitality of the Germanic people. Ask questions. Most locals are eager to point you in their idea of the right direction. Wear your money belt, pack along a pocket-size notebook to organize your thoughts, and practice the virtue of simplicity. Those who expect to travel smart, do. Plan ahead for banking, laundry, post office chores, and picnics. To maximize rootedness, minimize one-night stands. Mix intense and relaxed

Best Three-Week Trip

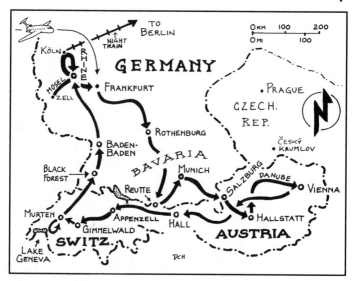

periods. Every trip (and every traveler) needs at least a few slack days. Pace yourself. Assume you will return.

As you read through this book, note special days (festivals, colorful market days, and days when sights are closed). Saturday morning feels like any bustling weekday morning, but at lunchtime, many shops close down through Sunday. Sundays have pros and cons, as they do for travelers in the United States (special events, limited hours, shops and banks closed, limited public transportation, no rush hours). Popular places are even more popular on weekends. Many sights are closed on Monday.

Tourist Information

The tourist information office is your best first stop in any new city. Try to arrive, or at least telephone, before it closes. In this book I'll refer to a tourist information office as a TI. Throughout Germany, Austria, and Switzerland, you'll find TIs are usually well organized with English-speaking staff.

As national budgets tighten, many TIs have been privatized. This means they become sales agents for big tours and hotels and their "information" becomes unavoidably colored. While TIs are eager to book you a room, you should use their room-finding service only as a last resort. TIs can as easily book you a bad room as a good one—they are not allowed to give hard opinions on the relative value of one place over another. The accommodations stakes are too high to go potluck through the TI. And with the listings in this book, there's no need to do so.

Tourist Offices, U.S. Addresses

Each country's national tourist office in the United States is a wealth of information. Before your trip, get their free general information packet and request any specifics you may want (such as regional and city maps and festival schedules).

German National Tourist Office: 122 E. 42nd St., 52nd floor, New York, NY 10168, tel. 212/661-7200, fax 212/661-7174, www.germany-tourism.de, e-mail: gntony@aol.com. Maps, Rhine schedules, events, city and regional information.

Austrian National Tourist Office: Box 1142, New York, NY 10108-1142, tel. 212/944-6880, fax 212/730-4568, www.experienceaustria.com, e-mail: info@oewnyc.com. Ask for their "Vacation Kit" with map. Fine hikes and Vienna material.

Swiss National Tourist Offices: Call nearest office: New York, tel. 212/757-5944, fax 914/682-9093; Chicago, tel. 312/332-9900; San Francisco, tel. 415/362-2260; Los Angeles, tel. 310/640-8900. Or write to 608 Fifth Ave., New York, NY 10020; www.myswitzerland.com, e-mail: info.usa@ switzerlandtourism.ch. Comprehensive "Welcome to the Best of Switzerland" brochure, great maps, and hiking material.

Czech Tourist Authority: 1109 Madison Ave., New York, NY 10028, tel. 212/288-0830, fax 212/288-0971, www.czechcenter.com, e-mail: travelczech@pop.net. To get a weighty information package, send a check for $3.20 to cover postage and specify places of interest. Basic information and map are free.

Recommended Guidebooks

You may want some supplemental information if you'll be traveling beyond my recommended destinations. When you consider the improvements they'll make in your $3,000 vacation, $25 or $35 for extra maps and books is money well spent. Especially for several people traveling by car, the weight and expense are negligible.

Students, backpackers, and those interested in the night scene should consider either the hip Rough Guides (British researchers, more insightful but not updated annually) or the Let's Go guides (by Harvard students, better hotel listings, updated annually). Lonely Planet's Germany, Austria, and Switzerland guides are well researched and mature. The popular, skinny, green Michelin Guides to Germany, Austria, and Switzerland are excellent, especially if you're driving. They're known for their city and sightseeing maps, dry but concise and helpful information on all major sights, and good cultural and historical background. English editions are sold locally at gas stations and tourist shops.

For background reading, consider *Germany and the*

Germans (by John Ardagh), *La Place de la Concorde Suisse* (by John McPhee, about Switzerland, in English), and *A Tramp Abroad* (by Mark Twain).

Rick Steves' Books and Videos

Rick Steves' Europe Through the Back Door 2001 gives you budget travel tips on minimizing jet lag, packing light, planning your itinerary, traveling by car or train, finding budget beds without reservations, changing money, avoiding rip-offs, outsmarting thieves, hurdling the language barrier, staying healthy, taking great photographs, using your bidet, and much more. The book also includes chapters on my 35 favorite "Back Doors," five of which are in Germany, Austria, Switzerland, and the Czech Republic.

Rick Steves' Country Guides are a series of seven guidebooks—including this book—covering Europe, Britain/Ireland, France/Belgium/Netherlands, Italy, Spain/Portugal, and Scandinavia. All are updated annually and come out in December.

My **City Guides** for London, Paris, and Rome (annually updated and available in January) give you all you'll need to make your trip a success: in-depth information on the sights, hotels, restaurants, and nightlife in these grand cities along with illustrated tours of their great museums.

Europe 101: History and Art for the Traveler (with Gene Openshaw, 2000) gives you the story of Europe's people, history, and art. Written for smart people who were sleeping in their history and art classes before they knew they were going to Europe, *101* really helps Europe's sights come alive.

Rick Steves' Mona Winks (with Gene Openshaw, 1998) gives you fun, easy-to-follow, self-guided tours of Europe's top 20 museums in London, Paris, Madrid, Amsterdam, Venice, Florence, and Rome.

Rick Steves' German Phrase Book (1999) is a fun, practical tool for independent budget travelers. This handy book has everything from beer-hall vocabulary, to a menu decoder, to sample telephone conversations for making hotel reservations.

My television series, *Travels in Europe with Rick Steves*, includes 11 half-hour shows on Germany, Austria, and Switzerland (two shows are on the Swiss and Austrian Alps and Prague). A brand-new series, called *Rick Steves' Europe*, airs in 2001 with 16 shows, including one on Germany's Black Forest and Baden-Baden. All 52 of the earlier shows run throughout the United States on public television stations and on the Travel Channel. The shows are also available as information-packed videotapes, along with my two-hour slideshow lecture on Germany, Austria, and Switzerland (call us at 425/771-8303 for our free newsletter/catalog).

Rick Steves' Postcards from Europe (1999), my autobiographical book, packs 25 years of travel anecdotes and insights into the ultimate 3,000-mile European adventure. Through my guidebooks, I share my favorite European discoveries with you. *Postcards* (much of which is set in Germany and Switzerland) introduces you to my favorite European friends.

All of my books are published by Avalon Travel Publishing (www.travelmatters.com).

Maps

The maps in this book, drawn by Dave Hoerlein, are concise and simple. Dave, who is well traveled in Germany, Austria, and Switzerland, has designed the maps to help you locate recommended places and get to the tourist offices, where you can pick up a more in-depth map (usually free) of the city or region. For an overall map of Europe, consider my new Rick Steves' Europe Planning Map—geared to travelers' needs—with sightseeing destinations listed prominently (for our free newsletter/catalog, contact us at 425/771-8303 or www.ricksteves.com).

European bookstores, especially in tourist areas, have good selections of maps. For drivers, I'd recommend a 1:200,000- or 1:300,000-scale map for each country. Train travelers usually manage fine with the freebies they get with their train pass and from the local tourist offices.

Tours of Germany, Austria, and Switzerland

Travel agents can tell you about all the normal tours, but they won't tell you about ours. At Europe Through the Back Door we offer 16-day tours of Germany, Austria, and Switzerland that feature most of the all-stars covered in this book (departures May–Sept, 26 people on a big roomy bus with 2 great guides). For details, call 425/771-8303 or see www.ricksteves.com.

Transportation

By Car or Train?

The train is best for single travelers, those who'll be spending more time in big cities, and those who don't want to drive in Europe. While a car gives you the ultimate in mobility and freedom, enables you to search for hotels more easily, and carries your bags for you, the train zips you effortlessly from city to city, usually dropping you in the center and near the tourist office. Cars are great in the countryside but a worthless headache in places like Munich, Prague, and Vienna.

Trains

The trains are punctual and cover cities well, but frustrating schedules make a few out-of-the-way recommendations (such

Major Train Lines

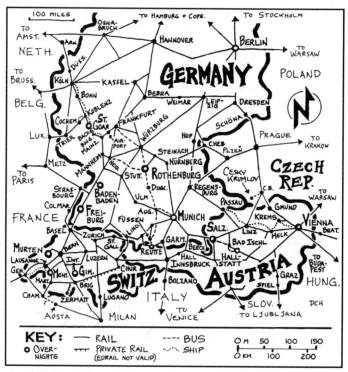

KEY:
- ○ OVER-NIGHTS
- —— RAIL
- ┬┬┬ PRIVATE RAIL (EURAIL NOT VALID)
- ---- BUS
- ⋯⋯ SHIP

0 M 50 100 150
0 KM 100 200

as the concentration camp at Mauthausen) not worth the time and trouble for the less determined. For timetables, visit http://bahn .hafas.de/english.html.

The most economical railpass for a focused tour of this region is the new Eurail Selectpass for $476, which gives you 10 travel days (within a two-month period) in three adjacent countries—such as Germany, Austria, and Switzerland. Other possibilities include a five-country Europass with an Austria add-on, or a 17-country Eurailpass (if you're doing a whirlwind trip of Europe). All of these passes give a 15 percent discount to two or more companions traveling together.

Each country has its own individual train passes. Patchworking several second-class country passes together (for example, a 10-day-in-a-month German railpass, a 3-days-in-15 Austrian pass, and a 8-day Swiss pass) is only about $100 less than a 21-day Eurailpass that covers first-class travel in 17 countries ($718). You can purchase Eurailpasses from your travel agent or Europe

GERMAN RAILPASS (2000)

	1st cl	1st twin	2nd cl	2nd twin	2nd youth*
4 days in a month	$252	$189	$174	$131	$138
Add-on days (6 max)	32	24	22	16.50	6-18

"Twin" pass prices are per person for 2 traveling together. Third person pays full fare. Covers Rhine and Mosel boats, 75% off Romantic Road bus ride. Kids 6-11 half of full fare.

2001 EURAIL SELECTPASSES

This pass covers travel in three adjacent countries. For details, visit www.ricksteves.com/rail or see *Rick Steves' Guide to European Railpasses* (see note below).

	1st class Selectpass	1st class Saverpass	2nd class Youthpass
5 days in 2 months	$328	$280	$230
6 days in 2 months	360	306	252
8 days in 2 months	420	358	294
10 days in 2 months	476	406	334

Saverpass prices are per person for 2 or more people traveling together. Prices subject to change.

Adjoining countries: These countries are connected by covered trains or ferries: **Austria**: to Germany, Hungary, Italy, Switzerland. **Benelux area**: to France, Germany, Ireland. **Denmark**: to Germany, Norway, Sweden. **Finland**: to Germany, Sweden. **France**: to Benelux, Germany, Ireland, Italy, Spain, Switzerland. **Germany**: to Austria, Benelux, Denmark, Finland, France, Sweden, Switzerland. **Greece**: to Italy. **Hungary**: to Austria. **Ireland**: to Benelux, France. **Italy**: to Austria, France, Greece, Switzerland. **Norway**: to Denmark, Sweden. **Portugal**: to Spain. **Spain**: to France, Portugal. **Sweden**: to Denmark, Finland, Germany, Norway. **Switzerland**: to Austria, France, Germany, Italy.

Germany:
Map shows approximate point-to-point one-way 2nd-class rail fares in $US.

2001 EURAILPASSES

	1st class Eurailpass	1st class Saverpass	2nd class Youthpass*
10 days in 2 months flexi	$654	$556	$458
15 days in 2 months flexi	862	732	599
15 consecutive days	554	470	388
21 consecutive days	718	610	499
1 month consec. days	890	756	623
2 months consec. days	1260	1072	882
3 months consec. days	1558	1324	1089

Eurailpasses Countries

Austria	Italy
Belgium	Luxembourg
Denmark	Netherlands
Finland	Norway
France	Portugal
Germany	Spain
Greece	Sweden
Hungary	Switzerland
Ireland	

These passes cover all 17 Eurail countries. Saverpass prices are per person for 2 or more traveling together.

Note: For a free copy of Rick Steves' Guide to European Railpasses, call us at 425/771-8303 or visit www.ricksteves.com/rail (you can order most passes online).

My free *Rick Steves' Guide to European Railpasses* has the latest on 2001 prices. To get the railpass guide, call us at 425/771-8303 or visit www.ricksteves.com/rail (you can order most passes online).

SWISS PASS AND SWISS FLEXIPASS (2000)

	1st cl	1st cl Saver	2nd cl	2nd cl Saver
4 consec. days	$245	$208	$160	$136
8 consec. days	330	281	220	187
15 consec. days	400	340	265	225
21 consec. days	458	390	305	260
1 month	525	445	345	294
3 days in 15 flexi	234	198	156	132
Add'l flexi days (first 3)	42	36	28	24
Add'l flexi days (next 3)	32	27	21	18

Saverpass prices are per person for 2 or more traveling together. Covers all trains, boats and buses with 25% off high mountain rides. Bonuses require use of a travel day on flexipasses. Kids under 16 free with parent.

AUSTRIAN FLEXIPASS (2000)

	1st cl	2nd cl
Any 3 days out of 15 days	$154	$104
Add-on days (max 5)	22	16

Kids 4-11 half adult fare, under 4: free

Austria

Switzerland

Maps show approximate point-to-point one-way 2nd class rail fares in $US.

Through the Back Door—call 425/771-8303 for our free Railpass Guide or find it at www.ricksteves.com.

Eurailers (including Euro and Selectpass users) should know what extras are included with their pass—such as any German buses marked "Bahn" (run by the train company); city S-Bahn systems; boats on the Rhine, Mosel, and Danube Rivers and Swiss lakes; and a 75 percent discount on the Romantic Road bus tour. Those traveling in the Swiss Alps can use their Eurailpass to get discounts (but not free passage) on some private trains and lifts in the mountains. If you want to focus on Switzerland (where many scenic rides are not covered by railpasses), consider the various Alps passes sold at Swiss train stations. The Swiss Junior Card allows children under 16 to travel free with their parents (20 SF per child at Swiss stations or free with Swiss train passes when requested with purchase in the United States).

If you decide to buy train tickets as you go, look into local specials. For instance, Germany offers a wild "Schönes Wochenende" ticket for 35 DM; it gives groups of up to five people unlimited travel on nonexpress trains all day Saturday or Sunday. Their "Guten-Abend" pass gives you unlimited travel on nonexpress trains any evening from 19:00 until 02:00 for 60 to 70 DM. Seniors (women over 60, men over 65) and youths (under 26) can enjoy substantial discounts. While Eurailers (over 26) automatically travel first class, those buying individual tickets should remember that second-class tickets, available to people of any age, provide the same transportation for 33 percent less.

Train schedules are generally slick and speedy with synchronized connections. Major German stations now have handy Service Points offering general help to travelers.

Hundreds of local train stations rent bikes for about $5 a day (40 percent discount in Austria for those with train tickets or passes) and sometimes have easy "pick up here and drop off there" plans. For mixing train and bike travel, ask at stations for information booklets: *Bahn & Bike* (Germany and Austria) and *Velo und Bahn* (Switzerland).

Car Rental

It's cheaper to arrange your car rental in advance in the United States than in Europe. You'll want a weekly rate with unlimited mileage. For three weeks or longer, leasing is cheaper because it saves you money on taxes and insurance. Comparison shop through your agent. DER, a German company, often has the best rates (tel. 800/782-2424, www.dertravel.com).

Expect to pay about $600 per person (based on 2 people sharing the car) for a small economy car for three weeks with unlimited mileage, including gas, parking, and insurance. I normally rent a small, inexpensive model like a Ford Fiesta. For a bigger, roomier, more powerful but inexpensive car, move up to a Ford Escort or VW Polo. If you drop your car off early or keep it longer, you'll be credited or charged at a fair, prorated price.

For peace of mind, I splurge for the CDW insurance (about $10–15 a day). A few "gold" credit cards cover CDW; quiz your credit-card company on the worst-case scenario. Travel Guard sells CDW insurance for $6 a day (tel. 800/826-1300, www.travelguard .com). With the luxury of CDW, you'll enjoy the autobahn knowing you can bring back the car in shambles and just say, "S-s-s-sorry."

For driving in Switzerland and the Czech Republic, your driver's license is all you need. For Austria and Germany, you're strongly advised to get an international driver's license (at your local AAA office—$10 plus 2 passport-type photos).

If you plan to drive your rental car from Germany or Austria into the Czech Republic, keep these tips in mind: State your travel plans up front to the rental company. Some won't allow any of their

Standard European Road Signs

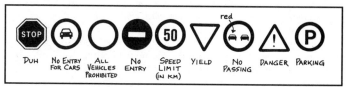

rental cars to enter eastern European countries due to the high theft rate. Some won't allow certain types of cars: BMWs, Mercedes, and convertibles. Ask about extra fees—some companies automatically tack on theft and collision coverage for a Czech excursion. To avoid hassles at the Czech border, ask the rental agent to mark your contract with the company's permission to cross.

Driving

Every long drive between my recommended destinations is via the autobahn (super freeway), and nearly every scenic backcountry drive is paved and comfortable.

Austria and Switzerland charge drivers who use their roads. For Austria, you'll need a sticker for your rental car (buy at the border)—105 AS for 10 days or 300 AS for two months. To use the autobahn in Switzerland, you'll pay a one-time 40-SF fee (at the border, a gas station, or a rental agency).

Learn the universal road signs (explained in charts in most road atlases and at service stations). Seat belts are required, and two beers under those belts are enough to land you in jail.

Use good local maps and study them before each drive. Learn which exits you need to look out for, which major cities you'll travel toward, where the ruined castles lurk, and so on. For parking, you can pick up the "cardboard clock" (*Parkscheibe*, available free at gas stations, police stations, and *Tabak* shops) and display your arrival time on the dashboard so parking attendants can see you've been there less than the posted maximum stay (blue lines indicate 90-minute zones on Austrian streets).

In Europe the shortest distance between any two points is the autobahn. Signs directing you to the autobahn are green in Austria and Switzerland, blue in Germany. To understand the complex but superefficient autobahn (no speed limit, toll free), pick up the *Autobahn Service* booklet at any autobahn rest stop (free, lists all stops, services, road symbols, and more). Learn the signs: *Dreieck* (literally "three corners") means a "Y" in the road; *Autobahnkreuz* is an intersection. Exits are spaced about every 20 miles and often have a gas station (*bleifrei* means unleaded), restaurant, a mini-market, and sometimes a tourist information desk. Exits and intersections refer to the next major or the nearest small town.

Study the map and anticipate which town names to look out for. Know what you're looking for—miss it and you're long autobahn-gone. When navigating, you'll see *nord, süd, ost, west,* or *mitte.* Don't cruise in the passing lane; stay right.

Get used to metric. A liter is about a quart, four to a gallon; a kilometer is six-tenths of a mile. Convert kilometers to miles by cutting them in half and adding back 10 percent of the original (120 km: 60 + 12 = 72 miles).

Telephones, Mail, and E-mail

Smart travelers learn the phone system and use it daily to reserve or reconfirm rooms, get tourist information, or phone home. Many European phone booths take cards but not coins. Each country sells phone cards good for use only in that country's phones. (For example, a Swiss phone card works for local and international calls from Switzerland, but is worthless in Austria.) Buy a phone card from post offices, newsstands, or tobacco shops. Insert the card into the phone, make your call, and the value is deducted from your card. If you use coins, have a bunch handy. Or look for a metered phone ("talk now, pay later") in the bigger post offices. Avoid using hotel room phones for anything other than local calls and toll-free "USA Direct" calling-card calls (see below).

Dialing Direct: You'll save money by dialing direct. You just need to learn to break the codes. When calling long distance within a country, first dial the area code (which starts with zero), then dial the local number. For example, Munich's area code is 089, and the number of one of my recommended Munich hotels is 264-043. To call it from Frankfurt, dial 089/264-043. When dialing internationally, dial the international access code (of the country you're calling from), the country code (of the country you're calling to), the area code (without the initial zero), and the local number. To call the Munich hotel from the United States, dial 011 (the U.S. international access code), 49 (Germany's country code), 89 (Munich's area code without the zero), and 264-043. To call my office from Munich, I dial 00 (Germany's international access code), 1 (U.S. country code), 425 (Edmonds' area code), and 771-8303. European time is six/nine hours ahead of the east/west coast of the United States. For a listing of international access codes and country codes, see the appendix. Don't be surprised if local phone numbers have differing numbers of digits within the same city or even the same hotel (e.g., a hotel can have a six-digit phone number and an eight-digit fax number).

USA Direct Services: New inexpensive direct-dial rates of less than a dollar a minute make the previously economical USA Direct Services (AT&T, MCI, or Sprint) a bad value. Still, many are comforted by their American phone card and hearing that Yankee operator. Each card company has a toll-free number in each European country that puts you in touch with an English-speaking operator. The operator asks for your card number and the number you want to call, puts you through, and bills your home phone number for the call (at the rate of $2.00 per minute plus a $4.00 service charge). Calling an answering machine is an expensive mistake ($6.00). First use a small-value coin or a German, Austrian, or Swiss phone card to call home for five seconds—long enough to make sure the answering machine is off so you can call back using your USA Direct number. For a list of AT&T, MCI, and Sprint operators, see the Appendix. Avoid using USA Direct for calls between European countries; it's far cheaper to call direct using coins or a German, Austrian, or Swiss phone card.

Mail: To arrange for mail delivery, reserve a few hotels along your route in advance and give their addresses to friends, or use American Express Company's mail services (available to anyone who has at least one Amex traveler's check). Allow 10 days for a letter to arrive. Phoning is so easy that I've dispensed with mail stops altogether.

E-mail: More and more hoteliers have e-mail addresses and Web sites (listed in this book). And cybercafés are available in most cities, giving you reasonably inexpensive and easy Internet access. Look for the cybercafés listed in this book, or ask at the local TI, computer store, or your hotel.

Sleeping

In the interest of smart use of your time, I favor hotels and restaurants handy to your sightseeing activities. Rather than list hotels scattered throughout a city, I describe two or three favorite neighborhoods and recommend the best accommodations values in each, from $10 bunks to $180 doubles.

While accommodations in Germany, Austria, and Switzerland are fairly expensive, they are normally very comfortable and come with breakfast. Plan on spending $70 to $120 per hotel double in big cities and $40 to $70 in towns and in private homes. Swiss beds are 20 percent more expensive than those in Austria and Germany.

A triple is much cheaper than a double and a single. While hotel singles are most expensive, private accommodations (*Zimmer*) have a flat per-person rate. Hostels and dorms always charge per person. Especially in private homes, where the boss changes the sheets, people staying several nights are most desirable. One-night stays are sometimes charged extra.

In recommending hotels, I favor small, family-run places that are central, inexpensive, quiet, clean, safe, friendly, English speaking, and not listed in other guidebooks. I also like local character and simple facilities that don't cater to American "needs." Obviously, a place meeting every criterion is rare, and all of my recommendations fall short of perfection—sometimes miserably.

Sleep Code

To save space while giving more specific information for people with special concerns, I've described my recommended hotels with a standard code. Prices listed are per room, not per person. When a range of prices is listed for a room, the price fluctuates with room size or season.

S = Single room (or price for one person in a double).

D = Double or Twin. Double beds are usually big enough for nonromantic couples.

T = Triple (often a double bed with a single bed moved in).

Q = Quad (an extra child's bed is usually cheaper).

b = Private bathroom with toilet and shower or tub.

t = Private toilet only (the shower is down the hall).

s = Private shower or tub only (the toilet is down the hall).

CC = Accepts credit cards (Visa, MasterCard, American Express). If CC isn't mentioned, assume you'll need to pay cash.

SE = Speaks English. This code is used only when it seems predictable that you'll encounter English-speaking staff.

NSE = Does not speak English. Used only when it's unlikely you'll encounter English-speaking staff.

According to this code, a couple staying at a "Db-120 DM, CC:V, SE" hotel would pay 120 Deutsche Marks (around $60) for a double room with a private bathroom. The hotel accepts Visa or German cash, and the staff speaks English.

But I've listed the best values for each price category, given the above criteria. The best values are family-run places with showers down the hall and no elevator.

Any room without a bathroom has access to a bathroom in the corridor (free unless otherwise noted). Except for pensions in Prague, all rooms have a sink. For environmental reasons, towels are often replaced in hotels only when you leave them on the floor. In cheaper places they aren't replaced at all, so hang them up to dry and reuse.

Unless I note otherwise, the cost of a room includes a continental breakfast. The price is usually posted in the room. Before accepting, confirm your understanding of the complete price. About tipping: the only tip the hotels I've listed would like is a friendly, easygoing guest. The accommodations prices listed in this book should be good through 2001. I appreciate feedback on your hotel experiences.

Making Reservations

It's possible to travel at any time of year without reservations, but given the high stakes, erratic accommodations values, and the quality of the gems I've found for this book, I'd highly recommend calling ahead for rooms at least several days in advance as you travel (but book well in advance for festivals such as Oktoberfest). If tourist crowds are down, you might make a habit of calling between 9:00 and 10:00 on the day you plan to arrive, when the hotel knows who'll be checking out and just which rooms will be available. I've taken great pains to list telephone numbers with long distance instructions (see "Telephones," above). Use the telephone and the convenient telephone cards. Most hotels listed are accustomed to English-only speakers. A hotel receptionist will trust you and hold a room until 16:00 without a deposit, though some will ask for a credit-card number. Honor (or cancel by phone) your reservations. Long distance is cheap and easy from public phone booths. Trusting people to show up is a hugely stressful issue and a financial risk for B&B owners. Don't let these people down—I promised you'd call and cancel if for some reason you can't show up. Don't needlessly confirm rooms through the tourist offices; they'll take a commission.

If you know exactly which dates you need and really want a particular place, reserve a room long before you leave home. To reserve from home, call, fax, or e-mail the hotel. Phone and fax costs are reasonable, and simple English is usually fine. To fax, use the form in the appendix (e-mailers can find it online at www.ricksteves.com/reservation). If you're writing, add the zip code and confirm the need and method for a deposit. A two-night stay in August would be "two nights, 16/8/01 to 18/8/01" (Europeans write the date day/month/year, and European hotel jargon uses your day of departure). You'll often receive a letter back requesting one night's deposit. A credit-card number and expiration date will usually be accepted as a deposit. If your credit card is the deposit, you can pay with your card or cash when you arrive; if you don't show up, you'll be billed for one night. Reconfirm your reservations a day in advance for safety.

Camping and Hosteling

Campers can manage with the Let's Go listings and help from the local TI (ask for a regional camping listing). Your hometown travel bookstore also has guidebooks on camping in Europe. You'll find campgrounds just about everywhere you need them. Look for "Campingplatz" signs. You'll meet lots of Europeans—camping is a popular, middle-class-family way to go. Campgrounds are cheap ($5–8 per person), friendly, safe, more central and convenient han rustic, and rarely full.

Hostelers can take advantage of the wonderful network of

hostels. Follow signs marked "Jugendherberge" (with triangles) or the "tree next to a house" logo. Generally, travelers without a membership card ($25 per year, sold at hostels in most U.S. cities) are admitted for an extra $5.

Hostels are open to members of all ages (except in Bavaria, where a maximum age of 26 is strictly enforced). They usually cost $10 to $20 per night (cheaper for those under 27, plus $4 sheet rental if you don't have your own) and serve good, cheap meals and/or provide kitchen facilities. If you plan to stay in hostels, bring your own sheet. While many hostels have couples' or family rooms available upon request for a little extra money, plan on segregated dorms with 4 to 20 beds per room. Hostels can be idyllic and peaceful, or school groups can raise the rafters. School groups are most common on summer weekends and on school-year weekdays. I like small hostels best. While many hostels may say over the telephone that they're full, most hold a few beds for people who drop in, or they can direct you to budget accommodations nearby.

Eating

Germanic cuisine is heavy and hearty. While it's tasty, it can get monotonous if you fall into the schnitzel or wurst-and-potatoes rut. Be adventurous. My German phrase book has a handy menu decoder that works well for most travelers, but galloping gluttons will prefer the meatier *Marling German Menu Master*. Each region has its specialties, which, while not cheap, are often good values.

There are many kinds of restaurants. Hotels often serve fine food. A *Gaststätte* is a simple, less-expensive restaurant. Ethnic restaurants provide a welcome break from Germanic fare. Foreign cuisine is either the legacy of a crumbled empire (Hungarian and Bohemian, from which Austria gets its goulash and dumplings) or a new arrival to feed the many hungry-but-poor guest workers. Italian, Turkish, and Greek food are good values. The cheapest meals are found in department-store cafeterias, *Schnell-Imbiss* (fast-food) stands, university cafeterias (*Mensas*), and hostels. For a quick, cheap bite, have a deli make you a *Wurstsemmel*, a meat sandwich.

Most restaurants tack a menu onto their door for browsers and have an English menu inside. Only a rude waiter will rush you. Good service is relaxed (slow to an American). When you want the bill, ask, "*Die Rechnung, bitte.*" (In Germany and Austria, you might be charged for bread you've eaten from the basket on the table.) Service is included, although it's common to round up the bill after a good meal (e.g., for an 18-DM meal, pay 20 DM). Rather than leaving coins on the table, Germans pay with paper, saying how much they'd like the bill to be (e.g., for a 9.20-DM meal, give a 20-DM bill and say "*Zehn Mark*"—10 marks). To wish others "Happy eating!" offer a cheery "*Guten Appetit!*"

For most visitors, the rich pastries, wine, and beer provide the fondest memories of Germanic cuisine. The wine (85 percent white) is particularly good from the Mosel, Rhine, Danube, eastern Austria, and southwestern Switzerland areas. Order wine by the *Viertel* (quarter liter) or *Achtel* (eighth liter). You can say, "*Ein Viertel Weisswein* (white wine), *bitte* (please)." Order it *süss* (sweet), *halbe trocken* (medium), or *trocken* (dry). *Rotwein* is red wine and *Sekt* is German champagne.

The Germans enjoy a tremendous variety of great beer. The average German, who drinks 40 gallons of beer a year, knows that *dunkles* is dark, *helles* is light, *Flaschenbier* is bottled, and *vom Fass* is on tap. *Pils* is barley based, *Weize* is wheat based, and *Malzbier* is the malt beer that children learn on. *Radler* is half beer and half lemon-lime soda. When you order beer, ask for *ein Halbe* for a half liter (not always available) or *eine Mass* for a whole liter (about a quart). Menus list drink size by the 10th of a liter, or deciliter. Tap water is *Leitungswasser*.

Back Door Manners

While updating this book, I heard over and over again that my readers are considerate and fun to have as guests. Thank you for traveling as temporary locals who are sensitive to the culture. It's fun to follow you in my travels.

Send Me a Postcard, Drop Me a Line

If you enjoy a successful trip with the help of this book and would like to share your discoveries, please fill out and send the survey at the end of this book to me at Europe Through the Back Door, Box 2009, Edmonds, Washington 98020. I personally read and value all feedback. Thanks in advance—it helps a lot.

For our latest information, visit our Web site: www.ricksteves.com. To check for any updates for this book, look into www.ricksteves.com/update. My e-mail address is rick@ricksteves.com. Anyone can request a free issue of our Back Door quarterly newsletter.

Judging from the happy postcards I receive from travelers, it's safe to assume you'll enjoy a great, affordable vacation—with the finesse of an independent, experienced traveler.

Thanks, and *gute Reise!*

BACK DOOR TRAVEL PHILOSOPHY
As Taught in *Rick Steves' Europe Through the Back Door*

Travel is intensified living—maximum thrills per minute and one of the last great sources of legal adventure. Travel is freedom. It's recess, and we need it.

Experiencing the real Europe requires catching it by surprise, going casual... "Through the Back Door."

Affording travel is a matter of priorities. (Make do with the old car.) You can travel—simply, safely, and comfortably—anywhere in Europe for $70 a day plus transportation costs. In many ways, spending more money only builds a thicker wall between you and what you came to see. Europe is a cultural carnival and, time after time, you'll find that its best acts are free and the best seats are the cheap ones.

A tight budget forces you to travel close to the ground, meeting and communicating with the people, not relying on service with a purchased smile. Never sacrifice sleep, nutrition, safety, or cleanliness in the name of budget. Simply enjoy the local-style alternatives to expensive hotels and restaurants.

Extroverts have more fun. If your trip is low on magic moments, kick yourself and make things happen. If you don't enjoy a place, maybe you don't know enough about it. Seek the truth. Recognize tourist traps. Give a culture the benefit of your open mind. See things as different but not better or worse. Any culture has much to share.

Of course, travel, like the world, is a series of hills and valleys. Be fanatically positive and militantly optimistic. If something's not to your liking, change your liking. Travel is addicting. It can make you a happier American, as well as a citizen of the world. Our Earth is home to 6 billion equally important people. It's humbling to travel and find that people don't envy Americans. They usually like us, but, with all due respect, they wouldn't trade passports.

Globetrotting destroys ethnocentricity. It helps you understand and appreciate different cultures. Travel changes people. It broadens perspectives and teaches new ways to measure quality of life. Many travelers toss aside their hometown blinders. Their prized souvenirs are the strands of different cultures they decide to knit into their own character. The world is a cultural yarn shop. And Back Door travelers are weaving the ultimate tapestry. Come on, join in!

GERMANY
(DEUTSCHLAND)

- Germany is 136,000 square miles (like Montana).
- Population is 77 million (about 650 per square mile, declining slowly).
- The West was 95,000 square miles (like Wyoming), with 61 million people. The East was 41,000 square miles (like Virginia), with 16 million people.
- 1 Deutsche Mark (DM) = 50 cents, and 2 DM = $1.

Deutschland is energetic, efficient, and organized, and Europe's muscleman—economically and wherever people are lining up (Germans have a reputation for pushing ahead). Its bustling cities hold 85 percent of its people, and average earnings are among the highest on earth. Ninety-seven percent of the workers get one-month paid vacations, and during the other 11 months, they create a gross national product that's about one-third of the United States' and growing. Germany has risen from the ashes of World War II to become the world's fifth-largest industrial power, ranking fourth in steel output and nuclear power and third in automobile production. Germany shines culturally, beating out all but two countries in production of books, Nobel laureates, and professors.

While its East-West division lasted about 40 years, historically Germany has been divided between north and south. While northern Germany was barbarian, is Protestant, and assaults life aggressively, southern Germany was Roman, is Catholic, and enjoys a more relaxed tempo of life. The American image of Germany is beer-and-pretzel Bavaria (probably because that was "our" sector after the war). This historic north-south division is less pronounced these days as Germany becomes a more mobile society. The big chore facing Germany today is integrating the wilted economy of what was East Germany into the powerhouse economy of the West. This monumental task has given the West higher taxes (and second thoughts).

Germany's tourist route today—Rhine, Romantic Road, Bavaria—was yesterday's trade route, connecting its most prosperous medieval cities. Germany as a nation is just 130 years old. In 1850 there were 35 independent countries in what is now Germany. In medieval times there were more than 300, each with its own weights, measures, coinage, king, and lotto.

Germans eat lunch and dinner about when we do. Order house specials whenever possible. Pork, fish, and venison are good, and don't miss the bratwurst and sauerkraut. Potatoes are the standard vegetable. The bread and pretzels in the basket on your table often cost extra. When I need a pork break, I order the *Saladteller*. Great beers and white wines abound. Go with whatever beer is on tap. Service and tips are included in your restaurant bills. Gummi Bears are local gumdrops with a cult following (beware of imitations— you must see the word *Gummi*), and Nutella is a chocolate-hazelnut spread that may change your life.

MUNICH (MÜNCHEN)

Munich, Germany's most livable and "yuppie" city, is also one of its most historic, artistic, and entertaining. It's big and growing, with a population of more than 1.4 million. Just a little more than a century ago, it was the capital of an independent Bavaria. Its imperial palaces, jewels, and grand boulevards constantly remind visitors that this was once a political and cultural powerhouse. And its recently bombed-out feeling reminds us that 75 years ago it provided a springboard for Nazism, and 55 years ago it lost a war.

Orient yourself in Munich's old center with its colorful pedestrian mall. Immerse yourself in Munich's art and history—crown jewels, Baroque theater, Wittelsbach palaces, great paintings, and beautiful parks. Munich evenings are best spent in frothy beer halls, with their oompah, bunny-hopping, and belching Bavarian atmosphere. Pry big pretzels from no-nonsense, buxom beer maids.

Planning Your Time

Munich is worth two days, including a half-day side trip to Dachau. If necessary, its essence can be captured in a day (walk the center, tour a palace and a museum, and enjoy a beer-filled evening). Those without a car and in a hurry can do the castles of Ludwig as a day trip from Munich by tour. Even Salzburg (2 hrs by train) can be a handy day trip from Munich.

Orientation (area code: 089)

The tourist's Munich is circled by a ring road (which was the town wall) marked by four old gates: Karlstor (near the train station, known as the Hauptbahnhof), Sendlinger Tor, Isartor (near the river), and Odeonsplatz (near the palace). Marienplatz is the city center. A great pedestrian-only street cuts this circle in half, running nearly from Karlstor and the train station through Marienplatz to Isartor. Orient yourself along this east-west axis. Most sights are within a few blocks of this people-filled walk. Ninety percent of the sights and hotels I recommend are within a 20-minute walk of Marienplatz and each other.

Tourist Information

Munich has two helpful TIs: in front of the station (with your back to the arrival/departure board, walk through the central hall and turn right outside; Mon–Sat 9:00–20:00, Sun 10:00–18:00, tel. 089/233-0300) and on Marienplatz (Mon–Fri 10:00–20:00, Sat 10:00–16:00, closed Sun, www.muenchen-tourist.de). Have a list of questions ready, confirm sightseeing plans, and pick up brochures. The excellent Munich city map is one of the handiest in Europe. Consider the *Monats-programm* (3 DM, a German-language list of sights and an events calendar), and the free twice-monthly magazine *In München* (lists in German all the movies and entertainment in town, available at TI or any big cinema until supply runs out). The TI can refer you to hotels for a 10 to 15 percent fee, but you'll get a better value with my recommended hotels—contact them directly. If the line at the TI is bad, go to EurAide (see below). The only essential item is the TI's great city map (also available at EurAide and many hotels).

   EurAide: The industrious, eager-to-help EurAide office in the train station is a godsend for Eurailers and budget travelers (daily in summer 7:45–12:00, 13:00–18:00; in winter it closes at 16:00 on weekdays, 12:00 on Sat, and all day Sun; Room 3 at track 11; tel. 089/593-889, fax 089/550-3965, www.euraide.de, see www.euraide.de/ricksteves for Romantic Road bus and Rhine cruise schedules, e-mail: euraide@compuserve.com). Alan Wissenberg and his staff know your train travel and accommodations questions and have answers in clear American English. The German rail company pays them to help you design your best train travels. They make train and Romantic Road bus reservations and sell train tickets, *couchettes*, and sleepers. They can find you a room for a 7-DM fee (but not at my hotels), and they offer a 1-DM city map and a free, useful newsletter. They sell a "Prague Excursion" train pass, convenient for Prague-bound Eurailers—good for train travel from any Czech border station to Prague and back to any border station within seven days (first class-90 DM, second class-60 DM, youth second class-45 DM; a bit cheaper through their U.S. office: tel. 941/480-1555, fax 941/480-1522). Every Wednesday in June and July, EurAide offers an excellent "Two Castle" tour of Neuschwanstein and Linderhof that includes Wieskirche (frustrating without a car, see "Sights—Near Munich" below).

Arrival in Munich

By Train: Munich's train station is a sight in itself—one of those places that can turn an accountant into a vagabond. For a quick orientation in the station, use the big wall maps showing the train station, Munich, and Bavaria (through the center doorway as you leave the tracks on the left). For a quick rest stop, the Burger King upstairs has toilets as pleasant and accessible as its hamburgers. Check out the new complex of restaurants and shops opposite Track 14. The Internationale Presse (across from track 24) is great for English-language books, papers, and magazines, including *Munich Found* (informative English-speaking residents' monthly, 5.50 DM). You'll also find two TIs (the city TI and EurAide, see above) and lockers (track 31). Europcar and Hertz are up the steps opposite track 21. The U-Bahn, S-Bahn, and buses connect the station to the rest of the city (though many hotels listed in this book are within walking distance of the station).

By Plane: There are two good ways to connect the airport and downtown Munich: Take an easy 40-minute ride on subway S-8 (from Marienplatz, 15.20 DM or free with train pass, every 10 min) or take the Lufthansa airport bus to (or from) the train station (16 DM, 3/hrly, 45 min, buy tickets on bus or from EurAide). Airport info: tel. 089/97500.

Getting around Munich

Much of Munich is walkable. To reach sights away from the city center, use the fine tram, bus, and subway systems. Taxis are expensive and generally unnecessary (except perhaps to avoid the time-consuming trip to Nymphenburg).

By Public Transit: Subways are called U- or S-Bahns. Subway lines are numbered (e.g., S-3 or U-5). Eurailpasses are good on the S-Bahn (actually an underground-while-in-the-city commuter railway). Regular tickets cost 3.80 DM and are good for two hours of changes in one direction. For the shortest rides (1 or 2 stops) buy the 1.90-DM ticket (*Kurzstrecke*). The 9-DM all-day pass is a great deal (valid until 6:00 the next morning). The Partner Daily Ticket (for 14 DM) is good all day for up to five adults and a dog (2 kids count as 1 adult, so 2 adults, 6 kids, and a dog can travel with this ticket). Tickets are available from easy-to-use ticket machines (which take bills and coins), subway booths, and TIs. The entire system (bus/tram/subway) works on the same tickets. You must punch your own ticket before boarding (stamping a date and time on it). Plainclothes ticket-checkers enforce this "honor system," rewarding freeloaders with stiff 60-DM fines.

Important: All S-Bahn lines connect the Hauptbahnhof (main station) with Marienplatz (main square). If you want to use the S-Bahn and you're either at the station or Marienplatz, follow signs to the S-Bahn (U is not for you) and concern yourself only with the direction—in German, *richtung* (Hauptbahnhof/Pasing or Marienplatz).

By Bike: Munich—level and compact, with plenty of bike paths—feels good on two wheels. Bikes can be rented quickly and easily at the train station at **Radius Tours** (May–mid-Oct daily 10:00–18:00, city bikes-5 DM/hr, 25 DM/day, 30 DM/24 hrs, 45 DM/48 hrs, mountain bikes 20 percent more; credit-card imprint, 100 DM, or passport for a deposit, in front of track 30, tel. 089/596-113). They also offer excellent Dachau tours (see "Sights—Near Munich" below) and dispense all the necessary tourist information (city map, bike routes), including a do-it-yourself bike tour booklet (free).

Helpful Hints

Monday Tips: Most Munich sights (including Dachau) are closed on Monday. If you're in Munich on Monday, here are some suggestions: visit the Deutsches Museum, Residenz, BMW Museum, or churches; take a walking tour or bus tour; climb high for city views; stroll the pedestrian streets; have lunch at the Viktualien Markt (see "Eating," below); rent a bike for a spin through Englischer Garten; day-trip to Salzburg or Ludwig's castles; or, if Oktoberfest is on, join the celebration.

Useful Phone Numbers: Pharmacy (at train station, tel. 089/594-119), EurAide train info (tel. 089/593-889, SE), U.S. consulate (Königinstrasse 5, tel. 089/28880), American Express Company (on main pedestrian drag at Kaufingerstrasse 24, tel. 089/2280-1387), taxi (tel. 089/21610).

Laundromat: A handy *Waschcenter* is near the station at Paul Heyse Strasse 21 (8 DM/load, daily 7:00–23:00).

Car Rental: Munich's cheapest is Allround Car Rental (Boschetsrieder Strasse 12, U-3 to Obersendling, tel. 089/723-8383).

Internet Access: There's plenty of on-line access in Munich. The best deal is across from the main entrance of the station on Bahnhofplatz at the Hertie department store (6 DM/hr, open weekdays until 20:00). Access at Times Square OnLine Bistro can be pricey (outside south exit of the station).

Sights—Central Munich

▲▲**Marienplatz and the Pedestrian Zone**—Riding the escalator out of the subway into sunlit Marienplatz (Mary's Square) gives you a fine first look at the glory of Munich: great buildings bombed flat and rebuilt, outdoor cafés, and people bustling and lingering like the birds and breeze they share this square with. Notice the ornate facades of the gray, pointy old city hall (Altes Rathaus) and the neo-Gothic new city hall (Neues Rathaus, built 1867–1910) with its *Glockenspiel*. The not-very-old *Glockenspiel* "jousts" on Marienplatz daily through the tourist season at 11:00, 12:00, and 17:00.

Munich Center

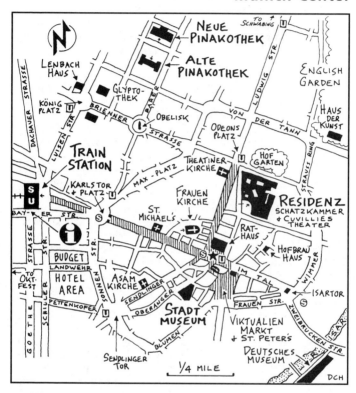

From here the pedestrian mall (Kaufingerstrasse and Neu-hauserstrasse) leads you through a great shopping area, past carnivals of street entertainers and good old-fashioned slicers and dicers, the twin-towering Frauenkirche (built in 1470, rebuilt after World War II), and several fountains, to Karlstor and the train station. As one of Europe's first pedestrian zones, the mall enraged shopkeepers when it was built in 1972. Today it is "Munich's living room." Nine thousand shoppers pass through it each hour . . . and the shopkeepers are happy. Imagine this street in hometown U.S.A.

In the pedestrian zone around Marienplatz, there are three noteworthy churches. **St. Michael's Church**, while one of the first great Renaissance buildings north of the Alps, has a brilliantly Baroque interior. You can borrow the tiny English booklet to read in a pew; see the interesting photos of the bombed-out city center near the entry; and go into the crypt to see the tomb of King Ludwig II, the "mad" king still loved by romantics (church open daily

8:30–19:00; crypt-2 DM, Sun–Fri 9:30–16:30, Sat 9:30–14:30, 40 stark royal tombs).

The twin onion domes of the 500-year-old **Frauenkirche** (Church of Our Lady) are the symbol of the city. While much of the church was destroyed in World War II, the towers survived. Gloriously rebuilt since, the church is worth a visit. It was built in Gothic style, but money problems meant the domes weren't added until Renaissance times. These domes were inspired by the arches of the Venetian Renaissance. And the church domes we think of as "typically Bavarian" were inspired by these.

St. Peter's Church, the oldest in town, overlooks Marien-platz. Built upon the hill where the first monks founded the city in the 12th century, it has a fine interior with photos of the WWII bomb damage near the entrance. It's a long climb to the top of the spire (no elevator), much of it with two-way traffic on a one-way staircase, but the view is dynamite (2.50 DM, Mon–Sat 9:00–19:00, Sun 10:00–19:00). Try to be two flights from the top when the bells ring at the top of the hour, and when your friends back home ask you about your trip, you'll say, "What?"

▲▲**City Views**—Downtown Munich's three best city viewpoints are from the tops of: 1) St. Peter's Church (described above); 2) Frauenkirche (also described above), the highest viewpoint at 350 feet (4 DM, elevator, Mon–Sat 10:00–17:00, closed Sun); and 3) the Neues Rathaus, or new city hall (3 DM, elevator from under the Marienplatz *Glockenspiel*, Mon–Fri 9:00–19:00, Sat–Sun 10:00–19:00).

▲**Münchner Stadtmuseum**—The Munich city museum has four floors of exhibits: first floor—life in Munich through the centuries (including World War II) illustrated in paintings, photos, and models; second floor—special exhibits (often more interesting than the permanent ones); third floor—historic puppets and carnival gadgets; and fourth floor—a huge collection of musical instru-ments from around the world (5 DM, 7.50 DM for families, Tue–Sun 10:00–18:00, closed Mon, no English descriptions, no crowds, bored and playful guards, 3 blocks off Marienplatz at St. Jakob's Platz 1, a fine children's playground faces the entry).

▲▲**Alte Pinakothek**—Bavaria's best painting gallery is newly renovated to show off a great collection of European masterpieces from the 14th to 19th centuries featuring work by Fra Angelico, Botticelli, da Vinci, Raphael, Dürer, Rubens, Rembrandt, El Greco, and Goya (7 DM, Tue–Sun 10:00–17:00, Thu until 22:00, closed Mon, U-2 to Königsplatz or tram #27, tel. 089/238-05216).

▲**Neue Pinakothek**—The Alte Pinakothek's hip sister is a twin building across the square, showing off paintings from 1800 to 1920: Romanticism, Realism, Impressionism, Jugendstil, Monet, Renoir, van Gogh, Goya, and Klimt (7 DM, Wed–Mon 10:00–17:00, closed Tue). During 2001, this museum will temporarily house some of Munich's modern art collection (which used to be in Haus der Kunst, below) until it moves next door to its new home—Pinakothek der Moderne—next year. In 2002, this powerful cluster of three museums (Alte, Neue, and Moderne Pinakotheks) will display art spanning from the 14th century to modern times.

Haus der Kunst—Built by Hitler as a temple of Nazi art, this bold and fascist building is now an impressive shell for various art exhibitions (8–12 DM, daily 10:00–22:00, Prinzregentenstrasse 1, at south end of Englischer Garden, tel. 089/211-27110, www.hausderkunst.de).

Bayerisches Nationalmuseum—This is an interesting collection of Riemenschneider carvings, manger scenes, traditional living rooms, and old Bavarian houses (8 DM, Tue–Sun 9:30–17:00, closed Mon, tram #20 or bus #53 or #55 to Prinzregentenstrasse 3).

▲▲▲Deutsches Museum—Germany's answer to our Smithsonian Institution, the Deutsches Museum traces the evolution of science and technology. With 10 miles of exhibits from astronomy to zymurgy—even those on roller skates will need to be selective. Blue dots on the floor mark someone's idea of the top 12 stops, but I had a better time just wandering through well-described rooms of historic bikes, cars (Benz's first car . . . a three-wheeler from the 1880s), trains, airplanes (Hitler's flying bomb from 1944), spaceships (step inside a rocket engine), mining, the harnessing of wind and water power, hydraulics, musical instruments, printing, photography, computers, astronomy, clocks . . . it's the Louvre of science and technology.

Most sections are lovingly described in English. The much-vaunted "high voltage" demonstrations (3/day, 15 min, all in German) show the noisy creation of a five-foot bolt of lightning—not that exciting. There's also a state-of-the-art planetarium (German only) and an adjacent IMAX theater (museum entry-12 DM, daily 9:00–17:00, self-serve cafeteria; S-Bahn to Isartor, then walk 300 meters over the river, following signs; tel. 089/21791). Save this for a Monday, when virtually all of Munich's museums are closed.

▲Müllersches Volksbad—This elegant Jugendstil (1901) public swimming pool is just across the river from the Deutsches Museum (5 DM, Rosenheimerstrasse 1, tel. 089/2361-3434).

Schwabing—Munich's artsy, bohemian university district, or "Greenwich Village," has been called "not a place but a state of mind." All I experienced was a mental lapse. The bohemians run the boutiques. I think the most colorful thing about Schwabing is the road leading back downtown. U-3 or U-6 will take you to the Münchener-Freiheit Center if you want to wander. Most of the jazz and disco joints are near Occamstrasse. The Haidhausen neighborhood (U-Bahn: Max Weber Platz) is becoming the "new Schwabing."

▲Englischer Garden—Munich's "Central Park," the largest on the Continent, was laid out in 1789 by an American. A huge beer garden sprawls near the Chinese pagoda. A rewarding respite from the city, it's especially fun on a bike under the summer sun (bike rental at train station). Caution: While a local law requires sun worshipers to wear clothes on the tram, this park is sprinkled with nude sunbathers—quite a spectacle to most Americans (they're the ones riding their bikes into the river and trees).

Asam Church—Near the Stadtmuseum, this private church of the Asam brothers is a gooey, drippy, Baroque-concentrate masterpiece by Bavaria's top two rococonuts. A few blocks away, the small Damenstift Church has a sculptural rendition of the Last Supper so real you feel you're not alone (at intersection of Altheimer Ecke and Damenstiftstrasse, a block south of the pedestrian street).

Sights—Residenz

▲**Residenz**—For a long hike through rebuilt corridors of gilded imperial Bavarian grandeur, tour the family palace of the Wittels-bachs, who ruled Bavaria for more than 700 years. With a worth-less English guidebook and not a word of English within, it's one of Europe's worst-presented palaces. Think of it as doing laps at the mall, with better art. Follow the "Führungslinie" signs: The first room shows a WWII exhibit. After long, boring halls of porcelain and dishes behind glass, you enter the king's apartments with a little throne-room action. The best Romantic-era dish art is on the top floor (8 DM, daily 10:00–16:30, enter on Max-Joseph Platz, 3 blocks north of Marienplatz).

▲▲**Schatzkammer**—This treasury, next door to the Residenz, shows off a thousand years of Wittelsbach crowns and knickknacks (another 8 DM from the same window, same hours as Residenz, the only English you'll encounter is the "do not touch" signs). Vienna's palace and jewels are better, but this is Bavaria's best, with fine 13th and 14th century crowns and delicately carved ivory and glass. For a more efficient ramble, consider the eight rooms as one big room and make a long clockwise circle.

▲**Cuvillies Theater**—Attached to the Residenz, this national theater designed by Cuvillies is dazzling enough to send you back to the days of divine monarchs. Visitors see simply the sumptuous interior; there is no real exhibit (3 DM, Mon–Sat 14:00–17:00, Sun 10:00–17:00; facing the Residenz entry, go left around the Residenz about a half block to reach the theater entrance).

Sights—Greater Munich

▲▲**Nymphenburg Palace**—This royal summer palace is impres-sive only by Bavarian standards. If you do tour it, meditate upon the theme: nymphs. Something about the place feels highly sexed in a Prince Charles kind of way. Two rooms deserve special attention:

Greater Munich

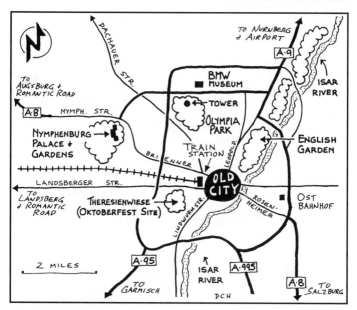

the riotous rococo Great Hall (at entry, 1756 by Zimmermann) and King Ludwig's Gallery of Beauties. The gallery (#15, 1825–1848) is stacked with portraits of 36 of Bavaria's loveliest women . . . according to Ludwig. If only these creaking floors could tell a story. Don't miss the photos (in the glass cases) of Ludwig II and his Romantic composer friend Richard Wagner.

The Amalienburg—another rococo jewel designed by Cuvillies and decorated by Zimmermann—is 300 meters from the palace. Every rich boy needs a hunting lodge like this. Above the pink-and-white grand entry, notice Diana, goddess of the chase, flanked by busts of satyrs. Tourists enter around back. Highlights in this tiny getaway include: first room—dog houses under gun cupboards; the fine yellow and silver bedroom—see Vulcan forging arrows for amorous cupids at the foot of the bed; the mini–Hall of Mirrors— a blue-and-silver commotion of rococo nymphs and a kitchen with blue Dutch Bible–scene tiles.

The sleigh and coach collection (Marstallmuseum, closes from 12:00–13:00) is a huge garage lined with gilded Cinderella coaches. It's especially interesting for Ludwig fans.

The palace park, which is good for a royal stroll or bike ride, contains more playful extras. You'll find things like a bathhouse, a pagoda, and artificial ruins (15 DM for everything, less for individual parts; Tue–Sun 9:00–18:00, shorter hours Oct–March; the 5-DM English guidebook does little to make the palace meaningful; U-1 direction: Westfriedhof to Rotkreuzplatz, then tram or bus #12 to Romanplatz and a 10-minute walk or tram #17 from downtown or the station direct; tel. 089/179-080).

BMW Museum—The BMW headquarters, located in a striking building across the street from the Olympic Grounds, offers a good museum popular with car buffs (5.50 DM, daily 9:00–18:00, last ticket sold at 17:00, closed much of Aug, U-3 to the end: Olympia-zentrum, tel. 089/3822-3307). BMW fans should ask about factory tours (often unreliable hours).

▲**Olympic Grounds**—Munich's great 1972 Olympic stadium and sports complex is now a lush park offering a tower (5 DM, commanding but so-high-it's-boring view from 820 feet, daily 9:00–24:00, last trip 23:30), an excellent swimming pool (5 DM, Fri–Wed 7:00–22:30, Thu 7:00–18:00), a virtual sports center where you can return Stefi Graf's serve, a good look at the center's striking "cobweb" style of architecture, and plenty of sun, grass, and picnic potential. Take U-3 to Olympia-zentrum direct from Marienplatz.

Tours of Munich: By Foot, Bike, and Bus

Walking Tours—Munich Walks offers two excellent walking tours: an introduction to the old town and "Infamous Third Reich Sites" (15 DM per tour, 3 hrs, tel. 0177-227-5901, e-mail: berlinwalks@berlin.de). The old-town tour starts daily at 10:15 early April through October (also at 14:15 May–Aug, but not Sun). The Third Reich tour is offered at 10:15 on Monday, Thursday, and Saturday from June through early October (less in off-season). Both tours depart from the EurAide office (track 11) in the train station. There's no need to register—just show up. For transportation during the tour, bring any subway ticket (like a Kurzstrecke) or buy one from your guide.

Renate Suerbaum is a good local guide (170 DM for private two-hour walking tour, tel. 089/283-374).

City Bus Tour—Panorama Tours offers one-hour orientation bus tours (19 DM, daily April–Oct, on the hour from 10:00–16:00; Nov–March 10:00 and 14:30; guide speaks German and English; Arnulfstrasse 8, near train station; tel. 089/5490-7560).

Radius Tours offers "alternative" Munich tours on a party tram—you and your friends can rent out a cable car that whisks you along the city's public tram lines. Live music is optional (at the station in front of track 30, tel. 089/596-113).

Bike Tours—If you miss your fraternity, consider Mike's four-hour and seven-hour bike tours (4-hr tour: 36 DM, June–July daily 10:30, 11:30, 15:00, 16:00; April–May and Aug–Sept daily 11:30, 16:00; mid-March–March 31 and Oct 12:30 only; 7-hr

tour: 49 DM, June–July daily 12:30, includes Nymphenburg
Palace, Olympic Park, and 2 beer gardens, meet at Old Town Hall
tower on east end of Marienplatz, guides can be crass—this isn't
for kids, tel. 089/651-4275, www.mikesbiketours.com).

Mike also runs bus day trips to Neuschwanstein (80 DM, castle
entry extra, daily May 15–Aug 15, 9:00 departure, 20:00 return to
Munich, tel. 089/2554-3987).

Oktoberfest

When King Ludwig I had a marriage party in 1810, it was such a
success that they made it an annual bash. These days the Oktoberfest lasts 16 days (Sept 22–Oct 7 in 2001), ending on the first full
weekend in October. It starts with an opening parade of more than
6,000 participants and fills eight huge beer tents with about 6,000
people each. A million gallons of beer later, they roast the last ox.

It's best to reserve a room early, but if you arrive in the morning (except Fri or Sat) and haven't called ahead, the TI can normally
help. The fairground, known as the "Wies'n" (south of the train
station), erupts in a frenzy of rides, dancing, and strangers strolling
arm-in-arm down rows of picnic tables while the beer god stirs tons
of beer, pretzels, and *wurst* in a bubbling caldron of fun. The three-
loops roller coaster must be the wildest on earth (best before the
beer drinking). During the fair, the city functions even better than
normal. It's a good time to sightsee, even if beer-hall rowdiness
isn't your cup of tea.

Sights—Near Munich

Castle Tours—Two of King Ludwig's castles, Neuschwanstein
and Linderhof, are a great day trip by tour. Without a tour, only
Neuschwanstein is easy (2 hrs by train to Füssen, 10-minute bus
ride to Neuschwanstein).

Panorama Tours offers all-day bus tours of the two castles
with 30 minutes in Oberammergau (78 DM, castles—24 DM
extra, daily April–Oct, Nov–March Tue, Thu, Sat, Sun, 8:30
departure from fountain on Elisenstrasse near botanical gardens,
10-min walk from station on Luisenstrasse, right on Elisenstrasse,
tickets at EurAide office, discount for railpass and ISIC holders,
tel. 089/593-889 or 089/5490-7560, www.autobusoberbayern.de).

On Wednesdays in June and July, EurAide operates an all-
day train/bus Neuschwanstein-Linderhof-Wieskirche day tour
(70 DM, 55 DM with railpass, admissions not included, departs at
7:30 from the EurAide office and beats most groups to avoid the
long line, tel. 089/593-889). For info on Ludwig's castles, see the
Bavaria and Tirol chapter.

Berchtesgaden—This resort, near Hitler's overrated Eagle's Nest
getaway, is easier as a day trip from Salzburg (just 20 kilometers
away). See the Salzburg chapter.

Munich Area

▲**Andechs Monastery**—Where can you find a fine Baroque church in a rural Bavarian setting at a monastery that serves hearty food and perhaps the best beer in Germany, in a carnival atmosphere full of partying locals? At the Andechs Monastery, which crouches quietly with a big smile between two lakes just south of Munich. Come ready to eat tender chunks of pork, huge pretzels, spiraled white radishes, savory sauerkraut, and Andecher monk-made beer that would almost make celibacy tolerable. Everything is served in medieval portions; two people can split a meal. The great picnic center offers first-class views and second-class prices (beer garden open daily 9:45–20:45, dinner until 18:30, church until 19:00, tel. 08152/3760). To reach Andechs from Munich without a car, take the S-5 train to Herrsching then catch a "Rauner" shuttle bus (hourly) or walk two miles. Don't miss a stroll up to the church, where you can sit peacefully and ponder the striking contrasts a trip through Germany offers....

▲▲**Dachau**—Dachau was the first Nazi concentration camp (1933). Today it's the most accessible camp to travelers and a very effective voice from our recent but grisly past, warning and pleading "Never Again," the memorial's theme. This is a valuable experience and, when approached thoughtfully, well worth the trouble. In fact, it may change your life. See it. Feel it. Read and think about it. After this most powerful sightseeing experience,

Dachau

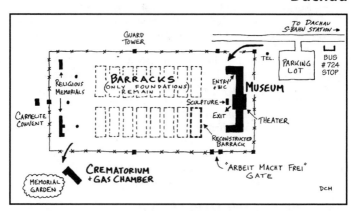

many people gain more respect for history and the dangers of not keeping tabs on their government.

Upon arrival, pick up the mini-guide and note when the next documentary film in English will be shown (25 min, normally shown at 11:30 and 15:30 and often at 14:00, verify times on board as you enter museum). Both the museum and the movie are exceptional. Notice the Expressionist fascist-inspired art near the theater, where you'll also find English books, slides, and a WC. Outside, see the reconstructed barracks and the memorial shrines at the far end (Tue–Sun 9:00–17:00, closed Mon). For maximum understanding, consider the English guided walk (daily in summer at 12:30, 2 hrs, donation, call 08131/1741 to confirm) or the Radius tour from Munich (see below). It's a 45-minute trip from downtown Munich: take S-2 (direction: Petershausen) to Dachau, then from the station, catch bus #724 or #726, Dachau-Ost, to Gedenkstätte (the camp). The two-zone 7.60-DM ticket covers the entire trip (one-way); with a train pass, just pay for the bus (1.90 DM one-way). Drivers follow Dachauerstrasse from downtown Munich to Dachau-Ost. Then follow the KZ-Gedenkstätte signs. The town of Dachau is more pleasant than its unfortunate image (TI tel. 08131/84566).

Radius Tours, in front of track 30 in the Munich train station, offers hassle-free and thoughtful tours of the Dachau camp from Munich (30 DM plus cost of public transportation, May–Sept, Tue–Sun at 10:00 and 13:00, allow 4 hrs for round-trip, reserve ahead, tel. 089/596-113).

Sleeping in Munich
(2 DM = about $1, country code: 49, area code: 089)
Sleep Code: **S** = Single, **D** = Double/Twin, **T** = Triple, **Q** = Quad

b = bathroom, **t** = toilet only, **s** = shower only, **CC** = Credit Card (Visa, MasterCard, Amex), **SE** = English spoken, **NSE** = No English. In Munich, hoteliers nearly always speak English, unless otherwise noted. Prices include breakfast and increase with conventions and festivals.

There are no cheap beds in Munich. Youth hostels strictly enforce their 26-year-old age limit, and side-tripping in is a bad value. But there are plenty of decent, moderately priced rooms. I've listed places in three areas: within a few blocks of the central train station (Hauptbahnhof), in the old center, and near the Deutsches Museum. Prices can triple during Oktoberfest (Sept 22–Oct 7 in 2001), when Munich is packed. While rooms can generally be found through the TI, Oktoberfest revelers should reserve in advance. Remember to book direct rather than pay the TI's hefty 10 to 15 percent commission.

Sleeping near the Train Station

Budget hotels (90-DM doubles, no elevator, shower down the hall) cluster in the area immediately south of the station. It's seedy after dark (erotic cinemas, barnacles with lingerie tongues, men with moustaches in the shadows) but dangerous only to those in search of trouble. Still, I've listed places in more polite neighborhoods, generally a 5- or 10-minute walk from the station, handy to the center, and usually include a breakfast buffet. Places are listed roughly in order of proximity to the station. The nearest **Laundromat** is at Paul Heyse Strasse 21, near the intersection with Landswehrstrasse (daily 7:00–23:00, 8 DM/load).

Hotel Haberstock, a classic old-European hotel less than a block from the station, is homey, a little worn, and relatively quiet (S-65–78 DM, Ss-85 DM, Sb-115 DM, D-120 DM, Ds-140 DM, Db-180 DM, good breakfast, CC:VMA, cable TV, Schillerstrasse 4, 80336 Munich, tel. 089/557-855, fax 089/550-3634, friendly Alfred at the desk). Ask about weekend and winter discounts.

Hotel Europäischer Hof München is a huge, impersonal business hotel with 160 fine rooms and elegant public spaces. They have three categories of rooms, ranging from moderately expensive to outrageous: standard, comfort, and business class (S-85–135 DM, Sb-155–425 DM, D-110–180 DM, Db-190–450 DM, 10 percent discount if you mention this book when you reserve, no discounts on Oktoberfest weekends, CC:VMA, Bayerstrasse 31, 80335 Munich, tel. 089/551-510, fax 089/5515-1222, www.heh.de).

Hotel Schweiz is plain outside and decent inside with 58 nonsmoking rooms and a good breakfast (Sb-120 DM, Db-169 DM, Tb-214 DM, garage–15-DM, CC:VMA, elevator, Goethestrasse 26, from the station walk 2 blocks down Goethestrasse, tel. 089/539-585, fax 089/543-69696, e-mail: info@hotel-schweiz.de).

Jugendhotel Marienherberge is clean and pleasant and

Hotels near the Train Station

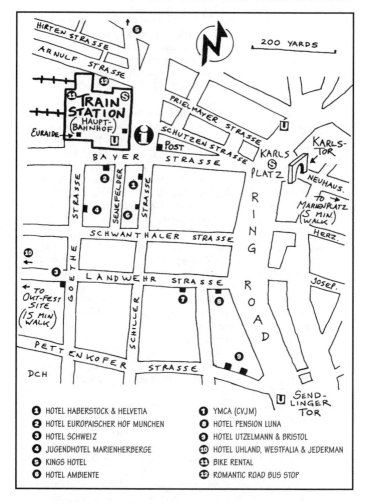

➊ HOTEL HABERSTOCK & HELVETIA	➐ YMCA (CVJM)
➋ HOTEL EUROPAISCHER HOF MUNCHEN	➑ HOTEL PENSION LUNA
➌ HOTEL SCHWEIZ	➒ HOTEL UTZELMANN & BRISTOL
➍ JUGENDHOTEL MARIENHERBERGE	➓ HOTEL UHLAND, WESTFALIA & JEDERMAN
➎ KINGS HOTEL	⑪ BIKE RENTAL
➏ HOTEL AMBIENTE	⑫ ROMANTIC ROAD BUS STOP

has the best cheap beds in town for young women only (25-year age limit can flex upward a couple of years for 10 DM extra, S-40 DM, 35 DM per bed in D and T, 30 DM per bed in 6-bed rooms, nonsmoking, office open 8:00–24:00, a block from station at Goethestrasse 9, tel. 089/555-805, fax 089/5502-8260).

Hotel Helvetia is an on-the-ball, backpacker's favorite (44 rooms, S-55–65 DM, D-78–99 DM, Ds-99–120 DM, T-110–129 DM, laundry service, free Internet access, elevator, Schillerstrasse

6, 80336 Munich, tel. 089/590-6850, fax 089/5906-8570, e-mail: hotel-helvetia@t-online.de).

Kings Hotel, a fancy, old, business-class hotel, is a good, elegant splurge on weekends. You'll get carved wooden ceilings, canopy beds, chandeliers, and a sauna (95 rooms, Db-295 DM; weekend special: Db-195 DM except during fairs; CC:VMA; some nonsmoking rooms; 500 meters north of station at Dachauer Strasse 13, 80335 Munich, tel. 089/551-870, fax 089/5518-7300, www.king-group.com).

Hotel Ambiente has dark halls but 46 clean, bright, newly refurbished rooms with all the comforts and a friendly professional staff (Sb-160 DM, Db-180 DM depending on season, CC:VMA, a block from station at Schillerstrasse 12, 80336 Munich, tel. 089/545-170, fax 089/5451-7200).

CVJM (YMCA), open to all ages and sexes, has modern rooms (79 beds, S-56 DM, D-90 DM, T-130 DM, 42 DM/bed in a shared triple, those over 26 pay 16 percent more, free showers, elevator, Landwehrstrasse 13, 80336 Munich, tel. 089/552-1410, fax 089/550-4282, www.cvjm-muenchen.org).

Hotel Pension Luna is a dumpy building with 16 cheery rooms (S-60 DM, Ss-75 DM, D-99 DM, Ds-115 DM, T and Ts-140 DM, CC:VMA, lots of stairs, free showers, Landwehrstrasse 5, tel. 089/597-833, fax 089/550-3761, Angelika SE).

Hotel Pension Utzelmann feels less cozy because of its huge rooms—especially the curiously cheap room #6—but the lacy rooms are richly furnished. It's in a pleasant neighborhood just a 10-minute walk from the station and a block off Sendlinger (S-50–85 DM, Ss-95 DM, Sb-125 DM, D-98 DM, Ds-115 DM, Db-145 DM, T-130 DM, Ts-150 DM, Tb-175 DM, hall showers-free, Pettenkoferstrasse 6, enter through iron gate, tel. 089/594-889, fax 089/596-228, Frau Schlee NSE).

Hotel Bristol, nearly next door to Hotel Utzelmann, has comfortable rooms and is a fine value (Sb-105 DM, Db-145 DM, Tb-170 DM; to get these cash-only prices—which are 20 to 30 DM below the hotel's normal rates—ask for friendly Johannes and mention this book; nonsmoking; hearty buffet breakfast on terrace, parking available, bike rental-15 DM/day, CC:VMA, Pettenkoferstrasse 2, 80336 Munich, one metro stop on U-1 or U-2 from station, tel. 089/595-151, fax 089/591-451, www.bristol-muc.com). Johannes also has an apartment (45 DM per person; up to 4 people) and a second hotel, Hotel Deutsches Theater (1 block away, same rates as Bristol).

Hotel Uhland, an elegant mansion, is a worthwhile splurge with 19 spacious rooms (Sb-110 DM, Db-160 DM, Tb-195 DM, breakfast, elevator, free bikes, cable TV, Internet access, free parking, Uhlandstrasse 1, 80336 Munich, near Theresienwiese Oktoberfest grounds, 15 minutes from station, walk up Goethestrasse and turn right on Pettenkoferstrasse, tel. 089/543-350, fax 089/ 5433-5250, www.hotel-uhland.de).

Pension Westfalia overlooks the Oktoberfest grounds from the top floor of a quiet and classy old building. Well run by Peter and Mary Deiritz, this is a great value if you prefer sanity and personal touches to centrality (S-65 DM, Sb-90 DM, D-90–95 DM, Db-115–135 DM, cheaper off-season, extra bed-25 DM, hallway showers-3 DM, buffet breakfast, CC:VA, elevator, easy parking, U-3 or U-6 to Goetheplatz, Mozartstrasse 23, 80336 Munich, tel. 089/530-377, fax 089/543-9120, e-mail: pension-westfalia@ t-online.de). Around the corner, tidy **Pension Schubert** rents four simple but elegant rooms (S-50 DM, D-85 DM, Db-95 DM, Schubertstrasse 1, tel. 089/535-087).

Hotel Jedermann is an old business hotel offering 56 comfortable rooms with baths and basic, well-worn rooms without baths (S-65–85 DM, Sb-95–160 DM, D-95–140 DM, Ds-120– 160 DM, Db-160–240 DM depending on season, T-130–180 DM, Tb-190–290 DM, kids' cot-15 DM, CC:VM, nonsmoking rooms available, buffet breakfast, Internet access, elevator, turn right out of station and walk 15 minutes to Bayerstrasse 95, or take tram #18 or #19, 80335 Munich, tel. 089/533-617, fax 089/536-506, www.hotel-jedermann.de).

Sleeping in the Old Center

Pension Lindner is clean, quiet, and modern, with pastel-bouquet rooms (S-65–80 DM, D-110 DM, Ds-135 DM, Db-150 DM, elevator, just off Sendlinger Strasse, Dultstrasse 1, 80331 Munich, tel. 089/263-413, fax 089/268-760, run by cheery Marion Sinzinger). One floor below, the quirky **Pension Stadt Munich** isn't as homey, but is OK if the Lindner is full (four Ds-120 DM, a tad smoky, Dultstrasse 1, tel. 089/263-417, fax 089/267-548, some English spoken).

Pension Seibel is ideally located with cozy rooms and a friendly, family atmosphere, two blocks off the Marienplatz in a fun neighborhood (S-70–90 DM, Sb-89–129 DM, D-99–139 DM, Db-129–169 DM, Tb-150–199 DM, these prices are promised through 2001 during nonfair periods if you show them this book and pay cash, family apartment for up to 5 people-65 DM each, good breakfast, CC to reserve but pay cash, tries to be smoke free, no elevator, Reichenbachstrasse 8, 80469 Munich, tel. 089/264-043, fax 089/267-803, www.seibel-hotels-munich.de, e-mail: pension.seibel@t-online.de, personable Moe and Kirstin). If you're stuck, ask about their not-as-central-but-still-comfortable Hotel Seibel on the fairgrounds (same rates).

Hotel Münchner Kindl is a jolly place with 16 decent rooms but high prices above a friendly local bar (S-90 DM, Ss-120 DM, Sb-130 DM, D-130 DM, Ds-150 DM, Db-170 DM, Tb-210 DM,

Munich Center Hotels and Restaurants

1. PENSION LINDNER & STADT MUNICH
2. PENSION SEIBEL
3. HOTEL MÜNCHNER KINDL
4. HOTEL ISARTOR
5. PENSION BECK
6. HOFBRÄUHAUS
7. WEISSES BRÄUHAUS
8. JODLERWIRT REST.
9. NÜRNBERGER BRATWURST GLÖCKL
10. ALTES HACKERHAUS
11. ALOIS DALLMAYR

Qb-240 DM, prices with this book, CC:VM, night noises travel up central courtyard, no elevator, easy telephone reservations, 2 blocks off main pedestrian drag from "Augustiner" sign at Damenstiftstrasse 16, 80331 Munich, tel. 089/264-349, fax 089/264-526, run by Gunter and English-speaking Renate Dittert).

Sleeping near Isartor, the Deutsches Museum, and Beyond

Hotel Isartor is a modern, comfortable, concrete-feeling place just a two-minute walk from the Isartor S-Bahn stop (38 rooms, Sb-from 145 DM, Db-from 170 DM, 5 percent discount with cash in July, August, and during slow times, parking—12 DM/day,

CC:VMA, elevator, Baaderstrasse 2, 80469 Munich, tel. 089/ 216-3340, fax 089/216-33420, e-mail: hotel-isartor@t-online.de, family Pangratz).

Pension Beck is well worn and farther away but a good budget bet (S-from 60 DM, D-86–95 DM, Db-125–135 DM, rooms for 3 to 5 people-40–55 DM each; family, youth, and two-night deals; CC:VM, 44 rooms on 5 floors with no elevator, lots of backpackers, east of Isartor, near river and Mariannenplatz, Thierschstrasse 36, take streetcar #17 direct from station or any S-Bahn to Isartor and 400-meter walk, tel. 089/220-708, fax 089/ 220-925, e-mail: pension.beck@bst-online.de).

American **Audrey Bauchinger** rents quiet, tidy rooms and spacious apartments east of the Deutsches Museum in a quiet residential area a 20-minute walk from Marienplatz (Ss-50 DM, D-80 DM, one D with private bath across hall-125 DM, Ds-105 DM, spacious one-bedroom apartment-160 DM, extra person-50 DM, no breakfast but bakery nearby, CC:VMA, corner of Schweigerstrasse, at Zeppelinstrasse 37, 81669 Munich, tel. 089/488-444, fax 089/489-1787, e-mail: 106437.3277@compuserve.com). From the station, take any S-Bahn to Marienplatz, then take bus #52 (the only bus there) to Schweigerstrasse.

Familie Jordan Zimmer, run by the Jordan family (now with an empty nest), rents two big apartments in their comfortable suburban home. This is ideal for those driving between Munich and Salzburg (Db-90 DM, 20 min from downtown on the S-5 to Vaterstetten, then a 2-minute walk; from the A-99 Autobahn, take exit 18 Haar Ebersberg when approaching from either direction, Luitpoldring 8, 85591 Vaterstetten, tel. 08106/358-032, fax 08106/358-033, SE).

Hostels and Cheap Beds

Munich's youth hostels charge 25 DM in dorms and 38 DM in doubles (including breakfast and sheets) and strictly limit admission to YH members who are under 27. **Burg Schwaneck Hostel** is a renovated castle (30 minutes from center—take the S-7 to Pullach and then follow signs to Burgweg 4, tel. 089/793-0643, fax 089/793-7922).

Munich's International **Youth Camp Kapuzinerhölzl** (a.k.a. "The Tent") offers 400 places on the wooden floor of a huge circus tent. You'll get a mattress (15 DM) or bed (19 DM), blankets, good showers, washing machines, and breakfast. It can be a fun experience—kind of a cross between a slumber party and Woodstock. There's a cool Ping-Pong-and-Frisbee atmosphere throughout the day, and no curfew at night (July–Aug only, confirm first at TI that it's open, then catch tram #17 from train station to Botanischer Garten, direction: Amalienburgstrasse, and follow crowd down Franz-Schrankstrasse, tel. 089/141-4300).

Eating in Munich

Munich cuisine is best seasoned with beer. For beer halls, you
have two basic choices: the Hofbräuhaus, where you'll find
music and tourists, or the mellower beer gardens, where you'll
find the Germans.

The world's most famous and touristy beer hall is the
Hofbräuhaus (daily 9:00–24:00, music during lunch and dinner,
Platzl 6, five-minute walk from Marienplatz, tel. 089/290-1360,
www.hofbraeuhaus.de). Even if you don't eat here, check it out;
it's fun to see 200 Japanese people drinking beer in a German beer
hall... across from a Planet Hollywood. Germans go for the entertainment—to sing "Country Roads," see how Texas girls party,
and watch salaried professionals from Tokyo chug beer. The
music-every-night atmosphere is thick, and the fat, shiny-leather
bands even get church mice to stand up and conduct three-quarter
time with breadsticks. Meals are inexpensive (for a light 10-DM
meal, I like the local favorite—2 *paar Schweinswurst mit Kraut*);
white radishes are salted and cut in delicate spirals; and surly beer
maids pull mustard packets from their cleavages. Huge liter beers
(called *eine Mass* in German or *"ein* pitcher" in English) cost 11.40
DM. You can order your beer *helles* (light but not "lite," which is
what you'll get if you say *"ein* beer"), *dunkles* (dark), or *Radler* (half
lemon-lime soda, half beer). Notice the vomitoriums in the WC.
(They host a gimmicky folk evening upstairs in the *Festsaal* nightly
at 19:00 for 9 DM, food and drinks are sold from same menu,
tel. 089/2901-3610.)

Weisses Bräuhaus is more local and features good food and
the region's fizzy wheat beer (daily 8:00–24:00, Tal 10, between
Marienplatz and Isartor, 2 blocks from Hofbräuhaus, 089/299-
875). Hitler met with fellow fascists here in 1920 when his Nazi
party had yet to ferment.

Augustiner Beer Garden is a sprawling haven for well-
established local beer lovers on a balmy evening (10:00–23:00,
across from train tracks, 3 loooong blocks from station, away
from the center, on Arnulfstrasse 52). For a true under-the-leaves
beer garden packed with locals, this is the best.

The tiny **Jodlerwirt** is a woodsy, smart-alecky, yodeling kind
of pub. The food is great and the ambience is as Bavarian as you'll
find. Avoid the basic ground-floor bar and climb the stairs into the
action (accordion act from 21:00, closed Sun, Altenhofstrasse 4,
between Hofbräuhaus and Marienplatz, tel. 089/221-249). Good
food, lots of belly laughs... completely incomprehensible to the
average tourist.

For a classier evening stewed in antlers and fiercely Bavarian,
eat under a tree or inside at the **Nürnberger Bratwurst Glöckl
am Dom** (daily 9:30–24:00, 25-DM dinners, Frauenplatz 9, at the
rear of the twin-domed cathedral, tel. 089/295-264). Almost next

door, the more trendy **Andechser am Dom** serves Andechs beer
to appreciative locals.

Locals enjoy the **Altes Hackerhaus** for traditional *Bayerischer*
fare with a dressier feel (daily until 24:00, 25–30 DM meals, Send-
lingerstrasse 14, tel. 089/260-5026).

For outdoor atmosphere and a cheap meal, spend an evening
at the Englischer Garden's **Chinesischer Turm** (Chinese pagoda)
Biergarten. You're welcome to BYO food and grab a table or buy
from the picnic stall (*Brotzeit*) right there. Don't bother to phone
ahead—they have 6,000 seats. For a more intimate place with
more local families and fewer tourists, venture deeper into the
garden (past Isarring road) to the **Hirschau Biergarten**.

For similar BYOF atmosphere right behind Marienplatz, eat
at **Viktualien Markt's** beer garden (closed Sun). Lunch or dinner
here taps you into about the best budget eating in town. Countless
stalls surround the beer garden and sell wurst, sandwiches, produce, and so on. This BYOF tradition goes back to the days when
monks were allowed to sell beer but not food. To picnic, choose a
table without a tablecloth. This is a good place to grab the most
typical meal in town: *Weisswurst* (white sausage) with *süss* (sweet)
mustard, a salty pretzel, and *Weissbier*. **Suppenküche** is fine for a
small, cozy, sit-down lunch (soup kitchen, 6–9-DM soup meals, in
Viktualien Markt near intersection of Frauenstrasse and Reichenbachstrasse, everyone knows where it is). For your strudel and coffee, consider **Marktcafe** (closed Sun, fresh strudel, on a tiny street
a block below market, Heiliggeiststrasse 2, tel. 089/227-816).

For a fun and easy (though not cheap) cafeteria meal near
Karlstor on the pedestrian mall, consider **Mövenpick Marche**.
Climb downstairs into the marketplace fantasy and pick up a card.
Your card will be stamped as you load your tray. Choose your
table from several typical Munich themes, and pay after you eat
(daily 8:00–22:00, smoke-free zones, reasonable small-plate veggie
and salad buffets, distracting men's room, on Neuhauser pedestrian street across from St. Michael's church).

The crown in its emblem indicates that the royal family
assembled its picnics in the historic and expensive **Alois Dallmayr**
delicatessen (Mon–Fri 9:30–19:30, Sat 9:00–16:00, closed Sun,
Dienerstrasse 14, behind the Neues Rathaus). An elegant café
serves light meals behind the bakery on the ground floor. Explore
this dieter's purgatory and put together a royal picnic to munch in
the nearby Hofgarten. To save money, browse at Dallmayr's but
buy in the basement **supermarkets** of the Kaufhof stores across
Marienplatz or at Karlsplatz.

Transportation Connections—Munich
Munich is a super transportation hub (one reason it was the
target of so many WWII bombs).

By train to: Füssen (10/day, 2 hrs; for a Neuschwanstein Castle day trip, depart at 6:50 and arrive at 9:00 with transfer in Buchloe; or go direct at 8:51 and arrive at 10:57—confirm times at station), **Berlin** (hrly, 7 hrs), **Würzburg** (hrly, 3 hrs), **Frankfurt** (hrly, 3.5 hrs), **Salzburg** (12/day, 2 hrs), **Vienna** (4/day, 5 hrs), **Venice** (4/day, 8 hrs), **Paris** (4/day, 9 hrs), **Prague** (3/day, 7–10 hrs), and just about every other point in western Europe. Munich is three hours from **Reutte**, Austria (every 2 hrs, 3 hrs, transfer in Garmisch). Night trains run daily to Berlin, Vienna, Venice, Paris, and Prague (at least 7 hrs to each city).

BAVARIA
AND TIROL

Two hours south of Munich, between Germany's Bavaria and
Austria's Tirol, is a timeless land of fairy-tale castles, painted
buildings shared by cows and farmers, and locals who still yodel
when they're happy.

In Germany's Bavaria, tour "Mad" King Ludwig's ornate
Neuschwanstein Castle, Europe's most spectacular. Stop by the
Wieskirche, a textbook example of Bavarian rococo bursting with
curly curlicues, and browse through Oberammergau, Germany's
wood-carving capital and home of the famous Passion Play.

In Austria's Tirol, hike to the Ehrenberg ruined castle,
scream down a nearby ski slope on an oversized skateboard, then
catch your breath for an evening of yodeling and slap dancing.

In this chapter I'll cover Bavaria first, then Tirol. Austria's
Tirol is easier and cheaper than touristy Bavaria. My favorite
home base for exploring Bavaria's castles is actually in Austria, in
the town of Reutte. Füssen, in Germany, is a handier home base
for train travelers.

Planning Your Time
While locals come here for a week or two, the typical speedy
American traveler will find two days' worth of sightseeing. With
a car and more time you could enjoy three or four days, but the
basic visit ranges anywhere from a long day trip from Munich to
a three-night, two-day visit. If the weather's good and you're not
going to Switzerland, be sure to ride a lift to an Alpine peak.

A good schedule for a one-day circular drive from Reutte is:
7:30–Breakfast, 8:00–Depart hotel, 8:15–Arrive at Neuschwanstein
to get admission times for two castles, tour both Hohenschwangau
and Neuschwanstein, 13:00–Drive to the Wieskirche (20-minute

Highlights of Bavaria and Tirol

stop) and on to Linderhof, 14:30–Tour Linderhof, 16:30–Drive along scenic Plansee back into Austria, 17:30–Back at hotel, 19:00–Dinner at hotel and perhaps a folk evening (or the Ludwig II Musical). In peak season you might arrive later at Linderhof to avoid the crowds. The next morning you could stroll through Reutte, hike to the Ehrenberg ruins, and ride the luge on your way to Innsbruck, Munich, Venice, Switzerland, or wherever.

Train travelers can base in Füssen and bus or bike the short distance to Neuschwanstein. Reutte, which will likely lose its train station in 2001, is connected by bus with Füssen (5/day, none on Sun). If you base in Reutte, you can bike to Neuschwanstein, Ehrenberg ruins, and the Tegelberg luge (and hike to Neuschwanstein from the recommended Gutshof zum Schluxen).

Getting around Bavaria and Tirol

By Car: This region is ideal by car. All the sights are within an easy 60-mile loop from Reutte or Füssen.

By Train and Bus: It can be frustrating by train. Local bus service in the region is spotty for sightseeing. If you're rushed and without wheels, Reutte, the Wieskirche, and the luge rides are probably not worth the trouble (but the Tegelberg luge near Neuschwanstein is within walking distance).

Füssen (with a 2-hour train ride to/from Munich every hour, transfer in Buchloe) is five kilometers from Neuschwanstein Castle with easy bus and bike connections. Reutte is a 30-minute bus ride from Füssen (5/day, not Sun). Oberammergau (2-hour trains from Munich every hour with 1 change) has decent bus connections to nearby Linderhof Castle. Oberammergau to Füssen is sparse (1 bus/day, 2 hrs).

By Rental Car: You can rent a car in Füssen (or in Reutte, if you're a guest at the Hotel Maximilian).

By Tour: If you're interested only in Bavarian castles, consider an all-day organized bus tour of the Bavarian biggies as a side trip from Munich (see Munich chapter).

By Bike: This is great biking country. Many shops near train stations (such as in Füssen) and hotels rent bikes for 15 to 20 DM per day. The rides from Reutte to Neuschwanstein, Ehrenberg ruins, and the luge are great for those with the time and energy.

By Thumb: Hitchhiking, always risky, is a slow-but-possible way to connect the public transportation gaps.

FÜSSEN

Füssen has been a strategic stop since ancient times. Its main street sits on the Via Claudia Augusta, which crossed the Alps (over Brenner Pass) in Roman times. The town was the southern terminus of the medieval trade route known among modern tourists as the "Romantic Road." Dramatically situated under a renovated castle on the lively Lech River, Füssen just celebrated its 700th birthday.

Unfortunately, in the summer Füssen is entirely overrun by tourists. Traffic can be exasperating, but by bike or on foot it's not bad. Off-season the town is a jester's delight.

Apart from Füssen's cobbled and arcaded town center, there's little real sightseeing here. The striking-from-a-distance castle houses a boring picture gallery. The mediocre city museum in the monastery below the castle exhibits lifestyles of 200 years ago and the story of the monastery, and offers displays on the development of the violin, for which Füssen was famous (5 DM, Tue–Sun 11:00–16:00, closed Mon, explanations in German only). Halfway between Füssen and the border (as you drive, or a woodsy walk from the town) is the Lechfall, a thunderous waterfall with a handy potty stop.

Orientation (area code: 08362)

Füssen's train station is a few blocks from the TI, the town center (a cobbled shopping mall), and all my hotel listings (see

"Sleeping," below). The TI has a room-finding service (Mon–Fri 9:00–18:00, Sat 9:00–14:00, shorter hours off-season, 3 blocks down Bahnhofstrasse from station, tel. 08362/93850, fax 08362/938-520, www.fuessen.de). After-hours the little self-service info pavilion near the front of the TI dispenses Füssen maps for 3 DM.

Arrival in Füssen: Exit left as you leave the train station (lockers available) and walk a few straight blocks to the center of town and the TI. To go to Neuschwanstein or Reutte, catch a bus from the station.

Bike Rental: Rent at Preisschranke next to the station (15 DM/day, Mon–Sat 9:00–20:00, tel. 08362/921-544) or, for a bigger selection and less convenient location, check out Rad Zacherl (14 DM/day, mountain bikes-20 DM, passport number for deposit, Mon–Fri 9:00–12:00, 14:00–18:00, Sat 9:00–13:00, 2 km out of town at Kempterstrasse 119, tel. 08362/3292).

Car Rental: Antes & Huber is more central (Kemptenenerstrasse 59, tel. 08362/91920) than Hertz (Füssenerstrasse 112, tel. 08362/986-580).

Sights—Neuschwanstein Castle Area, Bavaria

The most popular tourist destination in Bavaria is the "King's Castles" (Konigschlosser). With fairy-tale turrets in a fairy-tale Alpine setting built by a fairy-tale king, it's understandably popular. The well-organized visitor can have a great four-hour visit. Others will just stand in line and perhaps not even see the castle. The key: arrive early. You can see both castles, consider fun options nearby (mountain lift, luge course, Füssen town) and get out by early afternoon.

Ludwig II (a.k.a. "Mad" King Ludwig), a tragic figure, ruled Bavaria for 23 years until his death in 1886 at the age of 41. Politically, his reality was to "rule" either as a pawn of Prussia or a pawn of Austria. Rather than deal with politics in Bavaria's capital, Munich, Ludwig frittered away most of his time at his family's hunting palace, Hohenschwangau. He spent most of his adult life constructing his fanciful Neuschwanstein castle—much like a kid builds a tree house—on a neighboring hill upon the scant ruins of a medieval castle. Although Ludwig spent 17 years building Neuschwanstein, he lived in it only 172 days. Ludwig was a true Romantic living in a Romantic age. His best friends were artists, poets, and composers such as Richard Wagner. His palaces are wallpapered with misty medieval themes—especially those from Wagnerian operas. Eventually he was declared mentally unfit to rule Bavaria and taken away from Neuschwanstein. Two days after this eviction, Ludwig was found dead in a lake. To this day people debate whether the king was murdered or committed suicide.

▲▲▲**Neuschwanstein Castle**—Imagine King Ludwig as a boy, climbing the hills above his dad's castle, Hohenschwangau (below),

Neuschwanstein

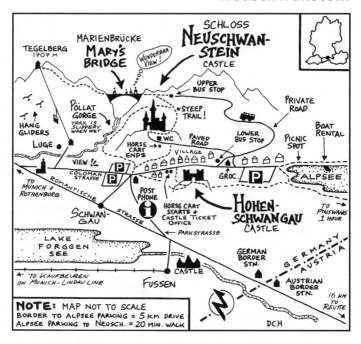

NOTE: MAP NOT TO SCALE
BORDER TO ALPSEE PARKING = 5 KM DRIVE
ALPSEE PARKING TO NEUSCH. = 20 MIN. WALK

dreaming up the ultimate fairy-tale castle. He had the power to make his dream concrete and stucco. Neuschwanstein was designed by a painter first…then an architect. It looks medieval, but it's only about as old as the Eiffel Tower. It feels like something you'd see at a home show for 19th-century royalty. Built from 1869 to 1886, it's a textbook example of the Romanticism that was popular in 19th-century Europe. Construction stopped with Ludwig's death (only a third of the interior was finished) and within six weeks, tourists were paying to go through it. Guides herd groups of 60 through the castle giving an interesting if rushed 30-minute tour. You'll go up and down more than 300 steps through lavish Wagnerian dream rooms, a royal state-of-the-19th-century-art kitchen, the king's gilded-lily bedroom, and his extravagant throne room. You'll see 15 rooms with their original furnishings and fanciful wall paintings. After the tour you'll see a room lined with fascinating drawings (described in English) of the castle plans, construction, and 1883 drawings of Falkenstein— a fanciful over-the-top but never-built castle which made Neuschwanstein look stubby and occupied Ludwig's fantasies the year he died. After the tour, a 20-minute slide show (alternating German and English) plays continuously. If English is on, pop in. If not, it's not worth waiting for.

▲▲**Hohenschwangau Castle**—Standing quietly below Neuschwanstein, the big yellow Hohenschwangau Castle was Ludwig's boyhood home. Originally built in the 12th century, it was ruined by Napoleon. Ludwig's father Maximilian rebuilt it, and you'll see it as it looked in 1836. It's more lived-in and historic, and excellent 30-minute tours actually give a better glimpse of Ludwig's life than the more visited and famous Neuschwanstein castle tour.

Getting Tickets for the Castles: Every tour bus in Bavaria converges on Neuschwanstein and tourists flush in each morning from Munich. A new reservation system sorts out the chaos for smart travelers. If you arrive late without a reservation you'll spend two hours in the ticket line and may find all tours for the day booked. A ticket center for both Neuschwanstein and Hohenschwangau castles is located a few blocks from the TI toward the Alpsee (street level between the 2 castles—not at either castle). The ticket booth opens at 7:30. Tickets come with admission times. (Miss this time and you don't get in.) First tours go at 8:45. Arrive by 8:30 (arriving before 8:00 accomplishes nothing) and you'll be touring by 9:00. To tour both castles you must do Hohenschwangau first (logical since this gives a better introduction to Ludwig's short life). You'll get two castle tour times: Hohenschwangau and then, two hours later, Neuschwanstein. The ticket office claims you can telephone for a reservation (minimum 48 hrs in advance, 08362/930-8322 or 08362/930-8324), but you'll likely get a long recording telling you first in German, then in English, how to fax or e-mail for a reservation (fax 08362/930-8320, www.ticket-center-hohenschwangau.de).

Cost and Hours: Each castle costs 14 DM, both castles are 26 DM, and children are free (April–Sept daily 8:30–17:30, Thu until 19:30, March and Oct 9:30–16:30, Neuschwanstein Nov–Feb 10:00–16:00, Hohenschwangau closed in winter, no photography inside).

Getting to the Castles: From the ticket booth, Hohenschwangau is an easy five-minute climb. Neuschwanstein is a steep 30-minute hike. To minimize hiking, you can take a shuttle bus or horse carriage, but neither gets you to the castle doorstep. The frequent shuttle buses drop you off at Mary's Bridge, leaving you a steep 10-minute downhill walk to the castle—be sure to see the view from Mary's Bridge before hiking down to castle (3.50 DM up; 5 DM round-trip not worth it since you have to hike up to bus stop for return trip). Horse carriages (8 DM up, 4 DM down) are slower than walking and stop below Neuschwanstein, leaving you a five-minute uphill hike. Note: If it's less than an hour until your Neuschwanstein tour time, you'll need to hike—at a brisk pace it's still 20 minutes.

Mary's Bridge: Before or after the tour, climb up to Mary's Bridge to marvel at Ludwig's castle, just as Ludwig did. This bridge was quite an engineering accomplishment 100 years ago. From the bridge, the frisky can hike even higher to the "Beware— Danger of Death" signs and an even more glorious castle view. For the most interesting descent (15 min longer and extremely slippery when wet), follow signs to the Pöllat Gorge.

Castle Village: The "village" at the foot of Europe's "Disney" castle feeds off the droves of hungry, shop-happy tourists. The Bräustüberl serves the cheapest grub (often with live folk music). The Alpsee lake is ideal for a picnic; the souvenir shop (open daily) nearest the Bräustüberl restaurant has a microwave fast-food machine and the makings for a skimpy lunch. Picnic at the lakeside park or in one of the old-fashioned rowboats (rented by the hour in summer). The bus stop, post/telephone office, and helpful TI cluster around the main intersection (TI open daily 9:00–18:00, until 16:00 Oct–March, tel. 08362/819-840).

Getting to the Castles from Füssen or Reutte: There's plenty of parking (all lots-7 DM). Get there early and you'll park conveniently at lot D next to the lake. Those without cars can bus from Füssen (2.50 DM one-way, 5 DM round-trip, 2/hrly, 10 min, 5 kilometers, from train station) or ride a rental bike. From Reutte, it's a bus ride to Füssen (5/day except Sun, 30 min, then city bus to castle).

For a romantic twist, hike or mountain bike from the trail-head at the recommended hotel Gutshof zum Schluxen in Pinswang (see "Sleeping near Reutte," below). When the dirt road forks at the top of the hill, go right (downhill), cross the Austria-Germany border (marked by a sign and deserted hut), and follow the narrow paved road to the castles. It's a 60- to 90-minute hike or a great circular bike trip (allow 90 min from Reutte or 30 min from Gutshof zum Schluxen; return by bus via Füssen).

▲**Tegelberg Gondola**—Just north of Neuschwanstein is a fun play zone around the mighty Tegelberg gondola. Hang gliders circle like vultures. Their pilots jumped from the top of the Tegelberg Gondola. For 28 DM you can ride high to the 5,500-foot summit and back down (daily from 9:00, last lift at 16:30, tel. 08362/98360). On a clear day you get great views of the Alps and Bavaria and the vicarious thrill of watching hang gliders and parasailors leap into airborne ecstasy. Weather permitting, scores of German thrill seekers line up and leap from the launch ramp at the top of the lift. With one leaving every two or three minutes, it's great spectating. Thrill seekers with exceptional social skills may talk themselves into a tandem ride with a parasailor. From the top of Tegelberg, it's a steep 2.5-hour hike down to Ludwig's castle. At the base of the gondola, you'll find a playground, cheery eatery, and a very good luge ride.

▲**Tegelberg Luge**—Next to the lift is a luge course. A luge is like a bobsled on wheels (for more details, see "Sights—Tirol, Near Reutte," below). The track, made of stainless steel, is often open when drizzly weather shuts down the concrete luges. It's not as scenic as Bichlbach and Biberwier (see below), but it's handy (5 DM per run, daily 10:00–18:00, closed in rain, tel. 08362/98360). A funky cable system pulls lugers to the top without a ski lift.

▲**Ludwig II Musical**—A spectacular opera/musical based on the romantic life and troubled times of Ludwig debuted in a grand new lakeside theater in 2000. While called a musical, "Ludwig II, Longing for Paradise" felt like opera to me—with an orchestra in the pit, creative stage sets, fine singing, wonderful acoustics, and an easy-to-follow story line about Ludwig abandoning the normal, guy-thing rush of political power to pal around with his muses (three vampy women dressed in purple). It's Bismarck the realistic politician on one side versus Wagner the romantic composer on the other as "art triumphs" (and Ludwig disappears into the lake).

   The music is wonderful and the show's a hit with Germans. It's clearly top classical quality, but the superscripts in English are tough to read and tickets are pricey. The state-of-the-art theater is romantically set on a lake (Forgensee) with a view of floodlit Neuschwanstein in the distance (85–230 DM per seat, Tue–Fri at 19:30, Sat–Sun at 13:00 and 18:00, Jan–Dec, English subtitles, 3 hrs including intermission, plenty of chances to eat a good light meal, parking-6 DM—have coins, about 1.5 kilometers north of Füssen—follow signs for "musical," book well in advance, for tickets call 01805/583-944, www.ludwigmusical.com).

More Sights—Bavaria

These are listed in driving order from Füssen.

▲▲**Wies Church (Wieskirche)**—Germany's greatest rococo-style church, Wieskirche ("the church in the meadow") is newly restored and looking as brilliant as the day it floated down from heaven. Overripe with decoration but bright and bursting with beauty, this church is a divine droplet, a curly curlicue, the final flowering of the Baroque movement. The ceiling depicts the Last Judgment—but the most positive one around. Jesus, rather than sitting on the throne to judge, rides high on a rainbow, giving any sinners the feeling that there is still time to repent and plenty of mercy on hand.

   This is a pilgrimage church. In the early 1700s a carving of Christ too graphic to be accepted by that generation's church was the focus of worship in a peasant's private chapel. Miraculously, it wept. And pilgrims came from all around.

   Bavaria's top rococo architects, the Zimmermann brothers, were then commissioned to build the Wieskirche, which features the amazing carving above its altar and still attracts countless pilgrims (donation requested, daily 8:00–20:00, less off-season).

Take a commune-with-nature-and-smell-the-farm detour back through the meadow to the car park.

Wieskirche is 30 minutes north of Neuschwanstein. The northbound Romantic Road bus tour stops here for 15 minutes. Füssen–Wieskirche buses run several times a day. By car, head north from Füssen, turn right at Steingaden, and follow the signs.

If you can't visit Wieskirche, visit one of the other churches that came out of the same heavenly spray can: Oberammergau's church, Munich's Asam Church, the Würzburg Residenz Chapel, or the splendid Ettal Monastery (free and near Oberammergau).

If you're driving from Wieskirche to Oberammergau, you'll cross the Echelsbacher Bridge, which arches 70 meters over the Pöllat Gorge. Thoughtful drivers let their passengers walk across (for the views) and meet them at the other side. Any kayakers? Notice the painting of the traditional village wood-carver (who used to walk from town to town with his art on his back) on the first big house on the Oberammergau side, a shop called Almdorf Ammertal. It has a huge selection of overpriced carvings and commission-hungry tour guides.

▲**Oberammergau**—The Shirley Temple of Bavarian villages and exploited to the hilt by the tourist trade, Oberammergau wears way too much makeup. If you're passing through anyway, it's worth a wander among the half-timbered houses painted with Bible scenes and famous fairy-tale characters. Browse through wood-carvers' shops—small art galleries filled with very expensive whittled works. Pilat's house on Ludwig Thomastrasse is a living workshop full of wood-carvers and painters in action (daily 13:00–18:00, off-season weekends only). Or see folk art at the town's Heimatmuseum (TI tel. 08822/92310, closed weekends off-season, www.oberammergau.de).

Visit the church, a poor cousin of the one at Wies. This church looks richer than it is. Put your hand on the "marble" columns. If they warm up, they're painted fakes. Wander through the graveyard. Ponder the deaths that two wars dealt Germany. Behind the church are the photos of three Schneller brothers, all killed within two years in World War II.

Passion Play: Still making good on a deal the townspeople made with God when they were spared devastation by the Black Plague 350 years ago, once each decade Oberammergau performs the Passion Play. It happened in 2000 when 5,000 people a day for 100 summer days attended Oberammergau's sold-out, all-day dramatic story of Christ's crucifixion. Until the next performance in 2010, you'll have to settle for reading the Book, seeing Nicodemus tool around town in his VW, or browsing through the theater's exhibition hall (4 DM, daily 9:30–12:00, 13:30–16:00, closed

Mon off-season, tel. 08822/32278). Consider a guided tour of the Passion Play theatre (call TI for details).

Sleeping: Gasthaus zum Stern is friendly, serves good food (closed Tue off-season), and is a good value for this touristy town (Sb-50 DM, Db-100 DM, Dorfstrasse 33, 82487 Oberammergau, tel. 08822/867, fax 08822/7027). **Hotel Bayerische Lowe** is central with a good restaurant and comfortable rooms (Db-99 DM, Dedlerstrasse 2, tel. 08822/1365). Oberammergau's modern **youth hostel** is on the river a short walk from the center (20-DM beds, open all year, tel. 08822/4114).

Driving into town from the north, cross the bridge, take the second left, follow "Polizei" signs, and park by the huge gray Passionsspielhaus. Leaving town, head out past the church and turn toward Ettal on Road 23. You're 30 kilometers from Reutte via the scenic Plansee. Oberammergau is connected to Füssen by six direct two-hour buses per day.

▲▲**Linderhof Castle**—This homiest of "Mad" King Ludwig's castles is small and comfortably exquisite—good enough for a minor god. Set in the woods 15 minutes from Oberammergau by car or bus (3 buses/day, fewer off-season) and surrounded by fountains and sculpted, Italian-style gardens, it's the only palace I've toured that actually had me feeling envious. Don't miss the grotto—15-minute tours included with palace ticket (11 DM, daily 9:00–17:30, Thu until 19:30, Oct–March 10:00–16:00 with lunch break, parking-4 DM, fountains often erupt on the hour, English tours when 20 gather—easy in summer but sparse off-season, tel. 08822/92030). Plan for lots of walking and a two-hour stop to fully enjoy this royal park. Pay at entry and get admission time. Visit outlying sights to pass any wait time.

▲▲**Zugspitze**—The tallest point in Germany is a border crossing. Lifts from Austria and Germany go to the 10,000-foot summit of the Zugspitze. Straddle the border between two great nations while enjoying an incredible view. Restaurants, shops, and telescopes await you at the summit.

On the German side, the 75-minute trip from Garmisch costs 79 DM round-trip; family discounts are available (buy a combo cogwheel train and cable car ride, tel. 08821/7970). Hikers enjoy the easy 10-kilometer walk around the lovely Elbsee lake (German side, 5 minutes downhill from cable "Seilbahn").

On the Austrian side, from the less crowded Talstation Obermoos above the village of Erwald, the tram zips you to the top in 10 minutes (420 AS or 61 DM round-trip, late May–Oct daily 8:40–16:40, tel. in Austria 05673/2309).

The German ascent is easier for those without a car, but buses do connect the Erwald train station and the Austrian lift almost every hour.

Sleeping in Füssen
(2 DM = about $1, country code: 49, area code: 08362, zip code: 87629)
Sleep Code: **S** = Single, **D** = Double/Twin, **T** = Triple, **Q** = Quad, **b** = bathroom, **t** = toilet only, **s** = shower only, **CC** = Credit Card (Visa, MasterCard, Amex).

Unless otherwise noted, breakfast is included, hall showers are free, and English is spoken. Prices listed are for one-night stays. Some places give a discount for longer stays. Always ask. Competition is fierce, and off-season prices are soft.

While I prefer sleeping in Reutte (see below), convenient Füssen is just five kilometers from Ludwig's castles and offers a cobbled, riverside retreat. But it also happens to be very touristy (notice *das* sushi bar). It has just about as many rooms as tourists, though, and the TI has a free room-finding service. All places I've listed (except the hostel) are within a few blocks of the train station and the town center. They are used to travelers getting in after the Romantic Road bus arrives (20:05) and will hold rooms for a telephone promise. Parking is easy at the station.

Hotel Kurcafé is deluxe, with spacious rooms and all of the amenities. Its bakery can ruin your budget any time of year (Sb-99–169 DM, Db-149–209 DM, Tb-179–249 DM, Q-199–279 DM, less off-season, CC:VM, on the tiny traffic circle a block in front of train station at Bahnhofstrasse 4, tel. 08362/6369, fax 08362/39424, www.kurcafe.com). The attached restaurant has good and reasonable daily specials.

Altstadt-Hotel zum Hechten offers all the modern comforts in a friendly, traditional shell right under the Füssen Castle in the old-town pedestrian zone (S-65 DM, Sb-80–90 DM, D-100 DM, Db-130–150 DM, Tb-180 DM, Qb-200 DM, these prices and free parking promised with this book in 2001, cheaper off-season and for multinight stays, fun mini–bowling alley in basement; from TI, walk down pedestrian street, take second right to Ritterstrasse 6, tel. 08362/91600, fax 08362/916-099, www.hotel-hechten.com, Frau Margaret has taken fine care of travelers for 40 years). The attached restaurant Zum Hechten serves hearty Bavarian specialties and specializes in pike (*Hecht*), pulled from the Lech River.

American **Suzanne's B&B,** run with an iron hand, offers backyard-fresh eggs, local cheese, a children's yard, affordable laundry, bright and spacious rooms, and feel-good balconies. Big families should ask about her "attic special," and the budget-conscious should ask about her "backpacker's special" (D-100 DM, Db-140 DM, Tb-180 DM, Qb-210 DM, room for up to six-220–240 DM, nonsmoking, backtrack 2 blocks from station, Venetianerwinkel 3, tel. 08362/38485, fax 08362/921-396, www .suzannes.org, e-mail: svorbrugg@t-online.de).

The funky, old, ornately furnished **Pension Garni Elisabeth**

Füssen

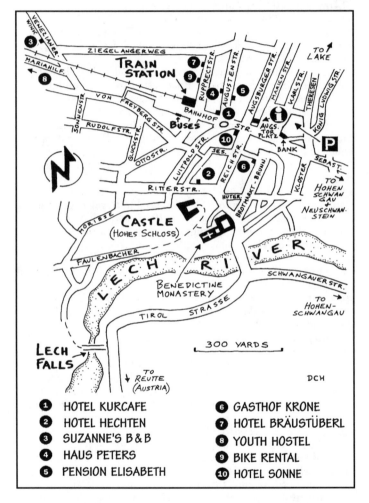

① HOTEL KURCAFE
② HOTEL HECHTEN
③ SUZANNE'S B & B
④ HAUS PETERS
⑤ PENSION ELISABETH
⑥ GASTHOF KRONE
⑦ HOTEL BRÄUSTÜBERL
⑧ YOUTH HOSTEL
⑨ BIKE RENTAL
⑩ HOTEL SONNE

exudes an Addams-family friendliness. Floors creak, dust balls wander, and the piano is never played (S-55 DM, D-90–100 DM, Db-120–180 DM, T-135 DM, Tb-180–195 DM, showers-6 DM, Augustenstrasse 10, 2 blocks from the station toward town, take second left, tel. 08362/6275).

Haus Peters, across the street, is comfy, smoke free, and friendly, but will be closed May, June, and September (Db-86 DM, Tb-120 DM, Augustenstrasse 5 1/2, tel. 08362/7171).

Gasthof Krone, a rare bit of pre-glitz Füssen in the pedestrian zone, has dumpy halls and stairs and standard, comfy rooms at good prices (S-58 DM, D-106 DM, extra bed-53 DM, prices drop 6 DM for 2-night stays, CC:VMA, reception in restaurant, from TI, head down pedestrian street, take first left to Schrannengasse 17, tel. 08362/7824, fax 08362/37505).

Hotel Bräustüberl, run with indifference, has decent rooms attached to a gruff and musty old beer hall–type place at fair rates (Sb-55 DM, Db-100 DM, Rupprechtstrasse 5, a block from the station, tel. 08362/7843, fax 08362/941-361).

Hotel Sonne is a splurge in the heart of the town with 32 quaint yet plush rooms with all the extras (Sb-160 DM, Db-195 DM, Tb-240 DM, CC:VMA, free parking, kitty-corner from TI on Reichenstrasse 37, tel. 08362/9080, fax 08362/908-100, www.hotel-sonne.de).

Füssen Youth Hostel, a fine, German-run youth hostel, welcomes travelers under 27 (2- to 6-bed rooms, bed and breakfast-23 DM, dinner-7 DM, sheets-5.50 DM, laundry-7 DM/load, nonsmoking, Mariahilferstrasse 5, tel. 08362/7754, fax 08362/2770). From the station, backtrack 10 minutes along the tracks.

Sleeping in Hohenschwangau, near Neuschwanstein Castle
(country code: 49, area code: 08362, zip code: 87645)
Inexpensive farmhouse *Zimmer* (B&Bs) abound in the Bavarian countryside around Neuschwanstein and are a good value. Look for signs that say "Zimmer Frei" ("room free," or vacancy). The going rate is about 80 DM per double including breakfast. **Pension Weiher** has lots of balconies and floodlit Neuschwanstein views (S-38 DM, D-80 DM, Db-100 DM, Hofwiesenweg 11, tel. & fax 08362/81161). **Pension Schwansee** has clean, basic rooms (Db-100–120 DM, CC:VM, bike rental, 2.5 kilometers from the castle, right on the road to Füssen at Parkstrasse 9, 87645 Alterschrofen, tel. 08362/8353, fax 08362/987-320, family Strössner).

For more of a hotel, try **Alpenhotel Meier**. It's located in a rural setting within walking distance of the castle, just beyond the lower parking lot. Its rooms have new furnishings and porches (Sb-80–90 DM, Db-130–150 DM, 2-night discounts, larger rooms available, easy parking, Schwangauerstrasse 37, tel. 08362/81152, fax 08362/987-028, e-mail: alpenhotelmeier@firemail.de).

Eating in Füssen
Infooday is a clever and modern self-service eatery that sells its hot meals and salad bar by weight and offers English newspapers (filling salad-6 DM, meals-10 DM, Mon–Fri 10:30–18:30, Sat 10:30–14:30, closed Sun, under Füssen Castle in Hotel zum Hechten, Ritterstrasse 6). Nearby **Ritterstuben** offers reasonable

and delicious fish and salads (Tue–Sun 11:30–14:30, 17:30–23:00, closed Mon, next to Altstadt-Hotel zum Hechten at Ritterstrasse 4, tel. 08362/7759). A couple of blocks away, **Pizza Blitz** is a dive that offers good take-out or eat-at-the-counter pizzas and hearty salads for about 10 DM apiece (Mon–Sat 11:00–23:00, Sun 12:00–23:00, Luitpoldstrasse 14). Picnickers can shop at **Woolworth's** plentiful supermarket (Mon–Fri 9:00–19:00, Sat 9:00–16:00, closed Sun, Reichenstrassse 11, tel. 083621/91840).

Transportation Connections—Füssen
To: Neuschwanstein (2 buses/hrly, 10 min, 2.50 DM one-way, 5 DM round-trip; taxis cost 20 DM), **Reutte** (5 buses/day, 30 min, no service on Sun; taxis cost 40 DM), **Munich** (hrly trains, 2 hrs, transfer in Buchloe).

Romantic Road Buses: The northbound Romantic Road bus departs Füssen at 8:00; the southbound bus arrives at Füssen at 20:05 (bus stops at train station). Railpasses get you a 75 percent discount on the Romantic Road bus (and, best of all, the ride doesn't use up a day of a flexipass)—this is a great value. For more information, see the Rothenburg chapter.

REUTTE, AUSTRIA
(15 AS = about $1)
Reutte (ROY-teh, rolled "r"), a relaxed town of 5,500, is located 20 minutes across the border from Füssen. It's far from the international tourist crowd, but popular with Germans and Austrians for its climate. Doctors recommend its "grade 1" air. Reutte's one claim to fame with Americans: As Nazi Germany was falling in 1945, Hitler's top rocket scientist Werner von Braun joined the Americans (rather than the Russians) here in Reutte. You could say the American space program began in Reutte.

Reutte isn't in any other American guidebook. Its charms are subtle, though its generous sidewalks are filled with smart boutiques and lazy coffeehouses. It never was rich or important. Its castle is ruined, its buildings have painted-on "carvings," its churches are full, its men yodel for each other on birthdays, and lately its energy is spent soaking its Austrian and German guests in *Gemütlichkeit*. Most guests stay for a week, so the town's attractions are more time-consuming than thrilling. If the weather's good, hike to the mysterious Ehrenberg ruins, ride the luge, or rent a bike. For a slap-dancing bang, enjoy a Tirolean folk evening. For accommodations, see "Sleeping," below.

Orientation (area code: 05672)
Tourist Information: Reutte's TI is a block in front of the train station (Mon–Fri 8:00–12:00, 14:00–18:00, Sat 8:30–12:00, tel. 05672/62336 or, from Germany, 0043-5672/62336). Go over your

sightseeing plans, ask about a folk evening, pick up city and biking maps, and ask about discounts with the hotel guest cards.

Bike Rental: In the center, the Heinz Glatzle rents good bikes (city and mountain bikes–200 AS, kids' bikes–100 AS, Obermarkt 61, tel. 05672/62752). Several recommended hotels loan or rent bikes to guests. Most of the sights described in this chapter make good biking destinations. Ask about the bike path (*Radwanderweg*) along the Lech River.

Kids' Play Areas: Reutte's excellent pool (see below) has a playground. The TI can recommend several others.

Laundry: Don't ask the TI about a Laundromat. Unless you can infiltrate the local campground, Hotel Maximilian, or Gutshof zum Schluxen (see "Sleeping," below), the town has none.

Sights—Reutte

▲▲**Ehrenberg Ruins**—The brooding ruins of Ehrenberg Castle are 1.5 kilometers outside of Reutte on the road to Lermoos and Innsbruck. This is a pleasant walk or a short bike ride from Reutte; bikers can use the trail—*Radwanderweg*—along the Lech River (the TI has a good map).

Ehrenberg, a 13th-century rock pile, provides a great contrast to King Ludwig's "modern" castles and a super opportunity to let your imagination off its leash.

At the parking lot at the base of the ruin-topped hill, you'll find the café/guest house Gasthor Klaus (closed Wed), which offers a German-language flyer about the castle and has a wall painting of the intact castle.

The parking lot lies on the ancient Roman road, Via Claudia, and the medieval salt road. The **fortification** at the parking lot was a castle built over the road to control traffic and levy tolls on all that passed this strategic valley. (This ruin will open as a museum of European castle ruins in about 2004.)

Hike up 20 minutes from the parking lot for a great view from your own private ruins. Facing the hill from the parking lot, find the gravelly road at the Klaus sign. Follow the road to the saddle between the two hills. From the saddle notice how the castle stands high on the horizon. This is Ehrenberg (which means "mountain of honor"), built in 1290. Thirteenth-century castles were designed to stand boastfully tall. With the advent of gunpowder, castles dug in. Notice the **ramparts** around you. They are 18th century. Approaching Ehrenberg castle, look for the small door to the left. It's the night entrance (tight and awkward, therefore safer in a surprise invasion).

Hiking up the hill you go through two doors. Castles allowed step-by-step retreat, giving defenders time to regroup and fight back against invading forces.

Before making the final and steepest ascent, follow the path

Reutte

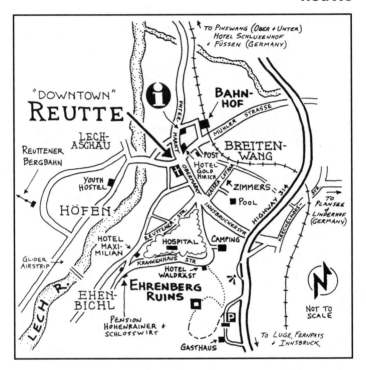

around to the right to a big, grassy courtyard with commanding views and a fat, newly restored **turret**. This stored gunpowder and held a big cannon that enjoyed a clear view of the valley below. In medieval times, all the trees approaching the castle were cleared to keep an unobstructed view.

Look out over the valley. The pointy spire marks **Breitenwang**, which was a stop on the ancient Via Claudia. In A.D. 46, there was a Roman camp here. In 1489, after the Reutte bridge crossed the Lech River, Reutte (marked by the onion-domed church) was made a market town and eclipsed Breitenwang in importance. Any gliders circling? They launch from just over the river in Hofen (see "Flying and Gliding," below).

For centuries, this castle was the seat of government—ruling an area called the "judgement of Ehrenberg" (roughly the same as today's "district of Reutte"). When the emperor came by, he stayed here. In 1604, the ruler moved downtown into more comfortable quarters and the castle was no longer a palace.

Climb the steep hill to the top of the castle. Take the high ground. There was no water supply here, just kegs of wine, beer, and a cistern to collect rain.

Ehrenberg repelled 16,000 Swedish soldiers in the defense of Catholicism in 1632. Ehrenberg saw three or four other battles, but its end was not glorious. In the 1780s, a local businessman bought the castle in order to sell off its parts. Later, when vagabonds moved in, the roof was removed to make squatting miserable. With the roof gone, deterioration quickened, leaving this evocative shell and a whiff of history.

Folk Museum—Reutte's Heimatmuseum, offering a quick look at the local folk culture and the story of the castle, is more cute than impressive and comes without English explanations (20 AS, Tue–Sun 10:00–12:00, 14:00–17:00, closed Mon and off-season, in the bright green building on Untermarkt, around corner from Hotel Goldener Hirsch, 1 block away).

▲▲**Tirolean Folk Evening**—Ask the TI or your hotel if there's a Tirolean folk evening scheduled. About three times a week in the summer, Reutte or a nearby town puts on an evening of yodeling, slap dancing, and Tirolean frolic usually worth the 80 to 120 AS and short drive. Off-season, you'll have to do your own yodeling. There are also weekly folk concerts in the park (summer only, ask at TI).

Swimming—Plunge into Reutte's Olympic-size swimming pool to cool off after your castle hikes (65 AS, daily 10:00–21:00, off-season 14:00–21:00 and closed Mon, new pool planned for 2001 at same site, 15 min on foot from Reutte center, head out Obermarkt and turn left on Kaiser-Lothar Strasse).

Reuttener Bergbahn—This mountain lift swoops you high above the tree line to a starting point for several hikes and an Alpine flower park with special paths leading you past countless local varieties (good bike ride with an uphill at the end).

Flying and Gliding—For a major thrill on a sunny day, drop by the tiny airport in Hofen across the river, and fly. A small single-prop plane can buzz the Zugspitze and Ludwig's castles and give you a bird's-eye peek at Reutte's Ehrenberg ruins (2 people for 30 min-1,350 AS, 1 hr-2,400 AS, tel. 05672/63207). Or, for something more angelic, how about *Segelfliegen*? For 370 AS you get 30 minutes in a glider for two (you and the pilot). Just watching the towrope launch the graceful glider like a giant, slow-motion rubber-band gun is thrilling (late May–Oct 11:00–19:00, in good weather only, tel. 05672/71550).

Sights—Tirol, Near Reutte

▲▲**The Luge (***Sommerrodelbahn***)**—Near Lermoos, on the road from Reutte to Innsbruck, you'll find two exciting luge courses, or *Sommerrodelbahn*. To try one of Europe's great $5 thrills, take the lift up, grab a sledlike go-cart, and luge down. The concrete course banks on the corners, and even a novice can go very, very fast. Most are cautious on their first run, speed demons on their second (and bruised and bloody on their third). A woman once showed me her journal illustrated with her husband's dried five-inch-long luge scab. He disobeyed the only essential rule of luging: Keep both hands on your stick. To avoid getting into a bumper-to-bumper traffic jam, let the person in front of you get way ahead before you start. No one emerges from the course without a windblown hairdo and a smile-creased face. Both places charge the same price (80 AS per run, 5- and 10-trip discount cards) and shut down at the least hint of rain (call ahead to make sure they're open; you're more likely to encounter an English-speaker if you call the TIs, numbers listed below). If you're without a car, these are not worth the trouble (consider the luge near Neuschwanstein instead, see "Tegelberg Luge," above).

The short and steep luge: Bichlbach, the first course (100-meter drop over 800-meter course), is six kilometers beyond Reutte's castle ruins. Look for a chair lift on the right and exit on the tiny road at the Almkopfbahn Rosthof sign (open only Sat–Sun 10:00–17:00 in mid-May, then daily June–Oct, call first, tel. 05674/5350, or contact the local TI at 05674/5354).

The longest luge: The Biberwier Sommerrodelbahn is a better luge and, at 1,300 meters, the longest in Austria (15 min farther from Reutte than Bichlbach, just past Lermoos in Biberwier—the first exit after a long tunnel). The only drawbacks are its short season and hours (open only Sat–Sun 9:00–16:30 from mid-May, then daily 9:00–16:30 through Sept, call first, tel. 05673/2111, TI tel. 05673/2922).

▲**Fallerschein**—Easy for drivers and a special treat for those who may have been Kit Carson in a previous life, this extremely remote log-cabin village is a 4,000-foot-high, flower-speckled world of serene slopes and cowbells. Thunderstorms roll down the valley like it's God's bowling alley, but the pint-size church on the high ground, blissfully simple in a land of Baroque, seems to promise that this huddle of houses will survive and the river and breeze will just keep flowing. The couples sitting on benches are mostly Austrian vacationers who've rented cabins here. Many of them, appreciating the remoteness of Fallerschein, are having affairs.

For a rugged chunk of local Alpine peace, spend a night in the local **Matratzenlager Almwirtschaft Fallerschein**, run by Kerle Erwin (about 120 AS per person with breakfast, 27 cheap beds in a very simple loft dorm, good, inexpensive meals; open, if weather permits, mid-May–Oct, 6671 Weissenbach Pfarrweg 18, Reutte, tel. 05678/5142, rarely answered, and then not in English). It's crowded only on weekends. Fallerschein, at the end of the two-kilometer Berwang Road, is near Namlos and about 45 minutes southwest of Reutte.

Sleeping in and near Reutte
(15 AS = about $1, country code: 43, area code: 05672, zip code: 6600)

Reutte is a mellow Füssen with fewer crowds and easygoing locals with a contagious love of life. Come here for a good dose of Austrian ambience and lower prices. Those with a car should home-base here; those without should consider it. (To call Reutte from Germany, dial 00-43-5672, then the local number.) You'll drive across the border without stopping. Reutte is popular with Austrians and Germans who come here year after year for one- or two-week vacations. The hotels are big, elegant, and full of comfy, carved furnishings and creative ways to spend so much time in one spot. They take great pride in their restaurants, and the owners send their children away to hotel management schools. All include a generally great breakfast but few accept credit cards.

Hotels and Guest Houses

Moserhof Hotel is a plush Tirolean splurge with polished service and facilities. The dining room is elegant (older but fine Db-900 AS, newer and larger Db-980 AS, extra person-460 AS, all rooms with balconies, elevator, from downtown Reutte walk to post office roundabout then to Planseestrasse 44, in village of Breitenwang, tel. 05672/62020, fax 05672/620-2040).

Hotel Goldener Hirsch, located in the center of Reutte just two blocks from the station, is a grand old hotel renovated with a mod Tirolean Jugendstil flair. It includes minibars, cable TV, and one lonely set of antlers (Sb-620 AS, Db-940 AS, 2-night discounts, CC:VMA, a few family rooms, elevator, quality food in their restaurant, 6600 Reutte-Tirol, tel. 05672/62508, fax 05672/625-087, www.goldener-hirsch.at, e-mail: gold.hirsch@netway.at, Monika, Helmut—who can be unpleasant, and daughter Vanessa).

The next four listings are a few miles upriver from Reutte in the village of Ehenbichl; all are along an enjoyable hike to Ehrenberg ruins.

Hotel Maximilian is a fine splurge. It includes free bicycles, Ping-Pong, a sauna, a children's playroom, and the friendly service of the Koch family. Daughter Gabi speaks flawless English and is clearly in charge. There always seems to be a special event here, and the Kochs host many Tirolean folk evenings (Sb-450–500 AS, Db-940–1,000 AS, cheaper for families, no CC, laundry service available even to nonguests, good restaurant, A-6600 Ehenbichl-Reutte, tel. 05672/62585, fax 05672/625-8554, www.maxihotel.com, e-mail: maxhotel@netway.at). From central Reutte, go south on Obermarkt and turn right on Reuttenerstrasse. They rent cars to guests only (one VW Golf, one VW van, must book in advance).

Pension Hohenrainer is a quiet, good value with some castle-view balconies (Sb-280–350 AS, Db-620–700 AS). The same family runs the simpler **Gasthof Schlosswirt** across the green field (S-180–200 AS, D-400–480 AS, no CC, traditional Tirolean-style restaurant). Both are up the road behind Hotel Maximilian (turn right and continue 100 meters to Unterreid 3, A-6600 Ehenbichl, tel. 05672/62544, fax 05672/62052, e-mail: hohenrainer@aon.at).

Gasthof-Pension Waldrast, separating a forest and a meadow, is run by the farming Huter family. The place feels hauntingly quiet and has no restaurant, but it does include 10 very nice rooms with sitting areas and castle-view balconies (Sb-400 AS, Db-700 AS, Tb-900 AS, Qb-1,200 AS, includes small breakfast, nonsmoking, a mile from Reutte just off the main drag toward Innsbruck, past the campground and under the castle ruins, on Ehrenbergstrasse, 6600 Reutte-Ehenbichl, tel. & fax 05672/62443, www.waldrast.com, e-mail: info@waldrast.com).

Closer to Füssen but still in Austria, **Gutshof zum Schluxen**, run by helpful Hermann, gets the "remote-old-hotel-in-an-idyllic-setting" award. This family-friendly working farm offers modern rustic elegance draped in goose down and pastels, and a chance to pet a rabbit and feed the deer. Its picturesque meadow setting will turn you into a dandelion picker, and its proximity to Neuschwanstein will turn you into a hiker (Sb-560 AS, Db-1,120 AS, extra person-300 AS, 3-night discounts, free pickup from Reutte, CC:VM, good restaurant, fun bar, self-service laundry, mountain bike rental, between Reutte and Füssen in village of Pinswang, A-6600 Pinswang-Reutte, tel. 05677/8903, fax 05677/890-323, www.schluxen.com, e-mail: welcome@schluxen.com).

Private Homes in Breitenwang, near Reutte

The Reutte TI has a list of more than 50 private homes (*Zimmer*) that rent out generally good rooms with facilities down the hall, pleasant communal living rooms, and breakfast. Most charge 200 AS per person per night and speak little if any English. Reservations are nearly impossible for one- or two-night stays. But short stops are welcome if you just drop in and fill in available gaps. Most *Zimmer* charge 15 AS to 20 AS extra for heat in winter (worth it). The TI can always find you a room when you arrive.

Right next door to Reutte is the older and quieter village of Breitenwang. It has all the best *Zimmer*, the recommended Moserhof Hotel (above), and a bakery (a 20-minute walk from the Reutte train station—at the post office roundabout, follow Planseestrasse past the onion dome to the pointy straight dome; unmarked Kaiser Lothar Strasse is the first right past this church). The following three *Zimmer* are comfortable, quiet, have few stairs, and are within two blocks of the Breitenwang church steeple: **Helene Haissl** (S-200 AS, D-400 AS, 2-night discounts, fine rooms, beautiful garden, separate entrance for rooms, across

from the big Alpenhotel at Planseestrasse 63, tel. 05672/67913);
Inge Hosp (S-220 AS, D-400 AS, an old-fashioned place, includes
antlers over the breakfast table, Kaiser Lothar Strasse 36, tel.
05672/62401); and **Walter and Emilie Hosp**, Inge's more formal
cousins, who have a modern house across the street (D-400 AS,
extra person-160 AS, Kaiser Lothar Strasse 29, tel. 05672/65377).

Hostel

The homey hostel **Jugendgästehaus Graben** has two to six beds
per room and includes breakfast and sheets. The Reyman family
keeps the place traditional, clean, and friendly and serves a great
90-AS dinner for guests only. This is a super value. If you've never
hosteled and are curious (and have a car or don't mind a bus ride),
try it. They accept nonmembers of any age (dorm bed-210 AS,
Db-570 AS, laundry service, no curfew, smoke-free rooms, bus
connection to Neuschwanstein; about 3 kilometers from Reutte,
from downtown Reutte, cross the bridge and follow the main road
left along the river, or take the bus—1 bus/hrly until 18:00, ask
for Graben stop; Graben 1, A-6600 Reutte-Höfen, tel. 05672/
626-440, fax 05672/626-444, www.tirol.com/jgh-hoefen, e-mail:
jgh-hoefen@tirol.com).

Eating in Reutte

Hotels in this region take great pleasure in earning the loyalty of
their guests by serving local cuisine at reasonable prices. Rather
than go to a cheap restaurant, eat at your hotel. For cheap food,
the **Metzgerei Storf** (Mon–Fri 8:30–15:00), above the deli across
from the Heimatmuseum on Untermarkt Street, is good. The
modern **Alina** restaurant in Breitenwang is a fine Italian establish-
ment with decent prices (near recommended *Zimmer*, 2 blocks
behind church at Bachweg 17).

Transportation Connections—Reutte

To: Füssen (5 buses/day, 30 min, no service on Sun; taxis cost 40
DM). In 2001 Reutte will probably lose its train service. Buses will
likely connect the town with Garmisch and Innsbruck from which
trains will connect to Munich and Salzburg.

BADEN-BADEN AND THE BLACK FOREST

Combine Edenism and hedonism as you explore this most romantic of German forests and dip into its mineral spas.

The Black Forest, or "Schwarzwald" in German, is a range of hills stretching 100 miles north-south along the French border from Karlsruhe to Switzerland. Its highest peak is the 4,900-foot-tall Feldberg. Because of its thick forests, people called it black.

Until the last century, the Schwarzwald had been cut off from the German mainstream. The poor farmland drove medieval locals to become foresters, glassblowers, and clock makers. Strong traditions continue to be woven through the thick dialects and thatched roofs. On any Sunday, you will find Germans in traditional costumes coloring the Black Forest on *Volksmärsche* (group hikes—open to anyone; for a listing, visit www.ava.org/clubs/germany).

Popular with German holiday-goers and those looking for some serious "R&R," the Black Forest offers clean air, cuckoo clocks, cherry cakes, cheery villages, and countless hiking possibilities.

The area's two biggest tourist traps are the tiny Titisee Lake (not quite as big as its tourist parking lot) and Triberg, a small town filled with cuckoo clock shops. In spite of the crowds, the drives are scenic, hiking is *wunderbar*, and the attractions listed below are well worth a visit. The two major (and very different) towns are Baden-Baden in the north and Freiburg in the south. Freiburg may be the Black Forest's capital, but Baden-Baden is Germany's greatest 19th-century spa resort. Stroll through its elegant streets and casino. Soak in its famous baths.

Planning Your Time

Save a day and two nights for Baden-Baden. Tour Freiburg but sleep in charming and overlooked Staufen. By train, Freiburg and

The Black Forest

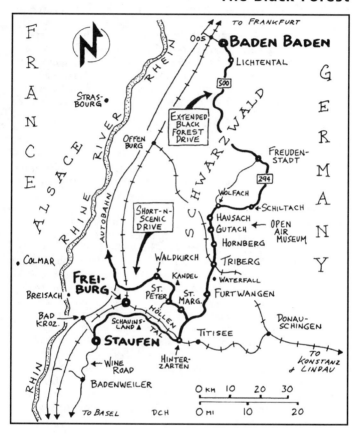

Baden-Baden are easy, as is a short foray into the forest from either. With more time, do the small-town forest medley between the two. With a car, I'd do the whole cuckoo thing: a night in Staufen, a busy day touring north, and two nights and a relaxing day in Baden-Baden.

A blitz day from Murten or Interlaken (Switzerland) would go like this: 8:30–Depart, 11:00–Staufen (stroll town, change money, buy picnic), 12:30–Scenic drive to Furtwangen with a scenic picnic along the way, 14:30–Tour clock museum, 15:30–Drive to Gütach, 16:30–Tour open-air folk museum, 18:00–Drive to Baden-Baden, 20:00–Arrive in Baden-Baden. With an overnight in Staufen, you could spend the morning in Freiburg and arrive in Baden-Baden in time for a visit to the spa (last entry 19:30).

BADEN-BADEN

Of all the high-class resort towns I've seen, Baden-Baden is the easiest to enjoy in jeans with a picnic. This was the playground of Europe's high-rolling elite 150 years ago. Royalty and aristocracy would come from all corners to take the *Kur*—a soak in the curative (or at least they feel that way) mineral waters—and enjoy the world's top casino. Today this lush town of 55,000 attracts a more middle-class crowd, both tourists in search of a lower pulse and Germans enjoying the fruits of their generous health-care system.

Orientation (area code: 07221)

Baden-Baden is made for strolling with a poodle. The train station is in a suburb called Baden-Oos, five kilometers from the center but easily connected with the center by bus. Except for the station and a couple of hotels on the opposite side of town, everything that matters is clustered within a 10-minute walk between the baths and the casino.

Tourist Information: At the TI, on the first floor of the Trinkhalle, pick up the good city map, Black Forest information, and monthly program (May–Oct Mon–Fri 9:00–17:30, Sat 9:00–15:00, tel. 07221/275-200; additional office on B-500 autobahn exit at Schwartzwaldstrasse 52, daily 9:00–19:00). It has enough recommended walks and organized excursions to keep the most energetic vacationer happy.

Internet Access: Check your e-mail at the town library across from the new post office in Wagener shopping center (8 DM/hr, best to call and reserve ahead, Tue–Fri 10:00–18:00, Sat 10:00–13:00, Langestrasse 43, tel. 07221/932-260).

Arrival in Baden-Baden: Walk out of the train station (lockers available on the platform) and catch bus #201 in front of the kiosks on your right. Get off in about 15 minutes at the Leopoldplatz stop (announced as "Stadtmitte"). Allow 20 DM for a taxi to the center.

Getting around Baden-Baden

Only one bus matters. Bus #201 runs straight through Baden-Baden, connecting its Oos train station, town center, and the east end of town (every 10 min until 19:00, then every 30 min until 01:00; buy tickets from driver: 3.50-DM ticket per person, or the 8-DM, 24-hr pass good for 2 adults or a family with kids under age 15). Tickets are valid for 90 minutes but only in one direction. With bus #201 you don't need to mess with downtown parking.

Sights-Sights—Baden-Baden

▲▲**Strolling Lichtentaler Allee**—Bestow a royal title on yourself and promenade down the famous Lichtentaler Allee, a pleasant, picnic-perfect, 1.5-mile lane through a park along the babbling,

Baden-Baden

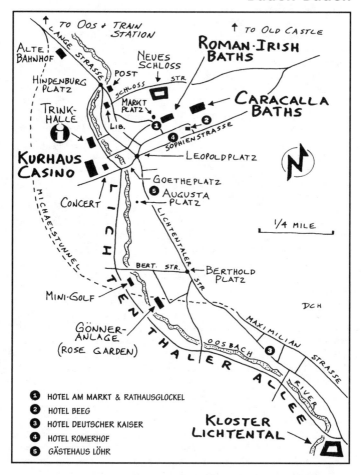

brick-lined Oos River, past old mansions and under hearty oaks and exotic trees (lit until 22:00), to the historic Lichtentaler Abbey (a Cistercian convent founded in 1245). At the mini-golf course (welcomes public) and elitist tennis courts, cross the bridge into the free Art Nouveau rose garden (*Gönneranlage*, 100 labeled kinds of roses, great lounge chairs, best in early summer). Either walk the whole length round-trip, or take city bus #201 one-way (runs between downtown and Klosterplatz, near the abbey). Many bridges cross the river, making it easy to shortcut to bus #201 anytime.

▲**Mini–Black Forest Walks**—Baden-Baden is at the northern end of the Black Forest. If you're not going south but want a taste of Germany's favorite woods, consider one of several hikes from town.

The best is probably the hike that starts from the old town past the Neues Schloss (new castle) to the Altes Schloss (ruined old castle), which crowns a hill above town, past cliffs tinseled with rock climbers and on to Ebersteinburg, a village with a ruined castle (allow 90 minutes and catch bus #214 back into town).

For less work and more view, consider riding the cogwheel Merkur Bergbahn to the 2,000-foot summit of Merkur (daily 10:00–22:00, closed Jan–Feb, take bus #204 from Augustaplatz or #205 from Leopoldsplatz to the end of the line and catch 7-DM funicular up, tel. 07221/31640). You can hike down, following the trails to Lichtentaler Abbey and then along Lichtentaler Allee into town.

▲▲**Casino and Kurhaus**—The impressive building called the Kurhaus is wrapped around a grand casino. Built in the 1850s in wannabe-French style, Marlene Dietrich declared this "the most beautiful casino." Inspired by the Palace of Versailles, it's filled with rooms honoring French royalty who never set foot in the place. But many French did. Gambling was illegal in 19th-century France... just over the border. The casino is licensed on the precondition that it pay about 90 percent of its earnings in taxes to fund state-sponsored social programs and public works. It earns $35 million a year... and is the toast of Baden-Baden, or at least its bread and butter. The staff of 300 is paid by tips from happy gamblers.

You can visit the casino on a tour (when it's closed to gamblers, see below), or you can drop by after 14:00 to gamble or just observe. (This is no problem—a third of the visitors only observe.) The place is most interesting in action; people watch under chandeliers. The scene is more subdued than at an American casino; anyone showing emotions is a tourist. Lean against a gilded statue and listen to the graceful reshuffling of personal fortunes. Do some imaginary gambling or buy a few chips at the window near the entry. The casino is open for gambling from 14:00 to 02:00 (5-DM entry, 5-DM minimum bet, 10-DM minimum Fri–Sun, no blue jeans or tennis shoes, tie and coat required and can be rented for 20 DM, passport absolutely required, liveliest after dinner and later, pick up English history and game rules as you enter).

Casino Tour: The casino gives 30-minute German-language tours every morning from 9:30 to 12:00 (6 DM, 2/hrly, last departure at 11:30, call to see if an English tour is scheduled, otherwise organize English-speakers in the group and aggressively lobby for information; pick up the paltry English brochure, tel. 07221/21060). Even peasants in T-shirts, shorts, and thongs are welcome on tours.

Town Orientation: From the steps of the casino, stand between big white columns #2 and #3 and survey the surroundings (left to right): find the ruined castle near the top of the hill, the rock-climbing cliffs next, the new castle (top of town) next to the salmon spire of the Catholic church (famous baths are just behind that), the Merkur peak (marked by tower, 2,000 feet above sea level), and the bandstand in the Kurhaus garden. The Baden-Baden orchestra plays here most days (free, usually at 16:00).

Trinkhalle: Beyond the colonnade on your left is the old Trinkhalle—a 300-foot-long entrance hall decorated with nymphs and romantic legends (explained by a book available inside) and the home of the TI.

The Baths

Baden-Baden's two much-loved but very different baths stand side by side in a park at the top of the old town. The Roman-Irish Bath is traditional, stately, indoors, not very social, and extremely relaxing...just you, the past, and your body. The perky, fun, and modern baths of Caracalla Baths are half the price, indoor and outdoor, fun, and more social. In each case, your admission ticket works like a subway token—you need it to get out. If you overstay your allotted time, you pay extra. You can relax while your valuables are stowed in very secure lockers. Both baths share a huge underground Kur-Garage, which is free only if you validate your parking ticket before leaving either bath. Caracalla is better in the sunshine. Roman-Irish is fine anytime. Most visitors do both. Save 10 to 15 percent by buying tickets from your hotel.

▲▲▲**Roman-Irish Bath (Friedrichsbad)**—The highlight of most Baden-Baden visits is a sober two-hour ritual called the Roman-Irish Bath. Friedrichsbad, on Römerplatz 1, pampered the rich and famous in its elegant surroundings when it opened 120 years ago. Today this steamy world of marble, brass columns, tropical tiles, herons, lily pads, and graceful nudity welcomes gawky tourists as well as locals. For 48 DM you get up to three hours and the works (36 DM without the eight-minute massage; some hotels sell a reduced-admission ticket).

Read this carefully before stepping out naked: In your changing cabin load all your possessions onto the fancy hanger (hang it in locker across the way, slip card into lock, strap key around wrist). As you enter (in the "crème" room), check your weight on the digital kilo scale. Do this again as you leave. You will have lost a kilo...all in sweat. The complex routine is written (in English) on the walls with recommended time—simply follow the room numbers from 1 to 15.

Take a shower; grab a towel and put on plastic slippers before hitting the warm-air bath for 15 minutes and the hot-air bath for five minutes; shower again; if you paid extra, take the soap-brush massage—rough, slippery, and finished with a Teutonic spank; play Gumby in the shower; lounge under sunbeams in one of several different thermal steam baths; glide like a swan under a divine dome in a royal pool (one of three "mixed" pools); don't skip the cold plunge; dry in warmed towels; and lay cocooned, clean, and thinking prenatal thoughts on a bed for 30 minutes in the mellow, yellow, silent room (don't skip the sleep room). You don't appreciate how really clean you are after this experience until you put your dirty socks back on. (Bring clean ones.)

All you need is money. You'll get a key, locker, and towel (Mon–Sat 9:00–22:00, Sun 12:00–20:00, men and women together Wed, Sat, Sun, and from 16:00–22:00 on Tue and Fri, last admission at 19:00 if you'll get a massage, at 19:30 otherwise, tel. 07221/275-920).

About the dress code: It's always nude. During "separate" times, men and women use parallel and nearly identical facilities. "Mixed" is still mostly separate, with men and women sharing only three pools in the center.

Afterward, before going downstairs, browse through the Roman artifacts in the Renaissance Hall, sip just a little terrible but "magic" hot water (*Thermalwasser*) from the elegant fountain, and stroll down the broad royal stairway feeling, as they say, five years younger—or at least 2.2 pounds lighter.

▲▲Caracalla Therme—For more of a modern experience, spend a few hours at the Baths of Caracalla (daily 8:00–22:00, last entry at 20:00), a huge palace of water, steam, and relaxed people (professional day care available).

Bring a towel (or pay 10 DM plus a 15-DM deposit to rent one) and swimsuit (shorts are OK for men). Buy a card (19 DM/2 hrs, 25 DM/3 hrs, 10 entries for a group or repeat visits cost only 155 DM) and put the card in the locker to get a key. Change clothes, strap the key around your wrist, and go play. Your key gets you into another poolside locker if you want money for a tan or a drink. The Caracalla Therme is an indoor/outdoor wonderland of steamy pools, waterfalls, neck showers, Jacuzzis, hot springs, cold pools, lounge chairs, exercise instructors, saunas, a cafeteria, and a bar. After taking a few laps around the fake river, you can join the kinky gang for water spankings (you may have to wait a few minutes to grab a vacant waterfall). Then join the gang in the central cauldron. The steamy "inhalation" room seems like purgatory's waiting room, with six misty inches of visibility, filled with strange, silently aging bodies.

The spiral staircase leads to a naked world of saunas, tanning lights, cold plunges, and sunbathing. There are three eucalyptus-scented saunas of varying temperatures: 80, 90, and 95 degrees. Follow the instructions on the wall. Towels are required, not for modesty but to separate your body from the wood bench. The highlight is the Arctic bucket in the shower room. Pull the chain. Only rarely will you feel so good. And you can do this over and over. As you leave, take a look at the Roman bath that Emperor Caracalla soaked in to conquer his rheumatism nearly 2,000 years ago.

Sleeping in Baden-Baden
(2 DM = about $1, country code: 49, area code: 07221, zip code: 76530)
Sleep Code: **S** = Single, D = Double/Twin, **T** = Triple, **Q** = Quad, **b** = bathroom, **t** = toilet only, **s** = shower only, **CC** = Credit Card (**V**isa, **M**asterCard, **A**mex), **SE** = Speaks English, **NSE** = No English.

The TI can nearly always find you a room, but don't use the TI for places listed here or you'll pay more. Go direct! The only tight times are during the horse races (May 19–27 and Aug 24–Sept 2 in 2001). If you arrive at Baden-Baden's Oos station, you can stay near the station (see below), but I'd hop on bus #201, which goes to the center of town (stop at Leopoldplatz—the first stop in the pedestrian zone—for Hotel am Markt, baths, casino, and the TI at the Trinkhalle; Augustaplatz for other hotels) and continues to Hotel Deutscher Kaiser (stop: Eckerlestrasse) on the east end of town. Hotel am Markt and Hotel Deutscher Kaiser, clearly the best values, are worth calling in advance.

Unless otherwise noted, assume a fine breakfast is included. Most hotels give a "guest card" offering small discounts on tourist admissions around town. All hotels and pensions are required to extract an additional 5-DM per-person per-night "spa tax."

Sleeping in the Center
Hotel am Markt is a warm, small, family-run hotel with all the comforts a commoner could want in a peaceful, central, nearly traffic-free location, two cobbled blocks from the baths (S-56 DM, Sb-75–90 DM, Dt-110 DM, Db-130–140 DM, Tb-160 DM, extra person-30 DM, CC:VMA, Marktplatz 18, tel. 07221/27040, fax 07221/270-444, e-mail: hotel.am.markt.bad@t-online.de, Herr und Frau Bogner-Schindler and Frau Jung all speak English). For romantics, the church bells blast charmingly through each room every quarter hour from 6:30 until 22:00; for others, they're a nuisance. Otherwise, quiet rules. The ambience and the clientele make killing time on their small terrace a joy. The daily menu offers a good dinner deal (orders 18:00–19:30, guests only). Walk from central Leopoldsplatz three minutes uphill to the red-spired church on Marktplatz.

Hotel Rathausglockel, around the corner and below the Hotel am Markt at Steinstrasse 7, is a 16th-century guest house with six cozy rooms and steep stairs (Db-150 DM, third person-40 DM, church bells every 15 min, cable TV, serves traditional regional fare at their classy restaurant, CC:VM, tel. 07221/90610, fax 07221/906-161, www.baden-baden.org/hotels/rathausgloeckel/main.htm, Michael Rothe SE).

Hotel Beeg rents 15 attractive and comfortable rooms, run (without a reception) from a delectable pastry shop/café on the ground floor. It's wonderfully located on a little square in a pedestrian zone, facing the baths (Sb-140 DM, Db-180 DM, extra person-50 DM, balcony-10 DM extra, CC:VMA, elevator, on Romerplatz, Gernsbacher Strasse 44, tel. 07221/36760, fax 07221/367-610, e-mail: hccbeeg@t-online.de).

Hotel Romerhof is an impersonal, central, and hotelesque alternative with 25 spacious and comfortable though dull rooms (Sb-90 DM, Db-170 DM, CC:VMA, parking garage-10 DM, 3 blocks up from Leopoldplatz on Sophienstrasse 25, tel. 07221/23415, fax 07221/391-707).

Gästehaus Löhr's 18 rooms are worthwhile only as a last resort (S-35 DM, Sb-65 DM, D-80–95 DM, Db-110 DM, CC:VMA, reception at Café Löhr, Lichtentaler Strasse 19, rooms 2 blocks away, tel. 07221/306-200, fax 07221/38308).

Sleeping on Southeast End of Lichtentaler Allee

Deutscher Kaiser offers some of the best rooms in town for the money. This big, traditional guest house is warmly run by Frau Peter, who enjoys taking care of my readers. Herr Peter cooks fine local-style meals (14–30 DM) in the hotel restaurant. It's right on the bus #201 line (Eckerlestrasse stop, 20 min from train station) or a 25-minute stroll from the city center down polite Lichtentaler Allee—cross the river at the green "Restaurant Deutscher Kaiser" sign, then turn right (S-60 DM, Sb-90 DM, D-80–90 DM, Db-110–120 DM, hall showers-3 DM, CC:VMA, some nonsmoking rooms, free and easy parking, Hauptstrasse 35, 76534 Baden-Baden Lichtental, tel. 07221/72152, fax 07221/72154, www.hoteldk.de, e-mail: info@hoteldk.de). Drivers: From autobahn, skip town center by following "Congress" signs into Michaelstunnel. Take first exit in tunnel (Lichtental) and another right inside tunnel. Outside, hotel is 300 meters on left. From Black Forest, follow "Zentrum" signs. Ten meters after Aral gas station, turn left down small road to Hauptstrasse.

Gasthof Cäcilienberg is farther out but still on the bus line at the end of Lichtentaler Allee. It's a good, comfortable fallback if the other recommended hotels are full (S-65 DM, Sb-78 DM, D-88 DM, Db-98 DM, take bus #201 and get off at Brahmsplatz, Geroldsauer Strasse 2, tel. 07221/72297, fax 07221/70459, NSE).

More Baden-Baden Accommodations

Near the Train Station: Gasthof Adler is clean, comfortable, friendly, and on a very busy intersection (ask for *"ruhige Seite,"* the quiet side, S-64 DM, Ss-69 DM, Sb-87 DM, D-114 DM, Ds-124 DM, Db-120–145 DM, CC:VMA, veer right from station, walk 3 blocks passing post office to stoplight, hotel is on corner, Ooser Hauptstrasse 1, 76532 Baden-Baden Oos, tel. 07221/61858 or 07221/61811, fax 07221/17145). Bus #201 stops across the street.

Hostel: The **Werner Dietz Hostel**, while not cheap, is a good value (beds in 2- to 6-bed rooms, sheets, and breakfast for 40 DM, 45 DM if you're 27 or older, add 6 DM if you have no hostel card, Hardbergstrasse 34, bus #201 from the station or downtown to Grosse Dollenstrasse—announced as "Jugendherberge Stop," about 8 stops from station, 5 from downtown; it's a steep, well-marked, 10-minute climb from there, tel. 07221/52223, SE). They give 4.60-DM discount coupons for both city baths, and serve cheap meals. Drivers: After the freeway to Baden-Baden ends, turn left at the first light and follow the signs. You'll wind uphill to the big, modern hostel next to a public swimming pool.

Eating in Baden-Baden

The recommended hotel, **Deutscher Kaiser**, serves a fine dinner (consider it as part of your evening Lichtentaler Allee stroll, but call to make sure the restaurant is open, tel. 07221/72152).

For beer-garden ambience in the town center, **Löwenbrau Baden-Baden** can't be beat (18–30 DM meals, nightly, leafy outdoors or antlered indoors, Gernsbacher Strasse 9, tel. 07221/22311). **La Provence**, with a romantic setting, an eclectic menu, and good food and prices, is popular, especially on weekends (daily 12:00–01:00, CC:VMA, from Marktplatz hike up Schloss Strasse #20, tel. 07221/25550). If you want to spend too much for an elegant 19th-century cup of coffee, **Café Koenig**, on Augustaplatz, is the place (tel. 07221/23573). For a cheap, good lunch or dinner, shuffle under the yellow awning of the **Stehcafe**, in the heart of the pedestrian area (Langestrasse 20)—get a salad and sandwich to enjoy on a nearby bench.

For a slice of Black Forest cake, try Café Koenig (see above) or **Café Bockelers** (Mon–Fri 8:00–18:30, Sat–Sun 9:30–18:00, Langestrasse 40, tel. 07221/949-594).

Transportation Connections—Baden-Baden

By train to: Freiburg (hrly, 60 min), **Triberg** (every 2 hrs, 60 min), **Heidelberg** (hrly, 60 min, catch Castle Road bus to Rothenburg), **Munich** (hrly, 4.5 hrs, with 2 changes, a few direct trains), **Frankfurt** (2/hrly, 1.5 hrs with a change), **Koblenz** (hrly, 2.5 hrs with a change), **Mainz am Rhine** (hrly, 90 min), **Strasbourg** (5/day, 45 min), **Bern** (hrly, 3.5 hrs, transfer in Basel).

FREIBURG

Freiburg (FRY-burg) is worth a quick look if for nothing else than to appreciate its thriving center and very human scale. Bikers and hikers seem to outnumber cars, and trams run everywhere. This "sunniest town in Germany," with 30,000 students, feels like the university town that it is. Freiburg, nearly bombed flat in 1944, skillfully put itself back together. And it feels cozy, almost Austrian; in fact, it was Hapsburg territory for 500 years. It's the "capital" of

the Schwarzwald, surrounded by lush forests and filled with environ-
mentally aware people and an "I could live here" appeal. Marvel at
the number of pedestrian-only streets. Freiburg's trademark is its
system of *Bächle*, tiny streams running down each street. These go
back to the Middle Ages (fire protection, cattle refreshment, constantly flushing disposal system). A sunny day turns any kid into a
puddle stomper. Enjoy the ice cream and street-singing ambience
of the cathedral square, which has a great produce and craft market
(Mon–Sat 8:00–14:30).

Orientation (area code: 0761)
Tourist Information: Freiburg's busy but helpful TI offers an
unnecessary 6-DM city guidebook, a workable free city map, a
better 1-DM map with a self-guided walking tour, a room-finding
service, 10-DM German-English walking tours (Wed–Mon at
10:30 and 14:30), and information on the Black Forest region
(Mon–Fri 9:30–20:00, Sat 9:30–17:00, Sun 10:00–12:00, less in
winter, WC around the corner, tel. 0761/388-1881).

   Arrival in Freiburg: Walk out of the bustling train station
(lockers available) and head straight up Eisenbahnstrasse, the
tree-lined boulevard (passing the post office). Within three blocks
you'll take an underpass under a busy road; as you emerge, the
TI is on your left and the town center is dead ahead.

Sights—Freiburg
▲**Church (Münster)**—This impressive church, completed in
1513, took more than three centuries to build, ranging in style
from late Romanesque to lighter, brighter Gothic. It was virtually
the only building in town to survive World War II bombs. The
lacy tower, considered by many the most beautiful around, is as
tall as the church is long...and not worth the 329-step ascent
(2 DM, Mon–Sat 9:30–17:00, Sun 13:00–17:00). From this lofty
perch, watchmen used to scan the town for fires. While you could
count the 123 representations of Mary throughout the church,
most gawk at the "mooning" gargoyle and wait for rain. Browse
the market in the square. The ornate Historisches Kaufhaus,
across from the church, was a trading center in the 16th century.
Augustiner Museum—This offers a good look at Black Forest
art and culture through the ages. Highlights are downstairs: a
close-up look at some of the Münster's original medieval stained
glass and statuary (6 DM, Tue–Sun 10:00–17:00, closed Mon).
Schauinsland—Freiburg's own mountain, while little more
than an oversized hill, offers the handiest panorama view of the
Schwarzwald for those without wheels. A gondola system, one of
Germany's oldest, was designed for Freiburgers relying on public
transportation (20 DM round-trip, June–Aug 9:00–18:00, Sept–
May 9:00–17:00, take tram #4 from town center to end, then bus

#21 seven stops to gondola, tel. 0671/292-930). At the 4,000-foot summit you'll find a view restaurant, pleasant circular walks, and the Schniederli Hof, a 1592 farmhouse museum. A tower on a nearby peak offers an even more commanding Black Forest view. This excursion will not thrill Americans from Colorado.

Sleeping and Eating in Freiburg
(2 DM = about $1, country code: 49, area code: 0761, zip code: 79098)
While I prefer nights in sleepy Staufen (see below), many will enjoy a night in lively Freiburg. The first two Freiburg listings are a 15-minute walk or easy bus ride from the station. Prices include breakfast, and English is spoken.

Hotel Alleehaus is tops. Located on the edge of the center on a quiet, leafy street in a big house that feels like home, it's thoughtfully decorated, comfy, and warmly run (S-85 DM, Ss-98 DM, Sb-98–120 DM, D-105 DM, Db-140–170 DM, Tb-185–220 DM, Qb-260 DM, parking-10 DM, includes good buffet breakfast, CC:VM, Marienstrasse 7, take tram #4 from station to Holzmarkt, near intersection with Wallstrasse, phone answered 8:00–20:00, tel. 0761/387-600, fax 0761/387-6099).

Hotel am Stadtgarten is on the opposite side of town (10-minute walk from TI) with comfortable rooms heavy on beige (S-92 DM, Ss-97 DM, Sb-102 DM, Db-139 DM, Tb-186 DM, Qb-228 DM, tram #5 two stops from station to Bernhardstrasse 5, near intersection with Karlstrasse, tel. 0761/282-9002, fax 0761/ 282-9022, Paul SE).

If you're willing to pay dearly to be near the station, stay at **Hotel Barbara**. Its rooms are brighter than its dark lobby (Sb-130 DM, Db-170–200 DM, some nonsmoking rooms, CC:VM, on quiet street 2 minutes from station, head towards TI but turn left to Poststrasse 4, tel. 0761/296-250, fax 0761/ 26688, www.hotel-barbara.de).

City Hotel is business sterile with 31 clean, modern rooms. It's near the main shopping street, a five-minute walk from the TI (Sb-145 DM, Db-190–205 DM, third person-45 DM, CC:VMA, Weberstrasse 3, tel. 0761/388-070, fax 0761/388- 0765, www.cityhotelfreiburg.de, e-mail: city.hotel.freiburg@ t-online.de).

The big, modern **Freiburg Youth Hostel** is on the east edge of Freiburg on the scenic road into the Black Forest (24 DM per bed with sheets and breakfast, "seniors" over 26 pay 32.50 DM, hostel card required, Kartuserstrasse 151, tram #1 to Römerhof, tel. 0761/67656).

Eating: Vegetarians will appreciate **Caruso's** large portions and fair prices (Mon–Sat 10:00–01:00, closed Sun, Kaiser Joseph Strasse 258, tel. 0761/36178).

Transportation Connections—Freiburg

By train to: Staufen (hrly, 30 min, 2/day are direct, others require easy change in Bad Krozingen, after 20:00 no trains to Staufen but shared taxis from Bad Krozingen station), **Baden-Baden** (8/day, 45 min), **Munich** (hrly, 4.5 hrs, transfer in Mannheim), **Mainz am Rhine** (hrly, 2.5 hrs), **Basel** (hrly, 45 min), **Bern** (hrly, 2.5 hrs, transfer in Basel).

STAUFEN

Staufen makes a peaceful and delightful home base for your exploration of Freiburg and the southern trunk of the Black Forest. Hemmed in by vineyards, it's small and off the beaten path, with a quiet pedestrian zone of colorful old buildings bounded by a happy creek that actually babbles. There's nothing to do here but enjoy the marketplace atmosphere, hike through the vineyards to the ruined castle overlooking the town, and savor a good dinner with local wine.

Orientation (area code: 07633)

Tourist Information: The TI, on the main square in the Rathaus, has a good (German only) map of the wine road and can help you find a room (Mon–Fri 8:00–12:30, 14:30–17:30, Sat 10:30–12:00, closed Sun, tel. 07633/80536).

Arrival in Staufen: Everything I list is within a 10-minute walk of the station (no lockers, try the Gasthaus Bahnhof, see "Sleeping," below). To get to town, exit the station with your back to the pond and angle right up Bahnhofstrasse. Turn right at the post office on Hauptstrasse for the town center, hotels, and TI.

Winery: The winery Weingot Wiesler offers *Weinprobes*—wine tastings (Mon–Fri 15:00–18:30, Sat 9:00–13:30, behind Gasthaus Bahnhof at base of castle hill, tel. 07633/6905).

Sights—Near Staufen

Wine Road (Badische Weinstrasse)—The wine road of this part of Germany staggers from Staufen through the tiny towns of Grunern, Dottingen, Sulzburg, and Britzingen, before sitting down in Badenweiler. If you're in the mood for some tasting, look for "Winzergenossenshaft" signs, which invite visitors in to taste and buy the wines, and often to tour the winery.

▲**Badenweiler**—If ever a town were a park, Badenweiler is it. This idyllic, poodle-elegant, and finicky-clean spa town is known only to the wealthy Germans who soak there. Its bath, Markgrafenbad, is next to the ruins of a Roman mineral bath in a park of imported and exotic trees (including a California redwood). This prize-winning piece of architecture perfectly mixes trees and peace with an elegant indoor/outdoor swimming pool (daily 8:00–18:00, Mon, Wed, and Fri until 20:00, tel. 07632/72110).

The locker procedure, combined with the language barrier, makes getting to the pool more memorable than you'd expect (14 DM/3 hrs; towels, required caps, and suits can be rented). Badenweiler is a 20-minute drive south of Staufen (take the train or bus to Mullheim and bus from there).

Sleeping in Staufen
(2 DM = about $1, country code: 49, area code: 07633, zip code: 79219)

The TI has a list of private *Zimmer*. Prices listed are for one night, but most *Zimmer* don't like one-nighters. Breakfast is usually included in the price.

Gasthaus Bahnhof is the cheapest, simplest place in town, with a dynamite castle view from the upstairs terrace, a self-service kitchen, and 15-DM dinners served in its tree-shaded patio (S-40 DM, D-80 DM, no breakfast, across from train station, tel. 07633/6190, fax 07633/5674, NSE). Seven comfortable and cheery rooms right out of grandma's house share two bathrooms. At night, master of ceremonies Lotte makes it the squeeze box of Staufen. People come from miles around to party with Lotte, so it can be noisy at night. If you want to eat red meat in a wine barrel under a tree, this is the place. For stays of three nights or longer, ask her about the rooms next door (Sb-50 DM, Db-80 DM).

Hotel Hirschen, with a storybook location in the old pedestrian center, has a cozy restaurant (closed Mon–Tue). It's family run with plush and thoughtfully appointed rooms, balconies, and a big roof deck (Sb-85 DM, Db-130 DM, Tb-180 DM, confirm your reservation, elevator, satellite TV, Hauptstrasse 19 on main pedestrian street, tel. 07633/5297, fax 07633/5295, e-mail: info@breisgaucity .com, SE). They have a huge luxury penthouse for six (240 DM).

Gasthaus Krone, across the street from the Hirschen, has nine rooms that gild the lily but is a good value in this price range (Sb-90 DM, Db-130 DM, Tb-170 DM, CC:VMA, Hauptstrasse 30, on main pedestrian street, tel. 07633/5840, fax 07633/82903, www .die-krone.de, e-mail: info@die-krone.de). Its restaurant appreciates vegetables and offers wonderful splurge meals (closed Fri–Sat).

Hotel Sonne is more simple with eight comfortable rooms at the edge of the pedestrian center (Sb-80 DM, Db-110 DM, elevator, continue straight past Hotel Krone, turn right at T-intersection, and take second left on Muhlegasse to reach Albert-Hugard Strasse 1, tel. 07633/95300, fax 07633/953-014, NSE).

Sights—Black Forest
▲▲**Short and Scenic Black Forest Joyride (by car or bus)**— This pleasant loop from Staufen (or Freiburg) takes you through the most representative chunk of the area, avoiding the touristy, overcrowded Titisee.

By Car: Leave Staufen on Schwarzwaldstrasse (signs to
Donaueschingen), which becomes Scenic Road 31 down the dark
Höllental (Hell's Valley) toward Titisee. Turn left at Hinterzarten
onto Road 500, follow signs to St. Margen, and then to St. Peter—
one of the healthy, go-take-a-walk-in-the-clean-air places that doctors actually prescribe for people from all over Germany. There is
a fine seven-kilometer walk between St. Margen and St. Peter,
with regular buses to bring you back.

By Bus: Several morning and late-afternoon buses connect
Freiburg's bus station (next to train station) with St. Peter and
St. Margen. Get off at St. Peter, hike seven kilometers to St.
Margen, and bus back to Freiburg (contact Freiburg TI for
details, tel. 0761/388-1881).

St. Peter: The TI, just next to the Benedictine Abbey (private),
can recommend a walk (Mon–Fri 8:00–12:00, 14:00–17:00, Sat
10:00–13:00, tel. 07660/910-224). Sleep at the traditional old
Gasthof Hirschen on the main square (Db-130–150 DM, CC:VM,
St. Peter/Hochschwarzwald, tel. 07660/204, fax 07660/1557) or
consider **Pension Kandelblick** (Ds-70 DM, Schweighofweg,
tel. 07660/349).

Extension for Drivers: From St. Peter, wind through
idyllic Black Forest scenery up to Kandelhof. At the summit is
the Berghotel Kandel. You can park here and take a short walk to
the 4,000-foot peak for a great view. Then the road winds steeply
through a dense forest to Waldkirch, where a fast road takes you
to the Freiburg Nord autobahn entrance. With a good car and no
stops, you'll get from Staufen/Freiburg to Baden-Baden via this
route in three hours.

▲▲**Extended Black Forest Drive**—Of course, you could spend
much more time in the land of cuckoo clocks and healthy hikes.
For a more thorough visit, still connecting with Baden-Baden,
try this drive: As described above, drive from Staufen or Freiburg
down Höllental. After a short stop in St. Peter, wind up in Furtwangen with the impressive Deutsches Uhrenmuseum (German
Clock Museum, 5 DM, April–Oct daily 9:00–18:00, less off-season,
tel. 07723/920-117). More than a chorus of cuckoo clocks, this
museum traces (with interesting English descriptions) the development of clocks from the Dark Ages to the space age. It has an
upbeat combo of mechanical musical instruments as well.

Triberg—Deep in the Black Forest, Triberg's famous for its
Gutach Waterfall (which falls 500 feet in several bounces, 3 DM
to see it) and, more important, the Heimatmuseum, which gives
a fine look at the costumes, carvings, and traditions of the local
culture (5 DM, Jan–Oct daily 10:00–17:00, Nov–Dec open only
on weekends 10:00–17:00, tel. 07722/4434). Touristy as Triberg
is, it offers an easy way for travelers without cars to enjoy the
Black Forest (TI tel. 07722/953-230).

▲**Black Forest Open-Air Museum (Schwarzwälder Freilichtermuseum)**—This offers the best look at this region's traditional folk life. Built around one grand old farmhouse, the museum is a collection of several old farms filled with exhibits on the local dress and lifestyles (8 DM, 50-DM guided tour with small groups but call first, daily April–Oct 8:30–18:00, last entry at 17:00, north of Triberg, through Hornberg to Hausach/Gutach, tel. 07831/93560). The surrounding shops and restaurants are awfully touristy. Try your *Schwarzwald Kirschtorte* (Black Forest cherry cake) elsewhere.

Continue north through Freudenstadt, the capital of the northern Black Forest, and onto the Schwarzwald-Hochstrasse, which takes you along a ridge through 30 miles of pine forests before dumping you right on Baden-Baden's back porch.

ROTHENBURG
AND THE
ROMANTIC ROAD

From Munich or Füssen to Frankfurt, the Romantic Road takes you through Bavaria's medieval heartland, a route strewn with picturesque villages, farmhouses, onion-domed churches, Baroque palaces, and walled cities.

Dive into the Middle Ages via Rothenburg (ROE-ten-burg), Germany's best-preserved walled town. Countless travelers have searched for the elusive "untouristy Rothenburg." There are many contenders (such as Michelstadt, Miltenberg, Bamberg, Bad Windsheim, and Dinkelsbühl), but none holds a candle to the king of medieval German cuteness. Even with crowds, over-priced souvenirs, Japanese-speaking night watchmen, and, yes, even with *Schneebälle*, Rothenburg is best. Save time and mileage and be satisfied with the winner.

Planning Your Time

The best one-day look at the heartland of Germany is the Romantic Road bus tour. Eurail travelers, who get a 60 percent discount, pay only 54 DM for the ride (daily, Frankfurt to Füssen and Munich to Rothenburg, and vice versa). Drivers can follow the route laid out in the tourist brochures (available at any TI). The only stop worth more than a few minutes is Rothenburg. Twenty-four hours is ideal for this town. Two nights and a day are a bit much, unless you're actually relaxing on this trip.

Rothenburg in a day is easy, with four essential experiences: the Medieval Crime and Punishment Museum, the Riemenschnei-der wood carving in St. Jakob's Church, the city walking tour, and a walk along the wall. With more time there are several mediocre but entertaining museums, walking and biking in the nearby countryside, and lots of cafés and shops. Make a point to

Rothenburg

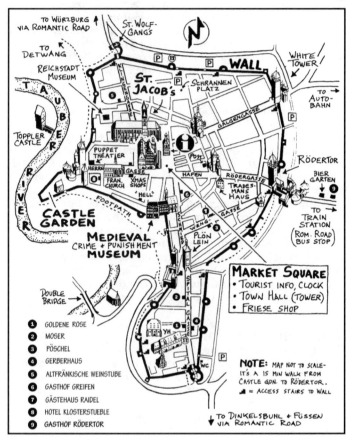

TO WÜRZBURG
VIA ROMANTIC ROAD

ST. WOLF-
GANGS

TO
DETWANG

REICHSTADT
MUSEUM

WHITE
TOWER

WALL

TAUBER

ST.
JACOB'S

SCHRANNEN
PLATZ

TO
AUTO-
BAHN

TOPPLER
CASTLE

GALGENGASSE

RÖDERTOR

RIVER

PUPPET
THEATER

HERRN GASSE

FRAN.
CHURCH

XMAS
SHOPS

"HELL"

POST

HAFEN

RÖDERGASSE

TRADES-
MANS
HAUS

BIER
GARTEN

CASTLE
GARDEN

FOOTPATH

SCH

WENG GASSE

TO
TRAIN
STATION
(ROM. ROAD
BUS STOP)

MEDIEVAL
CRIME + PUNISHMENT
MUSEUM

PLÖN
LEIN

MARKET SQUARE
• TOURIST INFO, CLOCK
• TOWN HALL (TOWER)
• FRIESE SHOP

DOUBLE
BRIDGE

SPITAL GASSE

YH

WC

NOTE: MAP NOT TO SCALE—
IT'S A 15 MIN WALK FROM
CASTLE GDN. TO RÖDERTOR.
▪ = ACCESS STAIRS TO WALL

① GOLDENE ROSE
② MOSER
③ PÖSCHEL
④ GERBERHAUS
⑤ ALTFRÄNKISCHE WEINSTUBE
⑥ GASTHOF GREIFEN
⑦ GÄSTEHAUS RAIDEL
⑧ HOTEL KLOSTERSTUEBLE
⑨ GASTHOF RÖDERTOR

TO DINKELSBUHL + FÜSSEN
VIA ROMANTIC ROAD

spend at least one night. The town is yours after dark when the groups vacate and the town's floodlit cobbles wring some romance out of any travel partner.

ROTHENBURG

In the Middle Ages, when Frankfurt and Munich were just wide spots on the road, Rothenburg was Germany's second-largest free imperial city, with a whopping population of 6,000. Today it's her best-preserved medieval walled town, enjoying tremendous tourist popularity without losing its charm. Get medievaled in Rothenburg.

During Rothenburg's heyday, from 1150 to 1400, it was the crossing point of two major trade routes: Tashkent–Paris and

Hamburg–Venice. Today the great trade is tourism; two-thirds of the townspeople are employed to serve you. Too often Rothenburg brings out the shopper in visitors before they've had a chance to appreciate the historic city. True, this is a great place to do your German shopping, but first see the town. While 2.5 million people visit each year, a mere 500,000 spend the night. Rothenburg is most enjoyable early and late, when the tour groups are gone.

Orientation (area code: 09861)

To orient yourself in Rothenburg, think of the town map as a human head. Its nose—the castle garden—sticks out to the left, and the neck is the skinny lower part, with the hostel and my favorite hotels in the Adam's apple. The town is a joy on foot. No sight or hotel is more than a 15-minute walk from the train station or each other.

Most of the buildings you'll see were built by 1400. The city was born around its long-gone castle—built in 1142, destroyed in 1356, and now the site of the castle garden. You can see the shadow of the first town wall, which defines the oldest part of Rothenburg, in its contemporary street plan. A few gates from this wall still survive. The richest and biggest houses were in this central part. The commoners built higgledy-piggledy (read: picturesquely) farther from the center near the present walls.

Tourist Information

The TI is on Market Square (Mon–Fri 9:00–12:30, 13:00–18:00, unreliably Sat–Sun 10:00–15:00, shorter hours off-season, tel. 09861/40492, after-hours board lists rooms still available). Pick up a map and the *Sights Worth Seeing and Knowing* brochure (a virtual walking guide to the town). The free "Hotels and Pensions of Rothenburg" map has the greatest detail and names all of the streets. Confirm sightseeing plans and ask about the daily 14:00 walking tour (April–Oct) and evening entertainment. The best town map is available free at the Friese shop, two doors from the TI in the direction of Rothenburg's "nose."

Arrival in Rothenburg: Exit left from the train station and turn right on the first busy street (Ansbacher Strasse). It'll take you to Rothenburg's Market Square within 10 minutes. Leave luggage in lockers at the station (2 DM). The travel agency in the station is the place to arrange train and *couchette*/sleeper reservations. Taxis wait at the station and can take you to any hotel for 10 DM. Drivers will find many parking lots outside the town walls that range from no charge up to 7 DM per day. Park outside of town and walk five minutes to the center. Only those with a hotel reservation can park within the walls after hours.

Helpful Hints
Festivals: Rothenburgers dress up in medieval costumes and beer gardens spill out into the street to celebrate Mayor Nusch's Meistertrunk victory (Whitsun, 6 weeks after Easter, see story below under "Sights—Meistertrunk Show") and 700 years of history in the Imperial City Festival (second weekend in September, with fireworks).

    Internet Access: Try Planet Internet (9 DM/hr, Paradeisgasse 5, tel. 09861/934-415).

Tours of Rothenburg
The TI on Market Square offers one-hour guided walking tours in English (6 DM, April–Oct daily at 14:00 from Market Square). A bit less informative but wonderfully entertaining, the **Night Watchman's Tour** takes tourists on his one-hour rounds each evening at 20:00 (6 DM, April–Dec, in English). This is the best evening activity in town. Or you can hire a **private guide**. For 98 DM, a local historian who's an intriguing character as well brings the ramparts alive. Eight hundred years of history are packed between Rothenburg's cobbles. Anita Weinzierl (tel. 09868/7993) and Manfred Baumann (tel. 09861/4146) are good guides. If you prefer riding to walking, **horse-and-buggy rides** last 30 minutes and cost 10 DM per person for a minimum of three people.

Sights—Rothenburg's Town Hall Square
▲▲**Town Hall Tower**—The best view of Rothenburg and the surrounding countryside and a close-up look at the interior of an old tiled roof are yours for 2 DM and a rigorous (214 steps, 180 feet) but interesting climb (daily 9:30–12:30, 13:00–17:00, off-season weekends 12:00–15:00 only). The entrance is on Market Square. Women, beware: Some men find the view best from the bottom of the ladder just before the top.

Meistertrunk Show—Be on Market Square at 11:00, 12:00, 13:00, 14:00, 15:00, 20:00, 21:00, or 22:00 for the ritual gathering of the tourists to see the less-than-breathtaking reenactment of the Meistertrunk story. In 1631 the Catholic army took the Protestant town and was about to do its rape, pillage, and plunder thing when, as the story goes, the mayor said, "Hey, if I can drink this entire three-liter tankard of wine in one gulp, will you leave us alone?" The invading commander, sensing he was dealing with an unbalanced person, said, "Sure." Mayor Nusch drank the whole thing, the town was saved, and the mayor slept for three days. Hint: For the best show, don't watch the clock; watch the open-mouthed tourists gasp as the old windows flip open. At the late shows, the square flickers with flash attachments. While you wait for the show, give yourself the spin tour below.

Market Square Spin Tour—Stand at the bottom of Market

Square (10 feet below the wooden post) and spin 360 degrees clockwise starting with the city hall tower. Now, do it slower following
these notes: 1) The city's tallest **tower**, at 200 feet, stands atop the
old city hall, a white, Gothic, 13th-century building. Notice the
tourists enjoying the view from the black top of the tower. 2) When
the town had more money and Gothic went out of style, a new **town
hall** was built in front of the old one. This is in Renaissance style
from 1570. (Access to the old town hall tower is through the middle
of the new town hall arcade.) 3) At the top of the square stands the
proud **Councilors' Tavern** (clock tower, from 1466). In its day, the
city council drank here. Today it's the TI and the focus of all the
attention when the little doors on either side of the clock flip open
and the wooden figures (from 1910) reenact the Meistertrunk.
4) Across the street, the green building is the oldest **pharmacy** in
town—Löwen Apotheke, from 1374—peek inside. 5) On the bottom
end of the square, the gray building is a fine **print shop** (see "Shopping," below, free brandy). 6) Adjoining that is the **Baumeister's
House** with its famous Renaissance facade featuring statues of the
seven virtues and the seven vices—the former supporting the latter.
7) The green house below that is the former house of Mayor Toppler, today the fine old **Greifen Hotel**; next to it is a famous Scottish
restaurant with golden arches. 8) Continue circling to the big 17th-
century **St. George's fountain**. The long metal gutters slid, routing
the water into the villagers' buckets. Rothenburg's many fountains
had practical functions beyond providing drinking water. The water
was used for fighting fires and the fountains were stocked with fish
during times of siege. Two fine buildings behind the fountain show
the old-time lofts with warehouse doors and pulleys on top for hoist-
ing. All over town, lofts were filled with grain and corn. A year's
supply was required by the city so they could survive any siege.
The building on the left is a free art gallery showing off the work of
Rothenburg's top artists. The other is another old-time pharmacy.
9) The broad street running under the town hall tower is **Herrngasse**. The town originated with its castle (1142). Herrngasse leads
from the castle (now gone) to Market Square where you stand now.
▲**Historical Town Hall Vaults**—Under the town hall tower is a
city history museum that gives a waxy but good look at medieval
Rothenburg. With the best English descriptions in town, it offers
a look at "the fateful year 1631," a replica of the famous Meistertrunk tankard, and a dungeon complete with three dank cells
and some torture lore (3 DM, 9:00–18:00, closed in winter, well
described in English).

Sights—Rothenburg
▲▲**Walk the Wall**—Just over a mile around, providing great
views and a good orientation, this walk can be done by those under
six feet tall and without a camera in less than an hour, and requires

no special sense of balance. Photographers go through lots of film, especially before breakfast or at sunset, when the lighting is best and the crowds are fewest. The best fortifications are in the Spitaltor (south end). Walk from there counterclockwise to the "forehead." Climb the Rödertor en route. The names you see along the way are people who donated money to rebuild the wall after World War II.

▲**Rödertor**—The wall tower nearest the train station is the only one you can climb. It's worth the hike up for the view and a fascinating rundown on the bombing of Rothenburg in the last weeks of World War II when the northeast corner of the city was destroyed (2 DM, daily 9:00–17:00, closed Nov–March, photos, English translation).

▲▲**St. Jakob's Church**—Built in the 14th century, it's been Lutheran since 1544. Take a close look at the Twelve Apostles altar in front (from 1546, left permanently in its open festival-day position). Six saints are below Christ. St. James (Jakob in German) is the one with the staff. He's the saint of pilgrims, and this was on the medieval pilgrimage route to Santiago de Compostela in Spain. Study the painted panels. Around the back (upper left) is a great painting of Rothenburg's Market Square in the 15th century looking like it does today. Before leaving the front of the church, notice the old medallions above the carved choir stalls featuring the coats of arms of Rothenburg's leading families and portraits of early Reformation preachers.

Next, climb the stairs in the back. Behind the pipe organ stands the artistic highlight of Rothenburg and perhaps the most wonderful woodcarving in all Germany: the glorious 500-year-old, 30-foot-high *Altar of the Holy Blood*. Tilman Riemenschneider, the Michelangelo of German wood-carvers, carved this from 1499 to 1504 to hold a precious rock crystal capsule set in a cross containing a drop of the holy blood (1270). Below, in the scene of the Last Supper, Jesus gives Judas a piece of bread marking him as the traitor while John lays his head on Christ's lap. On the left: Jesus entering Jerusalem. On the right: Jesus praying in the Garden of Gethsemane (2.50 DM, Mon–Sat 9:00–17:30, Sun 10:45–17:30, off-season 10:00–12:00, 14:00–16:00, free helpful English info sheet).

▲▲**Medieval Crime and Punishment Museum**—It's the best of its kind, full of fascinating old legal bits and *Kriminal* pieces, instruments of punishment and torture, even a special cage complete with a metal gag—for nags. Exhibits are well described in English (6 DM, 10 DM combo includes Imperial City Museum, daily 9:30–18:00, shorter hours in winter, fun cards and posters).

Museum of the Imperial City (Reichsstadt Museum)—This less sensational museum, housed in the former Dominican Convent, gives a more scholarly look at old Rothenburg. Highlights include *The Rothenburg Passion*, a 12-panel series of paintings from

1492 showing scenes leading up to Christ's crucifixion, an exhibit of Jewish culture through the ages in Rothenburg, and a 14th-century convent kitchen (5 DM, daily 9:30–17:30, Oct–March 13:00–16:00). The convent garden is a peaceful place to work on your tan.

▲**Toy Museum**—Two floors of historic *Kinder* cuteness is a hit with many (6 DM, 12 DM per family, daily 9:30–18:00, just off Market Square, downhill from the fountain, Hofbronneng 13).

▲▲**Herrngasse and the Castle Garden**—Any town's *Herrngasse*, where the richest patricians and merchants (the *Herren*) lived, is your chance to see its finest old mansions. Wander from Market Square down Herrngasse (past Rothenburg's old official measurement rods on the city hall wall) and drop into the lavish front rooms of a ritzy hotel or two. Pop into the Franciscan Church (free, Mon–Sat 10:00–12:00, 14:00–16:00, Sun 14:00–16:00, built in 1285—the oldest in town, with a Riemenschneider altar piece), continue on down past the old-fashioned puppet theater, through the old gate (notice the tiny after-curfew door in the big door and the frightening mask mouth from which hot Nutella was poured onto attackers), through the garden and to the end of what used to be the castle (great picnic spots and Tauber Riviera views at sunset). This is the popular kissing spot for romantic Rothenburg teenagers.

▲**Walk in the Countryside**—Just below the *Burggarten* (castle garden) in the Tauber Valley is the cute, skinny, 600-year-old castle/summer home of Mayor Toppler (2 DM, Fri–Sun 13:00–16:00, closed Mon–Thu, 1.5 kilometers from town center). On the top floor, notice the photo of bombed-out Rothenburg in 1945. Then walk on past the covered bridge and huge trout to the peaceful village of Detwang. Detwang (from 968, the second-oldest village in Franconia) is actually older than Rothenburg and also has a Riemenschneider altar piece in its church. For a scenic return, loop back to Rothenburg through the valley along the river, past a café with outdoor tables, great desserts, and a town view to match.

Swimming—Rothenburg has a fine modern recreation center with an indoor/outdoor pool and sauna. It's just a few minutes' walk down the Dinkelsbühl Road (Fri–Wed 9:00–20:00, Thu 10:00–20:00, tel. 09861/4565).

Sightseeing Lowlights—St. Wolfgang's Church is a fortified Gothic church built into the medieval wall at Klingentor. Its dungeonlike passages and shepherd's dance exhibit are pretty lame (2 DM, daily 10:00–13:00, 14:00–17:00, closed Nov–March). The cute-looking Bäuerliches Museum (farming museum) next door is even worse. The Rothenburger Handwerkerhaus (tradesman's house, 700 years old) shows the typical living situation of a Rothenburger in the town's heyday (3 DM, daily 10:00–18:00, closed in winter, Alter Stadtgraben 26, near the Markus Tower).

Sights—Near Rothenburg

Franconian Bike Ride—For a fun, breezy look at the countryside around Rothenburg, rent a bike from Rad & Tat (25 DM/day, Mon–Fri 9:00–18:00, Sat 9:00–14:00, closed Sun, Bensenstrasse 17, outside of town behind the "neck," near corner of Bensenstrasse and Erlbacherstrasse, no deposit except passport number, tel. 09861/87984). Return the bike the next morning before 10:00. For a pleasant half-day pedal, bike south down to Detwang via Topplerschlosschen. Go north along the level bike path to Tauberscheckenbach, then huff and puff uphill about 20 minutes to Adelshofen and south back to Rothenburg.

Franconian Open-Air Museum—A 20-minute drive from Rothenburg in the undiscovered "Rothenburgy" town of Bad Windsheim is a small, open-air folk museum that, compared with others in Europe, isn't much. But it's trying very hard and gives you the best look around at traditional rural Franconia (6 DM, Tue–Sun 9:00–18:00, closed Mon and Nov–Feb, tel. 09841/66800).

Shopping

Be careful... Rothenburg is one of Germany's best shopping towns. Do it here and be done with it. Lovely prints, carvings, wineglasses, Christmas-tree ornaments, and beer steins are popular. Warning: Shipping is so expensive that it's probably not worth it for purchases under $200.

The Käthe Wohlfahrt Christmas trinkets phenomenon is spreading across the half-timbered reaches of Europe. In Rothenburg tourists flock to two **Käthe Wohlfahrt Christmas Villages** (on either side of Herrngasse, just off Market Square). This Christmas wonderland is filled with enough twinkling lights to require a special electric hookup, instant Christmas mood music (best appreciated on a hot day in July), and American and Japanese tourists hungrily filling little woven shopping baskets with 10- to 15-DM goodies to hang on their trees. (OK, I admit it, my Christmas tree sports a few KW ornaments.) Note: Prices have hefty tour-guide kickbacks built into them. The Käthe Wohlfahrt discount store sells damaged and discontinued items. It's unnamed at Kirchgasse 5 across from the entrance of St. Jakob's Church (Mon–Fri 9:00–18:00, less on weekends, closed Jan–Feb, tel. 09861/4090).

The **Friese shop** offers a charming contrast (just off Market Square, west of TI, on corner across from public WC). Cuckoo with friendliness, it gives shoppers with this book tremendous service: a 10 percent discount, 16 percent tax deducted if you have it mailed, and a free map. Anneliese, who runs the place with her sons, Frankie and Berni, charges only her cost for shipping, changes money at the best rates in town with no extra charge, and lets tired travelers leave their bags in her back room for free.

For fewer crowds and better service, visit after 14:00. Her pricing is good, but to comparison shop, go here last.

The Ernst Geissendörfer **print shop** sells fine prints, etchings, and paintings. If you show this book they'll offer 10 percent off marked prices for all purchases in cash (or credit-card purchases of at least 100 DM) and a free shot of German brandy whether you buy anything or not (enter through bear shop in gray building on corner where Market Square hits Schmiedgasse; go to first floor).

For characteristic wineglasses and oinkology gear, drop by the **Weinladen am Plonlein** (Plonlein 27).

Shoppers who mail their goodies home can get handy boxes at the **post office** two blocks east of Market Square (Mon–Fri 9:00–12:30, 14:00–17:00, Milchmarkt 5) or the post office at the shopping center across from the train station (similar weekday hours and Sat 9:00–13:00).

Those who prefer to eat their souvenirs shop the *Bäckereien* (bakeries). Their succulent pastries, pies, and cakes are pleasantly distracting. Skip the bad-tasting Rothenburger *Schneebälle*.

Sleeping in Rothenburg
(2 DM = about $1, country code: 49, area code: 09861, zip code: 91541)
Sleep Code: **S** = Single, **D** = Double/Twin, **T** = Triple, **Q** = Quad, **b** = bathroom, **t** = toilet only, **s** = shower only, **CC** = Credit Card (Visa, MasterCard, Amex), **SE** = Speaks English, **NSE** = No English. Unless otherwise indicated, room prices include breakfast.

Rothenburg is crowded with visitors. But when the sun sets, most retreat to the predictable plumbing of their big-city high-rise hotels. Except for the rare Saturday night and festivals (see "Orientation," above), room finding is easy throughout the year. Unless otherwise noted, enough English is spoken.

Many hotels and guest houses will pick up desperate heavy packers at the station. You may be greeted at the station by *Zimmer* skimmers who have rooms to rent. If you have reservations, resist and honor your reservation. But if you haven't booked ahead, try talking yourself into one of these more desperate bed-and-breakfast rooms for a youth-hostel price. Be warned: These people are notorious for taking you to distant hotels and then charging you for the ride back if you decline a room.

A handy **Laundromat** is near the station (Johannitergasse 8, tel. 09861/2775).

Hotels
I like **Hotel Goldene Rose**, where scurrying Karin serves breakfast and stately Henni keeps everything in good order. Besides its annex and apartment, the hotel has one shower on each floor of rooms, but the rooms are clean, and you're surrounded by cobbles,

flowers, and red-tiled roofs (S-40 DM, D-68 DM, Ds-85 DM,
Db-90 DM; some triples, spacious family apartment: for four-200
DM, for five-240 DM; CC:VMA; streetside rooms can be noisy,
closed Jan–Feb, kid friendly, ground-floor rooms in annex, Spitalgasse 28, tel. 09861/4638, fax 09861/86417, Henni SE). The Fav-
etta family also serves good, reasonably priced meals. Remember
to keep your key to get in after they close (at the side gate in the
alley). The hotel is a 15-minute walk from the station or a seven-
minute walk downhill from Market Square.

Gasthof Greifen, once the home of Mayor Toppler, is a
big, traditional, 600-year-old place with large rooms and all the
comforts. It's run by a fine family staff and creaks just the way you
want it to (small Sb-64 DM, Sb-80 DM, one big D-74 DM with
no shower available, Db-115–135 DM, Tb-180 DM, fourth per-
son-30 DM, 10 percent off for three-night stay, CC:VMA, laundry
self- or full-service, free and easy parking, half a block downhill
from Market Square at Obere Schmiedgasse 5, tel. 09861/2281,
fax 09861/86374, Brigitte and Klingler family).

Gasthof Marktplatz, right on Market Square, has nine tidy
rooms and a cozy atmosphere (S-40 DM, D-72 DM, Ds-82 DM,
Db-90 DM, T-95 DM, Ts-108 DM, Tb-118 DM, Grüner Markt 10,
tel. & fax 09861/6722, www.gasthof-marktplatz.de, Herr Rosner SE).

Gästehaus Raidel, a creaky 500-year-old house packed with
antiques, offers 14 large rooms with cramped facilities down the
hall. Run by grim people who make me want to sing the *Addams
Family* theme song, it works in a pinch (S-35 DM, Sb-69 DM,
D-69 DM, Db-89 DM, Wenggasse 3, tel. 09861/3115, fax 09861/
935-255, www.romanticroad.com/raidel, e-mail: Gaestehaus
-Raidel@t-online.de, Herr Raidel speaks a little English).

Hotel Gerberhaus, a classy new hotel in a 500-year-old building, is warmly run by Inge and Kurt, who mix modern comforts
into bright and airy rooms while maintaining a sense of half-
timbered elegance. Enjoy the great buffet breakfasts and pleasant
garden in back (Sb-80 DM, Db-100–140 DM depending on size,
Tb-165 DM, Qb-185 DM, all with TV and telephones, CC:VM
or pay cash for 5 percent off and a free *Schneebälle*, Spitalgasse 25,
tel. 09861/94900, fax 09861/86555, www.gerberhaus.rothenburg
.de). The downstairs café serves good salads and sandwiches.

Hotel Klosterstueble, deep in the old town near the castle
garden, is even classier. Jutta greets her guests while husband
Rudolf does the cooking (Sb-100 DM, Db-130–170 DM, Tb-210
DM, some luxurious family rooms, 10 DM extra on weekends,
discounts for families, CC:VM, Heringsbronnengasse 5, tel.
09861/6774, fax 09861/6474, www.klosterstueble.de).

Bohemians enjoy the **Hotel Altfränkische Weinstube am
Klosterhof**. Mario and lovely Hanne run this dark and smoky pub
in a 600-year-old building. Upstairs they rent six cozy rooms with

upscale Monty Python atmosphere, TVs, modern showers, open-beam ceilings, and "*Himmel*" beds—canopied four-poster "heaven" beds (Sb-79 DM, Db-89 DM, Tb-109–119 DM, CC:VM, most rooms have tubs with hand-held showers, kid friendly, walk under St. Jakob's Church, take second left off Klingengasse at Klosterhof 7, tel. 09861/6404, fax 09861/6410). Their pub is a candlelit classic, serving hot food until 22:30 and closing at 01:00. Drop by on Wednesday evening (19:30–24:00) for the English Conversation Club.

Gasthof Rödertor offers 15 decent rooms in a quiet setting one block from the Rodertor tower (Sb-75–90 DM, Db-120–150 DM, third person-30 DM, most rooms with TV and phone, Ansbacher Strasse 7, tel. 09861/2022, fax 09861/86324, e-mail: hotel@roedertor.com).

Top Private Rooms

For the best real, with-a-local-family, comfortable, and homey experience, stay with **Herr und Frau Moser** (D-70 DM, T-100 DM, no single rooms, Spitalgasse 12, tel. 09861/5971). This charming retired couple speak little English but try very hard. Speak slowly, in clear, simple English. Reserve by phone and please reconfirm by phone one day ahead of arrival.

Pension Pöschel is friendly with seven cozy rooms on the second floor of a concrete but pleasant building (S-35 DM, D-60 DM, T-90 DM, small kids free, Wenggasse 22, tel. 09861/3430, e-mail: pension.poeschel@t-online.de).

Frau Guldemeister, who rents two simple ground-floor rooms, takes reservations by phone only, no more than a day or two in advance (Ss-40 DM, Ds with twin beds-60 DM, bigger Db-70 DM, breakfast in room, minimum two-night stay, off Market Square behind the Christmas shop, Pfaffleinsgasschen 10, tel. 09861/8988, some English).

Last-Resort Accommodations

These are all decent places, just lesser values compared to the places mentioned above. **Pension Kreuzerhof** has seven big, modern, ground-floor, motel-style rooms with views of parked cars on a quiet street (Sb-48–55 DM, Db-78–88 DM, Millergasse 6, tel. 09861/3424, fax 09861/936-730, http://home.debitel.net/user/maltz/Kreuzerhof). **Erich Endress** offers five airy, comfy rooms above his grocery store (S-45 DM, D-80 DM, Db-110 DM, nonsmoking, Rodergasse 6, tel. 09861/2331, fax 09861/935-355). The **Zum Schmolzer** restaurant at Rosengasse 21 rents 14 nice but drab-colored rooms (Sb-55 DM, Db-90 DM, Stollengasse 29, tel. 09861/3371, fax 09861/7204, e-mail: pension-hofmann-oe@t-online.de, SE). **Cafe Uhl** offers 10 fine, slightly frayed rooms over a bakery (Sb-58–75 DM, Db-98–120 DM, third person-35 DM, fourth person-25 DM, CC:VMA,

Plonlein 8, tel. 09861/4895, fax 09861/92820, e-mail: hotel@ uhl.de). **Gästehaus Flemming** has seven plain yet comfortable rooms behind St. Jakob's Church (Db-93 DM, Klingengasse 21, tel. & fax 09861/92380). **Gästehaus Viktoria** is a peaceful and cheery little place with a tiny garden and two rooms (Ds-75 DM, Klingenschütt 4, tel. 09861/87682, Hanne).

In the modern world, a block from the train station, **Pension Then** has six decent rooms and is worth a look (D-100 DM, Db-120 DM, Yohaneiter 8A, tel. 09861/5177, fax 09861/86014).

Hostel

Here in Bavaria, hosteling is limited to those under 27, except for families traveling with children under 18. The fine **Rossmühle Youth Hostel** has 184 beds in two buildings. The droopy-eyed building (the old town horse mill, used when the town was under siege and the river-powered mill was inaccessible) houses groups and the office. The adjacent hostel is mostly for families and individuals (dorm beds-28 DM, Db-66 DM, includes breakfast, dinner-10 DM, self-serve laundry, Muhlacker 1, tel. 09861/94160, fax 09861/ 941-620, www.djh.de, e-mail: jhrothenburg@djh-bayern.de, SE). This popular place takes reservations (even more than a year in advance) and will hold rooms until 18:00.

Sleeping in Nearby Detwang and Bettwar

The town of Detwang, a 15-minute walk below Rothenburg, is loaded with quiet *Zimmer*. The clean, quiet, and comfortable old **Gasthof zum Schwarzes Lamm** in Detwang (D-85 DM, Db-110– 130 DM, CC:VM, tel. 09861/6727, fax 09861/86899, e-mail: hotelschwarzeslamm@t-online.de) has 30 rooms and serves good food, as does the popular and very local-style **Eulenstube** next door. **Gästehaus Alte Schreinerei** offers good food and 18 quiet, comfy, reasonable rooms a little farther down the road in Bettwar (Db-76 DM, 9168 Bettwar, tel. 09861/1541, fax 09861/86710, e-mail: alte.schreinerei@t-online.de).

Eating in Rothenburg

Most places serve meals only from 11:30 to 13:30 and 18:00 to 20:00. At **Goldene Rose** (see "Sleeping," above), Reno cooks up traditional German fare at good prices (Tue 11:30–14:00, Wed–Mon 11:30–14:00, 17:30–21:00, in sunny weather the leafy garden terrace is open in the back, Spitalgasse 28).

Galgengasse (Gallows Lane) has two cheap and popular standbys: **Pizzeria Roma** (11:30–24:00, 12-DM pizzas and normal schnitzel fare, Galgengasse 19) and **Gasthof zum Ochsen** (Fri–Wed 11:30–13:30, 18:00–20:00, closed Thu, uneven service but decent 15-DM meals, Galgengasse 26). **Landsknechtstuben**, at Galgengasse 21, is pricey but friendly, with some cheaper schnitzel choices.

Gasthaus Siebersturm serves up tasty, reasonable meals in a bright, airy dining room (Spitalgasse, tel. 09861/3355). For a break from schnitzel, **Lotus China** serves good Chinese food daily (2 blocks behind TI near the church, Eckele 2, tel. 09861/86886). **Gasthaus Greifen** serves typical Rothenburg cuisine at moderate prices (just below Market Square, tel. 09861/2281).

Two **supermarkets** are near the wall at Rödertor (the one outside the wall to the left is cheaper; the one inside is nicer).

Evening Fun and Beer Drinking

For beer-garden fun on a balmy summer evening (dinner or beer), you have three fine choices: Nearby is **Gasthof Rödertor**, just outside the wall at the Rödertor (red gate, near discos, see below). In the valley along the river and worth the 20-minute hike is **Unter den Linden** beer garden. A more central and touristy beer garden is behind Hotel Eisenhut (nightly until 22:00, access from Burggasse or through the hotel off Herrngasse).

Trinkstube zur Hölle (Hell) is dark and foreboding. But they serve good ribs from 18:00 and offer thick wine-drinking atmosphere until late (a block past Criminal Museum on Burggasse, with devil hanging out front, tel. 09861/4229). For mellow ambience, try the beautifully restored **Alte Keller's Weinstube** under walls festooned with old pots and jugs (closed Tue, Alter Keller 8). Wine lovers enjoy the **Glocke Hotel's Stube** (Plonlein 1). And perhaps the most elegant place in town is the courtyard of **Baumeister Haus** (behind statue-festooned facade a few doors below Market Square).

Two popular **discos** are near the Gasthof Rödertor's beer garden, a few doors farther out near the Sparkasse bank (G-Spot at Ansbacher 15, in alley next to bank, open Wed, Fri–Sat; the other is Club 23, around the corner from the bank, open Wed, Fri–Sun).

For a rare chance to mix it up with locals who aren't selling anything, bring your favorite slang and tongue twisters to the **English Conversation Club** at Mario's Altfränkische Weinstube (Wed 19:30–24:00, Anneliese from the Friese shop is a regular). This dark and smoky pub is an atmospheric hangout any night but Tuesday, when it's closed (Klosterhof 7, off Klingengasse, behind St. Jakob's Church, tel. 09861/6404).

Transportation Connections—Rothenburg

The Romantic Road bus tour takes you in and out of Rothenburg each afternoon (April–Oct) heading to Munich, Frankfurt, or Füssen. See the Romantic Road bus schedule on page 98 (or check www.euraide.de/ricksteves).

A tiny train line runs between Rothenburg and Steinach (almost hrly, 15 min, last train at 21:00, train often leaves from the "B" section of track, away from the middle of the station).

Steinach by train to: Würzburg (hrly, 30 min), **Munich**

(hrly, 3 hrs), **Frankfurt** (hrly, 3 hrs, change in Würzburg). Train connections in Steinach are usually within a few minutes.

Route Tips for Drivers
Rothenburg to Füssen or Reutte, Austria: Get an early start to enjoy the quaint hills and rolling villages of what was Germany's major medieval trade route. The views of Rothenburg from the west, across the Tauber Valley, are magnificent.

After a quick stop in the center of Dinkelsbühl, cross the baby Danube River (Donau) and continue south along the Romantic Road to Füssen. Drive by Neuschwanstein Castle just to sweeten your dreams before crossing into Austria to get set up at Reutte.

If detouring past Oberammergau, you can drive through Garmisch, past Germany's highest mountain (Zugspitze), into Austria via Lermoos, and on to Reutte. Or you can take the small scenic shortcut to Reutte past Ludwig's Linderhof and along the windsurfer-strewn Plansee.

ROMANTIC ROAD
The Romantic Road (*Romantische Strasse*) winds you past the most beautiful towns and scenery of Germany's medieval heart-land. Once Germany's medieval trade route, now it's the best way to connect the dots between Füssen, Munich, and Frankfurt.

Wander through quaint hills and rolling villages, and stop wherever the cows look friendly or a town fountain beckons. My favorite sections are from Füssen to Landsberg and Rothenburg to Weikersheim. (If you're driving with limited time, you can connect Rothenburg and Munich by autobahn, but don't miss these two best sections.) Caution: The similarly promoted "Castle Road," which runs between Rothenburg and Mannheim, sounds intriguing but is nowhere near as interesting.

Throughout Bavaria you'll see colorfully ornamented may-poles decorating town squares. Many are painted in Bavaria's colors, blue and white. The decorations that line each side of the pole symbolize the crafts or businesses of that community. Each May Day they are festively replaced. Traditionally, rival communities try to steal each other's maypole. Locals will guard their new pole night and day as May Day approaches. Stolen poles are ransomed only with lots of beer for the clever thieves.

Getting around the Romantic Road
By Bus: The Europa Bus Company runs buses daily between Frankfurt and Füssen in each direction (April–Oct). A second route goes daily between Munich and Rothenburg (you can transfer at Rothenburg to the other route). Buses leave from train stations in towns served by a train. The 134-DM, 11-hour ride is offered at a 60 percent discount (only 54 DM plus

Romantic Road Bus Schedule (Daily, April–October)

These times are based on the 2001 schedule.
Check www.euraide.de/ricksteves for any changes.

Frankfurt	8:00	—
Würzburg	10:00	—
Arrive Rothenburg	12:45	—
Depart Rothenburg	14:30	14:30
Arrive Dinkelsbühl	15:25	15:25
Depart Dinkelsbühl	15:30	16:15
Munich	—	19:50
Füssen	20:15	—
Füssen	8:00	—
Arrive Wieskirche	8:42	—
Depart Wieskirche	8:55	—
Munich	—	9:00
Arrive Dinkelsbühl	12:45	12:45
Depart Dinkelsbühl	14:00	14:00
Arrive Rothenburg	14:30	14:50
Depart Rothenburg	16:15	—
Depart Würzburg	18:45	—
Frankfurt	20:30	—

3 DM per bag) to travelers who have a German railpass, Eurail-pass, Europass, or Eurail Selectpass—if Germany is one of the selected countries. Buses stop in Rothenburg (about 2 hrs) and Dinkelsbühl (about 1 hr) and briefly at a few other attractions, and have a usually mediocre guide who hands out brochures and narrates the journey in English. There is no quicker or easier way to get such a hearty dose of Germany's countryside. Bus reservations are free, easy, and smart—without one you can lose your seat to someone who has one (especially on summer weekends; call Munich's EurAide office at 089/593-889 at least one day in advance to reserve). You can start, stop, and switch over where you like, but you'll be guaranteed a seat only if you reserve each segment.

By Car: Follow the brown "Romantische Strasse" signs.

Romantic Road

Sights along the Romantic Road

These sights are listed from south to north.

Füssen—This town, the southern terminus of the Romantic Road, is two miles from the startlingly beautiful Neuschwanstein Castle, worthy of a stop on any sightseeing agenda. (See the Bavaria and Tirol chapter for description and accommodations.)

▲▲**Wieskirche**—This is Germany's most glorious Baroque-rococo church. Heavenly! It's in a sweet meadow and is newly restored. Northbound Romantic Road buses stop here for 15 minutes. (See the Bavaria and Tirol chapter.)

Rottenbuch—This is a nondescript village with an impressive church in a lovely setting.

▲**Dinkelsbühl**—Rothenburg's little sister is cute enough to merit a short stop. A moat, towers, gates, and a beautifully preserved medieval wall surround this town and its interesting local museum. The Kinderzeche children's festival turns Dinkelsbühl wonderfully on end in mid-July (TI tel. 09851/90240). On Neustädtlein you'll find 80-DM doubles with baths and TVs at friendly Haus Küffner (tel. 09851/1247) and Zur Linde (tel. 09851/3465).

▲▲▲**Rothenburg**—See opening of this chapter for information on Germany's best medieval town.

▲**Herrgottskapelle**—This peaceful church, graced with Tilman Riemenschneider's greatest carved altar piece (daily 9:15–17:30), is one mile from Creglingen and across the street from the Fingerhut thimble museum (daily 9:00–18:00). The southbound Romantic Road bus stops here for 15 minutes, long enough to see one or the other.

Weikersheim—This untouristy town has a palace with fine Baroque gardens (luxurious picnic spot), a folk museum, and a picturesque town square.

WÜRZBURG

A historic city, though freshly rebuilt since World War II, Würzburg is worth a stop to see its impressive Prince Bishop's Residenz, the bubbly Baroque chapel (Hofkirche) next door, and the palace's sculpted gardens.

Orientation (area code: 0931)

Tourist Information: Würzburg has a helpful TI on the Marktplatz (Mon–Sat 10:00–18:00, tel. 0931/372-355). Their wonderful little *Visitor's Guide* pamphlet covers the tourists' Würzburg well. The produce market near the Marktplatz TI bustles daily except Sunday.

Internet Access: The centrally located H@ckm@ck 2 has a friendly English-speaking staff (7 DM/hr, Sander Strasse 5, tel. 0931/52845).

Sights—Würzburg

▲▲▲**Residenz**—This Franconian Versailles, with grand rooms, 3-D art, and a tennis court–sized fresco by Tiepolo, is worth a tour. English tours are offered on weekends at 11:00 and 15:00 (April–Oct, confirm at TI or call ahead). During the week the best strategy is to take the TI's walking tour at 11:00, which includes a tour of the Residenz along with a walk through the "old" city (15 DM, daily May–Oct, 2 hrs, all in English, includes admission to Residenz; meet at Falken Haus). Or buy the 6-DM guide at the Residenz; it's dry and lengthy, but you can use the pictures to figure out which room you're in. No English labels or descriptions are provided. The top sights are the grand staircase with the Tiepolo ceiling, the reconstructed Room of Mirrors (destroyed during World War II), and the grandly Tiepoloed Imperial Hall (5 DM, April–Oct

Tue–Sun 9:00–18:00, Nov–March 10:00–16:00, last entry 30 min before closing, tel. 0931/355-170). The elaborate Hofkirche chapel is next door (as you exit the palace, go left) and the entrance to the picnic-worthy garden is just beyond. Easy parking is available. Don't confuse the Residenz (a 15-minute walk from the train station) with the fortress on the hilltop.

Fortress Marienberg—Along with a city history museum, the fortress contains the Mainfränkisches Museum, which highlights the work of Riemenschneider, Germany's top wood-carver and past mayor of Würzburg (5 DM, Tue–Sun 10:00–18:00, Nov–March 10:00–16:00, closed Mon, tel. 0931/43016). Riemenschneider fans will find his work throughout Würzburg's many churches (which look closed but are likely open; the sign on the door, "*Bitte Türe schliessen*," simply means "Please close the doors").

Veitshöchheim—Consider a cruise to Veitshöchheim, five kilometers away, to see the fanciful Baroque gardens and the Summer Residenz (gardens free and open daily 7:00–dusk, 3 DM for palace, Tue–Sun 9:00–12:00, 13:00–17:00, closed Mon). Catch the boat at the Würzburg dock (13 DM round-trip, leaves hrly, April–Oct daily 10:00–17:00, tel. 0931/91582) or bus #11 from the Würzburg station (4.20 DM, hrly, 10 min).

Sleeping in Würzburg
(2 DM = about $1, country code: 49, area code: 0931, zip code: 97070)
All listings include breakfast, and prices are soft off-season.

    Hotel-Pension Spehnkuch is the best budget hotel near the station. Overlooking a busy street but quiet behind double-paned windows, it's friendly and comfortable (S-50 DM, D-96 DM, T-140 DM, 2-minute walk from station, exit station and take a right on Rontgenring, at #7, elevator, tel. 0931/54752, fax 0931/54760, SE). **Pension Siegel** is a lesser option (S-46 DM, D-89 DM, from station, go straight on Kaiserstrasse and turn left at Muller store, Reisbrubengasse 7, tel. 0931/52941, fax 0931/52967, NSE).

    Three fine hotels cluster within a block on Theaterstrasse. Quieter rooms are in back; front rooms have street noise. **Hotel Barbarossa**, tucked away on the fourth floor, has 17 comfortable rooms (Ss-75 DM, Sb-95 DM, one Ds-110 DM, Db-140 DM, Tb-170 DM, CC:VMA, elevator, Theaterstrasse 2, tel. 0931/321-370, fax 0931/321-3737, e-mail: marchiorello@t-online.de, SE). **Hotel Schönleber** is a cheery vision of pastel yellow (S-70–100 DM, Sb-95–120 DM, D-110 DM, Ds-120 DM, Db-150 DM, hall showers-4 DM, CC:VMA, elevator, Theaterstrasse 5, tel. 0931/12068, fax 0931/16012), and the **Altstadt Hotel** is a slight cut above, with a wonderfully fragrant Italian restaurant below (Ss-85 DM, Sb-95 DM, Ds-110 DM, Db-140 DM, CC:VMA, Theaterstrasse 7, tel. 0931/321-640, fax 0931/321-6464, e-mail: marchiorello@t-online.de, SE).

Würzburg

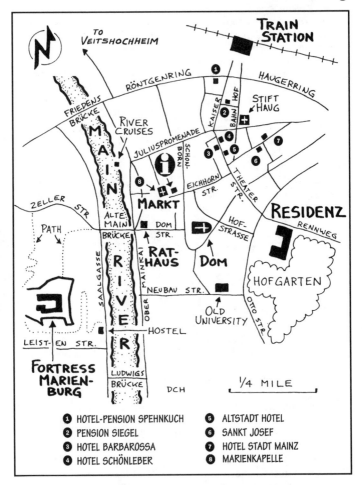

1 HOTEL-PENSION SPEHNKUCH
2 PENSION SIEGEL
3 HOTEL BARBAROSSA
4 HOTEL SCHÖNLEBER
5 ALTSTADT HOTEL
6 SANKT JOSEF
7 HOTEL STADT MAINZ
8 MARIENKAPELLE

Sankt Josef Hotel has a more Franconian feel, with a woody restaurant on a quieter street (Sb-90–95 DM, Db-150–170 DM, CC:VMA, Semmelstrasse 28, coming from station, take left off Theaterstrasse, tel. 0931/308-680, fax 0931/308-6860, e-mail: Hotel.St.Josef@t-online.de, Margit Casagrande and Connie speak some English). Across the street is the elaborately painted **Hotel zur Stadt Mainz**, dating from 1430. You'll pay 40 to 50 DM more for the privilege of sleeping here (CC:VMA, Semmelstrasse 39, tel. 0931/53155, fax 0931/58510, www.hotel-stadtmainz.de).

FRANKFURT

Frankfurt, the northern terminus of the Romantic Road, is actually pleasant for a big city and offers a good look at today's no-nonsense urban Germany.

Orientation (area code: 069)

Tourist Information: For a quick look at the city, pick up a 1-DM map at the TI in the train station (Mon–Fri 8:00–21:00, Sat–Sun 9:00–18:00, tel. 069/2123-8849).

It's a 20-minute walk from the station down Kaiserstrasse past Goethe's house (great man, mediocre sight, Grosser Hirschgraben 23) to Römerberg, Frankfurt's lively Market Square (or you can take subway U-4 or U-5 from the station to Römerberg). Just across the river along Schaumainkai is a string of museums (Tue–Sun 10:00–17:00, Wed until 20:00, closed Mon). The TI also has info on bus tours of the city (44 DM, 10:00 and 14:00 in summer, 14:00 only off-season, 2.5 hrs).

A browse through Frankfurt's red-light district offers a fascinating way to kill time between trains. Wander down Taunusstrasse two blocks in front of the station and you'll find 20 "eros towers," each a five-story-tall brothel filled with prostitutes. Climbing through a few of these may be one of the more memorable experiences of your European trip. It feels safe, the atmosphere is friendly, and browsing is encouraged (40 DM, daily).

Romantic Road Bus: If you're taking the bus out of Frankfurt, you can buy your ticket either at the train station or the Deutsches Touring office, which is part of the train station complex but has an entrance outside (Mon–Fri 7:30–18:00, Sat 7:30–14:00, Sun 7:30–14:00, CC:VMA, entrance at Mannheimer Strasse 4, to your left as you face the station, tel. 069/230-735); or pay cash when you board the bus.

Travelers with railpasses (German, Eurail, Europass, or Eurail Selectpass), who get a 60 percent discount, pay only 54 DM (plus 3 DM per bag). The bus waits at stall #9 (right of the train station as you leave).

Sleeping in Frankfurt
(2 DM = about $1, country code: 49, area code: 069, zip code: 60329)

Avoid driving or sleeping in Frankfurt, especially during the city's numerous trade fairs (about 5 days a month), which send hotel prices skyrocketing. Pleasant Rhine or Romantic Road towns are just a quick train ride or drive away. But if you must spend the night in Frankfurt, here are some places within a block of the train station (and its handy train to the airport). This isn't the safest neighborhood; be careful after dark. For a rough idea of directions to hotels, stand with your back to the main entrance of the station:

Using a 12-hour clock, Hotel Manhattan is across the street at 10:00, Pension Schneider at 12:00, Hotel Europa and Wiesbaden at 4:00, and Hotel Paris at 5:00. Breakfast is included in all listings and English is spoken.

Hotel Manhattan, with sleek, arty rooms, is expensive— best for a splurge on a first or last night in Europe (Sb-145 DM, Db-175 DM, show this book to get a break during nonconvention times, CC:VMA, elevator, riffraff in front of hotel, Düsseldorfer Strasse 10, tel. 069/269-5970, fax 069/2695-97777, e-mail: manhattan-hotel@t-online.de).

Pension Schneider is a strange little oasis of decency and quiet three floors above the epicenter of Frankfurt's red-light district, two blocks in front of the train station. The street is safe in spite of the pimps and pushers. Its 10 rooms are big, bright, and comfortable (S-70 DM, D-100 DM, Db-120 DM, Tb-150 DM, CC:VM, elevator, corner of Moselstrasse at Taunusstrasse 43, tel. 069/251-071, fax 069/259-228).

Hotel Europa, with 50 well-maintained rooms, is a fine value (Sb-80 DM, Db-120 DM, Tb-150 DM, prices soft on weekends, some nonsmoking rooms, garage, CC:VMA, Baseler Strasse 17, tel. 069/236-013, fax 069/236-203).

Hotel Wiesbaden has worn rooms and a kind manager (S-80 DM, Sb-115 DM, Db-140–165 DM depending on size, Tb-180–200 DM, CC:VMA, a little smoky, elevator, Baseler Strasse 52, tel. 069/232-347, fax 069/252-845).

Hotel Paris, with modern, Impressionist rooms, is the most cushy of my listings (Sb-110 DM, Db-150 DM, CC:VMA, Karlsruherstrasse 8, tel. 069/273-9963, fax 069/2739-9651).

Farther from the station is **Pension Backer** (S-50 DM, D-60 DM, showers-3 DM, near botanical gardens, take S-Bahn 2 stops to Hauptwache, then transfer to U-6 or U-7 for 2 stops to Westend; Mendelssohnstrasse 92, tel. 069/747-992).

The **hostel** is open to members of any age (8-bed rooms, 35 DM per bed with sheets and breakfast, bus #46 from station to Frankenstein Place, Deutschherrnufer 12, tel. 069/610-0150, fax 069/610-01599, e-mail: jugendherberge_frankfurt@t-online.de).

Transportation Connections—Frankfurt

By train to: Rothenburg (hrly, 3 hrs, changes in Würzburg and Steinach; the tiny Steinach–Rothenburg train often leaves from the "B" section of track, away from the middle of the station, shortly after the Würzburg train arrives), **Würzburg** (hrly, 90 min), **Munich** (hrly, 3.5 hrs), **Baden-Baden** (2/hr, 90 min), **Freiburg** (hrly, 2 hrs, change in Mannheim), **Bonn** (hrly, 2 hrs), **Koblenz** (hrly, 90 min), **Köln** (hrly, 2 hrs), **Berlin** (hrly, 5 hrs), **Amsterdam** (8/day, 5 hrs), **Bern** (14/day, 4.5 hrs, changes in Mannheim and Basel), **Brussels** (6/day, 5 hrs), **Copenhagen**

(3/day, 10 hrs), **London** (5/day, 9.5 hrs), **Milan** (6/day, 9 hrs), **Paris** (4/day, 6.5 hrs), **Vienna** (7/day, 7.5 hrs).

Frankfurt's Airport

The airport (*Flughafen*) is a 12-minute train ride from downtown (4/hrly, 6.10 DM, ride included in Frankfurt's 8.5-DM all-day city transit pass). The airport is user-friendly. It offers showers, a baggage check, fair banks with long hours, a grocery store, a train station, a lounge where you can sleep overnight, a business lounge (Europe City Club—30 DM for anyone with a plane ticket), easy rental-car pickup, plenty of parking, an information booth, and even McBeer. McWelcome to Germany. Airport English-speaking info: tel. 069/6901 (will transfer you to any of the airlines for booking or confirmation). Lufthansa—069/255-255, American Airlines—069/690-21781, Delta—069/690-28751, Northwest—0180-525-4650.

To Rothenburg: Train travelers can validate railpasses or buy tickets at the airport station and catch a train to Würzburg, connecting to Rothenburg via Steinach (hrly, 3 hrs). If driving to Rothenburg, follow autobahn signs to Würzburg.

Flying Home from Frankfurt: The airport has its own train station, and many of the trains from the Rhine stop there on their way into Frankfurt (e.g., hrly 90-min rides direct from Bonn; hrly 2-hr rides from Bacharach with a change in Mainz; earliest train from Bacharach to Frankfurt leaves just before 6:00). By car, head toward Frankfurt on the autobahn and follow the little airplane signs to the airport.

Route Tips for Drivers

Frankfurt to Rothenburg: The three-hour drive from the airport to Rothenburg is something even a jet-lagged zombie can handle. It's a 75-mile straight shot to Würzburg on A-3; just follow the blue autobahn signs. Leave the freeway at the Heidingsfeld-Würzburg exit. If going directly to Rothenburg, follow signs south to Stuttgart/Ulm/Road 19, then continue to Rothenburg via a scenic slice of the Romantic Road. If stopping at Würzburg, follow "Stadtmitte" then "Residenz" signs from the same freeway exit. From Würzburg, follow Ulm/Road 19 signs to Bad Mergentheim/Rothenburg.

RHINE AND MOSEL VALLEYS

These valleys are storybook Germany, a fairy-tale world of Rhine legends and robber-baron castles. Cruise the most castle-studded stretch of the romantic Rhine as you listen for the song of the treacherous Loreley. For hands-on castle thrills, climb through the Rhineland's greatest castle, Rheinfels, above the town of St. Goar. Then, for a sleepy and laid-back alternative, mosey through the neighboring Mosel Valley.

In the north you'll find the powerhouse city of Köln (Cologne), home to Germany's greatest Gothic cathedral and its best collection of Roman artifacts, a world-class art museum, and a healthy dose of German urban playfulness. Bustling Köln merits a visit, but spend your nights in a castle-crowned village. On the Rhine, stay in St. Goar or Bacharach. On the Mosel, choose Zell.

Planning Your Time

The Rhineland does not take much time to see. The blitziest tour is an hour at the Köln cathedral and an hour looking at the castles from your train window. For a better look, however, cruise in, tour a castle or two, sleep in a genuine medieval town, and take the train out. If you have limited time, cruise less and be sure to get into a castle.

Ideally, spend two nights here, sleep in Bacharach, cruise the best hour of the river (from Bacharach to St. Goar), and tour the Rheinfels Castle. Those with more time can ride the riverside bike path. With two days and a car, visit the Rhine and the Mosel. With two days by train, see the Rhine and Köln. With three days, do all three, and with four days include Trier and a sleepy night in the Mosel River Valley.

Rhine and Mosel Valleys

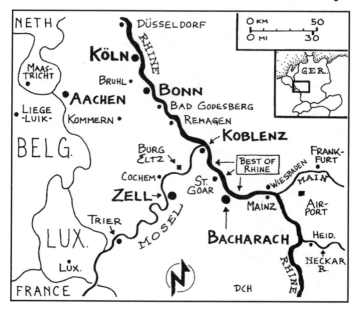

THE RHINE

Ever since Roman times, when this was the Empire's northern boundary, the Rhine has been one of the world's busiest shipping rivers. You'll see a steady flow of barges with 1,000- to 2,000-ton loads. Tourist-packed buses, hot train tracks, and highways line both banks.

Many of the castles were "robber-baron" castles, put there by petty rulers (there were 300 independent little countries in medieval Germany) to levy tolls on passing river traffic. A robber baron would put his castle on, or even in, the river. Then, often with the help of chains and a tower on the opposite bank, he'd stop each ship and get his toll. There were 10 customs stops between Mainz and Koblenz alone (no wonder merchants were early proponents of the creation of larger nation-states).

Some castles were built to control and protect settlements, and others were the residences of kings. As times changed, so did the lifestyles of the rich and feudal. Many castles were abandoned for more comfortable mansions in the towns.

Most Rhine castles date from the 11th, 12th, and 13th centuries. When the pope successfully asserted his power over the German emperor in 1076, local princes ran wild over the rule of their emperor. The castles saw military action in the 1300s and 1400s, as emperors began reasserting their control over Germany's many silly kingdoms.

The castles were also involved in the Reformation wars, in which Europe's Catholic and "protesting" dynasties fought it out using a fragmented Germany as their battleground. The Thirty Years' War (1618–1648) devastated Germany. The outcome: Each ruler got the freedom to decide if his people would be Catholic or Protestant, and one-third of Germany was dead. Production of Gummi Bears ceased entirely.

The French—who feared a strong Germany and felt the Rhine was the logical border between them and Germany—destroyed most of the castles prophylactically (Louis XIV in the 1680s, the revolutionary army in the 1790s, and Napoleon in 1806). They were often rebuilt in neo-Gothic style in the Romantic Age—the late 1800s—and today are enjoyed as restaurants, hotels, hostels, and museums.

For more information on the Rhine, visit www.loreleytal.com (heavy on hotels but has maps, photos, and a little history).

Getting around the Rhine

While the Rhine flows north from Switzerland to Holland, the stretch from Mainz to Koblenz hoards all the touristic charm. Studded with the crenelated cream of Germany's castles, it bustles with boats, trains, and highway traffic. Have fun exploring with a mix of big steamers, tiny ferries, bikes, and trains.

By Boat: While many travelers do the whole trip by boat, the most scenic hour is from St. Goar to Bacharach. Sit on the top deck with your handy Rhine map-guide (or the kilometer-keyed tour in this book) and enjoy the parade of castles, towns, boats, and vineyards.

There are several boat companies, but most travelers sail on the bigger, more expensive and romantic Köln-Düsseldorf (K-D) line (free with a consecutive-day Eurailpass or a dated Eurail Flex-ipass, Europass, Eurail Selectpass, or German railpass, otherwise about 15.40 DM for the first hr, then progressively cheaper per hr; the recommended Bacharach–St. Goar trip costs 15.40 DM one-way, 18.80 DM round-trip; tel. 06741/1634 in St. Goar, www.k-d.com, schedule at www.euraide.de/ricksteves). Boats run daily in both directions from April through October; no boats run off-season. Complete, up-to-date schedules are posted in any station, Rhineland hotel, TI, or current Thomas Cook Timetable. Purchase tickets at the dock up to five minutes before departure. The boat is rarely full. (Confirm times at your hotel the night before.)

The smaller Bingen-Rüdesheimer line is 25 percent cheaper than K-D (railpasses not valid, buy tickets on boat,

tel. 06721/14140), with three two-hour round-trip St. Goar–
Bacharach trips daily in summer (about 12 DM one-way, 17 DM
round-trip; departing St. Goar at 11:00, 13:10, and 16:10, departing Bacharach at 10:10, 12:30, and 15:00).

Drivers have these options: (1) skip the boat; (2) take a round-
trip cruise from St. Goar or Bacharach; (3) draw pretzels and let
the loser drive, prepare the picnic, and meet the boat; (4) rent a
bike, bring it on the boat for free, and bike back; or (5) take the
boat one-way and return by train.

By Train: Hourly milk-run trains down the Rhine hit every
town: St. Goar–Bacharach, 12 min; Bacharach–Mainz, 60 min;
Mainz–Frankfurt, 45 min. Some train schedules list St. Goar but
not Bacharach as a stop, but any schedule listing St. Goar also
stops at Bacharach. Tiny stations are unmanned—buy tickets at
the platform machines or on the train.

By Bike: In Bacharach try Hotel Hillen (10 DM/half day,
15 DM/day, cheaper for guests, 20 bikes) or Hotel Gelberhof
(25 DM/day for 10-speeds, 25 DM for trekking bikes, 5 DM
for child's seat, tel. 06743/910-100, ring bell when closed). In
St. Goar, it's Hermy's Garden (18 DM/day, Reine Strasse, tel.
06741/1360). The best riverside bike path is from Bacharach to
Bingen (leaving Bacharach, after you pass campground, head down
to path bordering river). The path is also good from St. Goar to
Bacharach, but it's closer to the highway. Consider renting a bike
in Bacharach and taking it on the boat to Bingen and biking back,
visiting Rheinstein Castle (you're on your own to wander the
well-furnished castle) and Reichenstein Castle (admittance with
groups), and maybe even taking a ferry across the river to Kaub
(where a tiny boat shuttles sightseers to the better-from-a-distance
castle on the island). While there are no bridges between Koblenz
and Mainz, several small ferries do their job constantly and cheaply.

Sights—The Romantic Rhine

These sights are listed from north to south, Koblenz to Bingen.
▲▲▲**Der Romantische Rhein Blitz Zug Fahrt**—One of
Europe's great train thrills is zipping along the Rhine in this fast
train tour. Here's a quick and easy, from-the-train-window tour
(also works for car, bike, or best by boat, you can cut in anywhere)
that skips the syrupy myths that fill normal Rhine guides. For
more information than necessary, buy the handy *Rhine Guide from
Mainz to Cologne* (7-DM book with foldout map, at most shops).

Sit on the left (river) side of the train or boat going south
from Koblenz. While nearly all the castles listed are viewed from
this side, clear a path to the right window for the times I yell,
"Crossover!"

You'll notice large black-and-white kilometer markers along
the riverbank. I erected these years ago to make this tour easier

Best of the Rhine

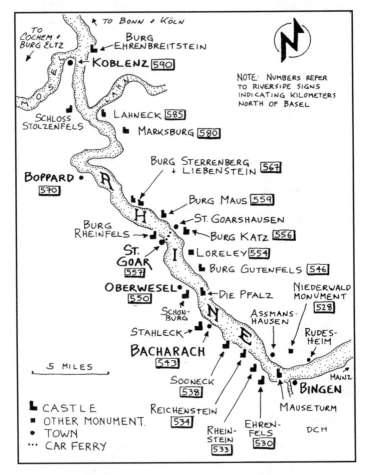

TO BONN + KÖLN

TO COCHEM + BURG ELTZ

BURG EHRENBREITSTEIN

KOBLENZ 590

NOTE: NUMBERS REFER TO RIVERSIDE SIGNS INDICATING KILOMETERS NORTH OF BASEL

SCHLOSS STOLZENFELS

LAHNECK 585

MARKSBURG 580

BOPPARD 570

BURG STERRENBERG + LIEBENSTEIN 567

BURG MAUS 559

ST. GOARSHAUSEN

BURG RHEINFELS

BURG KATZ 556

ST. GOAR 557

LORELEY 554

BURG GUTENFELS 546

OBERWESEL 550

DIE PFALZ

NIEDERWALD MONUMENT 528

SCHON-BURG

ASSMANS-HAUSEN

STAHLECK

RUDES-HEIM

BACHARACH 543

SOONECK 538

BINGEN

MAUSETURM

REICHENSTEIN 534

RHEIN-STEIN 533

EHREN-FELS 530

MAINZ

DCH

5 MILES

🯈 CASTLE
■ OTHER MONUMENT.
● TOWN
⋯ CAR FERRY

to follow. They tell the distance from the Rhinefalls where the Rhine leaves Switzerland and becomes navigable. Now the river-barge pilots have accepted these as navigational aids as well. We're tackling just 36 miles of the 820-mile-long Rhine. Your Blitz Rhine Tour starts at Koblenz and heads upstream to Bingen. If you're going the other direction, it still works. Just hold the book upside down.

Km 590: Koblenz—This Rhine blitz starts with Romantic Rhine thrills—at Koblenz. Koblenz is not a nice city (it was really hit hard in World War II), but its place as the historic

2001 Rhine Cruise Schedule

Koblenz	Boppard	St. Goar	Bacharach
—	9:00	10:15	11:25
9:00	11:00	12:20	13:35
11:00	13:00	14:15	15:25
14:00	16:00	17:15	18:25
11:00*	11:30*	11:50*	12:10*
13:00	11:50	10:55	10:15
14:20	12:50	11:55	11:15
—	13:50	12:55	12:15
18:00	16:50	15:55	15:15
20:00	18:50	17:55	17:15

* Hydrofoil, Koblenz–Bacharach, 25 DM one-way and 45 DM round-trip with Eurail, 90 DM without.
Note: Schedule applies May through September and mostly April and October; no boats run November through March.

Deutsche-Ecke (German corner)—the tip of land where the Mosel joins the Rhine—gives it a certain historic charm. Koblenz, Latin for "confluence," has Roman origins. Walk through the park, noticing the reconstructed memorial to the Kaiser. Across the river, the yellow Ehrenbreitstein Castle now houses a hostel. It's a 30-minute hike from the station to the Koblenz boat dock.

Km 585: Burg Lahneck—Above the modern autobahn bridge over the Lahn River, this castle (*Burg*) was built in 1240 to defend local silver mines, ruined by the French in 1688 and rebuilt in the 1850s in neo-Gothic style. Burg Lahneck faces the yellow Schloss Stolzenfels (out of view above the train, a 10-minute climb from tiny car park, open for touring, closed Mon).

Km 580: Marksburg—This castle (black and white with the three modern chimneys behind it, just after town of Spay) is the best looking of all the Rhine castles and the only surviving medieval castle on the Rhine. Because of its commanding position, it was never attacked. It's now open as a museum with a medieval interior second only to the Mosel's Burg Eltz (9 DM, daily 10:00–17:00, call ahead to see if a rare English tour is scheduled, tel. 02627/206).

Km 570: Boppard—Once a Roman town, Boppard has

some impressive remains of fourth-century walls. Notice the Roman towers and the substantial chunk of Roman wall near the Boppard's train station. Boppard is worth a stop. Just above the main square are the remains of the Roman wall. Below the square is a fascinating church. Notice the carved Romanesque crazies at the doorway. Inside, to the right of the entrance, you'll see Christian symbols from Roman times. Also notice the painted arches and vaults. Originally most Romanesque churches were painted this way. Down by the river, look for the high water (*Hochwasser*) marks on the arches from various flood years. (You'll find these flood marks throughout the Rhine and Mosel Valleys.)

Km 567: Burg Sterrenberg and Burg Liebenstein— These are the "Hostile Brothers" castles, across from Bad Salzig. Take the wall between the castles (actually designed to improve the defenses of both castles), add two greedy and jealous brothers and a fair maiden, and create your own legend. The castles are restaurants today.

Km 559: Burg Maus— The Maus ("Mouse") got its name because the next castle was owned by the Katzenelnbogen family. ("Katz" means "cat.") In the 1300s it was considered a state-of-the-art fortification...until Napoleon had it blown up in 1806 with state-of-the-art explosives. It was rebuilt true to its original plans around 1900.

Km 557: St. Goar and Rheinfels Castle— Cross to the other side of the train. The pleasant town of St. Goar was named for a sixth-century hometown monk. It originated in Celtic times (really old) as a place where sailors would stop, catch their breath, send home a postcard, and give thanks after surviving the seductive and treacherous Loreley crossing. St. Goar is worth a stop to explore its mighty Rheinfels Castle. (For information on a guided castle tour and accommodations, see below.)

Km 556: Burg Katz— From the town of St. Goar, you'll see Burg Katz (Katzenelnbogen) across the river. Together, Burg Katz (built in 1371) and Rheinfels Castle had a clear view up and down the river and effectively controlled traffic. There was absolutely no duty-free shopping on the medieval Rhine. Katz got Napoleoned in 1806 and rebuilt around 1900. Today it's a convalescent home.

About Km 555: You'll see the statue of the Loreley, the beautiful but deadly nymph (see next listing for legend), at the end of a long spit—built to give barges protection from vicious icebergs that occasionally rage down the river in the winter. The actual Loreley, a cliff, is just ahead.

Km 554: The Loreley— Steep a big slate rock in centuries of legend and it becomes a tourist attraction, the ultimate Rhinestone. The Loreley (two flags on top, name painted near shoreline), rising 450 feet over the narrowest and deepest point of the Rhine, has long been important. It was a holy site in pre-Roman

River Trade and Barge Watching

The river is great for barge watching. Since ancient times this has been a highway for trade. Today the world's biggest port (Rotterdam) waits at the mouth of the river. Barge workers are almost a subculture. Many own their own ships. The captain (and family) live in the stern. Workers live in the bow. The family car often decorates the bow like a shiny hood ornament. In the Rhine town of Kaub there's even a boarding school for the children of the Rhine merchant marine. The flag of the boat's home country flies in the stern (German, Swiss, Dutch—horizontal red, white, and blue; or French—vertical red, white, and blue). Logically, imports go upstream (Japanese cars, coal, and oil) and exports go downstream (German cars, chemicals, and pharmaceuticals). A clever captain manages to ship goods in each direction.

At this point tugs can push a floating train of up to five barges at once. Upstream it gets steeper and they can push only one at a time. Before modern shipping, horses dragged boats upstream (the faint remains of the tow-paths survive at points along the river). From 1873 to 1900 they actually laid a chain from Bonn to Bingen, and boats with cogwheels and steam engines hoisted themselves slowly upstream. Today 265 million tons are shipped each year along the 528 navigable miles from Basel on the Swiss border to Rotterdam on the Atlantic.

While riverside navigational aids are ignored by camera-toting tourists, they are of vital interest to captains who don't wish to meet the Loreley. Boats pass on the right unless they clearly signal otherwise with a large blue sign. Since downstream ships can't stop or maneuver as freely, upstream boats are expected to do the tricky do-si-do work. Cameras monitor traffic all along and relay warnings of oncoming ships via large triangular signals posted before narrow and troublesome bends in the river. There may be two or three triangles per sign-post, depending upon how many "sectors," or segments, of the river are covered. The lowest triangle indicates the nearest stretch of river. Each triangle tells if there's a ship in that sector. When the bottom side of a triangle is lit, that sector is empty. When the left side is lit, an oncoming ship is in that sector.

days. The fine echoes here—thought to be ghostly voices—
fertilized the legendary soil.

Because of the reefs just upstream (at kilometer 552), many
ships never made it to St. Goar. Sailors (after days on the river)
blamed their misfortune on a *wunderbares Fräulein* whose long
blonde hair almost covered her body. Heinrich Heine's *Song of
Loreley* (the Cliffs Notes version is on local postcards) tells the
story of a count who sent his men to kill or capture this siren
after she distracted his horny son, causing him to drown. When
the soldiers cornered the nymph in her cave, she called her father
(Father Rhine) for help. Huge waves, the likes of which you'll
never see today, rose from the river and carried Loreley to safety.
And she has never been seen since.

But alas, when the moon shines brightly and the tour buses
are parked, a soft, playful Rhine whine can still be heard from the
Loreley. As you pass, listen carefully ("Sailors . . . sailors . . . over
my bounding mane").

Km 552: Killer reefs, marked by red-and-green buoys, are
called the "Seven Maidens."

Km 550: Oberwesel—Cross to the other side of the train.
Oberwesel was a Celtic town in 400 B.C., then a Roman military
station. It now boasts some of the best Roman wall and tower
remains on the Rhine and the commanding Schönburg Castle.
Notice how many of the train tunnels have entrances designed
like medieval turrets—they were actually built in the Romantic
19th century. OK, back to the riverside.

**Km 546: Burg Gutenfels and Pfalz Castle: The Classic
Rhine View**—Burg Gutenfels (see the white painted "Hotel" sign)
and the shipshape Pfalz Castle (built in the river in the 1300s)
worked very effectively to tax medieval river traffic. The town of
Kaub grew rich as Pfalz raised its chains when boats came and
lowered them only when the merchants had paid their duty. Those
who didn't pay spent time touring its prison, on a raft at the bottom
of its well. In 1504 a pope called for the destruction of Pfalz, but a
six-week siege failed. Notice the overhanging "outhouse" (tiny white
room with the faded medieval stains between the two wooden ones).
Pfalz is tourable but bare and dull (3-DM ferry from Kaub, 4 DM,
Tue–Sun 9:00–13:00, 14:00–18:00, closed Mon, tel. 06774/570).

In Kaub a green statue honors the German General Blücher.
He was Napoleon's nemesis. In 1813, as Napoleon fought his way
back to Paris after his disastrous Russian campaign, he stopped at
Mainz—hoping to fend off the Germans and Russians pursuing
him—by controlling that strategic bridge. Blücher tricked Napoleon. By building the first major pontoon bridge of its kind,
here at the Pfalz Castle, he crossed the Rhine and outflanked the
French. Two years later Blücher and Wellington teamed up to
defeat Napoleon once and for all at Waterloo.

Km 544: The "Raft Busters"—Immediately before Bacharach, at the top of the island, buoys mark a gang of rocks notorious for busting up rafts. The Black Forest is upstream. It was poor, and wood was its best export. Black Foresters would ride log booms down the Rhine to the Ruhr (where their timber fortified coal-mine shafts) or to Holland (where logs were sold to shipbuilders). If they could navigate the sweeping bend just before Bacharach and then survive these "raft busters," they'd come home reckless and romantic, the German folkloric equivalent of American cowboys after payday.

Km 543: Bacharach and Burg Stahleck—Cross to the other side of the train. Bacharach is a great stop (see details and accommodations below). Some of the Rhine's best wine is from this town, whose name means "altar to Bacchus." Local vintners brag that the medieval Pope Pius II ordered it by the cartload. Perched above the town, the 13th-century Burg Stahleck is now a hostel.

Km 540: Lorch—This pathetic stub of a castle is barely visible from the road. Notice the small car ferry (3/hrly, 10 min), one of several between Mainz and Koblenz, where there are no bridges.

Km 538: Castle Sooneck—Cross back to the other side of the train. Built in the 11th century, this castle was twice destroyed by people sick and tired of robber barons.

Km 534: Burg Reichenstein, and **Km 533: Burg Rheinstein**—Stay on the other side of the train to see two of the first castles to be rebuilt in the Romantic era. Both are privately owned, tourable, and connected by a pleasant trail.

Km 530: Ehrenfels Castle—Opposite Bingerbrück and the Bingen station, you'll see the ghostly Ehrenfels Castle (clobbered by the Swedes in 1636 and by the French in 1689). Since it had no view of the river traffic to the north, the owner built the cute little *Mäuseturm* (Mouse Tower) on an island (the yellow tower you'll see near the train station today). Rebuilt in the 1800s in neo-Gothic style, today it's used as a Rhine navigation signal station.

Km 528: Niederwald Monument—Across from the Bingen station on a hilltop is the 120-foot-high Niederwald monument, a memorial built with 32 tons of bronze in 1877 to commemorate "the reestablishment of the German Empire." A lift takes tourists to this statue from the famous and extremely touristy wine town of Rüdesheim.

Our tour is over. From Bingen you can continue your journey (or return to Koblenz) by train or boat.

BACHARACH

Once prosperous from the wine and wood trade, Bacharach is now just a pleasant half-timbered village working hard to keep its tourists happy.

The slick new **TI** is on the main street in the Posthof court-yard next to the church (Mon–Fri 9:00–17:00, Sat 10:00–16:00, closed Sun, Internet access-12 DM/hr, Oberstrasse 45, from station turn right and walk down main street with castle high on your left and walk about 5 blocks, tel. 06743/919-303).

The **Jost beer stein "factory outlet"** carries most everything a shopper could want. It has one shop across from the church in the main square and a slightly cheaper shop (housing the post office) a block away on Rosenstrasse 16 (Mon–Fri 8:30–18:00, Sat 8:30–17:00, Sun 10:00–17:00, ships overseas, 10 percent discount with this book, CC:VMA, tel. 06743/1224).

Get acquainted with Bacharach by taking a **walking tour**. Charming Herr Rolf Jung, retired headmaster of the Bacharach school, is a superb English-speaking guide (50 DM, 90 min, call him to reserve a tour, tel. 06743/1519). The TI also has a list of other guides, or take the self-guided walk, described below. For accommodations, see "Sleeping on the Rhine," below.

Sights—Bacharach

▲▲**Introductory Bacharach Walk**—Start at the Köln-Düssel-dorf ferry dock (next to a fine picnic park). View the town from the parking lot—a modern landfill. The Rhine used to lap against Bacharach's town wall, just over the present-day highway. Every few years the river floods, covering the highway with several feet of water. The **castle** on the hill is a youth hostel. Two of its original 16 towers are visible from here (up to five if you look real hard). The huge roadside wine keg declares this town was built on the wine trade.

Reefs up the river forced boats to unload upriver and reload here. Consequently, Bacharach became the biggest wine trader on the Rhine. A riverfront crane hoisted huge kegs of prestigious "Bacharach" wine (which in practice was from anywhere in the region). The tour buses next to the dock and the flags of the biggest spenders along the highway remind you today's economy is basically tourism.

At the big town map and public WC, take the underpass, ascend on the right, make a U-turn, then walk under the train tracks through the medieval gate (one out of an original six 14th-century gates) and to the two-tone Protestant **church**, which marks the town center.

From this intersection, Bacharach's main street (Oberstrasse) goes right to the half-timbered, red-and-white Altes Haus (from 1368, the oldest house in town) and left way down to the train station. To the left (or south) of the church, the golden horn hangs over the old **Posthof** (and new TI). The post horn symbolizes the postal service throughout Europe. In olden days, when the postman blew this, traffic stopped and the mail sped through.

Bacharach

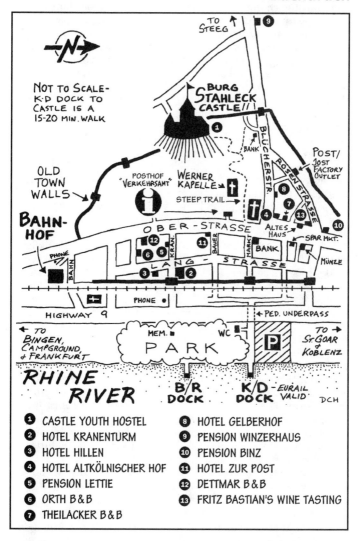

Step into the courtyard. Notice the fascist eagle (from 1936, on the left as you enter) and the fine view of a chapel and church. This post station dates from 1724, when stagecoaches ran from Köln to Frankfurt.

Two hundred years ago this was the only road along the

Rhine. Napoleon widened it to fit his cannon wagons. The steps alongside the church lead to the castle. Return to the church.

Inside the church you'll find grotesque and brightly painted capitals and a mix of round Romanesque and pointed Gothic arches. In the upper left corner some medieval frescoes survive where an older Romanesque arch was cut by a pointed Gothic one.

Continue down Oberstrasse past the Altes Haus to the **old mint** (*Münze*), marked by a crude coin in its sign. Across from the mint, the wine garden of Fritz Bastian is the liveliest place in town after dark. Above you in the vineyards stands a ghostly black-and-gray tower—your destination.

Take the next left (Rosenstrasse) and wander 30 meters up to the **well**. Notice the sundial and the wall painting of 1632 Bacharach with its walls intact. Climb the tiny-stepped lane behind the well up into the vineyard and to the tower. The slate steps lead to a small path that deposits you at a viewpoint atop the stubby remains of the old town wall, just above the tower's base (if signs indicate that the path is closed, get as close to the tower base as possible).

A grand medieval town spreads before you. When Frankfurt had 15,000 residents, medieval Bacharach had 6,000. For 300 years (1300–1600) Bacharach was big, rich, and politically powerful.

From this perch you can see the chapel ruins and six of the nine surviving **city towers**. Visually trace the wall to the castle, home of one of seven electors who voted for the Holy Roman Emperor in 1275. To protect their own power, these elector princes did their best to choose the weakest guy on the ballot. The elector from Bacharach helped select a two-bit prince named Rudolf von Hapsburg (from a two-bit castle in Switzerland). The underestimated Rudolf brutally silenced the robber barons along the Rhine and established the mightiest dynasty in European history. His family line, the Hapsburgs, ruled the Austro-Hungarian Empire until 1918.

Plagues, fires, and the Thirty Years' War (1618–1648) finally did Bacharach in. The town has slumbered for several centuries, with a population of about a thousand.

In the mid-19th century, artists and writers such as Victor Hugo were charmed by the Rhineland's romantic mix of past glory, present poverty, and rich legend. They put this part of the Rhine on the old "grand tour" map as the "Romantic Rhine." Victor Hugo pondered the ruined 15th-century chapel, which you can see under the castle. In his 1842 travel book, *Rhein Reise* (*Rhine Travels*), he wrote, "No doors, no roof or windows, a magnificent skeleton puts its silhouette against the sky. Above it, the ivy-covered castle ruins provide a fitting crown. This is Bacharach, land of fairy tales, covered with legends and sagas." If you're enjoying the Romantic Rhine, thank Victor Hugo and company.

To get back into town, take the path that leads along the wall up the valley to the next tower, then down onto the street. Follow the road under the gate and back into the center.

ST. GOAR

St. Goar is a classic Rhine town—its hulk of a castle overlooking a half-timbered shopping street and leafy riverside park busy with sightseeing ships and contented strollers. From the boat dock, the main drag—a pedestrian mall—cuts through town before winding up to the castle. Rheinfels Castle, once the mightiest on the Rhine, is the single best Rhineland ruin to explore.

The St. Goar **TI**, which offers a free left-luggage service, is on the pedestrian street, three blocks from the K-D boat dock (May–Oct Mon–Fri 8:00–12:30, 14:00–17:00, Sat 10:00–12:00, closed Sun and earlier in winter; if you're coming from train station, take a quick right, go around church, walk toward river and turn left on Herr Strasse, TI is 100 meters down on the right; tel. 06741/383).

St. Goar's waterfront park is hungry for a picnic. The small EDEKA **supermarket** on the main street is great for picnic fixings (Mon–Fri 8:00–19:00, Sat 8:00–16:00, limited hours on Sun in summer). Bike rental is available from Hermy's Garden (18 DM/day, Reine Strasse, tel. 06741/1360).

The friendly and helpful Montag family in the shop under Hotel Montag has Rhine guidebooks (Koblenz-Mainz), fine steins, and copies of this year's *Rick Steves' Germany, Austria & Switzerland* guidebook. They offer 10 percent off any of their souvenirs for travelers with this book (10 DM minimum purchase) and offer Internet access (12 DM/hr).

For a good two-hour **hike** from St. Goar to the Loreley viewpoint, catch the ferry across to St. Goarshausen (2.5-DM round-trip, 4/hrly), hike up past the Katz castle (now a convalescent home), and traverse along the hillside, always bearing right toward the river. You'll pass through a residential area, hike down a 50-meter path through trees, then traverse a wheat field until you reach an amphitheater adjacent to the Loreley overview (restaurant available). From here it's a steep 15-minute hike down to the river where a riverfront trail takes you back to the St. Goarshausen-to-St. Goar ferry.

Sights—St. Goar's Rheinfels Castle

▲▲▲**Self-Guided Tour**—Sitting like a dead pit bull above St. Goar, this mightiest of Rhine castles rumbles with ghosts from its hard-fought past. Burg Rheinfels (built in 1245) withstood a siege of 28,000 French troops in 1692. But in 1797 the French Revolutionary army destroyed it.

Rheinfels was huge. In fact, it was the biggest castle on

St. Goar

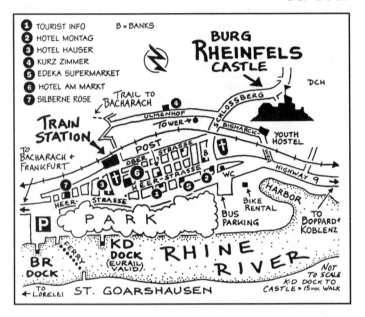

the Rhine and was used as a quarry. Today this hollow but interesting shell offers your single best hands-on ruined castle experience on the river (6 DM, daily 9:00–18:00, last entry at 17:00, only Sat–Sun in winter, gather 15 English-speaking tourists and get a nearly free English tour, tel. 06741/7753). The castle map is mediocre (.30 DM); the English booklet is better, with history and illustrations (3.50 DM).

If planning to explore the underground passages, bring a flashlight, buy a tiny one (5 DM at entry), or do it by candlelight (museum sells candles with matches, 1 DM). To get to the castle from St. Goar's boat dock or train station, take a steep 15-minute hike, a 9-DM taxi ride (11 DM for a minibus, tel. 06741/93100), or the goofy tourist train (5 DM, 3/hrly, 10:00–18:00, runs from square between station and dock, complete with lusty music). A handy WC is in the castle courtyard by the restaurant entry. If it's damp, be careful of slippery stones.

Rather than wander aimlessly, visit the castle by following this tour: From the ticket gate walk straight and uphill. Pass Grosser Keller on the left (where we'll end this tour), walk through an internal gate past the *"zu den gedeckten Wehrgängen"* sign on the right (where we'll pass later) to the museum (daily 9:00–12:00, 13:00–17:30) in the only finished room of the castle.

1. Museum and castle model: The seven-foot-tall carved stone ("*Keltische Säule von Pfalzfeld*") immediately inside the door—a tombstone from a nearby Celtic grave—is from 600 years before Christ. There were people here long before the Romans...and this castle. The chair next to the door is an old library chair. Fold it up and it becomes stairs for getting to the highest shelves.

The castle history exhibit in the center of the room is well described in English. The massive fortification was the only Rhineland castle to withstand Louis XIV's assault during the 17th century. At the far end of the room is a model reconstruction of the castle showing how much bigger it was before French revolutionary troops destroyed it in the 18th century. Study this. Find where you are (hint: look for the tall tower). This was the living quarters of the original castle, which was only the smallest ring of buildings around the tiny central courtyard (13th century, marked by red well). The ramparts were added in the 14th century. By 1650, the fortress was largely complete. Ever since its destruction by the French in 1797, it's had no military value. While no WWII bombs were wasted on this ruin, it served St. Goar as a quarry for generations. The basement of the museum shows the castle pharmacy and an exhibit on Rhine region odds and ends, including tools and an 1830 loom.

Exit the museum and walk 30 meters directly out, slightly uphill into the castle courtyard.

2. Medieval castle courtyard: Five hundred years ago the entire castle circled this courtyard. The place was self-sufficient and ready for a siege with a bakery, pharmacy, herb garden, animals, brewery, well (top of yard), and livestock. During peacetime, 300 to 600 people lived here; during a siege there would be as many as 4,500. The walls were plastered and painted white. Bits of the original 13th-century plaster survive.

Continue through the courtyard, out "*Erste Schildmauer,*" turn left into the next courtyard, and walk to the two old, black, upright posts. Find the pyramid of stone catapult balls.

3. Castle garden: Catapult balls like these were too expensive not to recycle. If ever used, they'd be retrieved after the battle. Across from the balls is a well—essential for any castle during the age of sieging. The old posts are for the ceremonial baptizing of new members of the local trading league. While this guild goes back centuries, today it's a social club that fills this court with a huge wine party the first weekend of each August.

If weary, skip to 5; otherwise, climb the cobbled path up to the castle's best viewpoint up where the German flag waves.

4. Highest castle tower lookout: Enjoy a great view of the river, castle, and the forest that was once all part of this castle. Remember, the fortress once covered five times the land it does today. Originally this castle was no bigger than the two you see over the river. Notice how the other castles don't poke above the top of the Rhine canyon. That would make them easy for invading armies to see.

Return to the catapult balls, walk down the road, go through the tunnel, veer left through the arch marked "*zu den Gedeckten Wehrgängen*," go down two flights of stairs, and turn left into the dark covered passageway. We now begin a rectangular walk taking us completely around the perimeter of the castle.

5. Covered defense galleries: Soldiers—the castle's "minutemen"—had a short commute: defensive positions on the outside, home in the holes below on the left. Even though these living quarters were padded with straw, life was unpleasant. A peasant was lucky to live beyond age 28.

Continue straight through the gallery and to the corner of the castle, where you'll see a white painted arrow at eye level.

6. Corner of castle: Look up. A three-story, half-timbered building originally rose beyond the highest stone fortification. The two stone tongues near the top just around the corner supported the toilet. (Insert your own joke here.) Turn around. The crossbow slits below the white arrow were once steeper. The bigger hole on the riverside was for hot pitch, etc.

Follow that white arrow along the outside to the next corner. Midway you'll pass stairs leading down "*zu den Minengängen*" (sign on upper left). Adventurers with flashlights can detour here. You may come out around the next corner. Otherwise, stay with me, walking level to the corner. At the corner, turn left.

7. Thoop…you're dead. Look ahead at the smartly placed crossbow arrow slit. While you're lying there, notice the stone work. The little round holes were for scaffolds used as they built up. They indicate this stonework is original. Notice also the fine stonework on the chutes. More boiling oil…now you're toast too. Continue along. At the railing, look up the valley and uphill where the fort existed. Below, just outside the wall, is land where attackers would gather.

To the left you'll find a metal gate and stairs. Walk down into small, dark tunnels that were once filled with explosives and ran under the land just outside the walls. Keep your bearings by following the faded white marks on the ceiling. To protect their castle, the Rheinfellers cleverly built tunnels topped by thin slate roofs and packed with explosives. By detonating the explosives when under attack, they could kill hundreds of approaching invaders without damaging the castle. In 1626 a handful of underground Protestant Germans blew 300 Catholic Spaniards to—they figured—hell.

Continue along the perimeter, jog left, go down five steps and into an open field, and walk toward the wooden bridge. You may detour here into the passageway marked "13 Hals Graben." The old wooden bridge is actually modern. Angle left through two arches and through the rough entry to "*Verliess*" on the left.

8. Prison: This is one of six dungeons. You walked through a door prisoners only dreamed of 400 years ago. They came and went through the little square hole in the ceiling. The holes in the walls supported timbers that politely gave as many as 15 residents something to sit on to keep them out of the filthy slop that gathered on the floor. Twice a day they were given bread and water. Some prisoners actually survived five years in here. The town could torture and execute. The castle had permission only to imprison criminals in these dungeons.

Continue through the next arch, under the white arrow, and turn left and walk 40 yards to the *Schlachthaus*.

9. Slaughterhouse: A castle was prepared to survive a six-month siege. With 4,000 people, that's a lot of provisions. The cattle that lived within the walls were slaughtered here. Notice the drainage gutters for water and blood. "Running water" came through from above...one bucket at a time.

Back outside, climb the modern stairs to the left. A skinny passage leads you into...

10. The big cellar: This "Grosser Keller" was a big pantry. When the castle was smaller, this was the original moat—you can see the rough lower parts of the wall. The original floor was five feet deeper. When the castle expanded, the moat became the cellar. Above the entry, holes mark spots where timbers made a storage loft, perhaps filled with grain. Kegs of wine lined the walls. Part of a soldier's pay was three liters of wine a day. In the back, an arch leads to the wine cellar where finer wine was kept. The castle consumed 200,000 liters of wine a year. The count owned the surrounding farmland. Farmers got to keep 20 percent of their production. Later, in more liberal feudal times, the nobility let them keep 40 percent. Today the German government leaves the workers with 60 percent...and provides a few more services.

Climb out, turn right, and leave. For coffee on a great view terrace, visit the Rheinfels Castle Hotel, opposite the entrance (good WC at base of steps).

Sleeping on the Rhine
(2 DM = about $1)

Sleep Code: **S** = Single, **D** = Double/Twin, **T** = Triple, **Q** = Quad, **b** = bathroom, **t** = toilet only, **s** = shower only, **CC** = Credit Card (**V**isa, **M**asterCard, **A**mex), **SE** = Speaks English, **NSE** = No English. All hotels speak some English. Breakfast is included unless otherwise noted.

The Rhine is an easy place for cheap sleeps. *Zimmer* and *Gasthäuser* with 40-DM beds abound (and *Zimmer* normally discount their prices for longer stays). A few exceptional Rhine-area hostels offer 20-DM beds (for travelers of any age). Each town's TI is eager to set you up, and finding a room should be easy any time of year (except for wine-festy weekends in September and October). Bacharach and St. Goar, the best towns for an overnight stop, are about 10 miles apart, connected by milk-run trains, riverboats, and a riverside bike path. Bacharach is more interesting and less touristy, but St. Goar has the famous castle (see "St. Goar," above). Parking in Bacharach is simple along the highway next to the tracks (3-hour daytime limit is generally not enforced) or in the boat parking lot. Parking in St. Goar is tighter; ask at your hotel.

Sleeping in Bacharach
(country code: 49, area code: 06743, zip code: 55422)

Hotels

Hotel Kranenturm gives you castle ambience without the climb. It offers a good combination of comfort and hotel privacy with *Zimmer* coziness, a central location, and a medieval atmosphere. Every room is different. Run by hardworking Kurt Engel, his intense but friendly wife, Fatima, and faithful Schumi, this hotel is actually part of the medieval fortification. Its former *Kran* (crane) towers are now round rooms—great for medievalists. When the riverbank was higher, cranes on this tower loaded barrels of wine onto Rhine boats. Hotel Kranenturm is five meters from the train tracks, but a combination of medieval sturdiness, triple-paned windows, and included earplugs makes the riverside rooms sleepable (Sb-75–80 DM, Db-105–110 DM, Tb-145–150 DM, Qb-175–180 DM with this book, prices include breakfast, the lower price is for off-season or stays of at least 3 nights in high season, CC:VMA but prefer cash, Rhine views come with ripping train noise, back rooms—some with castle views—are quieter, all rooms with cable TV, kid friendly, Langstrasse 30, tel. 06743/1308, fax 06743/1021, e-mail: hotel-kranenturm@t-online.de). Kurt, a good cook, serves 12- to 27-DM dinners; try his ice-cream special for dessert. Trade travel stories on the terrace with new friends over dinner, letting screaming trains punctuate your conversation. Drivers park along the highway at the Kranenturm tower. Eurailers walk down Oberstrasse, then turn right on Kranenstrasse.

Hotel Hillen, a block south of the Hotel Kranenturm, has less charm and more train noise, with friendly owners, great food, and lots of rental bikes. To minimize train noise, ask for "*ruhige Seite*," the quiet side (S-50 DM, Sb-65 DM, D-80 DM, Ds-85 DM, Db-90–100 DM, Tb-140 DM, includes breakfast, 10 percent less for 2 nights, Langstrasse 18, tel. 06743/1287, fax 06743/1037, Iris speaks some English).

Hotel Altkölnischer Hof, a grand old building near the church, rents 20 rooms with modern furnishings and bathrooms, some with balconies over an Old World restaurant. Public rooms are old-time elegant (Sb-90–95 DM, Db-120–130 DM, Db with terrace-160–170 DM, with balcony-150–170 DM, CC:VA, TV in rooms, elevator, tel. 06743/1339 or 06743/2186, fax 06743/2793, e-mail: tscherba@sparkasse.net, SE).

Hotel Gelberhof, a few doors up from the Jost store, has spiffy public spaces but unimaginative rooms (S-55 DM, Sb-75–85 DM, small Db-110 DM, Db-120–140 DM, 3-night discounts, CC:VM, popular with groups, elevator, bike rental, Blücherstrasse 26, tel. 06743/910-100, fax 06743/910-1050, www.hotelgelberhof.com).

Pensions and Private Rooms
At **Pension Lettie**, effervescent and eager-to-please Lettie offers four modern, bright rooms (Sb-60 DM, Db-80 DM, Tb-110 DM with this book and cash, discount for 3-night stays, strictly nonsmoking, no train noise, a few doors inland from Hotel Kranenturm, Kranenstrasse 6, tel. & fax 06743/2115, e-mail: pension.lettie@ t-online.de). Lettie speaks English (worked for the U.S. Army before we withdrew) and does laundry (18 DM per load).

Delightful **Ursula Orth** rents five, airy rooms—a great value, around the corner from Pension Lettie (Sb-35 DM, Db-60–65 DM, Tb-75 DM for 1 night and less for 2, nonsmoking, Rooms 4 and 5 on ground floor—easy access, from Hotel Hillen walk up Spurgasse, her *Zimmer* is on the right at #3, tel. 06743/1557, minimal English spoken).

On the main street, the cozy home of **Herr und Frau Theilacker** is a German-feeling *Zimmer* offering comfortable rooms and a pleasant stay. It's likely to have a room when others don't (S-30 DM, D-60 DM, in the town center, walk 30 steps straight out of Restaurant Braustube to Oberstrasse 57, no outside sign, tel. 06743/1248, NSE).

Pension Winzerhaus, a 10-room place run by Herr and Frau Petrescu, is 200 meters up the valley from the town gate, so the location is less charming, but it has no train noise and easy parking. Rooms are simple, clean, and modern (Sb-50 DM, Db-85 DM, Tb-90 DM, Qb-95 DM, 10 percent off with this book, free bikes for guests, Blücherstrasse 60, tel. 06743/1294, fax 069/283-927).

Pension Binz offers slightly older rooms and an apartment in a serene location (Sb-65 DM, Db-98 DM, third person-35 DM, apartment-120–150 DM, fine breakfast, CC:VM, Koblenzer Strasse 1, tel. 06743/1604, cheery Carla SE).

Hotel zur Post has 16 quiet rooms, fine furniture, dark hallways, and a hint of character (Sb-85 DM, Db-95–110 DM, Tb-135 DM, Qb-145 DM, CC:V, Oberstrasse Strasse 38, tel. 06743/1277, fax 06743/2807, e-mail: hzp.scherschlicht@t-online.de).

Annelie und Hans Dettmar, entrepreneurial and curiously lacking in warmth, rent several smoke-free rooms and two great family rooms with kitchenette (20 DM to use it) in a modern house on the main drag (big Sb-50 DM, Db-55–70 DM, Tb-75–90 DM, Qb-100–120 DM, includes breakfast, free use of 2 old bikes, laundry-17 DM, Oberstrasse 8, tel. 06743/2661, fax 06743/919-396, a little English spoken). Readers give this couple mixed reviews, but their rooms are good. Their son **Jürgen Dettmar**, who smiles occasionally, rents five fine, very central rooms with a common kitchen and small bathrooms, near the church behind Restaurant Braustube. Ask for a room with balcony for a bird's-eye view over the town center (D-60 DM, Db-80 DM, Tb-105 DM, Oberstrasse 64, tel. & fax 06743/1715, www.pension-dettmar.bacharach-rhein.de, SE).

Bacharach's hostel, **Jugendherberge Stahleck**, is a 12th-century castle on the hilltop—500 steps above Bacharach—with a royal Rhine view. Open to travelers of any age, this is a newly redone gem with eight beds and a private modern shower and WC in each room. A steep 15-minute climb on the trail from the town church, the hostel is warmly run by Evelyn and Bernhard Falke (FALL-kay), who serve hearty, 9.70-DM buffet, all-you-can-eat dinners. The hostel pub serves cheap local wine until midnight (26-DM dorm beds with breakfast and sheets, 6 DM extra without a card or in a double, couples can share rooms, groups pay 35.40 DM per bed with breakfast and dinner, no smoking in rooms, easy parking, beds normally available but call and leave your name, they'll hold a bed until 18:00, tel. 06743/1266, fax 06743/2684, e-mail: jh-bacharach@djh-info.de, SE).

Eating in Bacharach

Several places offer good, inexpensive, and atmospheric indoor or outdoor dining in Bacharach, all for about 20 to 30 DM. The oldest building in town, **Altes Haus** (dead center by the church, closed Wed), and **Kurpfälzische Münze** (open daily, in the old mint, a half block down from Altes Haus; claims to be even older) are both good values with great ambience. **Weingut zum Gruner Baum** offers delicious appetizers (also next to Altes Haus with good ambience indoors and out). **Hotel Kranenturm** is another good value with hearty meals and good main course salads (see hotel listing above).

Wine Tasting: Drop in on entertaining Fritz Bastian's **Weingut zum Grüner Baum** wine bar (just past Altes Haus, eves only, closed Thu, tel. 06743/1208). As the president of the local vintner's club, Fritz's mission is to give travelers an understanding of the subtle differences among the Rhine wines. Groups of two to six people pay 26 DM for a "carousel" of 15 glasses of 14 different white wines, one lonely red, and a basket of bread. Your mission: Team up with others with this book to rendezvous here after dinner. Spin the lazy Susan, share a common cup, and discuss the taste. Fritz insists, "After each wine, you must talk to each other."

Sleeping in St. Goar
(country code: 49, area code: 06741, zip code: 56329)

Hotel am Markt, well run by Herr and Frau Velich, is rustic with all the modern comforts. It features a hint of antler with a pastel flair and bright rooms and a good restaurant. It's a good value and a stone's throw from the boat dock and train station (Ss-65 DM, Sb-80 DM, Db-110 DM, Tb-140 DM, Qb-160 DM, cheaper off-season, closed Dec–Feb, CC:VMA, Am Markt 1, tel. 06741/1689, fax 06741/1721, e-mail: hotel.am.markt@gmx.de).

Hotel Hauser, facing the boat dock, is another good deal, warmly run by another Frau Velich and Sigrid (S-42 DM, D-88 DM, Db-98 DM, great Db with Rhine-view balconies-110 DM, small bathrooms, show this book to get these prices, cheaper in off-season, CC:VMA, Heerstrasse 77, telephone reservations easy, tel. 06741/333, fax 06741/1464, SE).

Hotel Montag is on the castle end of town just across the street from the world's largest free-hanging cuckoo clock. Manfred and Maria Montag and their son Mike speak New Yorkish. Even though the hotel gets a lot of bus tours, it's friendly, laid-back, and comfortable; ask about its luxurious apartments (Sb-70 DM, Db-130 DM, price can drop if things are slow, CC:VMA, Internet access-12 DM/hr, Heerstrasse 128, tel. 06741/1629, fax 06741/2086, e-mail: hotelmontag@1019freenet.de). Check out their adjacent crafts shop (heavy on beer steins).

A few doors away, the strangely vacant **Rhein Hotel** has modern, unimaginative rooms (Sb-70–80 DM, Db-90–130 DM, Heerstrasse 71, tel. 06741/355, fax 06741/2835, e-mail: blecic@ t-online.de). Next door, **Hotel Silberne Rose** is musty with older decor and some rooms with Rhine views (Sb-60–70 DM, Db-100–120 DM, Tb-125–140 DM, cheaper price for longer stays, CC:VM, across from K-D dock, Heerstrasse 63, tel. 06741/7040, fax 06741/2865).

St. Goar's best *Zimmer* deal is the home of **Frau Kurz**, "which comes with a breakfast terrace, garden, fine view, easy parking, and most of the comforts of a hotel (S-37 DM, D-60–64 DM, Db-70 DM, showers-5 DM, 1-night stays cost extra, free parking, confirm prices, honor your reservation or call to cancel, Ulmenhof 11, tel. & fax 06741/459, some English spoken). It's a steep five-minute hike from the train station (exit left from station, take immediate left at the yellow phone booth, go under tracks to paved path, take a right partway up stairs, climb a few more stairs to Ulmenhof).

The Germanly run **St. Goar Hostel**, the big beige building under the castle (veer right off the road up to the castle), has two to twelve beds per room, a 22:00 curfew, and hearty 10-DM dinners (22-DM beds with breakfast, open all day, check-in preferred 17:00–18:00 and 19:00–20:00, Bismarckweg 17, tel. 06741/388, e-mail: jl-st-goar@djh-info.de, SE).

Rheinfels Castle Hotel is the town splurge. Actually part of the castle, but an entirely new building, this luxury place is good for those with money and a car (Db-240–285 DM depending on river views and balconies, CC:VMA, elevator, free parking, dress-up restaurant, Schlossberg 47, tel. 06741/8020, fax 06741/802-802, www.schlosshotel-rheinfels.de, e-mail: rheinfels.st.goar@t-online.de).

Eating in St. Goar

Hotel Am Markt and **Hotel Hauser** offer excellent meals at fair prices. For your Rhine splurge, walk, taxi, or drive up to **Rheinfels Castle Hotel** for its incredible view and elegant setting, and consider a sunset drink on the view terrace (see hotel listing above; reserve a table by the window).

Transportation Connections—Rhine

Milk-run trains stop at all Rhine towns each hour starting as early as around 6:00. Koblenz, Boppard, St. Goar, Bacharach, Bingen, and Mainz are each about 15 minutes apart. From Koblenz to Mainz takes 75 minutes. To get a faster big train, go to Mainz or Koblenz.

From Mainz by train to: Bacharach/St. Goar (hrly, 1 hr), **Cochem** (hrly, 2.5 hrs, changing in Koblenz), **Köln** (3/hrly, 90 min), **Baden-Baden** (hrly, 2.5 hrs), **Munich** (hrly, 4 hrs), **Frankfurt** (3/hrly, 45 min), **Frankfurt Airport** (3/hrly, 25 min).

From Frankfurt by train to: Koblenz (hrly, 90 min), **Rothenburg** (hrly, 3 hrs, transfers in Würzburg and Steinach), **Würzburg** (hrly, 90 min), **Munich** (hrly, 3.5 hrs), **Amsterdam** (8/day, 5 hrs), **Paris** (4/day, 6.5 hrs).

MOSEL VALLEY

The misty Mosel is what some visitors hoped the Rhine would be—peaceful, sleepy, romantic villages slipped between the steep vineyards and the river; fine wine; a sprinkling of castles; and lots of friendly *Zimmer*. Boat, train, and car traffic here is a trickle compared to the roaring Rhine. While the swan-speckled Mosel moseys 300 miles from France's Vosges Mountains to Koblenz, where it dumps into the Rhine, the most scenic piece of the valley lies between the towns of Bernkastel-Kues and Cochem. I'd savor only this section. Zell makes a pleasant home base.

Throughout the region on summer weekends and during the fall harvest time, wine festivals with oompah bands, dancing, and colorful costumes are powered by good food and wine.

Getting around the Mosel Valley

By Train and Bus: The train zips you to Cochem, Bullay, or Trier in a snap. Frequent buses connect Zell with the Bullay

Mosel Valley

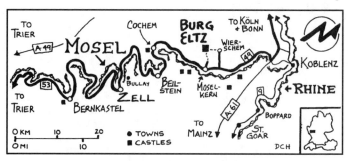

station in 10 minutes, and six buses a day connect tiny Beilstein with Cochem in 20 minutes (last bus about 15:10). Four buses a day link Zell and Beilstein.

By Boat: A few daily departures allow you to cruise the most scenic stretch between Cochem, Beilstein, and Zell: between Cochem and Zell (2/day, May–Oct, but none on Fri and Mon May–June, 3 hrs, 23 DM one-way, 35 DM round-trip, on Kolb-Line); between Cochem and Beilstein (5/day, 60 min, 14 DM one-way, 19 DM round-trip, tel. 02671/7387); and between Zell and Beilstein (1/day May–Oct, 2 hrs, 18 DM one-way, 26 DM round-trip). The K-D (Köln-Düsseldorf) line sails once a day in each direction but only as far as Cochem (May–Sept, Koblenz to Cochem 10:00–14:30, or Cochem to Koblenz 15:40–20:10, free with consecutive-day Eurailpass or a dated Eurail flexipass, Europass, Eurail Selectpass, or German railpass).

By Bike: You can rent bikes in most Mosel towns (see village listings below).

Cochem

With a majestic castle and picturesque medieval streets, Cochem is the very touristic hub of this part of the river.

Tourist Information: The information-packed TI is by the bridge at the main bus stop. They book rooms (same day only) and keep a thorough 24-hour room listing in the window. Their free map includes the town's history and a walking tour. Ask about public transportation to Burg Eltz (see below) and pick up the well-done *Moselle Wine Road* brochure and info on area hikes (May–Oct Mon–Sat 10:00–17:00, Sun 10:00–12:00, off-season closed weekends and at lunch, tel. 02671/60040). For accommodations, see "Sleeping," below.

Arrival in Cochem: Make a hard right out of the station (lockers available) and walk about 10 minutes to the town center and TI (just past the bus lanes). Drivers can park near the bridge

(TI right there). To get to the main square (*Markt*), continue under the bridge, then angle right and follow Bernstrasse.

Sights: The pointy Cochem Castle is the work of overly imaginative 19th-century restorers (7 DM, daily mid-March–Oct 9:00–17:00, 15-minute walk from Cochem, follow one of the frequent German-language tours while reading English explanation sheets or call ahead to see if any English tours are planned, tel. 02671/255).

Stroll along the pleasant paths that line the river and hike up to the Aussichtspunkt (the cross on the hill) for a great view. You can rent bikes from the K-D boat kiosk at the dock (summers only) or year-round from Kreutz near the station on Ravenstrasse 42 (7 DM/4 hrs, 14 DM/day, no deposit required, just your passport number, tel. 02671/91131). Consider taking a bike on the boat and riding back. If stranded, many hitchhike.

Connections: Cochem has frequent train service to Koblenz (hrly, 60 min), Bullay (hrly, 10 min), and Trier (hrly, 60 min).

Sights—Mosel Valley

▲▲▲**Burg Eltz**—My favorite castle in all of Europe lurks in a mysterious forest. It's been left intact for 700 years and is furnished throughout as it was 500 years ago. Thanks to smart diplomacy and clever marriages, Burg Eltz was never destroyed. (It survived one five-year siege.) It's been in the Eltz family for 820 years. The countess arranges for new flowers in each room weekly. The only way to see the castle is with a one-hour tour (included in admission ticket). German tours (with helpful English fact sheets, 1 DM) go constantly. Call ahead to see if an English-language tour is scheduled, or organize your own by corralling 20 English-speakers in the inner courtyard—they'll thank you for it. Then push the red button on the white porch and politely beg for an English guide. This is well worth a short wait (9 DM, April–Oct daily 9:30–17:30, tel. 02672/950-500, www.burg-eltz.de). To get to Burg Eltz from Cochem, you can taxi (70 DM, 02671/980-098), drive, or train-and-hike.

Arrival by Train: Get off at the Moselkern station midway between Cochem and Koblenz (no lockers at station, but, if you ask politely, clerk will store luggage in office). When leaving the station, exit right and follow Burg Eltz signs for about 15 minutes through town, then take the marked trail (slippery when wet, slightly steep near end). It's a pleasant 60-minute hike between the station and castle through a pine forest where sparrows carry crossbows, and maidens, disguised as falling leaves, whisper "watch out."

Arrival by Car: Drivers often get lost on the way to Burg Eltz. Use your map and do this: Leave the river at Hatzenport (shortest drive) following the white "Burg Eltz

Park & Ride" signs
through the towns of
Münstermaifeld and
Wierschem. The castle
parking lot is two kilo-
meters past Wierschem.
From the lot, hike 10
minutes downhill or
wait for the red castle
shuttle bus (2 DM).
There are three "Burg
Eltz" parking lots; only
the lot two kilometers
south of Wierscheim is
close enough for an
easy walk. Another
option is to park at the
Moselkern station and
follow the "park and
walk" signs (see "Arrival
by Train," above).

Burg Eltz Area

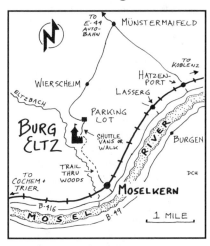

▲**Beilstein**—Farther upstream is the quaintest of all Mosel towns
(see "Sleeping," below). Beilstein is Cinderella land. Explore the
narrow lanes, ancient wine cellar, resident (and very territorial)
swans, and ruined castle. The small 2-DM ferry goes constantly
back and forth across the river. A shop rents bikes for the pleasant
riverside ride (toward Zell is best). The TI is in Café Klapperburg
(summer Tue–Sun 9:00–18:00, closed Mon, tel. 02673/1417).
Four buses a day connect Zell and Beilstein.

▲**Zell**—This is the best Mosel town for an overnight stop (see
"Sleeping," below). It's peaceful, with a fine riverside promenade,
a pedestrian bridge over the water, plenty of *Zimmer*, and a long
pedestrian zone filled with colorful shops, restaurants, *Weinstuben*
(wine bars), and a fun oompah folk band on weekend evenings on
the main square.

The TI is on the pedestrian street, four blocks downriver
from the pedestrian bridge (Mon–Fri 8:00–12:30, 13:30–17:00,
Sat 10:00–13:00, off-season closed Sat, tel. 06542/4031). The
fine little Wein und Heimatmuseum features Mosel history
(same building as TI, Wed and Sat 15:00–17:00). Walk up
to the medieval wall's gatehouse and through the cemetery
to the old munitions tower for a village view. You can rent
bikes from Frau Klaus (Hauptstrasse 5, tel. 06542/2589). For
Internet access, try the relaxing Berliner Kaffe-Kannchen (30
min/5 DM, 7:00–18:30 Thu–Tue, closed Wed, across pedestrian bridge opposite bus stop at Baldninen Strasse 107, tel.
06542/5450).

Locals know Zell for its Schwarze Katz (Black Cat) wine. Franz Josef Weis (who was once a POW in England) and his son Peter give an entertaining and free tour of their 40,000-bottle-per-year wine cellar. The clever tour starts at 17:00 (call ahead to reserve, tel. 06542/41398); buy a bottle or two to keep this fine tour going. A green flag marks their *Weinkeller* south of town, past the bridge, at Notenau 30. They also rent two fine apartments (see "Sleeping in Zell," below).

Sleeping on the Mosel
(2 DM = about $1)

Sleeping in Cochem
(country code: 49, area code: 02671, zip code: 56812)
All rooms come with breakfast.

Weingut Rademacher offers a good value and beautiful rooms, wedged between vineyards and train tracks, with a pleasant garden and a big common kitchen. Charming hostess Andrea (SE) and her husband sometimes give tours of their wine cellar; houseguests enter for free. If there is no tour, visitors are welcome to taste the wine (Sb-50 DM, Db-90 DM, family deals, ground-floor rooms, from station take a quick right on Ravenestrasse, turn right on Pinnerstrasse, pass under train tracks, curve right for another 50 meters, Pinnerstrasse 10, tel. 02671/4164, fax 02671/91341).

Just above a local *Weinstube*, the light-hearted and ever-so-funky **Gasthaus Ravene** offers six rooms varying in size and comfort (several are spacious and airy). The stairway needs new carpeting, but the rooms are fine (Sb-60 DM, Db-80–100 DM, Tb-135 DM, CC:VM, Ravenestrasse 43, tel. 02671/980-177, fax 02671/91119, www.gasthaus-ravene.de, NSE).

The rustic **Hotel Lohspeicher**, just off the main square on a tiny-stepped street, is for those who want a real hotel—with much higher prices—in the thick of things (Sb-95 DM, Db-170 DM, CC:VMA, some nonsmoking rooms, includes breakfast, restaurant, elevator, closed Feb, Obergasse 1, tel. 02671/3976, fax 02671/1772, Ingo SE).

Haus Andreas has many small but modern rooms at fair prices (S-25 DM, Sb-40 DM, Db-60 DM, Schlosstrasse 9, tel. 02671/1370 or 02671/5155, fax 02671/1370). From the main square, take Herrenstrasse; after a block, angle right uphill on Schlosstrasse.

For a top-dollar view of Cochem, cross the bridge and find the balconied rooms at **Hotel Am Hafen** (110–190 DM, skip cheaper no-view rooms, Uferstrasse 3, cross bridge to reach hotel, tel. 02671/97720, fax 02671/977-227, e-mail: hotel-am-hafen@t-online.de).

Sleeping in Zell
(country code: 49, area code: 06542, zip code: 56856)
If the Mosel charms you into spending the night, do it in Zell. By car, this is a natural. It's also easy by boat (2/day from Cochem) or train (go to Bullay—hrly from Cochem or Trier; from Bullay the bus takes you to little Zell—2.80 DM, 2/hrly, 15 min; bus stop is across street from Bullay train station, check yellow MB schedule for times, last bus at about 19:00). The central Zell stop is called Lindenplatz.

Zell's hotels are a disappointment, but its private homes are great. The owners speak almost no English and discount their rates if you stay more than one night. They can't take reservations long in advance for one-night stays; just call a day ahead. My favorites are on the south end of town, a five-minute walk from the town hall square (TI) and the bus stop. Breakfast is included unless otherwise noted. These places are listed in the order you would find them from the pedestrian bridge.

Friendly **Natalie Huhn** (no sign), your German grand-mother, has the cheapest beds in town in her simple but comfort-able house (S-35 DM, D-60 DM, cheaper for 2-night stays, 2 blocks to left of church at Jakobstrasse 32, tel. 06542/41048).

Weinhaus zum Fröhlichen Weinberg offers cheap, basic rooms (D-70 DM, 60 DM for 2 or more nights, family *Zimmer*, Mittelstrasse 6, tel. 06542/4308, fax 06542/5781) above a *Wein-stube* disco (noisy on Friday and Saturday nights).

Homey **Gästehaus am Römerbad** is a few blocks from the church and a decent value (Db-80 DM, Am Römerbad 5, tel. 06542/41602, Elizabeth Münster).

Zell's best *Zimmer* values lie at the end of the pedestrian street about five blocks from the pedestrian bridge:

Gasthaus Gertrud Thiesen is classy, with a TV-living-breakfast room and a river view. The Thiesen house has big, bright rooms and is on the town's first corner overlooking the Mosel from a great terrace (S or D-70 DM, Balduinstrasse 1, tel. 06542/4453, SE). Notice the high-water flood marks on the wall across the street.

Gästezimmer Rosa Mesenich is another little place facing the river (S-35 DM, Sb-40 DM, D-76 DM, Db-80 DM, Branden-burg 48, tel. 06542/4297, NSE).

Almost next door, the vine-strewn doorway of **Gastehaus Eberhard** leads to gregarious owners, cushy rooms, and potential wine tastings (Db-70 DM, Brandenburg 42, tel. 06542/41216, NSE).

If you're looking for room service, a sauna, a pool, and an ele-vator, sleep at **Hotel Grüner Kranz** (Sb-85 DM, Db-160 DM, CC:VMA, tel. 06542/98610, fax 06542/986-180).

Weinhaus Mayer, a classy—if stressed-out—old pen-sion next door, is perfectly central with Mosel-view rooms

(Db-120–160 DM, Balduinstrasse 15, tel. 06542/4530, fax 06542/61160). They have newly renovated rooms with top comforts, many with river-view balconies (ask for *Neues Gastehaus*, view Db-180 DM, big Tb-240 DM, tel. & fax 06542/61169).

The freshly remodeled **Hotel Ratskeller** (above a classy pizzeria) has rooms on the pedestrian street that are less cozy but sharp with tile flooring and fair rates (Sb-70–85 DM, Db-120–145 DM, CC:VM, Balduinstrasse 36, tel. 06542/98620, fax 06542/986-244).

Franz Josef Weis and son Peter of the **Schwarze Katz** winery rent two luxurious apartments with kitchens and fireplaces and free use of a funky old grape-pressing room (Db-100 DM, extra person-20 DM, breakfast-10 DM, CC:VMA, look for green flag marking their *Weinkeller* south of town, past bridge, at Notenau 30, tel. 06542/41398, fax 06542/961-178, e-mail: f.j.weis@t-online.de).

Sleeping in Beilstein
(country code: 49, area code: 02673, zip code: 56814)
Cozier and farther north, Beilstein (BILE-shtine) is very small and quiet (no train; 5 buses/day to nearby Cochem, fewer buses on weekends, 15 min; taxi from Cochem-25 DM). Breakfast is included.

Hotel Haus Lipmann is your chance to live in a medieval mansion with hot showers and TVs. A prizewinner for atmosphere, it's been in the Lipmann family for 200 years. The creaky wooden staircase and the elegant dining hall, with long wooden tables surrounded by antlers, chandeliers, and feudal weapons, will get you in the mood for your castle sightseeing, but the riverside terrace may mace your momentum (5 rooms, Db-140–160 DM, tel. 02673/1573, fax 02673/1521, e-mail: hotel.haus.lipmann@t-online.de).

Gasthaus Winzerschenke an der Klostertreppe is comfortable and a great value, right in the tiny heart of town (Db-75 DM, bigger Db-95 DM, discount for 2-night stays, tel. & fax 02673/1354, Frau Sausen).

The half-timbered, riverfront **Altes Zollhaus Gästezimmer** has packed all the comforts into eight tight, bright, and modern rooms (Db-110 DM, deluxe Db-145 DM, closed Nov–Feb, tel. 02673/1574, fax 02673/1287, e-mail: lipmann@t-online.de).

Hotel Gute Quelle offers more half-timbers, 13 comfortable rooms, and a good restaurant (Db-80–120 DM, CC:VMA, Marketplatz 34, tel. 02673/1437, fax 02673/1399, Susan SE).

TRIER
Germany's oldest city lies at the head of the scenic Mosel Valley, near the Luxembourg border. An ancient Roman capital, Trier brags that it was inhabited for 1,300 years before the Romans

came. Today Trier feels very young and thriving. A short stop
here offers you a look at Germany's oldest Christian church, one
of its most enjoyable market squares, and its best Roman ruins.

Founded by Augustus in 15 B.C., Trier was the Roman
"Augusta Treverorum" for 500 years. When Emperor Diocletian
(who ruled A.D. 285–305) divided his overextended Roman empire
into four sectors, he made Trier the capital of the West: modern-
day Germany, France, Spain, and England. For most of the fourth
century, this city of 80,000, with a four-mile-long wall, four great
gates, and 47 round towers, was the favored residence of Roman
emperors. Emperor Constantine used the town as the capital of
his fading western Roman Empire. Much of the building was built
under Constantine before he left for Constantinople. In 480 Trier
fell to the Franks. Today Trier's Roman sights include the huge
city gate (Porta Nigra), basilica, baths, and amphitheater.

Orientation (area code: 0651)

Tourist Information: Trier's helpful TI is just through the Porta
Nigra. You can pay 3 DM for an easily readable map or get the free
map, which suffices (barely) for navigating Trier's key sights. The
TI sells a useful little guide to the city called *Trier: A Guide to Monu-
ments* (6.50 DM). They usually have bus schedules for Cochem and
Zell areas and organize a two-hour walking tour in English (10 DM,
May–Oct daily at 13:30; TI open April–Oct Mon–Sat 9:00–18:30,
Sun 9:00–15:30, less off-season, tel. 0651/978-080, www.trier.de).

Internet Access: Try the Net Cafe (30 min/5 DM, Mon–
Fri 13:00–01:00, Sat 15:00–01:00, closed Sun, Saarstrasse 51,
0651/970-9918).

Arrival in Trier

By Train: From the train station (lockers available), walk 15
boring minutes four blocks up Theodor-Heuss Allee to the big
black Roman gate, and turn left under the gate where you'll find
the TI. From here the main pedestrian mall leads into the town's
charm: the market square, cathedral, and basilica—all within a
five-minute walk.

By Car: Drivers get off at Trier Verteilerring and follow
signs to "Zentrum." There is parking near the gate and TI.

Sights—Trier

▲**Porta Nigra**—Roman Trier was built as a capital. Its architecture mirrored the grandeur of the empire. Of the four-mile wall's
four huge gates, only this north gate survives. This most impressive Roman fortification in Germany was built without mortar—
only iron pegs hold the sandstone blocks together. While the
other three gates were destroyed by medieval metal and stone
scavengers, this "black gate" survived because it became a church.

Trier

1 KOLPINGHAUS   **4** HOTEL ROMISCHER KAISER   **7** LAUNDROMAT

2 HOTEL FRANKENTURM   **5** HOTEL MONOPOL

3 HOTEL CHRISTOPHEL   **6** HOTEL PIEPER

Saint Simeon—a pious Greek recluse—lived inside the gate for seven years. After his death in 1035, the Simeon monastery was established and the gate was made into a two-story church—lay church on the bottom, monastery church on top. While Napoleon had the church destroyed in 1803, the 12th-century Romanesque apse—the round part that you can see at the east end—survived. You can climb around the gate, but there's little to see (4 DM, April–Oct 9:00–18:00, Nov–March 9:00–17:00).

Trier's main pedestrian drag, which leads away from the gate, is named for Saint Simeon. The arcaded courtyard and buildings of the monastery of Saint Simeon survive. They now house the city museum and TI.

▲▲**Market Square**—Trier's Hauptmarkt square is a people-filled swirl of fruit stands, flowers, painted facades, and fountains—with a handy public WC. This is one of Germany's most in-love-with-life marketplaces. Its centerpiece, a market cross from 958 (with an ancient Roman pedestal), celebrates the trading rights given to the town by King Otto the Great. The adjacent Renaissance St. Peter's Fountain (1595) symbolizes thoughtful city government with allegorical statues of justice (sword and scale), fortitude (broken column), temperance (wine and water), and prudence (snake and mirror). From this square you can survey a textbook of architectural styles. Overlooking it all (as its fire watchman did in medieval times) is the Gothic tower of the church of St. Gangolf.

▲▲**Cathedral (Dom)**—One block east of the market square, this church, the oldest in Germany, goes back to Roman times. St. Helena, the mother of Emperor Constantine (who legalized Christianity in the Roman Empire in A.D. 312) and an important figure in early Christian history, let part of her palace be used as the first church on this spot. (A fine Roman-painted ceiling survives under today's altar.) In 326, to celebrate the 20th anniversary of his reign, Constantine began the construction of St. Peter's in Rome and this huge cathedral in Trier (daily April–Oct 6:30–18:00, Nov–March 6:30–17:30). The cathedral's most important relic is the "Holy Robe" of Christ (rarely on display, found by St. Helena on a pilgrimage to Jerusalem). The treasury, or *Dom Schatzkammer*, has huge bishops' rings and a "holy nail" supposedly from the Crucifixion (2 DM, Mon–Sat 10:00–17:00, Sun 13:30–17:00).

The Leibfrau Church, connected to the *Dom*, dates from 1235 and claims to be the oldest Gothic church in Germany (daily 8:00–12:00, 14:00–18:00).

▲▲**Basilica**—Two blocks south of the *Dom*, this 200-foot-long and 100-foot-high building is the largest intact Roman structure outside of Rome. Picture this hall of justice in ancient times, decorated with golden mosaics, rich marble, colorful stucco, and busts of Constantine and his family filling the niches. The emperor sat in majesty under a canopy on his altarlike throne. The last emperor moved out in 395, and petty kings set up camp in the basilica throughout the Middle Ages. The building became a church in 1856.

Long after its Roman days, Trier was important enough to have a prince "elector" who helped elect the legal successors of the "Holy Roman Emperor." A rococo wing, the Elector's Palace, was added to the basilica in the 18th century. This faces a fragrant garden, which leads to a mildly interesting archeological museum (Rheinisches Landesmuseum, 7 DM, Tue–Sun 9:30–17:00, closed Mon), the remains of a Roman bath, and a 25,000-seat amphitheater.

Trier's newest sight is a modern glass box covering interesting Roman bath excavations at the Viehmarkt Museum (3 DM, Tue–Sun 9:00–18:00, some models of Roman streets, 10-minute walk from market square down Brofstrasse on Viehmarktplatz).

Karl Marx's House—Communists can lick their wounds at Karl Marx's house. Early manuscripts, letters, and photographs of the influential economist/philosopher fill several rooms of his birth house. Oblivious to their slide out of a shrinking middle class, people still sneer (3 DM, Tue–Sun 10:00–18:00, Mon 13:00–18:00, lunch breaks in winter, 15-min film at 20 min after each hr, a reasonable amount of English description). From the market square, it's a 10-minute walk down Fleischstrasse—which becomes Brückenstrasse—to the house at Brückenstrasse 10.

Sleeping in Trier
(2 DM = about $1, country code: 49, area code: 0651, zip code: 54290)
A handy self-service **Laundromat** is near the Marx Museum (daily 8:00–22:00, 11 DM for the works, English instructions, Brükenstrasse 19).

Kolpinghaus Warsberger Hof is the best value for cheap sleeps in town. This Catholic Church–run place is clean, with 150 beds—some in single and double rooms, and a pleasant restaurant serving inexpensive meals in its open-to-anyone restaurant (28 DM per bed with sheets and breakfast in 2- to 6-bed dorm rooms, 40 DM per person in S, D, or T hotel rooms, showers down the hall, a block to the right at the end of the market square, Dietrichstrasse 42, tel. 0651/975-250, fax 0651/975-2540, e-mail: info@warsberger-hof.de).

Hotel Frankenturm, plain, comfortable, and simple, is on the same street, above a lively saloon (S-70 DM, Sb-110 DM, D-110 DM, Db-140 DM, CC:VMA, Dietrichstrasse 3, tel. 0651/978-240, fax 0651/978-2449).

At the Porta Nigra, the cozy **Hotel zum Christophel** offers top comfort in its 11 sharp rooms above a fine restaurant (Sb-90–115 DM, Db-160–170 DM, CC:VMA, elevator, cable TV, Am Porta Nigra Platz, tel. 0651/979-4200, fax 0651/74732, www.zumchristophel.de). Next door, **Hotel Romischer Kaiser** offers luxurious accommodations with a polished lobby and restaurant, professional staff, and spaciously elegant rooms (Sb-130–150 DM, Db-190–210 DM, includes breakfast and parking, CC:VMA, Am Porta Nigra Platz, tel. 0651/97700, fax 0651/977-099).

Hotel Monopol, at the train station, is dark but handy (S-75 DM, Sb-90 DM, D-130 DM, Db-150 DM, T-165 DM, Tb-195 DM, CC:VM, buffet breakfast, Bahnhofsplatz 7, tel. 0651/714-090, fax 0651/714-0910).

The less central **Hotel Pieper** is family run and rents 20 comfortable rooms over a pleasant restaurant (Sb-80 DM, Db-130 DM, Tb-165 DM, CC:VM, 2 blocks north of main drag between station and Roman gate, Thebäerstrasse 39, tel. 0651/23008, fax 0651/12839).

Transportation Connections—Trier

By train to: Cochem (hrly, 45 min), **Köln** (7/day, 2.5 hrs), **Koblenz** (hrly, 75 min), **Bullay** (with buses to Zell, hrly, 38 min), **St. Goar/Bacharach** (hrly, 2.5 hrs), **Baden-Baden** (hrly, 4 hrs).

KÖLN (COLOGNE) AND THE UNROMANTIC RHINE

Romance isn't everything. Köln is an urban Jacuzzi that keeps the Rhine churning. The small town of Remagen had a bridge that helped defeat Hitler in World War II, and unassuming Aachen (near the Belgian border) was once the capital of Europe.

Getting around the Unromantic Rhine

Fast and frequent super-trains connect Köln, Trier, Koblenz, and Frankfurt. All major sights are within a reasonable walk from each city's train station.

KÖLN

Germany's fourth-largest city, big, no-nonsense Köln has a compact and lively center. The Rhine was the northern boundary of the Roman Empire and, 1,700 years ago, Constantine—the first Christian emperor—made "Colonia" the seat of a bishopric. Five hundred years later, under Charlemagne, Köln became the seat of an archbishopric. With 40,000 people living within its walls, it was the largest German city and an important cultural and religious center throughout the Middle Ages. To many, the city is most famous for its toilet water. "Eau de Cologne" was first made here by an Italian chemist in 1709. Even after World War II bombs destroyed 95 percent of it (population down from 800,000 to 40,000), Köln has remained, after a remarkable recovery, a cultural and commercial center as well as a fun, colorful, and pleasant-smelling city.

Orientation (area code: 0221)

Köln's old-town core, bombed out then rebuilt quaint, is traffic free and includes a park and bike path along the river. From the cathedral/TI/train station, Hohe Strasse leads into the shopping action. The Roman arch in front of the cathedral reminds us that even in Roman times this was an important trading street and a main road through Köln. In medieval times, when Köln was a major player in the heavyweight Hanseatic Trading League, two major trading routes crossed here. This "high street" thrived. After complete destruction in World War II, it has emerged—the first pedestrian shopping mall in Germany—once again as a thriving trading street. For a quick old-town ramble, stroll down Hohe Strasse and take a left at the city hall (Rathaus) to the river (where K-D Rhine cruises start). Enjoy the quaint old town and

Köln

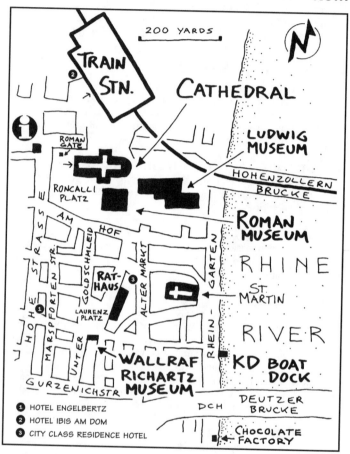

200 YARDS

TRAIN STN.

CATHEDRAL

LUDWIG MUSEUM

ROMAN GATE

HOHENZOLLERN BRUCKE

RONCALLI PLATZ

AM HOF

RHINE

ROMAN MUSEUM

HOHE STRASSE

GOLDSCHLEID STR.

MARSPFORTEN STR.

RAT-HAUS

ALTER MARKT

RHEIN-GARTEN

ST. MARTIN

LAURENZ PLATZ

RIVER

UNTER

KD BOAT DOCK

WALLRAF RICHARTZ MUSEUM

GURZENICHSTR

1 HOTEL ENGELBERTZ
2 HOTEL IBIS AM DOM
3 CITY CLASS RESIDENCE HOTEL

DCH

DEUTZER BRUCKE

CHOCOLATE FACTORY

the waterfront park. The Hohenzollernbrücke, crossing the Rhine at the cathedral, is the busiest railway bridge in the world (30 trains per hour all day long).

Tourist Information: Köln's energetic TI, opposite the church entry, has a list of reasonable private guides and a wealth of brochures (Mon–Sat 8:00–22:30, Sun 9:00–22:30, closes at 21:00 in winter, tel. 0221/19433).

Arrival in Köln: Köln couldn't be easier to visit: Its three important sights cluster within two blocks of its TI and train station (lockers available). This super pedestrian zone is a constant carnival of people. If you drive to Köln, follow signs to "Zentrum" then continue to the huge Parkhaus Am Dom pay lot under the cathedral (2 DM/hr, 25 DM/day).

Internet Access: Try Future Power (6 DM/30 min, Richard Strasse, tel. 0221/206-7206).

Sights—Köln's Cathedral

▲▲▲**Cathedral**—The Gothic *Dom*, or cathedral, Germany's most exciting church, looms immediately up from the train station (daily 7:00–19:00, tel. 0221/9258-4730). The one-hour English-only tours are reliable and excellent (7 DM, Mon–Sat at 10:30 and 14:30, Sun at 14:30). If you are unable to follow a local guide, follow this eight-stop walk:

1. Roman gate and cathedral exterior: The square in front of the cathedral has been a busy civic meeting place since ancient times. A Roman temple stood where the cathedral stands today. The north gate of the Roman city, from A.D. 50, marks the start of Köln's 2,000-year-old main street.

Look for the life-size replica tip of a spire. The real thing is 515 feet above you. The cathedral facade, while finished according to the original 13th-century plan, is "neo-Gothic" from the 19th century.

Postcards show the church after the 1945 bombing. The red brick building—to your right as you face the church—is the Diocesan Museum. The Roman museum is beside the church on the right and the art museum is behind that.

Step inside the church. Grab a pew in the center of the nave.

2. Nave: If you feel small, you're supposed to. The 140-foot-tall ceiling reminds us of our place in the vast scheme of things. Lots of stained glass—enough to cover three football fields—fills the church with light, representing God.

The church was begun in 1248. The choir—the lofty area from the center altar to the far end ahead of you—was finished in 1322. Later, with the discovery of America and routes to the Indies by sea, trade shifted away from inland ports like Köln. Funds dried up and eventually the building stopped. For 300 years the finished end of the church was walled off and functioned as a church while the unfinished torso (where you now sit) waited. For centuries the symbol of Köln's skyline was a huge crane that sat atop the unfinished west spire.

With the rise of German patriotism in the early 1800s, Köln became a symbol of German unity. And the Prussians—the movers and shakers behind German unity—mistakenly considered Gothic a German style. They initiated a national tax that funded the speedy completion of this gloriously Gothic German church. Seven hundred workers (compared to 100 in the 14th century) finished the church in just 38 years (1842–1880). The great train station was built in the shadow of the cathedral's towering spire.

The glass windows in the front of the church are medieval. The glass surrounding you in the nave is not as old, but it's precious nevertheless. The glass on the left is Renaissance. That on the right—a gift from Ludwig I, father of "Mad" King Ludwig of touristic fame—is 19th-century Bavarian.

Köln Cathedral

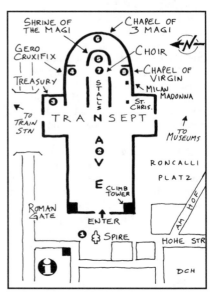

While 95 percent of Köln was destroyed by WWII bombs, the structure of the cathedral survived fairly well. In anticipation of the bombing, the glass and art treasures were taken to shelters and saved. The new "swallow's nest" organ above you was installed to celebrate the cathedral's 750th birthday in 1998. Relics (mostly skulls) fill cupboards on each side of the nave.

3. Treasury: The treasury is one room filled with mostly medieval reliquaries (bits of chain, bone, cross, cloth, and so on, in gold-crusted glass capsules—3 DM, daily 9:00–17:00). It's fine medieval art but—with no English descriptions—pretty meaningless. The fine little 6-DM book at the door helps (cheapskates read it on the leash).

4. Gero-Crucifix: The Chapel of the Cross features the oldest surviving monumental crucifix from north of the Alps. Carved in 976 with a sensitivity 300 years ahead of its time, it shows Jesus not suffering and not triumphant—but with eyes closed...dead. He paid the price for our sins. It's quite a two-fer: great art and powerful theology in one. The cathedral has three big pilgrim stops: this crucifix, the Shrine of the Magi, and the *Madonna of Milan* (both coming up).

As you step into the oldest part of the church, look for the mosaic of the ninth-century church on the floor. It shows a saint holding the Carolingian Cathedral, which stood on this spot for several centuries before this one was built.

Continue to the front end of the church, stopping to look at the glass case behind the high altar.

5. Shrine of the Magi: Relics were a big deal in the Middle Ages. Köln's acquisition of the bones of the Three Kings in the 12th century put it on the pilgrimage map and brought in enough money to justify the construction of this magnificent place. By some stretch of medieval Christian logic, these relics also justified the secular power of the local king. This reliquary, made in about 1200, is the biggest and most splendid I've seen. It's seven feet of gilded silver, jewels, and enamel. Old Testament prophets line the bottom, and 12 New Testament apostles—with a wingless angel in the center—line the top.

Inside sit the bones of the Magi...three skulls with golden crowns. So what's the big deal about these three kings of Christmas carol fame? They were the first to recognize Jesus as the savior and the first to come as pilgrims to worship him. They inspired medieval pilgrims and countless pilgrims since. For a thousand years, a theme of this cathedral has been that life is a pilgrimage...a search for God.

6. Chapel of the Three Magi: The center chapel, at the far end, is the oldest. It also has the church's oldest window (center, from 1265). It has the typical design: a strip of Old Testament scenes on the left with a theologically and visually parallel strip of New Testament scenes on the right (e.g., on bottom panels: to the left, the birth of Eve; to the right, the birth of Mary with her mother Anne on the bed).

Later, glass (which you saw lining the nave) was painted and glazed. This medieval window is actually colored glass, which is assembled like a mosaic. It was very expensive. The size was limited to what pilgrim donations could support. Notice the plain, budget design higher up.

7. Choir: Try to get into the center zone between the high altar and the carved wooden central stalls. This is surrounded by 13th- and 14th-century art: carved oak stalls, frescoed walls, statues painted as they would have been, and original stained glass high above. Study the fanciful oak carvings. The woman cutting the man's hair is a Samson-and-Delilah warning to the sexist men of the early Church.

8. Chapel of the Virgin: The nearby chapel faces one of the most precious paintings of the important Gothic "School of Köln." *The Patron Saints of Köln* was painted in 1442 by Stefan Lochner. Notice the photographic realism and believable depth. There are literally dozens of identifiable herbs in the grassy foreground. During the 19th century the city fought to have it in the museum. The Church went to court to keep it. The judge ruled that it can stay in the cathedral only as long as a Mass is said before it every day. For over a hundred years, that has happened at 18:00. Lochner was a leader in the School of Köln art style. (For lots more, see Wallraf-Richartz Museum below.)

Overlooking the same chapel, the *Madonna of Milan* (1290) was associated with miracles and a focus of pilgrims for centuries. As you head for the exit, find the statue of St. Christopher (with Jesus on his shoulder and the pilgrim's staff). Since 1470, pilgrims and travelers have looked up at him and taken solace in the hope that their patron saint is looking out for them. Go in peace.

Church Spire Climb—For 509 steps and 3 DM you can enjoy a fine city view from the cathedral's south tower. From the *Glockenstube* (only 400 steps up) you can see the *Dom's* nine huge bells including Dicke Peter (24-ton "Fat Peter"), claimed to be the largest free-swinging church bell in the world.

Dom Forum—This new visitor center is across from the entry of the church (plenty of info, welcoming lounge with 1-DM coffee, free WC downstairs). They offer an English-language "multivision" video on the history of the church daily at 11:30 and 15:30 (starts slow but gets a little better, 20 min, 3 DM or included with church tour).

Diocesan Museum—This contains some of the cathedral's finest art (free, Fri–Wed 10:00–18:00, closed Thu, English description sheet).

More Sights—Köln

▲▲**Römisch-Germanisches Museum**—Germany's best Roman museum offers not a word of English among its elegant and fascinating display of Roman artifacts: fine glassware, jewelry, and mosaics (5 DM, Tue–Sun 10:00–17:00, closed Mon, tel. 0221/24590). The permanent collection is downstairs and upstairs. Temporary exhibits (extra ticket) are on the main floor. Budget travelers can view its prize piece, a fine mosaic floor, free from the front window. Once the dining-room floor of a rich merchant, this is actually its original position (the museum was built around it). It shows scenes from the life of Dionysus . . . wine and good times, Roman style. The tall monument over the Dionysus mosaic is the mausoleum of a first-century Roman army officer. Upstairs you'll see a reassembled, arched original gate to the Roman city with the Roman initials for the town, "CCAA," still legible, and incredible glassware that Roman Köln was famous for producing.

▲▲**Wallraf-Richartz and Ludwig Museums**—Next door and more enjoyable, you'll find three museums in one slick and modern building (10 DM, Tue 10:00–20:00, Wed–Fri 10:00–18:00, Sat–Sun 11:00–18:00, closed Mon, exhibits are fairly well described in English, classy but pricey cafeteria with a reasonable salad bar at entry level, tel. 0221/221-22379). Don't worry about which museum you're in—the floor plan is a mess. Just enjoy the art. (In January 2001, the Wallraf-Richartz collection is scheduled to move to its own building near the city hall on Laurenz Platz, and the Ludwig will take over this entire building.)

The **Wallraf-Richartz** features a world-class collection of old masters arranged chronologically, from medieval to northern Baroque and Impressionist. You'll see the best collection anywhere of Gothic School of Köln paintings (1300–1550), offering an intimate peek into those times. Then comes German, Dutch, Flemish, and French art with masters such as Dürer, Rubens, Rembrandt, Hals, Steen, van Gogh, Renoir, Monet, Munch, and Cézanne.

The **Ludwig Museum** offers a stimulating trip through the art of the last century (upstairs) and American Pop and post–WWII art (in the basement). Artists featured include German and Russian expressionists, the Blue Rider school, and Picasso.

The **Agfa History of Photography** exhibit is three rooms with no English. (Look for the pigeon with the tiny vintage camera strapped to its chest.)

Assorted Museums and Tours—The TI has information on lots more museums. For a thorough visit, consider Köln's two-day museum and transit pass (20 DM, family-36 DM).

The **Käthe Kollwitz Museum** offers the largest collection of this woman's powerful expressionist art, welling from her experiences living in Berlin during the tumultuous first half of the last century (Tue–Fri 10:00–18:00, Sat–Sun 11:00–18:00, Neumarkt 18, tel. 0221/227-2363).

Chocoholics love the **Chocolate Museum**, which takes you on a well-described-in-English tour from the origin of the cocoa bean to the finished product. View displays on the culture of chocolate and watch treats trundle down the conveyor belt in the functioning chocolate factory. Sample sweets from the chocolate fountain (Rheinauhafen 1a, an easy walk south on riverfront between Deutzer and Severins bridges, tel. 0221/931-8880).

Two-hour German/English **city bus tours** leave from the TI daily (26 DM, at 10:30, 11:00, and 14:30).

Sleeping and Eating in Köln
(2 DM = about $1, country code: 49, area code: 0221, zip code: 50667)

Köln is *the* convention town in Germany. Consequently, the town is either jam-packed with hotel prices in the 300-DM range, or empty and hungry. In 2001, conventions are scheduled for these dates: January 15–21, January 28–February 4, March 7–10 and 27–31, April 1–4 and 27–30, May 18–22, June 13–17, all of August, September 2–4 and 19–21, October 13–18, and all of November. Outside of convention times the TI can always get you a discounted room in a business-class hotel, and the hotels listed below will honor their fair rates.

Hotel Engelbertz is a fine family-run, 40-room place a five-minute walk from the station and cathedral at the end of the pedestrian mall (specials for readers with this book during non-convention times: Db-110 DM if you call to book on same day or day before, Db-158 DM if you reserve in advance; regular rate Db-188 DM, convention rate Db-330 DM, CC:VMA, elevator, just off Hohe Strasse at Obenmarspforten 1–3, tel. 0221/257-8994, fax 0221/257-8924).

Hotel Ibis am Dom, a huge budget chain with a 71-room modern hotel right at the train station, offers all the comforts in a tidy affordable package without the convention price gouge (Db-170 DM, no breakfast, CC:VMA, some nonsmoking rooms, elevator, Hauptbahnhof, tel. 0221/912-8580, fax 0221/138-194, www.ibis-hotel.de).

City Class Residence Hotel is a modern, practical place buried nicely in the old town (Db-190–240 DM, CC:VMA, elevator, Alter Markt 55, tel. 0221/920-1980, fax 0221/9201-9899, e-mail: cityclass@t-online.de).

For the best outdoor dining on a balmy summer evening, consider the eateries lining Alter Markt (2 blocks off river); **Gaffel Haus** serves good local food with Kölsch, a uniquely Köln-style beer.

Transportation Connections—Köln
By train to: Cochem (every 2 hrs, 1.75 hrs), **Bacharach** or **St. Goar** (hrly, 90 min with 1 change), **Frankfurt airport** (hrly, 2 hrs), **Koblenz** (5/hrly, 1 hr), **Bonn** (6/hrly, 20 min), **Trier** (7/day, 2.5 hrs), **Aachen** (3/hrly, 1 hr), **Paris** (6/day, 4 hrs), **Amsterdam** (8/day, 2.5 hrs).

Sights—Unromantic Rhine
▲**Bonn**—Bonn was chosen for its sleepy, cultured, and peaceful nature as a good place to plant Germany's first post-Hitler government. After Germany became one again, Berlin took over its position as capital.

Today Bonn is sleek, modern, and, by big-city standards, remarkably pleasant and easygoing. Stop here not to see the sparse exhibit at **Beethoven's House** (8 DM, Mon–Sat 10:00–18:00, Sun 11:00–16:00, free English brochure, tel. 0228/981-7525), but to come up for a smoggy breath of the real world after the misty, romantic Rhine.

The pedestrian-only old town stretches out from the station and makes you wonder why the United States can't trade in its malls for real, people-friendly cities. The market square and Münsterplatz—filled with street musicians—are a joy. People watching doesn't get much better. The TI faces the station (Mon–Fri 9:00–18:30, Sat 9:00–16:00, Sun 10:00–14:00, room-finding service-5 DM, tel. 0228/773-466).

Hotel Eschweiler is plain but well located, just off the market square on a pedestrian street above a taco joint and next door to Beethoven's House (S-70 DM, Ss-80 DM, Sb-115 DM, Ds-140 DM, Db-160 DM, show this book for a 10 percent discount, great breakfasts, 7-minute walk from the station, Bonngasse 7, tel. 0228/631-760 or 0228/631-769, fax 0228/694-904).

▲**Remagen**—Midway between Koblenz and Köln are the scant remains of the Bridge at Remagen, of World War II (and movie) fame. But the memorial and the bridge stubs are enough to stir the emotions of Americans who remember when it was the only bridge that remained, allowing the Allies to cross the Rhine and race to Berlin in 1945. The small museum tells the bridge's fascinating story in English. Built during World War I to help supply the German forces on the Western Front, it's ironic that this was the bridge Eisenhower said was worth its weight in gold for its service against Germany. Hitler executed four generals for their failure to blow it up. Ten days after the Americans arrived, it did collapse, killing 28 Americans (2.50 DM, March–Oct daily 10:00–17:00, on Rhine's west bank, south side of Remagen town, follow *"Brücke von Remagen"* signs, Remagen TI tel. 02642/2010).

▲**Aachen (Charlemagne's Capital)**—This city was the capital of Europe in A.D. 800, when Charles the Great (Charlemagne) called it Aix-la-Chapelle. The remains of his rule include an impressive Byzantine/Ravenna–inspired church with his sarcophagus and throne. See the headliner newspaper museum and great fountains, including a clever arrange-'em-yourself version.

Sightseeing Lowlights
Heidelberg—This famous old university town attracts hordes of Americans. Any surviving charm is stained almost beyond recognition by commercialism. It doesn't make it in Germany's top 20 days.

Mainz, Wiesbaden, and Rüdesheim—These towns are all too big or too famous. They're not worth your time. Mainz's Gutenberg Museum is also a disappointment.

BERLIN

No tour of Germany is complete without a look at its historic and reunited capital, a construction zone called Berlin. Stand over ripped-up tracks and under a canopy of cranes and watch the rebirth of a European capital. Enjoy the thrill of walking over what was the Wall and through Brandenburg Gate.

Berlin has had a tumultuous history. The city was devastated in World War II then divided by the Allied powers: with the American, British, and French sectors being West Berlin, and the Russian sector, East Berlin. The division was set in stone when the East built the Berlin Wall in 1961. The Berlin Wall lasted 28 years. In 1990, less than a year after the Wall fell, Germany was formally reunited. When the dust settled, Berliners from both sides of the once-divided city faced the monumental challenge of reunification.

The last decade has taken Berlin through a frenzy of rebuilding. And, while there's still plenty of work to be done, a new Berlin is emerging. Berliners joke they don't need to go anywhere because the city's always changing. Spin a postcard rack to see the news. A five-year-old guidebook on Berlin covers a different city.

Unification has had its negative side, and the Wall survives in the minds of some people. Some "Ossies" (impolite slang for Easterners) miss their security. Some "Wessies" miss their easy ride (military deferrals, subsidized rent, and tax breaks). To free spirits, walled-in West Berlin was a citadel of freedom within the East.

The city government has been eager to charge forward with little nostalgia for anything that was "Eastern." Big corporations and the national government have moved in, and the dreary swath of land that was the Wall has been transformed. City planners are boldly taking Berlin's reunification and the return of the national government as a good opportunity to make Berlin a great capital once again.

During the grind of World War II, Hitler enjoyed rolling out the lofty plans for a post-war Berlin as capital of a Europe united under his rule. As Europe unites, dominated by a muscular Germany with its shiny new capital in the works, Hitler's dream of a grand post-war Berlin seems about to come true....

Planning Your Time

Because of the city's location, try to enter and/or leave by either night train or plane. On a three-week trip through Germany, Austria, and Switzerland, I'd give Berlin two days and spend them this way:

Day 1: 10:00-Take a guided walking tour (offered by Original Berlin Walks, see "Tours of Berlin," below). After lunch, take my Do-It-Yourself Orientation Tour, stopping midway to scale the new dome of the Reichstag building, then finishing with a walk through Eastern Berlin. Stop at the Deutscher Dom (German Cathedral) to devour the "Questions on Germany History" exhibit. Finish your day at the Pergamon Museum.

Day 2: Spend the morning lost in the painted art of the Gemäldegalerie, explore Potsdamer Platz center, hike to the Topography of Terror exhibit and along the surviving Zimmerstrasse stretch of Wall to the Museum of the Wall at Checkpoint Charlie.

If you are maximizing your sightseeing you could start Day 2 with a visit to the Egyptian and Picasso museums at Charlottenburg. Remember that the Museum of the Wall is open late and most museums are closed on Monday.

Orientation (area code: 030)

Berlin is huge, with nearly four million people. But the tourist's Berlin can be broken into four digestible chunks:

1. The area around Bahnhof Zoo and the grand Kurfürstendamm (called Ku'damm) Boulevard (transportation, tours, information, hotel, shopping hub).

2. Former downtown East Berlin (Brandenburg Gate, Unter den Linden Boulevard, Pergamon Museum, and the area around Oranienburger Strasse).

3. The new center: Kulturforum museums, Potsdamer Platz, and Wall-related sights.

4. Charlottenburg Palace and museums.

Tourist Information

Berlin's TIs are run by a for-profit agency working for the city's big hotels, which colors the information they provide. The main TI is five minutes from the Bahnhof Zoo train station, in the Europa Center (with Mercedes symbol on top, enter outside to left, on Budapester Strasse, Mon–Sat 8:30–20:30, Sun 10:00–18:00,

Berlin Sightseeing Modules

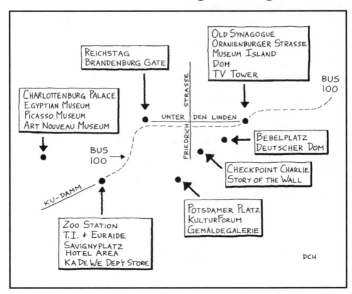

tel. 030/250-025, www.btm.de). A smaller TI is in the Brandenburg Gate (daily 9:30–18:00). The TIs sell city maps (1 DM—get
it), the *Berlin Programm* (a 3-DM German-language monthly listing upcoming events and museum hours, www.berlin.de), the
Museumspass (16-DM, 3-day pass to state museums, see "Helpful
Hints," below), and the German-English quarterly *Berlin* magazine
(4 DM, with timely features on Berlin and a partial calendar of
events). Ask for the free *What's On in Berlin* monthly entertainment magazine. The TIs also offer a 5-DM room-finding service
(but only to hotels that give them kickbacks—many don't). Most
hotels have free city maps.

   EurAide's information office, in the Bahnhof Zoo, provides a
great service. They have answers to all your questions about Berlin
or train travel around Europe. Staffed by Americans, communica-
tion is simple and they have a knack for predicting your needs and
then publishing free fliers to answer them (daily 10:00–18:00 with
a 12:00–13:00 lunch break in summer, off-season Mon–Sat 10:00–
16:30, closed Sun, at the back of station near lockers, great opportunity to get all future *couchette* reservations nailed ahead of time,
Prague Excursion passes available, www.euraide.de). EurAide also
sells one-day bus/metro passes and city maps (making a trip to the
TI probably unnecessary). To get the most out of EurAide, organize your questions and needs before your visit.

Arrival in Berlin

By Train at Bahnhof Zoo: Berlin's central station is called Bahnhof Zoologischer Garten (because it's near Berlin's famous zoo)..."Zoo" for short. Coming from Western Europe, you'll probably land at Zoo (rhymes with "toe"). It's small, well organized, and handy.

Upon arrival by train, orient yourself like this: Inside the station, follow signs to Hardenbergplatz. Step into this busy square filled with city buses, taxis, the transit office, and derelicts. "The Original Berlin Walks" start from the curb immediately outside the station at the top of the taxi stand (see "Tours of Berlin," below). Between you and the McDonald's across the street is the stop for bus #100 (departing to the right for the Do-It-Yourself Orientation Tour, described below). Turn right and tiptoe through the riffraff to the eight-lane highway, Hardenbergstrasse. Walk to the median strip and stand with your back to the tracks. Ahead you'll see the black, bombed-out hulk of the Kaiser Wilhelm Memorial Church and the Europa Center (Mercedes symbol spinning on roof), which houses the main TI. Just ahead on the left amid the traffic is the BVG transport information kiosk. (Buy a 8.70-DM day pass covering the subway and buses, and pick up a free subway map.) If you're facing the church, my recommended hotels are behind you to your right.

If you arrive at Berlin's other train stations (trains from most of Eastern Europe arrive at Ostbahnhof), no problem: Ride another train (fastest option) or the S-Bahn or U-Bahn (runs every few minutes) to Bahnhof Zoo and pretend you arrived here.

By Plane: See "Transportation Connections," below.

Getting around Berlin

Berlin's sights spread far and wide. Right from the start, commit yourself to the fine public transit system. The *On the Move* booklet (from BVG and EurAide) explains it all.

By Subway and Bus: The U-Bahn, S-Bahn, and all buses are consolidated into one "BVG" system that uses the same tickets. Here are your options:

• Basic ticket (*Einzel Fahrschein*) for two hours of travel on buses or subways (4 DM; *Erwachsener* means adult—anyone 14 or older).

• A day pass (*Tages Karte*) covering zones A and B—the city proper—8.70 DM, good till 03:00 the morning after. To get out to Potsdam you need a ticket covering zone C (9.90 DM). Small groups from three to five people should consider the all-day "*Kleingruppenkarte*" which costs 21 DM (25 DM to include Zone C for Potsdam).

• A cheap short-ride ticket (*Kurzstrecke Erwachsener*) for a single short ride of six bus stops or three subway stations, with one transfer (2.50 DM).

• Berlin/Potsdam WelcomeCard gives you three days of transportation and three days of minor sightseeing discounts (32 DM, valid for an adult and up to 3 kids—generally only worthwhile for traveling families).

Buy your tickets or cards from machines at U- or S-Bahn stations or at the BVG pavilion in front of Bahnhof Zoo. To use the machine, first select the type of ticket you want, then load in the coins or paper. Punch your ticket in a red or yellow clock machine to validate it (or risk a 60-DM fine). The double-decker buses are a joy (can buy ticket on bus) and the subway is a snap. The S-Bahn is free with a validated Eurailpass.

By Taxi: Taxis are easy to flag down, and taxi stands are common. A typical ride within town costs 15 DM. A local law designed to help people get safely and affordably home from their subway station late at night is handy for tourists any time of day: A short ride of no more than two kilometers is a flat 5 DM. (Ask for "*Kurzstrecke, fünf Mark, bitte.*")

By Bike: In western Berlin you can rent bikes at the Bahnhof Zoo; in the east, go to Fahrradstation at Hackesche Höfe (25 DM/day, Mon–Fri 10:00–19:00, Sat 10:00–16:00, closed Sun, Rosenthaler Strasse 40). Be careful, in Berlin motorists don't brake for bikers.

Helpful Hints

Most museums are closed on Monday. Save Monday for Berlin Wall sights, the Reichstag building, the Do-It-Yourself Orientation Tour (see below), walking/bus tours, churches, the zoo, or shopping along Kurfurstendamm (Ku'damm) Boulevard or at the Kaufhaus des Westens (KaDeWe) department store. (When Monday is a holiday—as it is several times a year—museums are open then and closed Tuesday.)

City museums—such as the Käthe Kollwitz Museum, Bröhan Museum, and Jewish Museum—are free on the first Sunday of each month. All state museums, including the Pergamon Museum and Gemäldegalerie (plus others noted in "Sights," below), are covered by one Museumspass (8 DM/1 day, 16 DM/3 consecutive days, not valid for special exhibitions, purchase at TI or participating museum).

Many Berlin streets are numbered with odd and even numbers on the same side of the street, often with no connection to the other side (i.e., Ku'damm #212 can be across the street from #14). To save steps, check the white street signs on curb corners; many list the street numbers covered on that side of the block.

Reiseburo im Europa Center specializes in last-minute tickets (e.g., fly to London tomorrow for 200 DM, next to TI in Europa Center, tel. 030/2655-1050, www.lastminuteflugboerse.de).

Do-It-Yourself Orientation Tour

Here's an easy ▲▲▲ introduction to Berlin. Half the tour is by bus; the other half is on foot. Berlin's bus #100 is a sightseer's dream, stopping at Bahnhof Zoo, Europa Center/Hotel Palace, Siegessäule, Reichstag, Brandenburg Gate, Unter den Linden, Pergamon Museum, and ending at Alexanderplatz. If you have the 33 DM and 90 minutes for a hop-on hop-off bus tour (described below), take that instead. But this short 4-DM tour is a fine city introduction. Buses leave from Hardenbergplatz in front of the Zoo Station (and nearly next door to the Europa Center TI, in front of Hotel Palace). Buses come every 10 minutes, and single tickets are good for two hours—so take advantage of hop on and off privileges. Climb aboard, stamp your ticket (giving it a time), and grab a seat on top. You could ride the bus all the way, but I'd get out at the Reichstag and walk to Alexanderplatz.

Part 1: By Bus #100 from Bahnhof Zoo to the Reichstag

(This is about a 10-minute ride.)

☛ Around the corner, then straight ahead, before descending into the tunnel, you'll see: the bombed-out hulk of the Kaiser Wilhelm Memorial Church, with its post-war sister church (described below) and the Europa Center. This is the west end shopping district with the big department stores nearby.

☛ At the stop in front of Hotel Palace: on the left, the Berlin Zoo entrance and its aquarium (described below).

☛ Driving down Kurfürstenstrasse, turning left into Tiergarten: The Victory Column (Siegessäule, with the gilded angel, described below), towers above a vast city park once a royal hunting grounds, now nicknamed the "green lungs of Berlin."

☛ On the left a block after leaving the Siegessäule: The 18th-century late-rococo Bellevue Palace is the German "White House," once a Nazi VIP guesthouse, now the residence of the federal president (whose "power" is mostly ceremonial). If the flag's out, he's in.

☛ Driving along the Spree River: This park area was a residential district before World War II. Now, on the left-hand side, it's filled with the buildings of the new national government. The huge brick "brown snake" complex was built to house government workers—but it didn't sell—so now its apartments are available to anyone. Beyond that is the new and huge chancellory. A Henry Moore sculpture floats in front of the slope-roofed House of World Cultures (left side, nicknamed "the pregnant oyster"). The modern tower (next on left) is a carillon with 68 bells (1987).

☛ While you could continue on bus #100, it's better on foot from here. Leap out at the House of World Cultures (Haus der Kulturen der Welt). Before you stands the Reichstag. Visit this and continue the walk below.

Berlin

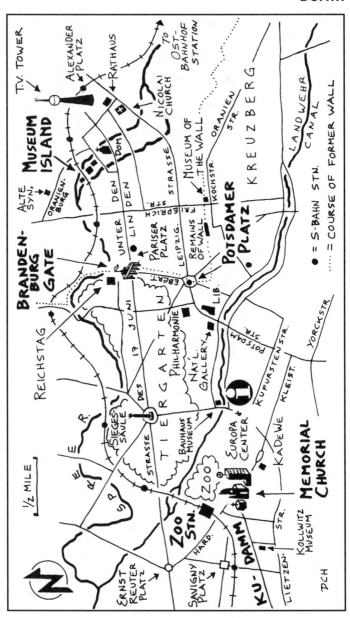

▲▲▲**Reichstag Building**—This building—the heart of German democracy—has a short but complicated and emotional history. When inaugurated in the 1890s, the last emperor, Kaiser Wilhelm, disdainfully called it the "house for chatting." It was from this Parliament building that the German Republic was proclaimed in 1918. In 1933 this symbol of democracy nearly burned down. It's believed Hitler planned the fire, using it as a handy excuse to frame the Communists and grab power. As WWII drew to a close, Stalin ordered his troops to take the Reichstag from the Nazis by May 1 (the worker's holiday). More than 1,500 Nazis made their last stand here—extending WWII by two days. On April 30, 1945, it fell to the Allies. It was not used from 1933 to 1999. For its 101st birthday, in 1995, the Bulgarian artist Christo wrapped it in silvery-gold cloth. It was then wrapped again in scaffolding, rebuilt by British architect Sir Norman Foster, and turned into the new parliamentary home of the Bundestag (Germany's lower house). To many Germans, the proud resurrection of the Reichstag—which no longer has a hint of Hitler—symbolizes the end of a terrible chapter in German history.

The **glass cupola** rises 48 meters above the ground, and a double staircase winds 230 meters to the top for a grand view. Inside the dome a cone of 360 mirrors reflects natural light into the legislative chamber. Lit from inside at night, this gives Berlin a memorable new night-light.

Visit the Reichstag (free, daily 8:00–22:00, most crowded 10:00–16:00, wait in line to go up—good street musicians, some hour-long English tours, tel. 030/2273-2152). As you approach the building, look above the door, surrounded by stone patches from WWII bomb damage, to see the motto and promise: "*Dem Deutschen Volke*" (to the German people). The open and airy lobby towers 30 meters (about 30 yards) high with 20-meter tall colors of the German flag. Glass doors show the **central chamber**. The message: there will be no secrets in government. Look inside. The seats are "Reichstag blue," a lilac blue color designed by the architect to brighten the otherwise gray interior. The German eagle (a.k.a. the "fat hen") spreads his wings behind the podium. Notice the doors marked "yes," "no," or "abstain"... the Bundestag's traditional "sheep jump" way of counting votes (for critical and close votes, all 669 members leave and vote by walking through the door of their choice).

Ride the elevator to the base of the glass dome. Take time to study the photos and read the circle of captions—an excellent exhibition telling the Reichstag story. Then study the surrounding architecture: a broken collage of old on new, like Germany's history. Notice the dome's giant and unobtrusive sunscreen that moves as necessary with the sun. Peer down through the skylight to look over the shoulders of the elected representatives at work.

For Germans, the best view is down—keeping a close eye on their government.

Wind up to the top of the double staircase. Take a 360-degree survey of the city as you hike: First, the big park is the Tiergarten, the "green lung" of Berlin. Beyond that is the Teufelsberg—Devil's Hill (built of rubble from the bombed city in the late 1940s and famous during the Cold War as a powerful ear of the West—notice the telecommunications tower on top). Given the violent and tragic history of Berlin, a city blown apart by bombs and covered over by bulldozers, locals say, "You have to be suspicious when you see the nice green park." Find the Seigessäule, the Victory Column (moved by Hitler in the 1930s from in front of the Reichstag to its present position in the Tiergarten). Next, scenes of the new Berlin spiral into your view—Potsdamer Platz marked with the conical glass tower that houses Sony's European headquarters. The yellow building to the right is the Berlin Philharmonic Concert Hall. Continue circling left, and find the green chariot atop the Brandenburg Gate. A monument to the Gypsy Holocaust will be built between the Reichstag and Brandenburg Gate. (Gypsies, as disdained by the Nazis as the Jews, lost the same percentage of their population to Hitler.) Next, you'll see former East Berlin and what will become the city's next huge construction zone, with a forest of 100-meter-tall skyscrapers in the works. Notice the TV tower (with the Pope's Revenge—explained below), the Berlin Cathedral's massive dome, the red tower of the city hall, the golden dome of the New Synagogue, and the Reichstag's roof garden restaurant (Dachgarten, 25-DM meals with a view, open until 17:00, tel. 030/2262-9933). Follow the train tracks in the distance to the left toward a huge construction zone marking the future central Berlin train station. Complete your spin tour with the blocky Chancellory. It may look like a pharaoh's tomb, but it's the office of Germany's most powerful person, the Chancellor and his team.

Part 2: Walking Tour from Brandenburg Gate up Unter den Linden to Alexanderplatz

Allow a comfortable hour for this walk through Eastern Berlin, including time for dawdling but not museum stops.

▲▲**Brandenburg Gate**—The historic Brandenburg Gate (1791, the last survivor of 14 gates in Berlin's old city wall), crowned by a majestic four-horse chariot with the Goddess of Peace at the reins, was the symbol of Berlin and then the symbol of divided Berlin. Napoleon took the statue to the Louvre in Paris in 1806. When the Prussians got it back, she was renamed the Goddess of Victory. The gate sat, part of a sad circle dance called The Wall, for more than 25 years. (TI within gate, open daily 9:30–18:00.)

Now postcards all over town show the ecstatic day—November 9, 1989—when the world enjoyed the sight of happy

Berliners jamming the gate like flowers on a parade float. Pause a minute and think about struggles for freedom—past and present.
▲**Pariser Platz**—From Brandenburg Gate, face Pariser Platz (into the east). Unter den Linden leads to the TV tower in the distance (the end of this walk). The space used to be filled with important government buildings—all bombed to smithereens. Today, Pariser Platz is unrecognizable from the deserted no-man's land it became under the Communist regime. Sparkling new banks, embassies (the French embassy rebuilt where it was pre–WWII), and a swanky hotel have filled in the void.

Crossing through the Gate, look to your right to a stretch of empty land—formerly the "death strip." The U.S. Embassy once stood here. Plans to rebuild it here are stalled because of new American setbacks for embassy safety requirements. The new Holocaust memorial (probably under construction in 2001) will stand behind that.

Brandenburg Gate, the center of old Berlin, sits on a major boulevard, running east-west through Berlin. The western segment, called Strasse des 17 Juni, stretches for 10 miles from the Siegessäule to the Olympic Stadium. For our walk, we'll follow this city axis in the opposite direction, east, up what is known as Unter den Linden, into the core of old imperial Berlin and past what was once the palace of the Hohenzollern family of Prussia, and then of Germany's imperial rulers. The palace—the reason for just about all you'll see—is a phantom sight... long gone.
▲▲**Unter den Linden**—This is the heart of former East Berlin. In Berlin's good old days, Unter den Linden was one of Europe's grand boulevards. In the 15th century, this horseway led from the palace to the hunting grounds (today's big park). In the 17th century, Hohenzollern princes and princesses moved in and built their palaces here so they could be near the Prussian emperor.

Named centuries ago for its thousand linden trees, this was the most elegant street of Prussian Berlin before Hitler's time and the main drag of East Berlin after his reign. Hitler replaced the venerable trees—many 250 years old—with Nazi flags. Popular discontent actually drove him to replant linden trees. Today Unter den Linden is no longer a depressing Cold War cul-de-sac, and its pre-Hitler strolling café ambience is returning.

As you walk toward the giant TV tower, the first big building you see on your right is the **Hotel Adlon**. It hosted such notables as Charlie Chaplin, Albert Einstein, and Greta Garbo. (This was where Garbo said, "I want to be alone," during the filming of *Grand Hotel*.) Destroyed in World War II, the grand Adlon was rebuilt in 1996. See how far you can get inside.

On your right, several doors down (past the S-Bahn station), is the **Russian embassy** (guarded by German police)—not quite as important now as it was a few years ago, but immense as ever. It

Unter den Linden

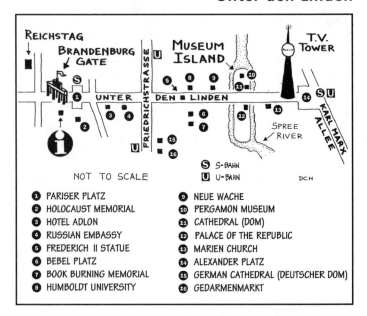

NOT TO SCALE

S S-BAHN
U U-BAHN

DCH

1. PARISER PLATZ
2. HOLOCAUST MEMORIAL
3. HOTEL ADLON
4. RUSSIAN EMBASSY
5. FREDERICK II STATUE
6. BEBEL PLATZ
7. BOOK BURNING MEMORIAL
8. HUMBOLDT UNIVERSITY
9. NEUE WACHE
10. PERGAMON MUSEUM
11. CATHEDRAL (DOM)
12. PALACE OF THE REPUBLIC
13. MARIEN CHURCH
14. ALEXANDER PLATZ
15. GERMAN CATHEDRAL (DEUTSCHER DOM)
16. GEDARMENMARKT

flies the Russian white, red, and blue. Find the hammer-and-sickle motif decorating the window frames. Continuing past the Aeroflot Airline offices, you come to the back of the Komische Oper (comic opera, program, and view of ornate interior posted in window). While the exterior is ugly, the fine old theater interior, amazingly missed by WWII bombs, survives.

The West lost no time in consuming the East; consequently, some are feeling a wave of nostalgia—**Ost-algia**—for the old days of East Berlin. But one symbol of that era has been given a reprieve. At Friedrichstrasse, look at the DDR–style pedestrian lights and you'll realize someone had a sense of humor back then. The perky red and green men—*Ampelmannchen*—were under threat of replacement by the far less jaunty Western signs. Fortunately, the DDR lights will be kept after all.

At **Friedrichstrasse**, look right. Before the war, the Unter den Linden/Friedrichstrasse intersection was the heart of Berlin. In the '20s this was the cabaret drag, a springboard to stardom for young and vampy entertainers like Marlene Dietrich. Today, this boulevard, lined with super department stores (like Galeries Lafayette—with its cool marble and glass waste-of-space interior) and big-time hotels (like Hilton and Four Seasons)—hopes to replace Ku'damm as the grand commerce and café boulevard of Berlin. Unfortunately, no one expects the new Friedrichstrasse to have the café/strolling ambience of the old one. It's a no-man's-land after dark.

Continue down Unter den Linden a few more blocks, past the large equestrian statue of **Frederick II** ("the Great"), and turn right into the square (Bebelplatz). Stand on the glass window in the center.

Frederick the Great—who ruled from 1740 to 1786—established Prussia as a military power. This square was center of Frederick's Berlin. Much of Frederick's palace actually survived World War II but was torn down by the Communists since it symbolized the imperialist past.

Look around: **Bebelplatz** is bounded by the German State Opera, former state library, and the round Catholic St. Hedwig's Church.

Humboldt University (across Unter den Linden) was one of Europe's greatest. Marx and Lenin (not the brothers or the sisters) studied here along with Grimm (both brothers) and 22 Nobel Prize winners. Einstein taught here until taking a spot at Princeton in 1932 (smart guy).

Look down through the glass you're standing on: The room of empty bookshelves is a memorial to the notorious Nazi **book burning**. It was on this square in 1933 that staff and students from the university threw 20,000 newly forbidden books (like Einstein's) into a huge bonfire on the orders of the Nazi propaganda minister Joseph Goebbels. Continue down Unter den Linden. The next square on your right holds the Opernpalais' restaurants (see "Eating," below).

On the university side of Unter den Linden, the Greek templelike building is the **Neue Wache** (New Guardhouse, from 1816). When the Wall fell, this memorial to the victims of fascism was transformed into a new national memorial. Look inside where a replica of the Käthe Kollwitz statue, *Mother with Her Dead Son*, is surrounded by thought-provoking silence. The inscription in front reads, "To the victims of war and tyranny."

Just before the bridge (where the pink German History Museum will reopen in 2002), wander left along the canal through the tiny but colorful flea market (weekends only). Canal tour boats leave from here.

Cross the bridge to **Museum Island**, home of Germany's first museums and today famous for its Pergamon Museum (described below). The museum complex starts with an imposing neoclassical facade on the left (a musty museum of antiquities). For 300 years the square has flip-flopped between military parade ground and people-friendly park. In 1999 it was made into a park again.

The towering church (ahead, before the next bridge) is the 100-year-old **Berlin Cathedral**, or *Dom* (8 DM, 10 DM including access to the dome, organ concerts offered most Wed, Thu, and Fri at 15:00 for free with regular admission). Inside, the great reformers stand around the brilliantly restored dome like stern saints guarding their theology. Frederick I rests in an ornate tomb (right transept, near entry to dome). The crypt downstairs is not worth a look.

Across the street is the **Palace of the Republic** (with the copper-tinted windows). A symbol of the Communist days, it was East Berlin's parliament building and futuristic entertainment complex. Although it officially has a date with the wrecking ball, many easterners want it saved, and its future is still uncertain.

Before crossing the next bridge (and leaving Museum Island), look right. The pointy twin spires of the 13th-century Nikolai Church mark the center of medieval Berlin. This *Nikolai-Viertel* (district) was restored by the DDR and was trendy in the last years of socialism. Today it's dull and, with limited time, not worth a visit.

As you cross the bridge, look left in the distance to see the gilded **New Synagogue**, rebuilt after WWII bombing (described below).

Walk toward **Marien Church** (from 1270, interesting but very faded old *Dance of Death* mural inside door) at the base of the TV tower. The big, red brick building past the trees on the right is the city hall, built after the revolution of 1848 and arguably the first democratic building in the city.

The 400-meter-tall **Fernsehturm (TV Tower)** offers a fine view from 200 meters (9 DM, daily 9:00–01:00). Consider a kitchsy trip to the top for the view and lunch in its revolving restaurant. Built (with Swedish know-how) in 1969, the tower was meant to show the power of the atheistic state at a time when DDR leaders were having the crosses removed from church domes and spires. But when the sun shines on their tower, the greatest spire in East Berlin, a huge cross reflects on the mirrored ball. Cynics called it "The Pope's Revenge."

Farther east, pass under the train tracks into **Alexanderplatz**. This, especially the Kaufhof, was the commercial pride and joy of East Berlin. Today it's still a landmark, with a major U-Bahn and S-Bahn station.

For a ride through workaday eastern Berlin, with its Lego-hell apartments (dreary even with their new face-lifts), hop back on bus #100 from here. It loops five minutes to the end of the line and then, after a couple minutes break, heads on back. (This bus retraces your route, finishing back at Bahnhof Zoo.) Consider extending this foray into eastern Berlin to Karl Marx Allee (described below).

Tours of Berlin
▲▲▲**City Walking Tours**—"The Original Berlin Walks" offers a variety of worthwhile tours led by enthusiastic guides who are native English speakers. The company, run by Englishman Nick Gay, offers a three-hour "Discover Berlin" introductory walk daily

at 10:00 (all year) and 14:30 (April–Oct) for 18 DM (14 DM if you're under 26). Just show up at the taxi rank in front of Zoo Station. Their high-quality, high-energy guides also offer tours of "Infamous Third Reich Sites," most mornings in high season at 10:00, "Jewish Life in Berlin," and Potsdam. Many of the Third Reich and Jewish history sites are difficult to pin down without these excellent walks. Confirm the schedule at EurAide or by phone with Nick or his wife and partner Serena (private tours also available, tel. 030/301-9194, www.berlinwalks.com).

▲**City Bus Tours**—For bus tours you have two choices:
1) Full-blown, three-hour bus tours. Contact Severin & Kühn (39 DM, live guides in 2 languages, daily 10:00 and 14:00, 2/day in summer, from Ku'damm 216, tel. 030/880-4190) or take BVG buses from Ku'damm 225 (tel. 030/885-9880).
2) Hop-on hop-off circle tours. Several companies do the "City-Circle Sightseeing" tour. The tour offers unlimited hop-on hop-off privileges for its 12-stop route (33 DM, 2/hrly, 2-hr loop, April–October, taped guides, frequent buses). The TI has the brochures. Just hop on where you like and pay the driver. On a sunny day when the double-decker buses go topless, these are a photographer's delight.

Sights—Western Berlin

Western travelers still think of Berlin's "West End" as the heart of the city. While it's no longer that, the West End still has the best infrastructure to support your visit and works well as a home base. Here are a few sights within an easy walk of your hotel and the Zoo station.

▲**Kurfürstendamm**—In the 1850s, when Berlin became a wealthy and important capital, her new rich chose Kurfürsten-damm as their street. Bismarck made it Berlin's Champs-Élysées. In the 1920s it became a chic and fashionable drag of cafés and boutiques. During the Third Reich, as home to an international community of diplomats and journalists, it enjoyed more freedom than the rest of Berlin. Throughout the Cold War, economic subsidies from the West made sure that capitalism thrived on Ku'damm, as western Berlin's main drag is popularly called. And today, while much of the old charm has been hamburgerized, Ku'damm is still a fine place to feel the pulse of the city and enjoy the elegant shops (around Fasanenstrasse), department stores, and people watching. Ku'damm, starting at Kaiser Wilhelm Memorial Church, does its commercial cancan for two miles.

▲**Kaiser Wilhelm Memorial Church (Gedächtniskirche)**— The church was originally a memorial to the first emperor of Germany, who died in 1888. Its bombed-out ruins have been left standing as a memorial to the destruction of Berlin in World War II. Under a fine mosaic ceiling, a small exhibit features interesting

Western Berlin

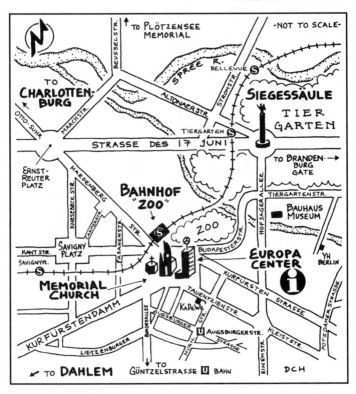

photos about the bombing (free, Mon–Sat 10:00–16:00, closed Sun). Next to it, a new church (1961) offers a world of 11,000 little blue windows. The blue glass was given to the church by the French as a reconciliation gift. The lively square between this and the Europa Center (a shiny high-rise shopping center built as a showcase of Western capitalism during the Cold War) usually attracts street musicians.

▲**Käthe Kollwitz Museum**—This local artist (1867–1945), who experienced much of Berlin's stormiest century, conveys some powerful and mostly sad feelings about motherhood, war, and suffering through the black-and-white faces of her art (8 DM, Wed–Mon 11:00–18:00, closed Tue, free on first Sun of month, a block off Ku'damm at Fasanenstrasse 24).

▲**Kaufhaus des Westens (KaDeWe)**—The "department store of the West," with a staff of 2,400 to help you sort through its vast selection of 380,000 items, is the biggest department store

on the Continent. You can get everything from a haircut and
train ticket to souvenirs (third floor). A cyber bar is on the fourth
floor (5 DM/30 min). The theater and concert box office on the
sixth floor charges an 18 percent booking fee, but they know all
your options. The sixth floor is also a world of gourmet taste
treats. This biggest selection of deli and exotic food in Germany
offers plenty of classy opportunities to sit down and eat. Ride the
glass elevator to the seventh floor's glass-domed Winter Garden
self-service cafeteria—fun but pricey (Mon–Fri 9:30–20:00,
Sat 9:00–16:00, closed Sun, tel. 030/21210, U-Bahn: Wittenbergplatz). The Wittenbergplatz U-Bahn station (in front of
KaDeWe) is a unique opportunity to see an old-time station in
Berlin. Enjoy its interior.

Berlin Zoo—More than 1,400 different kinds of animals call
Berlin's famous zoo home—or so the zookeepers like to think.
Germans enjoy seeing the pandas at play (straight in from the
entry). I enjoy seeing the Germans at play (13 DM for zoo or
world-class aquarium, 21 DM for both, children half price, daily
9:00–18:30, feeding times—*Fütterungszeiten*—posted on map just
inside entry, enter near Europa Center in front of Hotel Palace,
Budapester Strasse 32, tel. 030/254-010).

Erotic Art Museum—This offers three floors of graphic (mostly
18th-century) Oriental art, a tiny theater showing erotic silent
movies from the early 1900s, and a special exhibit on the queen
of German pornography, Beate Uhse. This amazing woman, a
former test pilot for the Third Reich and ground-breaking
purveyor of condoms and sex ed in the 1950s, is now the female
Hugh Hefner of Germany and CEO of a huge chain of porn
shops. If you're traveling far and are sightseeing selectively, the
sex museums in Amsterdam or Copenhagen are much better.
This one, while well described in English, is little more than
prints and posters (10 DM, daily 9:00–24:00, hard-to-beat gift
shop, at corner of Kantstrasse and Joachimstalerstrasse, a block
from Bahnhof Zoo). If you just want to see sex, you'll see much
more for half the price in a private video booth next door.

Sights—Central Berlin
Hitler and The Third Reich—While many come to Berlin to see
Hitler sights, these are essentially invisible. The German Resistance
Museum (described below) is in German only and difficult for the
tourist to appreciate. The Topography of Terror (Gestapo headquarters) is a fascinating exhibit but—again—only in German, and
all that remains of the building is its foundation. "Hitler's Bunker" is
completely gone and built over. Your best bet for "Hitler sights" is
to take the "Infamous Third Reich Sites" walking tour offered by
Berlin Walks (see "City Walking Tours," above). EurAide has a
good flier listing and explaining sights related to the Third Reich.

Tiergarten/Siegessäule—Berlin's "Central Park" stretches two miles from Bahnhof Zoo to Brandenburg Gate. Its centerpiece, the Siegessäule (Victory Column), was built to commemorate the Prussian defeat of France in 1870. The pointy-helmeted Germans rubbed it in, decorating the tower with French cannons and paying for it all with francs received as war reparations. The three lower rings commemorate Bismarck's victories. I imagine the statues of Moltke and other German military greats goose-stepping around the floodlit angel at night. Originally standing at the Reichstag, the Siegessäule was moved to this position by Hitler to complement his anticipated victory parades. Climbing its 285 steps earns you a fine Berlin-wide view (2 DM, Mon–Thu 9:30–18:30, Fri–Sun 9:30–19:00, bus #100). From the tower, the grand Strasse des 17 Juni (named for a workers' uprising against the DDR government in the 1950s) leads to the Brandenburg Gate.

German Resistance Memorial (Gedenkstätte Deutscher Widerstand)—This memorial and museum tells the story of the German resistance to Hitler. The Benderblock was a military headquarters where an ill-fated attempt to assassinate Hitler was plotted. Stauffenberg and his co-conspirators were shot in the courtyard. While explanations are in German only, the spirit that haunts the place is multilingual (free, Mon–Fri 9:00–18:00, Thu until 20:00, Sat–Sun 10:00–18:00, printed English translation for sale, just south of Tiergarten at Stauffenbergstrasse 13, bus #129, tel. 030/2699-5000).

▲**Potsdamer Platz**—The Times Square of Berlin and possibly the busiest square in Europe before World War II, it was cut in two by the Wall and left a deserted no-man's-land for 40 years. This immense commercial/residential/entertainment center (with the European corporate headquarters of Sony and others) sitting on a futuristic transportation hub was a vision begun in 1991 when it was announced that Berlin would resume its position as capital of Germany. Sony, Daimler-Chrysler, and other huge corporations have turned it once again into a center of Berlin. Stroll the arcade (like any huge modern American mall) and find the Sony Center Platz under the towering tent roof. The "Sony Music Box" is a huge interactive center for music fun.

Sights—Kulturforum, in Central Berlin

Just off Potsdamer Platz, with several top museums and Berlin's concert hall, is the city's cultural heart (admission to all sights covered by 8-DM day card, free on first Sun of month, S- and U-Bahn: Potsdamer Platz). Of its sprawling museums, only the Gemäldegalerie is a must.

▲▲▲**Gemäldegalerie**—Germany's top collection of 13th-through 18th-century European paintings (over a thousand canvases) is beautifully displayed in a building which is a work of art in itself. The central hall is part medieval (like three parallel naves) and part Renaissance (pillars converge as they move toward the back wall, giving the place the illusion of greater depth—a trick popular with the Renaissance artists). Follow the excellent and free audioguide. The North Wing starts with German paintings of the 13th to 16th centuries—including eight by Dürer. Then come the Dutch and Flemish—Jan van Eyck, Brueghel, Rubens, Van Dyck, Hals, and Vermeer. The wing finishes with German, English, and French 18th-century art—Gainsborough and Watteau. An octagonal hall at the end features one of the best collections of Rembrandts anywhere. The South Wing is saved for the Italians—Giotto, Botticelli, Titian, Raphael, and Caravaggio (8 DM, covered by Museumspass, Tue–Sun 10:00–18:00, closed Mon, S- and U-Bahn: Potsdamer Platz, or bus #200 to Philharmonie).

New National Gallery (Neue Nationalgalerie)—This features 20th-century art (8 DM, covered by Museumspass, Tue–Fri 10:00–18:00, Sat–Sun 11:00–18:00, closed Mon, Potsdamer Strasse 50, tel. 030/266-2662).

Museum of Arts and Crafts (Kunstgewerbemuseum)—This shows off a thousand years of applied arts—porcelain, fine Jugendstil furniture, art deco, and reliquaries. There are no crowds and no English descriptions (4 DM, covered by Museumspass, Tue–Fri 10:00–18:00, Sat–Sun 11:00–18:00, closed Mon). The huge National Library is across the courtyard (free, English periodicals).

▲**Music Museum**—This impressive hall is filled with 600 exhibits from the 16th century to modern times. Wander among old keyboard instruments and funny-looking tubas. There's no English, but it's fascinating if you're into pianos (4 DM, Tue–Fri 9:00–17:00, Sat–Sun 10:00–17:00, closed Mon, facing the Philharmonic Concert Hall, circle around to left, tel. 030/254-810). Poke into the lobby of Berlin's Philharmonic Concert Hall and see if there are tickets available for your stay (must purchase tickets in person, box office tel. 030/2548-8132).

Sights—Eastern Berlin

▲▲**Pergamon Museum**—Of the museums on Museumsinsel (Museum Island), just off Unter den Linden, only the Pergamon Museum is essential. Its highlight is the fantastic Pergamon Altar. From a second-century B.C. Greek temple, it shows the Greeks under Zeus and Athena beating the giants in a dramatic pig pile of mythological mayhem. Check out the action spilling onto the stairs. The Babylonian Ishtar Gate (glazed blue tiles from sixth century B.C.) and many ancient Greek and Mesopotamian treasures are also impressive (8 DM, covered by Museumspass, free

Eastern Berlin

on first Sun of month, Tue–Sun 10:00–18:00, Thu until 22:00, closed Mon, café, tel. 030/2090-5555). The excellent audioguide (free with admission) cover the museum's highlights.

Old National Gallery—Also on the museum island, this gallery shows German paintings of the 19th century (closed for renovation until Dec 2001).

▲▲**The Berlin Wall**—The 100-mile "Anti-Fascist Protective Rampart," as it was called by the East German government, was erected almost overnight in 1961 to stop the outward flow of people (3 million leaked out between 1949 and 1961). It was 13 feet high with a 16-foot tank ditch, 30 to 160 feet of no-man's-land, and 300 sentry towers. In its 28 years there were 1,693 cases when border guards fired, more than 250 deaths, 3,221 arrests, and 5,043 documented successful escapes (565 of these were East German guards). The carnival atmosphere of those first years after the Wall fell has faded away, but hawkers still sell "authentic" pieces of the Wall, DDR (East German) flags, and military paraphernalia to gawking tourists.

▲▲▲**Haus am Checkpoint Charlie Museum**—While the famous border checkpoint between the American and Soviet sectors is long gone, its memory is preserved by one of Europe's most interesting museums: The House at Checkpoint Charlie. During the Cold War it stood defiantly—spitting distance from the border guards—showing off all the clever escapes over, under, and through the Wall.

Today, while the drama is over and hunks of the Wall stand like victory scalps at its door, the museum still tells a gripping history of the Wall, recounts the many ingenious escape attempts, and includes plenty of video and film coverage of those heady days when people-power tore down the Wall (10 DM, daily 9:00–22:00, U-Bahn to Kochstrasse, Friedrichstrasse 44, tel. 030/253-7250). If you're pressed for time, this is a good after-dinner sight.

Americans and Russians, the major forces behind the Cold War, have the biggest appetite for Wall-related sights. Where the gate once stood, notice the thought-provoking post with a young American soldier facing east and a young Russian soldier facing west. What do their young faces tell us? A few meters away (on Zimmerstrasse) a glass panel describes the former Checkpoint. From there a double row of cobbles in Zimmerstrasse marks where the Wall once stood. Follow it down Zimmerstrasse to a surviving stretch of Wall.

When it fell, the Wall was literally carried away by the euphoria. What survived has been nearly devoured by a decade of persistent "wall peckers." The park behind the Zimmerstrasse Wall marks the site of the command center of Hitler's Gestapo and SS (explained by English plaques throughout). It's been left undeveloped as a memorial to the tyranny once headquartered here. In the park is...

The Topography of Terror—Now temporarily housed in the excavated foundations of the Gestapo and SS buildings, this exhibit tells the story of National Socialism and its victims in Berlin (free, info booth open daily 10:00–18:00, English translation-2 DM, tel. 030/2548-6703).

East Side Gallery—The biggest remaining stretch of the Wall is now "the world's longest art gallery." It stretches for a mile and is covered with murals painted by artists from around the world. The murals are routinely whitewashed so new ones can be painted. This length of the Wall makes a poignant walk. From Schlesisches Tor (end of Kreuzberg), walk across the river on the bridge, turn left, and follow the Wall to the Ostbahnhof. For a quick look, just go to Ostbahnhof station and look around. The gallery only survives until a land ownership dispute can be solved when it will likely be developed like the rest of the city. (Given the recent history, imagine the complexity of finding rightful owners of all this suddenly very valuable land.)

Kreuzberg—This district—once butted against the dreary Wall and inhabited largely by poor Turkish guest laborers and their families—is still run-down, with graffiti-riddled buildings and plenty of student and Turkish street life. It offers a great look at melting-pot Berlin in a city where original Berliners are as rare as old buildings. Berlin is the fourth-largest Turkish city in the world, and Kreuzberg is its "downtown." But to call it a "little Istanbul" insults the big one. You'll see mothers wearing scarves, *döner kebab* stands, and spray paint–decorated shops. For a dose of Kreuzberg without getting your fingers dirty, joyride on bus #129. For a colorful stroll, take U-bahn to Kottbusser Tor and wander— ideally on Tuesday and Friday from 12:00 to 18:00, when the Turkish Market sprawls along the bank of the Maybachufer Canal.

▲▲**German Cathedral**—The Deutscher Dom houses the great and thought-provoking "Questions on German History" exhibit, a wonderful coverage of the story of German nationalism from medieval times to unification. It's impressive how openly and hon- estly Germany is dealing with its fascist past. There are no English descriptions, but you can follow a fine and free hour-long audio- guide or buy the excellent 10-DM book (free, Tue–Sun 10:00– 18:00, summer until 19:00, closed Mon, on Gendarmenmarkt just off Friedrichstrasse, tel. 030/2273-2141).

▲▲**New Synagogue**—A shiny gilded dome marks the New Synagogue, now a museum and cultural center on Oranienburger Strasse. Only the dome and facade have been restored, and a window overlooks a vacant field marking what used to be the synagogue. The largest and finest synagogue in Berlin before World War II, it was desecrated by Nazis on "Crystal Night" in 1938, bombed in 1943, and partially rebuilt in 1990. Inside, past tight security, there's a small but moving exhibit on the Berlin Jewish community through the centuries with some good English descriptions (ground floor and first floor). The *"Vergesst es nie"* message on its facade means "Never forget." It was put up by East Berlin Jews in 1966. East Berlin had only a few hundred Jews, but now that the city is united, the Jewish community numbers about 10,000 (8 DM, Sun–Thu 10:00–18:00, Fri 10:00–14:00, closed Sat, at Oranienburger Tor U-Bahn stop). Oren, a popular near- kosher café, is next to the synagogue (see "Eating," below). Note: If you're heading for the Pergamon Museum, take the shortcut (leaving synagogue, turn left, then right on Monbijoustrasse, cross canal, and turn left to museum).

A block from the Synagogue, go 50 meters down Grosse Hamburger Strasse to a little park. This street was known for 200 years as the "street of tolerance" for its many religions. Hitler turned it into the street of death (*"Todes Strasse"*), bulldozing 12,000 graves of the city's oldest Jewish cemetery and turning a Jewish old-folks home into a deportation center. Note the two memorials—one erected by the former East Berlin government and one built later by the city's unified government. Somewhere nearby, a plainclothes police officer keeps watch on this park.

▲**Oranienburger Strasse**—Berlin is developing so fast it's impossible to predict what will be "in" next year. The area around Oranienburger Strasse is definitely trendy (but is being challenged by hip Friedrichshain farther east).

While the area immediately around the Synagogue is dull, 100 meters away things get colorful. The streets behind Grosse Hamburger Strasse flicker with atmospheric cafés, *Kneipen* (pubs), and art galleries.

At night "techno-prostitutes" line Oranienburger Strasse. Prostitution is legal here, but there's a big debate about taxation. Since they don't get unemployment insurance, why should they pay taxes?

A block in front of the Hackescher Markt S-Bahn station is Hackesche Höfe—with eight courtyards bunny-hopping through a wonderfully restored 1907 Jugendstil building. It's full of trendy restaurants, theaters, and cinema (playing movies in their original languages). This is a fine example of how to make huge city blocks livable—Berlin's apartments are organized around courtyard after courtyard off the main roads.

Jewish Museum Berlin—Berlin's new Jewish museum opens in October 2001. The striking zinc-walled building (built 1993–1998) is already drawing crowds. Designed by the American architect Daniel Libeskind, the building's zigzag shape is pierced by voids symbolic of the irreplaceable cultural loss caused by the Holocaust. While it promises to be a great museum, it's in a nondescript neighborhood a 10-minute walk from the Checkpoint Charlie museum. Unless you're an architect, see the wonderful exhibits at the New Synagogue before trekking out here (Lindenstrasse 9).

Karl Marx Allee—The buildings along Karl Marx Allee in east Berlin (just beyond Alexanderplatz) were completely leveled by the Soviets in 1945. When Stalin decided this main drag should be a showcase street, he had it rebuilt with lavish Soviet aid and named Stalin Allee. Today, this street, done in the bold Stalin Gothic style so common in Moscow back in the 1950s, has been restored (and named after Karl Marx), providing a rare look at Berlin's communist days. Cruise down Karl Marx Allee by taxi or ride the U-bahn to Strausberger Platz and walk to Schillingstrasse. You might cap the experience with a stop at the ice cream shop across the street from the Moskwa restaurant—it was an institution in communist times.

Natural History Museum (Museum für Naturkunde)—This

place is worth a visit just to see the largest dinosaur skeleton ever assembled. While you're there, meet "Bobby," the stuffed ape (5 DM, Tue–Sun 9:30–17:00, closed Mon, U-6 to Zinnowitzer Strasse, at Invalidenstrasse 43).

Sights—Around Charlottenburg Palace

The Charlottenburg District—with a cluster of fine museums across the street from a grand palace—makes a good side trip from downtown. Ride U-1 to Sophie-Charlotte Platz and walk 10 minutes up the tree-lined boulevard (following signs to "Schloss"), or—much faster—catch bus #145 direct from Bahnhof Zoo. For a Charlottenburg lunch, the Luisen Brau is a comfortable brew-pub restaurant with a copper and woody atmosphere, good local "microbeers" (*dunkles*—dark, *helles*—light), and traditional German grub (10-DM meals, fun for groups, daily 9:00–24:00, across from palace at Luisenplatz 1, tel. 030/341-9388).

▲**Charlottenburg Palace (Schloss)**—If you've seen the great palaces of Europe, this Baroque Hohenzollern palace comes in at about number 10 (behind Potsdam, too). It's even more disappointing since the main rooms can be toured only with a German guide (8 DM, 45-minute tour, Tue–Fri 10:00–18:00, Sat–Sun 11:00–18:00, closed Mon, tel. 030/3209-1275).

The **Knöbelsdorff Wing** of the palace is used for two painting galleries. Facing the palace, walk to the right wing where one desk sells tickets to two galleries. For a quick look at a few royal apartments, go upstairs (5 DM) and take a substantial hike through restored-since-the-war, gold-crusted, white rooms filled with Frederick the Great's not-so-great collection of Baroque paintings. The ground floor of the Knöbelsdorff wing is the **Galerie der Romantik**, a delightful collection of 19th-century German Romantic art: man against nature, Greek ruins dwarfed in enchanted forests, medieval churches, and powerful mountains (5 DM, covered by Museumspass).

▲▲**Egyptian Museum**—Across the street from the palace, the Egyptian Museum offers one of the great thrills in art appreciation—gazing into the still-young and beautiful face of 3,000-year-old Queen Nefertiti, the wife of King Akhenaton (8 DM, covered by Museumspass, Tue–Sun 10:00–18:00, closed Mon, Schlosstrasse 70).

This bust of Queen Nefertiti, from 1340 B.C., is perhaps the most famous piece of Egyptian art in Europe. Discovered in 1912, she was the Marilyn Monroe of the early 20th century, with all the right beauty marks: long neck, symmetrical face, and just the right makeup. The bust never left its studio but served as a master model for all other portraits of the queen. (That's probably why the left eye was never inlaid.) Buried over 3,000 years, she was found by a German team who, by agreement with the Egyptian government, got to take home any workshop models they found.

Charlottenburg Palace Area

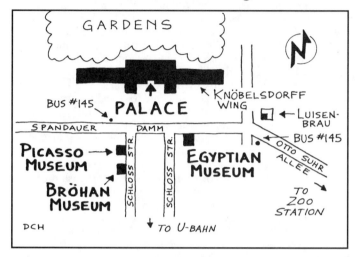

Although this bust is not representative of Egyptian art, it's
become a symbol for Egyptian art by popular acclaim. Don't
overlook the rest of the impressive museum: wonderfully lit and
displayed but with little English.

▲▲**Berggruen Collection: Picasso and His Time**—This tidy
little museum is a pleasant surprise. Climb three floors through a
fun and substantial collection of Picasso. Along the way you'll see
plenty of notable work by Matisse, van Gogh, and Cézanne, and
enjoy a great chance to meet Paul Klee (8 DM, covered by Museumspass, Tue–Fri 10:00–18:00, Sat–Sun 11:00–18:00, closed Mon,
tel. 030/2090-5566).

▲**Bröhan Museum**—Wander through a dozen beautifully
furnished Art Nouveau (Jugendstil) and art deco living rooms,
a curvy organic world of lamps, glass, silver, and posters. While
you're there, go to the second floor to see a fine collection of
Impressionist paintings by Karl Hagemeister (6 DM, free first
Sun of month, Tue–Sun 10:00–18:00, closed Mon, next to Egyptian Museum, across street from Charlottenburg Palace).

Sights—Near Berlin
▲**Sanssouci Palace and Park, Potsdam**—With a lush park
strewn with the extravagant whimsies of Frederick the Great,
the sleepy town of Potsdam has long been Berlin's holiday retreat.
Frederick's super-rococo Sanssouci Palace is one of Germany's
most dazzling. His equally extravagant New Palace (Neues Palais),
built to disprove rumors that Prussia was running out of money

after the costly Seven Years' War, is on the other side of the park. While Potsdam is easy to reach (30 min direct on S-Bahn from Bahnhof Zoo to Potsdam Stadt), Sanssouci Palace can be visited only by German-language tour—which can be booked for hours (unless you take TI tour; see below). The palaces of Vienna, Munich, and even Würzburg offer equal sightseeing thrills with fewer headaches. Even though *Sanssouci* means "without a care," get your appointment immediately upon arrival so you know how much time to kill or if you need to come back and try again tomorrow (Sanssouci: 10 DM, Tue–Sun 9:00–12:30, 13:00–17:00, closed Mon, shorter hours off-season, tel. 0331/969-4190; New Palace: 8 DM, Sat–Thu 9:00–12:30, 13:00–17:00, closed Fri). Sanssouci Palace and the New Palace are a 30-minute walk apart.

Potsdam's TI offers a handy walking tour that includes Sanssouci Palace (39 DM covers guided German/English tour of palace park and admission and tour of Sanssouci without any wait, 11:00 except Mon, 5-minute walk from S-Bahn stop, depart from Film Museum in downtown Potsdam, 3.5 hrs, book by phone, tel. 0331/291-100). Otherwise, upon arrival, catch bus #695 from S-Bahn to the palace. Use the same bus (3/hrly) to shuttle between the sights in the park. Potsdam's much-promoted Wannsee boat rides are torturously dull.

An interesting "Discover Potsdam" walking tour, offered by "The Original Berlin Walks" and led by a well-qualified English-speaking guide, leaves from Berlin Tuesday, Thursday, and Satur-day (28 DM, or 21 DM if under age 26, meet at 9:00 at taxi stand at Zoo Station, public transportation not included but can buy ticket from guide, no booking necessary, tel. 030/301-9194). This tour takes you to Cecilienhof Palace (site of post-war Potsdam conference attended by Churchill, Stalin, and Truman), through pleasant green landscapes to the historic heart of Potsdam for lunch, and to Sanssouci Park (palace not included).

Other Day Trips—EurAide has researched and printed a "Get Me Outta Here" flier describing good day trips to small towns and another on the nearby Sachsenhausen Concentration Camp.

Nightlife in Berlin

"What's On in Berlin" is a small, free English entertainment listing available at EurAide. For the young and determined sophisticate, *Zitty* and *Tip* are the top guides to alternative culture (German, sold at kiosks). The TI's *Berlin Programm* lists the nonstop parade of concerts, plays, exhibits, and cultural events (www.berlin.de).

Tourists stroll the Ku'damm after dark. Oranienburger Strasse's trendy scene (described above) is already being eclipsed by the action at Friedrichshain and Kollwitzplatz farther east.

Visit KaDeWe's ticket office for your music and theater

Greater Berlin

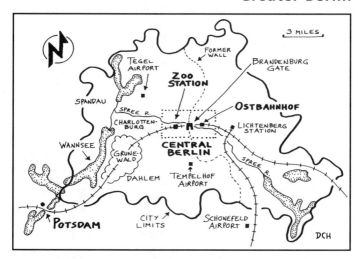

options (sixth floor, 18 percent fee but access to all tickets). Ask about "competitive improvisation" and variety shows.

For jazz (blues and boogie, too) near recommended Savigny-platz hotels, consider **A Trane Jazz Club** (Bleibtreustrasse 1, tel. 030/313-4629) and **Quasimodo Live** (Kantstrasse 12a, under Delphi Cinema, tel. 030/312-8086). For quality blues and New Orleans–style jazz, stop by **Ewige Lampe** (from 21:00, Niebuhr-strasse 11a, tel. 030/324-3918).

Sleeping in Berlin
(2 DM = about $1, country code: 49, area code: 030)
Sleep Code: **S** = Single, **D** = Double/Twin, **T** = Triple, **Q** = Quad, **b** = bathroom, **t** = toilet only, **s** = shower only, **CC** = Credit Card (**V**isa, **M**asterCard, **A**mex), **SE** = Speaks English, **NSE** = No English. Unless otherwise noted, a buffet breakfast is included.

I've concentrated my hotel recommendations around Savigny-platz. While the Bahnhof Zoo and Ku'damm are no longer the center of Berlin, trains, TI, and walking tours are all still handy to Zoo. And the streets around the tree-lined Savignyplatz (a five-minute walk behind the station) have a neighborhood charm. While towering new hotels are being built in the new center, simple, small, and friendly good value places abound only here. My listings are generally located a couple of flights up in big, run-down buildings. Inside they are clean, quiet, and spacious enough so that their well-worn character is actually charming. Rooms in back are on quiet courtyards.

The city is packed and hotel prices go up on holidays, including Green Week in mid-January, Easter weekend, first weekend in May, Ascension weekend in May, the Love Parade (a huge techno-Woodstock, second weekend in July), Germany's national holiday (Oct 2–4), Christmas, and New Year's.

During slow times, the best values are actually business-class rooms on the push list booked through the TI. But as the world learns what a great place Berlin is to visit, a rising tide of tourists will cause these deals to fade away.

Sleeping near Zoo Station at Savignyplatz
(zip code: 10623, unless otherwise noted)

These hotels and pensions are a 5- to 15-minute walk from Bahnhof Zoo (or take S-Bahn to Savignyplatz). Hotels on Kantstrasse have street noise. Ask for a quieter room in back. The area has an artsy charm going back to the cabaret days in the 1920s, when it was the center of Berlin's gay scene. Wasch Salon is a handy **Laundromat** (daily 6:00–22:00, 8–16 DM wash and dry, Leibnizstrasse 72, near intersection with Kantstrasse).

Business-Class Splurges near Zoo

Hotel Astoria is a friendly, three-star, business-class hotel with 32 comfortably furnished rooms and affordable summer and weekend rates (high season Db-289 DM, prices drop to Sb-186 DM, Db-220 DM during low season of July–Aug, Nov–Feb, or any 2 weekend nights or if slow; rooms with showers are cheaper than rooms with baths, CC:VMA, around corner from Bahnhof Zoo at Fasanenstrasse 2, tel. 030/312-4067, fax 030/312-5027, www.home.t-online.de/home/astoriahotel, e-mail: astoriahotel@t-online.de).

Heckers Hotel is an ultramodern, three-star business hotel with all the sterile Euro-comforts (Sb-260 DM, Db-310 DM, breakfast-25 DM, summer and weekends breakfast included, CC:VMA, smoke-free rooms, between Savignyplatz and Ku'damm at Grolmanstrasse 35, tel. 030/88900, fax 030/889-0260, www.heckers-hotel.com).

Hotel Askanisherhof is the oldest *Zimmer* in Berlin. Posh as can be, you get porters, valet parking, and 16 sprawling antique-furnished rooms. Photos on the walls brag of famous movie-star guests. Frau Glinicke offers Old World service and classic Berlin atmosphere (Sb-195 DM, Db-250 DM, CC:VMA, no-smoking rooms, elevator, Kurfurstendamm 33, tel. 030/881-8033, fax 030/881-7206).

Inexpensive Pensions near Savignyplatz

These hotels are clean but well worn, unless otherwise stated.
Pension Peters, run by a German-Swedish couple, is sunny

Berlin's Savignyplatz Neighborhood

❶ PENSION PETERS	❽ HOTEL ASTORIA	⓮ HOTEL BOGOTA
❷ HOTEL CRYSTAL GARNI	❾ PENSION SAVOY	⓯ HOTEL PENSION FUNK
❸ PENSION ALEXIS	❿ HOTEL ATLANTA	⓰ DICKE WIRTIN
❹ HOTEL CARMER 16	⓫ HECKERS HOTEL	⓱ ZILLEMARKT RESTAURANT
❺ JUGENDGASTEHAUS AM ZOO	⓬ HOTEL ASKANISHERHOF	⓲ SCHELL RESTAURANT
❻ PENSION KNESEBECK	⓭ HOTELS AUSTRIANA, RÜGEN,	⓳ KÄTHE KOLLEWITZ MUSEUM
❼ PENSION SILVA	CURTIS, HOTEL-PENSION BELLA,	⓴ TAXI STAND
	WEYERS CAFE RESTAURANT	

and central with a cheery breakfast room. Decorated sleek Scandinavian, with every room renovated, it's a winner (S-60–80 DM, Ss-90–100 DM, D-100–110 DM, Ds-120–130 DM, Db-130–150 DM, extra bed-15 DM, kids under 12 free, family room, CC:VMA, 10 meters off Savignyplatz at Kantstrasse 146, tel. 030/3150-3944, fax 030/312-3519, e-mail: penspeters@aol.com, Annika and Christoph SE). They also rent apartments (ideal for small groups and longer stays) and bikes (10 DM/day).

Hotel Crystal Garni is professional, with small, well-worn but comfortable rooms and a *vollkorn* breakfast room (S-70 DM, Sb-80 DM, D-90 DM, Ds-110 DM, Db-130–150 DM, CC:VMA, elevator, a block past Savignyplatz at Kantstrasse 144, tel. 030/312-9047, fax 030/312-6465, run by John and Dorothy Schwarz-rock and Herr Glasgow Flasher).

Pension Alexis is a classic old-European four-room pension in a stately 19th-century apartment run by Frau and Herr

Schwarzer. This, more than any other Berlin listing, has you feeling at home with a faraway aunt (S-75 DM, D-110 DM, T-155 DM, Q-220 DM, big rooms, Carmerstrasse 15, tel. 030/312-5144, enough English spoken).

Hotel Carmer 16, with 40 bright, airy rooms, feels like a big professional hotel (S-90–110 DM, Sb-130–140 DM, D-130 DM, Db-180–200 DM, CC:VMA, smoke-free rooms, Carmerstrasse 16, tel. 030/3110-0500, fax 030/3110-0510, e-mail: carmer16@t-online.de).

Pension Knesebeck rents nine comfy—if cheaply furnished—rooms just off Savignyplatz (S-65–75 DM, Ss-85 DM, D-120 DM, Ds-130–140 DM, Ts-180 DM, Qs-200 DM, laundry-8 DM/load, Knesebeckstrasse 86, tel. 030/312-7255, fax 030/313-9507, Brigitta SE).

Pension Silva is another basic place just off Savignyplatz with 15 spacious well-furnished rooms (S-55 DM, Sb-90 DM, Db-100 DM, Tb-150 DM, 10 DM less without breakfast, CC:VM, Knesebeckstrasse 29, tel. 030/881-2129, fax 030/885-0435).

Pension Savoy rents 16 rooms with all the amenities. You'll love the cheery old pastel breakfast room (S-120 DM, Ss-140 DM, Db-195 DM, CC:VM, Meinekestrasse 4, 10719 Berlin, elevator, tel. 030/881-3700, fax 030/882-3746).

Hotel Atlanta is in an older building half a block south of Ku'damm. It's next to Gucci, on an elegant shopping street, with big leather couches (Sb-130–165 DM, Db-160–195 DM, extra person-10 DM, family friendly, smoke-free rooms, CC:VMA, Fasanenstrasse 74, 10719 Berlin, tel. 030/881-8049, fax 030/881-9872, e-mail: hatlanta68266759@aol.com).

Hotel Bogota has 125 big and comfortable rooms in a sprawling, well-worn old building. The service is brisk and hotel-esque (S-78 DM, Ss-100 DM, Sb-130 DM, D-125 DM, Ds-145 DM, Db-170–190 DM, extra person-45 DM, children under 15 free, elevator, CC:VMA, smoke-free rooms, bus #109 from Bahnhof Zoo to Schlüterstrasse 45, tel. 030/881-5001, fax 030/883-5887, e-mail: hotel.bogota@t-online.de).

Hotel-Pension Funk is the former home of a 1920s silent-movie star. It offers 14 elegant, richly furnished old rooms (S-70 DM, Ss-100 DM, Sb-120 DM, D-120 DM, Ds-140 DM, Db-160 DM, extra person-45 DM, CC:VMA but prefer cash, Fasanenstrasse 69, a long block south of Ku'damm, tel. 030/882-7193, fax 030/883-3329).

Hotel Pension Eden am Zoo is another nondescript place with well-worn rooms in a big, old, well-located building (25 rooms, D-100 DM, Ds-120 DM, Db-150 DM, Uhlandstrasse 184, tel. 030/881-5900, www.rheingold-hotel.de).

Jugendgastehaus am Zoo is a bare-bones, cash-only youth hostel that takes no reservations and hardly has a reception desk.

It's far less comfortable and only marginally cheaper than simple hotels (85 beds, 40 DM dorms, S-52 DM, D-90 DM, with sheets, without breakfast, Hardenbergstrasse 9a, tel. 030/312-9410).

Sleeping South of Ku'damm
(zip code: 10707)
Several small hotels are nearby in a charming, café-studded neighborhood 300 meters south of Ku'damm near the intersection of Sächsische Strasse and Pariser Strasse (bus #109 from Bahnhof Zoo). They are less convenient from the station than the Savigny-platz listings above.

Hotel Austriana, with 25 modern and bright rooms, is warmly and energetically run by Thomas (S-65 DM, Ss-85 DM, Sb-100 DM, Ds-120 DM, Db-150 DM, cheaper off-season, CC:VMA, Pariser Strasse 39, tel. 030/885-7000, fax 030/8857-0088, e-mail: Austriana@t-online.de). Two other pensions are in the same building: the ornate and eastern-feeling **Hotel Rügen** (Ds-130 DM, CC:VM, Pariser Strasse 39, tel. 030/884-3940, fax 030/884-39-437); and hip, piney, and basic **Pension Curtis** (S-70 DM, Ds-110–130 DM, cheaper for slow-time drop-ins, Pariser Strasse 39, tel. 030/883-4931, fax 030/885-0438).

Hotel-Pension Bella, a clean, simple, masculine-feeling place with high ceilings and an cheery, attentive management, rents nine big, comfortable rooms (S-80 DM, D-110 DM, Ds-140–150 DM, Ts-170 DM, Qs-200 DM, CC:VM, bus #249 from Zoo, Ludwigkirchstrasse 10a, tel. 030/881-6704, fax 030/8867-9074, e-mail: pension.bella@t-online.de).

More Berlin Hotels
Near Augsburgerstrasse U-Bahn stop: Consider **Hotel-Pension Nürnberger Eck** (D-130 DM, Db-150 DM, Nürnberger Strasse 24a, tel. 030/235-1780, fax 030/2351-7899) or, just upstairs, **Pension Fischer** (D-70 DM, Ds-90–130 DM, breakfast-10 DM, Nürnberger Strasse 24a, tel. 030/218-6808, fax 030/213-4225), or **Hotel Arco** (S-110–140 DM, Db-140–175 DM, Geisbergerstrasse 30, tel. 030/235-1480, fax 030/2147-5178, www.arco-hotel.de).

Near Güntzelstrasse U-Bahn stop: The **Hotel Pension München** (D-80 DM, Db-115–130 DM, breakfast-9 DM, Güntzelstrasse 62, tel. 030/857-9120, fax 030/8579-1222), **Pension Güntzel** (Ds-100–140 DM, also Guntzelstrasse 62, tel. 030/857-9020, fax 030/853-1108), or **Pension Finck** (Ds-110 DM, Güntzelstrasse 54, tel. 030/861-2940).

In eastern Berlin: The **Hotel Unter den Linden** is ideal for those nostalgic for the days of Soviet rule, although nowadays at least, the management tries to be efficient and helpful. Formerly one of the best hotels in the DDR, this huge blocky hotel, right on Unter den Linden in the heart of what was East Berlin, is reasonably comfortable and reasonably priced. Built in 1966 with prisonlike corridors, its 331 rooms are modern, plain, and comfy (Sb-110–220 DM, standard Db-160–230 DM, superior Db-180–290 DM, only a tiny difference between standard and superior, some nonsmoking rooms, CC:VMA, at intersection of Friedrichstrasse, Unter den Linden 14, 10117 Berlin, tel. 030/238-1100, fax 030/2381-1100).

Studenten Hotel Berlin is open to all and has no curfew (D-84 DM, 40-DM-per-bed quads with sheets and breakfast, near city hall on JFK Platz, Meiningerstrasse 10, U-Bahn: Rathaus Schoneberg, tel. 030/784-6720, fax 030/788-1523).

Eating in Berlin

Don't be too determined to eat "Berlin style." The city is known only for its mildly spicy sausage, curry wurst. Still there is a world of restaurants in this ever-changing city to choose from. Your best approach may be to choose a neighborhood rather than a particular restaurant.

For quick and easy meals, colorful pubs—called *Kneipen*—offer light meals and the fizzy local beer, Berliner Weiss. Ask for it *mit Schuss* for a shot of fruity syrup in your suds. If the kraut is getting wurst, try one of the many Turkish, Italian, or Balkan restaurants. Eat cheap at *Imbiss* snack stands, bakeries (sandwiches), and falafel/kebab places. Bahnhof Zoo has several bright and modern fruit-and-sandwich bars and a grocery (daily 6:00–24:00).

Self-Service Cafeterias near Bahnhof Zoo

The top floor of the famous department store, **KaDeWe**, holds the Winter Garden Buffet view cafeteria, and its sixth-floor deli/food department is a picnicker's nirvana. Its arterials are clogged with more than 1,000 kinds of sausage and 1,500 types of cheese (hours similar to Wertheim's, below). The **Wertheim** department store, a half block from the Memorial Church, has cheap food counters in the basement and a city view from its fine self-service cafeteria, Le Buffet, located up six banks of escalators (Mon–Fri 9:30–20:00, Sat 9:00–16:00, closed Sun, U-Bahn: Ku'damm). The **Marche**, popping up in big cities all over Germany, is another decent self-service cafeteria within a half block of the church (daily 8:00–24:00, CC:VMA, Ku'damm 14, enter on ground floor of mall).

Eating near Savignyplatz

Several good places are within 100 meters of Savignyplatz:

Dicke Wirtin is a smoky old pub with good *Kneipe* atmosphere and famous *Gulaschsuppe* for 6 DM (daily from noon until

late, just off Savignyplatz at Carmerstrasse 9). **Die Zwölf Apostel**
restaurant is trendy for leafy candlelit ambience and Italian food.
A dressy local crowd packs the place for 20-DM pizzas and
30-DM meals. Late-night party goers appreciate Apostel's great
breakfast (daily 24 hrs, immediately across from Savigny S-Bahn
entrance, Bleibtreustrasse 49, tel. 030/312-1433). **Ristorante San
Marino** is another good Italian place, this one on the square and
serving cheaper pasta and pizza (Savignyplatz 12, tel. 030/313-
6086). **Zillemarkt Restaurant** feels like an old-time Berlin beer
garden. It offers seating in the garden or in the rustic candlelit
interior and serves traditional Berlin specialties (20-DM meals,
daily until late, no English menu—that's good—a block from
Savigny S-Bahn station, under the tracks at Bleibtreustrasse 48a,
tel. 030/881-7040).

   Schell Restaurant is a dressy place (named for a gas station
that once stood there) serving high Italian cuisine to a completely
German crowd that seems in-the-know (40-DM dinner plates,
daily, a block off Savignyplatz at Knesebackstrasse 22, tel. 030/
312-8310). **Bistrot Hegel** is a mellow little Russian piano bar
with light meals right on Savignyplatz. Late at night there may
be some balalaika music (open from 18:00 on, Savignyplatz 2,
tel. 030/312-1948).

   Weyers Cafe Restaurant, serving quality international/
German cuisine, is a great value and worth a short walk. It's trendy
with white tablecloths but not stuffy (20-DM dinner plates, daily,
seating indoors or outside on the leafy square, Pariser Strasse 16,
reservations smart after 20:00, tel. 030/881-9378).

   Ullrich Supermarkt is the neighborhood grocery store
(Mon–Sat 9:00–20:00, Sun 9:00–16:00, Kantstrasse 7, under
the tracks near Bahnhof Zoo). There's plenty of fast food near
Bahnhof Zoo and on Ku'damm.

Eating along Unter den Linden
near Pergamon Museum

The Opernpalais, preening with fancy pre-war elegance, hosts a
number of pricey restaurants. Its **Operncafé** has the best desserts
(longest dessert bar in Europe, across from university and war
memorial at Unter den Linden 5). The shady beer/tea garden in
front has a cheap self-service *Imbiss* (wurst, meatball sandwiches,
and so on) and a *creperie*. More students and fewer tourists eat in
the café at Humboldt University across the street (off courtyard,
enter building, café on right).

   Oren Restaurant/Café is a trendy, stylish, near-kosher/
vegetarian place next to the New Synagogue. The food is pricey
but good, and the ambience is happening (daily 12:00–24:00,
north of Museum Island about 5 blocks away at Oranienburger
Strasse 28, tel. 030/282-8228).

Transportation Connections—Berlin

Berlin has three train stations. Bahnhof Zoo was the West Berlin train station and still serves Western Europe: Frankfurt, Munich, Hamburg, Paris, and Amsterdam. The Ostbahnhof (former East Berlin's main station) still faces east, serving Prague, Warsaw, Vienna, and Dresden. The Lichtenberg Bahnhof (eastern Berlin's top U- and S-Bahn hub) also handles a few eastbound trains. Expect exceptions. All stations are conveniently connected by subway and even faster, by train. Train info: tel. 0180/599-6633.

By train to: Frankfurt (14/day, 5 hrs), **Munich** (8/day, 7 hrs, 10 hrs overnight), **Köln** (hrly, 6.5 hrs), **Amsterdam** (4/day, 7 hrs), **Budapest** (3/day, 13 hrs), **Copenhagen** (4/day, 8 hrs), **London** (4/day, 15 hrs), **Paris** (6/day, 13 hrs), **Zurich** (12/day, 10 hrs), **Prague** (8/day, 4.5 hrs), **Warsaw** (4/day, 8 hrs), **Vienna** (2/day, 12 hrs via Czech Republic; for second-class ticket, Eurailers pay an extra 45 DM if under age 26 or 60 DM if age 26 or above; otherwise, take the Berlin-Vienna via Passau train—nightly at 20:00), **Prague** (5/day, 6 hrs, no overnight); Eurailpasses don't cover the Czech Republic. The Prague Excursion pass picks up where Eurail leaves off, getting you from any border into Prague and then back out to Eurail country again within seven days (60 DM-second class, 90 DM-first class, buy at EurAide in Berlin and get reservations—5 DM—at the same time).

Berlin is connected by overnight trains from Bonn, Köln, Frankfurt, Munich, and Vienna. A *Liegeplatz*, or berth (30–40 DM), is a great deal; inquire at EurAide at Bahnhof Zoo for details. Beds cost the same whether you have a first- or second-class ticket or railpass. Trains are rarely full, but get your bed reserved a few days in advance from any travel agency or major train station in Europe. Note: Since the Paris–Berlin night train goes through Belgium, Europass or Eurail Selectpass holders can't travel on it unless they've added or selected Belgium.

Berlin's Three Airports

Allow 25 DM for a taxi ride to or from any of Berlin's airports. **Tegel Airport** handles most flights from the United States and Western Europe (6 kilometers from center, catch the faster bus #X9 to Bahnhof Zoo or bus #109 to Ku'damm and Bahnhof Zoo for 3.90 DM). Flights from the east usually arrive at **Schönefeld Airport** (20 km from center, short walk to S-Bahn, catch S-9 to Zoo Station). **Templehof Airport**'s future is uncertain (in Berlin, bus #119 to Ku'damm or U-Bahn 6 or 7). The central telephone number for all three airports is 0180-500-0186. British Air (tel. 030/254-0000), Delta (tel. 0180-333-7880), SAS and Lufthansa (tel. 0180-6951-2841).

PRAGUE

It's amazing what 10 years of freedom can do. Prague has always been historic. Now it's fun, too. No place in Europe has become so popular so quickly. And for good reason: The capital of the Czech Republic—the only major city of central Europe to escape the bombs of the last century's wars—is Europe's best-preserved Baroque city. It's slinky with sumptuous Art Nouveau facades, it offers tons of cheap Mozart and Vivaldi, and it brews the best beer in Europe. But more than the architecture and traditional culture, it's an explosion of pent-up entrepreneurial energy jumping for joy after 50 years of Communist rule. And its low prices will make your visit enjoyable and nearly stressless.

For a relaxing pause between the urban bustle of Vienna and Prague, visit the Czech town of Český Krumlov, the perfect big-city antidote, peaceful and happily hemmed in by its lazy river.

Planning Your Time

Two days (with 3 nights, or 2 nights and a night train) makes the long train ride in and out worthwhile and gives you time to get beyond the sightseeing and enjoy Prague's fun-loving ambience. Many wish they'd scheduled three days for Prague. From Munich, Berlin, and Vienna, it's a six-hour train ride (during the day) or an overnight ride.

With two days in Prague, I'd spend a morning seeing the castle and a morning in the Jewish Quarter—the only two chunks of sightseeing that demand any brainpower. Spend your afternoons loitering around the Old Town, Charles Bridge, and the Little Quarter and your nights split between beer halls and live music. Keep in mind that state museums close on Monday, and Jewish sites close on Saturday.

Prague

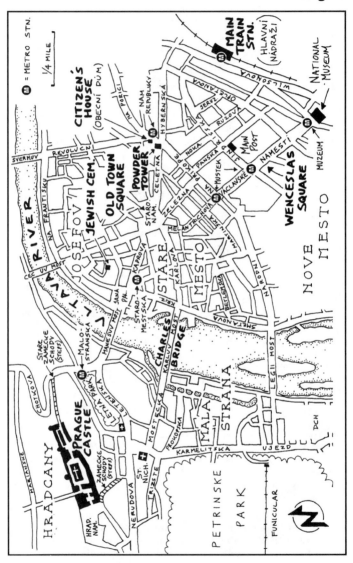

Český Krumlov, 2.5 hours from Prague by train, could be a day trip, but I'd spend the night (consider visiting Český on your way to or from Prague).

History

Medieval Prague: Prague's castle put it on the map in the ninth century. In the 10th century the region was incorporated into the German "Holy Roman" Empire. The 14th century was Prague's Golden Age, when Holy Roman Emperor Charles IV ruled from here, and Prague was one of Europe's largest and most highly cultured cities. During this period Prague built St. Vitus Cathedral and Charles Bridge and established the first university in central Europe.

Bucking the Pope and Germany: Jan Hus was a local preacher who got in trouble with the Vatican a hundred years before Martin Luther. Like Luther, he preached in the people's language rather than Latin. To add insult to injury, he complained about church corruption. Tried for heresy and burned in 1415, Hus roused nationalist (Bohemian) as well as religious feelings and became a symbol of Czech martyrdom. His followers are Hussites.

Religious Wars: The reformist times of Jan Hus (around 1400, when Czechs rebelled against both German and Roman Catholic control) led to a period of religious wars and ultimately subjugation under Austrian rule. Prague stagnated under the Hapsburgs of Austria with the brief exception of Rudolf II's reign.

Under the late 16th-century rule of the Hapsburg King Rudolf II, Prague emerged again as a cultural and intellectual center. Johannes Kepler, Tycho Brahe, and others worked here. Much of Prague's great art can be attributed to this Hapsburg king who lived not in Vienna but in Prague.

The Thirty Years' War (1618–1648) began in Prague when locals tossed two Catholic/Hapsburg officials (Czechs sympathetic to the Germans) out the window of the Prague Castle. Often called "the first world war" because it engulfed so many nations, these 30 years were particularly tough on Prague. During this period its population dropped from 60,000 to 25,000. The result of this war was 300 years of Hapsburg rule: German and Catholic culture, not Czech. Prague became a backwater of Vienna.

Czech Nationalist Revival: The 19th century was a time of nationalism for people throughout Europe, including the Czechs, as the age of divine kings and ruling families was coming to a fitful end. The arts (such as the paintings by Mucha and the building of the massive National Museum atop Wenceslas Square) stirred the national spirit. With the end of World War I, the Hapsburgs were history, and in 1918 the independent country of Czechoslovakia was proclaimed with Prague as its capital.

Troubled 20th Century: Independence lasted only until 1939 when the Nazis swept in. Prague escaped the bombs of World War II but went almost directly from the Nazi frying pan into the Communist fire. Almost. A local uprising freed the city from the Nazis on May 8, 1945. The Russians "liberated" them again on May 9.

The Communist chapter of Czech subjugation (1948–1989) was grim. The student- and artist-led "Prague Spring" revolt in 1968 was crushed. The charismatic leader Alexander Dubcek was exiled into a job in the backwoods, and the years after 1968 were particularly tough. But eventually the Soviet empire crumbled. Czechoslovakia regained its freedom in the 1989 "Velvet Revolution" (so called because there were no casualties). Until 1989, May 9 was the Czech day of liberation. Now Czechs celebrate their liberation on May 8. In 1993, the Czech and Slovak Republics agreed on the "Velvet Divorce" and became two separate countries.

Today, while not without its problems, the Czech Republic is enjoying a growing economy and a strong democracy. Prague has emerged as one of the most popular tourist destinations in Europe. It's a huge entrepreneurial spanking machine...and it's your turn.

Orientation (tel. code: 02)

Locals call their town "Praha." It's big, with 1.2 million people, but for a quick visit, focus on its small old-town core. I will refer to the tourist landmarks in English (with the Czech name in parentheses). Study the map and learn these key places:

Main Train Station:	*Hlavní Nádraží* (hlav-nee nah-dra-shzee)
Old Town:	*Staré Město* (sta-rey mnyess-toh)
Old Town Square:	*Staroměstské Náměstí* (starro-min-yes-ststi-keh nah-mnyess-tee)
New Town:	*Nové Město* (no-vay mnyess-toh)
Little Quarter:	*Malá Strana* (mah-lah strah-nah)
Jewish Quarter:	*Josefov* (yoo-zef-fohf)
Castle Area:	*Hradčany* (hrad-chah-nee)
Charles Bridge:	*Karluv Most* (kar-loov most)
Wenceslas Square:	*Václavske Náměstí* (vah-slawf-skeh nah-mnyess-tee)
The River:	*Vltava* (vul-tah-vah)

The Vltava River divides the west side (castle and Little Quarter) from the east side (train station, Old Town, New Town, and nearly all of the recommended hotels). Prague addresses come with a general zone. Praha 1 is in the old center on either side of the river. Praha 2 is in the new city south of Wenceslas Square. Praha 3 and higher indicates a location farther from the center.

Tourist Information

TIs are at four key locations: main train station, Old Town Square, below Wenceslas Square at Na Príkope 20, and the castle side of Charles Bridge (generally 9:00–18:00 or 19:00, tel. 02/2448-2202). They offer maps, information on guided walks and bus tours, and bookings for concerts, hotel rooms, and rooms in private homes. Get the brochure listing all of Prague's museums and hours.

Helpful Hints

Formalities: Travel in Prague is like travel in Western Europe—
15 years ago and for half the price. Americans and Canadians need
no visa. Just flash your passport at the border. The U.S. embassy
in Prague is near the Little Quarter Square, or Malostranske
Náměstí (Trziste 15, tel. 02/5753-0663). Since Eurailpasses don't
cover the Czech Republic, you'll need to buy train tickets or a
Prague Excursion pass for your travels to and from Prague (see
"Transportation Connections," below).

 Rip-offs: Prague's new freedom comes with new scams.
There's no particular risk of violent crime, just green, rich tourists
getting taken by con artists. Simply be on guard: on trains (thieves
on overnight trains and corrupt conductors intimidating Western
tourists for a bribe); changing money (tellers anywhere with bad
arithmetic and inexplicable pauses while counting back your
change); and dealing with taxis (see "Getting around Prague,"
below). In restaurants, understand the price clearly before order-
ing. Plainclothes policemen "looking for counterfeit money" are
con artists. Don't show them your cash.

 Telephoning: Czech phones work like any in Europe. For
international calls, buy a phone card at a kiosk or your hotel
(180 kč). It costs about $1 a minute to call the United States
directly (dial 001, the area code, and the number) from a public
phone booth that accepts the local phone card. To call Prague
from abroad, dial the international code (00 in Europe or 011 in
the U.S.), the Czech Republic code (420), then Prague's area code
(2), followed by the local number. Hotels often list phone numbers
with the country code (420), a number you don't need to dial
when inside the Czech Republic.

 Money: 38 koruna (kč) = about U.S. $1. There is no black mar-
ket. Assume anyone trying to sell money on the streets is peddling
obsolete currency. Buy and sell easily at the station (5 percent fees),
banks, or hotels. ATMs are everywhere. Czech money is tough to
change in the West. Before leaving the Czech Republic, change your
remaining koruna into your next country's currency (at Prague's
train station change bureaus or Český Krumlov's banks).

 American Express: Václavske Náměstí 56, Praha 1 (9:00–
19:00, closed Sun) or Mosteka 12, Praha 1 (open 9:30–19:30,
tel. 02/5731-3636).

 Internet Access: Internet cafés beg for business all along
Karlova street on the city side of the bridge.

 Local Help: Magic Praha is a tiny travel service run by
hardworking, English-speaking Lida Steflova. A charming jack-of-
all-trades who takes her clients' needs seriously, she's particularly
helpful with accommodations, private tours, and airport or train
station transfers anywhere in the Czech Republic (tel. 02/302-
5170, cellular 060-420-7225, e-mail: mp.ludmila@post.cz).

Best Views: Enjoy "the golden city of a hundred spires" during the early evening when the light is warm and the colors are rich. Good viewpoints include the castle square, the top of the east tower of Charles Bridge, the Old Town Square clock tower, and the steps of the National Museum overlooking Wenceslas Square.

Language: Czech, a Slavic language, has little resemblance to Western European languages. These days, English is "modern" and you'll find the language barrier minimal. If you speak German, it's helpful. An acute accent means you linger on that vowel. The little smile above the c, s, or z makes it ch, sh, or zh.

Learn these key Czech words:

Hello/Goodbye (familiar)	*Ahoj* (ah-hoi)
Good day, Hello (formal)	*Dobrý den* (DOH-bree den)
Yes/No	*Ano* (AH-no)/*Ne* (neh)
Please	*Prosím* (proh-zeem)
Thank you	*Děkuji* (dyack-quee)
You're welcome	*Prosím* (proh-zeem)
Where is...?	*Kde je...?* (gday yeh)
Do you speak English?	*Mluvíte anglicky?*
	(MLOO-vit-eh ANG-litz-key)
krown (the money)	*koruna* (koh-roo-nah)

Arrival in Prague

Prague unnerves many travelers—it's relatively run-down, it's behind the former Iron Curtain, and you've heard stories of rip-offs and sky-high hotel prices. But, in reality, Prague is charming, safe, and welcomes you with open cash registers and smiles.

By Train: Most travelers coming from and going to the West use the main station (Hlavní Nádraží) or the secondary station (Holešovice Nádraží). Trains to other points within the country use Masarykovo or Smíchov stations. Trains to/from Český Krumlov usually use Prague's main station, sometimes the Smíchov station.

Upon arrival, change money. Rates vary—compare by asking at two exchange windows what you'll get for $100. Count carefully. At the same window, buy a city map (50 kč, with trams and metro lines marked and tiny sketches of the sights for ease in navigating). You'll be constantly referring to this map. Confirm your departure plans at the train information window. Consider arranging a room or tour at the TI or AVE travel agency. The left-luggage counter is reportedly safer than the lockers.

At Prague's main train stations, anyone arriving on an international train will be met at the tracks by room hustlers (snaring tourists for cheap rooms). The orange low-ceilinged main hall is a fascinating mix of travelers, kiosks, loitering teenagers, and older riffraff.

From the main station, it's a 10-minute walk to Wenceslas

Square (turn left out of the station and follow Washingtonova to the huge Narodini Museum and you're there). You can also catch trams #5, #9, or #26 (to find the stop, walk into park, head 2 minutes to right), or take the metro (inside station, look for the red "M" with 2 directions: Muzeum or Florenc; take Muzeum, then transfer to the green line—direction Dejvicka—and get off at either Můstek or Staroměstske; these stops straddle the Old Town). The courageous and savvy get a cabby to treat them fairly and get to their hotel fast and sweat-free for no more than 130 kč (see "Getting around Prague," below; to avoid the train station taxi stand, go out the front door and downhill through the park to the first street for a rank of less criminal cabbies or ride the metro a stop and catch one on the street).

Holešovice Nádraží station is suburban mellow. The main hall has all the services of the main station in a compact area. Outside the first glass doors, the ATM is on the left, the metro is straight ahead (follow "Vstup" which means "entrance," take it 3 stops to the main station, 4 stops to the city center Muzeum stop), and taxis and trams are outside to the right (allow 150 kč for a cab to the center).

By Plane: Your hotel can arrange for a shuttle minibus to take you economically to the airport. Airport info tel. 02/367-814.

Getting around Prague

You can walk nearly everywhere. But the metro is slick, the trams fun, and the taxis quick and easy once you're initiated.

Public Transport: The trams and metro work on the same cheap tickets. Buy from machines (press enter after the ticket type before inserting coins) at kiosks or purchase at hotels. For convenience, buy all the tickets you think you'll need: 15-minute ticket—8 kč, 60-minute ticket—12 kč, 24-hour ticket—70 kč, three-day pass—180 kč. Cheaters, when caught, are fined 800 kč. The metro closes at midnight, but some trams keep running all night (identified with white numbers on blue backgrounds at tram stops).

City maps show the tram/bus/metro lines. The metro system is handy and simple (just 3 lines) but doesn't get to many hotels and sights. Trams are also easy to use; track your route with your city map. They run every 5 to 10 minutes, less on weekends. Get used to hopping on and off. Validate your ticket on the bus by sticking it in the machine (which stamps a time on it).

Taxis: Prague's taxis—notorious for meters that spin for tourists like pinwheels—are being tamed. Still, many cabbies consider one sucker a good day's work. While most hotel receptionists and guidebooks advise avoiding taxis, this is defeatist. I find Prague is a great taxi town and use them routinely. Get the local rate, and they're cheap. Use only registered taxis: These are marked by a fixed (not magnetic) roof lamp with the word "TAXI"

Prague Metro

in black on both sides, and the front doors sport a company name, license number, and rates (3 rows: drop charge—25 kč, per-kilometer charge—17 kč, and wait time per minute—4 kč). The key is the tiny "*sazba*" box on the magic meter showing the rate. This should read "1," unless you called for a pickup (which adds 30 to 50 kč). If a cabby tries to rip you off, simply pay 100 kč or 150 kč for a long ride. Let him follow you into the hotel if he insists you owe him more. (He won't.) The receptionist will defend you. Don't bother with any taxi parked in a touristed zone. To remind him to turn on the meter, say "*Zapnete taximetr*" (zapp-nyet-ay tax-ah-met-er). The AAA and ProfiTaxi companies are considered honest. Any taxi with an excuse not to use the meter ("personal transport") is ripping you off. In 2001, 150 kč is the most any Old Town ride should cost.

Tours of Prague
Walking Tours—Prague Walks offers walking tours of the Old Town, the castle, and Jewish Quarter (mostly 2 hrs, 250 kč, tel. 02/627-0981, e-mail: pwalks@comp.cz). Consider their clever

Good Morning Walk (7:00, before the crowds hit). Several decent companies give guided walks. For the latest, pick up the walking tour fliers at the TI. The TI has plenty of private guides available for hire on very short notice (3 hrs for 1,000 kč, desk at Old Town Square TI, tel. 02/2448-2562).

Bus Tours—Cheap big-bus orientation tours provide an efficient once-over-lightly look at Prague and a convenient way to see the castle. Premiant City Tours offers 15 different tours including: quick city (350 kč, 2 hrs, 5/day), grand city (590 kč, 3.5 hrs, 2/day), Jewish Quarter (620 kč, 2 hrs), Prague by night, Bohemian glass, Terezin Concentration Camp memorial, Karlštejn Castle, Český Krumlov (1,600 kč, 8 hrs), and a river cruise. The tours feature live guides (in German and English) and depart from near the bottom of Wenceslas Square at Na Príkope 23. Get tickets at an AVE travel agency, hotel, on the bus, or at Na Príkope 20 (tel. 02/2494-6922, www.premiant.cz).

Tram Joyride—Tram #22 makes a fine joyride through town. Consider this as a scenic lead-up to touring the castle. Catch it at metro: Náměstí Míru, roll through a bit of new town, the old town, across the river, and hop out just above the castle (at Pyramid Hotel and hike down the hill into castle area).

Self-Guided Walking Tour

The King's Walk (Královská cesta), the ancient way of coronation processions, is touristy but great. Pedestrian friendly and full of playful diversions, it connects the essential Prague sites. The king would be crowned in St. Vitus Cathedral in the Prague Castle, walk through the Little Quarter to the Church of St. Nicholas, cross Charles Bridge, and finish at the Old Town Square. If he hurried, he'd be done in 20 minutes. Like the main drag in Venice between St. Mark's and the Rialto bridge, this walk mesmerizes tourists. Use it as a spine, but venture off it—especially to eat.

While you could cover this route in the same direction, the king's long gone and it's a new morning in Prague, so I'll lay out Prague's essential sights in walking order, starting where modern independence was proclaimed, on Wenceslas Square, proceeding through the Old Town, across the bridge, and finishing at the castle. This walk laces together all the following recommended sights except the Jewish Quarter.

▲▲**Wenceslas Square (Václavske Náměstí)**—More a broad boulevard than a square (until recently trams rattled up and down its parklike median strip), it's named for the equestrian statue of King Wenceslas that stands at the top of the boulevard.

The square is a stage for modern Czech history: The Czechoslovak state was proclaimed here in 1918. In 1968 the Soviets put down huge popular demonstrations here. Starting at the top (metro: Muzeum), stroll down the square:

The **National Museum** stands grandly at the top. The only thing exciting about it is the view (80 kč, daily 10:00–18:00, halls of Czech fossils and animals).

The metro stop (Muzeum) is the cross point of two metro lines. From here you could roll a ball straight down the boulevard and through the heart of Prague to Charles Bridge.

St. Wenceslas (Václave), commemorated by the statue, is the "good king" of Christmas carol fame. He was never really a king but the wise and benevolent 10th-century Prince of Bohemia. After being assassinated in 929, he became a symbol of Czech nationalism. Now his equestrian statue is a popular meeting point. Locals say, "I'll see you under the horse's ass."

Thirty meters below the big horse is a small round garden with a low-key **memorial** "to the victims of Communism." Pictured here is Jan Palach. In 1969, a group of patriots decided a self-immolation would stoke the fires of independence. They drew straws and Jan Palach got the short one. He set himself on fire for the cause of Czech independence. Twenty years later massive demonstrations here led to the overthrow of the Czech Communist government. From the balcony of Melantrich (opposite the Grand Hotel Europa—farther down), Vaclav Havel stood with Alexander Dubcek, hero of the 1968 revolt, and declared the free Republic of Czechoslovakia in December 1989.

Havel is still president and popular, although his popularity took a hit when he married for the second time to an actress 17 years his junior (some say his brain dropped about one meter). His second (and last) five-year term ends in 2003.

As you wander, notice the fun mix of **architectural styles**, all post-1850: Romantic neo-Gothic, neo-Renaissance, neo-Baroque from the 19th century, Art Nouveau from 1900, ugly functionalism from the mid-20th century, and Stalin Gothic from the "Communist epoch." The Grand Hotel Europa (halfway down Wenceslas Square) is hard to miss with its dazzling Art Nouveau exterior.

▲**Na Príkope (the Moat)**—The bottom of Wenceslas Square meets another spacious pedestrian mall. Na Príkope (meaning "the moat") leads from Wenceslas Square right to the Powder Tower (the Powder Tower sounds interesting but is a dud). While probably not worth the detour on this walk, consider these reasons to explore the Tower area later: City tour buses leave from along this street. A fancy Bohemian crystal shop, Moser's (described below in "Shopping"), is at #12. Next to the Powder Tower is the dazzling **Municipal House**, with a great Art Nouveau facade and three recommended restaurants.

▲**Havelská Market**—Central Prague's best open-air flower and produce market scene is a block toward the Old Town Square from the bottom of Wenceslas Square. Laid out in the

Prague

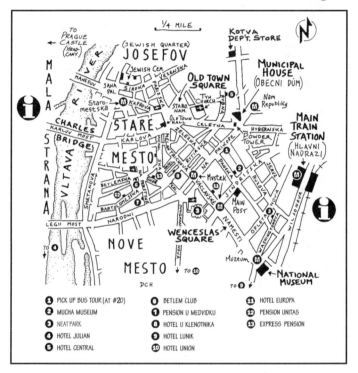

❶ PICK UP BUS TOUR (AT #20)	❻ BETLEM CLUB	⑪ HOTEL EUROPA
❷ MUCHA MUSEUM	❼ PENSION U MEDVIDKU	⑫ PENSION UNITAS
❸ NEAT PARK	❽ HOTEL U KLENOTNIKA	⑬ EXPRESS PENSION
❹ HOTEL JULIAN	❾ HOTEL LUNIK	
❺ HOTEL CENTRAL	⑩ HOTEL UNION	

13th century by King Wenceslas for the German trading community, it keeps hungry locals and vagabonds fed cheaply today.

▲▲▲Old Town Square (Staroměstske Náměstí)—The focal
point for most visits, this has been a market square since the
11th century. It became the nucleus of a town (Staré Město) in
the 13th century when its city hall was built. Today the old-time
market stalls have been replaced by cafés, touristic horse buggies,
and souvenir hawkers.

The **Hus Memorial**—erected in 1915, 500 years after his
burning—marks the center of the square and symbolizes the long
struggle for Czech freedom. Walk around the memorial. The
Czech reformer Jan Hus stands tall between two groups of people:
victorious Hussite patriots and Protestants defeated by the Hapsburgs. One of the patriots holds a cup—in the medieval Church,
only priests could drink the wine at communion. Hussites fought
for the right to take both the wine and the bread. A mother with
her children behind Hus represents the ultimate rebirth of the

Czech nation. Hus was excommunicated and burned in Germany a century before the age of Martin Luther.

Do a spin tour in the center of the square to get a look at architectural styles: Romanesque, Gothic, Renaissance, Baroque, and Art Nouveau.

Spin clockwise, from the green domes of the Baroque Church of St. Nicholas. There has been a church on this site since the 12th century. This one, dating from the early 18th century, is now a Hussite church (evening concerts). The Jewish Quarter (Josefov) is a few blocks behind it down the uniquely tree-lined Paris Street (Parizska), a festival of mostly Art Nouveau facades. Spin to the right past the Hus Memorial and the fine golden and mosaic Art Nouveau facade of the Ministry of the Economy. Notice the Gothic Tyn Church (described below) with its Disneyesque spires flanking a solid gold effigy of the Virgin Mary. Lining the uphill side of the square is an interesting row of pastel houses with Gothic, Renaissance, and Baroque facades. The pointed 75-meter-tall spire marks the 14th-century Old Town Hall, famous for its astronomical clock (described below). In front of the city hall, 27 white inlaid crosses mark the spot where 27 Protestant nobles and intellectuals were beheaded in 1621 after rebelling against the Catholic Hapsburgs.

Tyn Church—The fanciful church (pronounced "teen") facing the Old Town Square was rebuilt fancier than the original—but enjoy it. For 200 years after Hus's death, this was Prague's leading Hussite church. Enter through the Gothic arcade facing the square (a diagram at the door locates spots of interest, such as the tomb of astronomer Tycho Brahe).

The lane leading to the church from the Old Town Square has a public WC and the most central box office in town (see "Entertainment," below).

▲**Old Town Hall Astronomical Clock**—Join the gang—ignoring the ridiculous human sales racks—for the striking of the hour (daily 8:00–20:00) on the 15th-century town hall clock. As you wait, see if you can figure out how the clock works.

With revolving disks, celestial symbols, and sweeping hands, this clock keeps several versions of time. Two outer rings show the hour: Bohemian time (Gothic numbers, counts from sunset—find the zero, next to 23 ... supposedly the time of tonight's sunset) and modern time (24 Roman numerals, XII at the top being noon, XII at the bottom being midnight). Five hundred years ago, everything revolved around the earth (the fixed middle background).

To indicate the times of sunrise and sunset, arcing lines and moving spheres combine with the big hand (a sweeping golden sun) and the little hand (the moon showing various stages). Look for the orbits of the sun and moon as they rise through day (the blue zone) and night (the black zone).

If this seems complex today, it must have been a marvel 500 years ago. The circle below (added in the 19th century) shows the zodiac, scenes from the seasons of a rural peasant's life, and a ring of saints' names—one for each day of the year with a marker showing today's special saint (out of order).

Four statues flanking the clock represent 15th-century Prague's four biggest worries: invasion (a Turkish conqueror... his hedonism symbolized by a mandolin), death (a skeleton), greed (a miserly moneylender, which used to have "Jewish" features until after World War II, when anti-Semitism became politically incorrect), and vanity (enjoying the mirror).

At the top of the hour (don't blink—the show lasts 20 seconds): (1) Death tips his hourglass and pulls the cord ringing the bell; (2) the windows open and the Twelve Apostles parade by acknowledging the gang of onlookers; (3) the rooster crows; and (4) the hour is rung. The hour is often off because of daylight saving time (completely senseless to 15th-century clockmakers). At the top of the next hour, stand under the tower—protected by a line of banner-wielding, powdered-wigged concert salespeople— and watch the tourists.

Left of the clock is the main TI, a local guides' desk, and an opportunity to pay three admissions: for the city hall (by tour only), a Gothic chapel (only interesting for a close-up of the Twelve Apostles, and the clock mechanism well described in English), and the tower (long climb, fine view).

To reach the bridge, turn your back to the fancy Tyn Church and march with the crowds.

Karlova Street—This street winds through medieval old Prague from the City Hall Square to the Charles Bridge. This is a commercial gauntlet, and it's here that the touristic feeding frenzy of Prague is most ugly. Street signs keep you on track and "Karluv Most" signs point to the bridge. Obviously, you'll find great people watching but no good values on this drag.

Torture Museum—This gimmicky moneymaker is no different from any other European torture museum—but nevertheless interesting, showing 60 models of gruesome medieval tortures with well-written English descriptions (100 kč, daily 10:00–22:00, just before the bridge at Karlova 2).

▲▲▲Charles Bridge (Karluv Most)—This much-loved bridge, commissioned by the Holy Roman Emperor Charles IV in 1357, offers one of the most pleasant 500-meter strolls in Europe. Until 1850 it was the only bridge crossing the river here. Be on the bridge when the sun is low for the warmest people watching and best photo opportunities.

Before crossing the bridge, step into the little square on the right with the statue of the Holy Roman Emperor Charles IV (Karlo Quatro). Charles ruled his vast empire from Prague in the

14th century. He's holding a contract establishing Prague university—the first in central Europe. The women around his pedestal symbolize the university's four faculties: medicine, law, theology, and the arts. The statue was erected in 1848 to celebrate the university's 500th birthday. Enjoy the view across the river. The bridge tower above you—once a toll booth—is considered one of the finest Gothic gates anywhere. Climb it for a fine view but nothing else (30 kč, daily 10:00–22:00).

Charles Bridge is famous for its statues. But those you see today are replicas—the originals are in city museums and out of the pollution.

Two statues on the bridge are worth a comment: the crucifix (facing the castle, near the start on the right) is the spot where convicts would pause to pray on their way to execution on the Old Town Square. Further on (midstream, on right) the statue of John Nepomuk—patron saint of the Czech people—draws a crowd (look for the guy with the five golden stars and the shiny dog). Back in the 14th century, he was the priest to whom the queen confessed all her sins. The king wanted to know her secrets but John dutifully refused to tell. He was tortured, eventually killed, and tossed off the bridge. When he hit the water five stars appeared. The shiny spot on the base of the statue shows the heave-ho. Locals touch it to help wishes come true. The shiny dog killed the queen . . . but that's another story. From the end of the bridge (TI in tower on castle side), the street leads two blocks to the Little Quarter Square at the base of the huge St. Nicholas church.

▲▲**Little Quarter (Malá Strana)**—This is the most characteristic, fun-to-wander old section of town. It's one of four medieval towns (along with Hradčany, Staré Město, and Nové Město) that united in the 1700s to make modern Prague. It centers on the Little Quarter Square (Malostranské Náměstí, on downhill side of huge St. Nicholas church) with its plague monument facing the entry to the commanding church, at the upper end of the square.

Church of St. Nicholas—Dominating the Little Quarter, this is the best example of High Baroque in town. It's a Jesuit church, giddy with curves and illusions. The altar features a lavish gold-plated Nicholas flanked by the two top Jesuits: St. Ignatius Loyola and St. Francis Xavier (45 kč, daily 9:00–16:00, built 1703–1760, 75-meter-high dome, tower climbable from outside right transept). From here, hike 10 minutes uphill to the castle.

Sights—Prague's Castle Area

▲▲**Prague Castle**—For a thousand years, Czech rulers have ruled from the Prague Castle. It's huge (by some measures, the biggest castle on earth) and confusing—with plenty of sights not worth seeing. Rather than worry about rumors that you should spend all day here with long lists of museums to see, keep things simple. Five stops matter and are explained here: Castle Square, St. Vitus Cathedral, the old Royal Palace, Basilica of St. George, and the Golden Lane. One 120-kč ticket gets you into all these sights (Tue–Sun 9:00–17:00, last entry at 16:00, closed Mon; the 145 kč audioguide is good but requires 2 hrs and, since you need to return it where you got it, makes it impossible to exit the castle area from the bottom).

To reach the castle, choose one of four ways: metro to Malostranská (and climb up); tram #22 or #23 (which stop above the castle, and hike down); take a cab directly to Castle Square; or—the best—walk through the Little Quarter from the bridge.

Castle Square (Hradčanske Náměstí)—The big square facing the castle feels like the castle's entry, but it's actually the central square of a fortified town called Prague Castle, which until the 1700s was independent. Enjoy the awesome city view and the Prague Fun Fair Orchestra—a string quartet which plays regularly at the gate (their CD is terrific, say hello to friendly, mustachioed Josef). A tranquil café hides a few steps down immediately to the right as you face the castle. From here stairs lead into the Lesser Town. Uphill from the gate is a plague monument in the center, the Renaissance Schwarzenberg Palace (on the left, now an armory museum), a lane on the right leading to the Sternberg Palace (filled with the National Gallery's skippable collection of European paintings—mostly minor works by Dürer, Rubens, Rembrandt, El Greco, 90 kč, Tue–Sun 10:00–18:00, closed Mon).

Survey the castle from this square—the tip of a 500-meter-long series of courtyards, churches, and palaces. The offices facing this first courtyard belong to the Czech president, Vaclav Havel (left side). The guard changes on the hour (with the most ceremony at noon). Walk under the fighting giants, under an arch, to the ticket booth. You can walk through the castle and enter the cathedral without a ticket, but you'll need a ticket to see the castle properly (120-kč ticket covers cathedral apse and spire, Old Royal Palace, Basilica of St. George, and Powder Tower; hour-long, 60-kč English tours depart from ticket office regularly but cover Cathedral and Old Palace only; private guides-500 kč, tel. 02/2437-3368).

▲**St. Vitus Cathedral**—This Roman Catholic cathedral symbolizes the Czech spirit. Started in 1344, Prague's top church wasn't finished until 1929 in time for the 1,000th anniversary of the assassination of St. Wenceslas, patron saint of the Czechs. It looks all Gothic, but it's two distinct halves: modern neo-Gothic first and the original 14th-century Gothic from the high altar to the far end. Wars and plagues stalled the building, and for 400 years a temporary wall sealed off the unfinished cathedral. With the 19th-century rise of Czech nationalism, it was finally finished in the last century.

In the neo-Gothic section, the stained glass is all 20th century. The masterful Art Nouveau window on the left is from

Prague's Castle Area

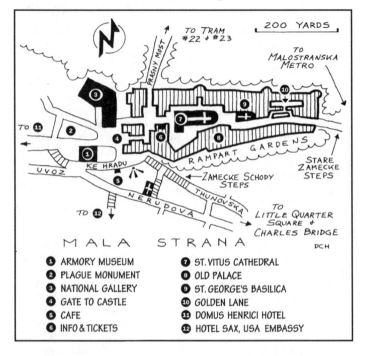

1 ARMORY MUSEUM
2 PLAGUE MONUMENT
3 NATIONAL GALLERY
4 GATE TO CASTLE
5 CAFE
6 INFO & TICKETS
7 ST. VITUS CATHEDRAL
8 OLD PALACE
9 ST. GEORGE'S BASILICA
10 GOLDEN LANE
11 DOMUS HENRICI HOTEL
12 HOTEL SAX, USA EMBASSY

1931 by Czech artist Alfons Mucha (if you like this, you'll love the Mucha museum downtown—described below in "Art Nouveau").

Show your ticket and circulate around the apse past a carved wood relief of Prague in 1630, lots of faded Gothic paintings, and tombs of local saints. A fancy roped-off chapel (right transept) houses the tomb of Prince Wenceslas surrounded by murals showing scenes of his life, and a locked door leading to the crown jewels. More kings are buried in the royal mausoleum in front of the high altar and in the crypt underneath. You can climb the spire for a fine view (daily except Sunday morning, 9:00–17:00, 287 steps).

Leaving the cathedral, turn left. Find the 14th-century mosaic of the Last Judgment outside on the right transept. Across from that is the...

Old Royal Palace—This was the seat of the Bohemian princes in the 12th century. While extensively rebuilt, the large hall is late Gothic. It's big enough for jousts—even the staircase was designed to let a mounted soldier gallop in. Look up at the impressive vaulted ceiling, look down on the chapel from the end, and go out on the balcony for a fine Prague view. Is that Paris in the distance?

No, it's an observation tower built for an exhibition in 1891 (60 meters tall; a quarter of the height of its Parisian big brother that was built in 1889). The spiral stairs on the left lead up to several rooms with painted coats of arms and no English explanations. There's nothing to see downstairs in the palace. Across from the palace exit is the basilica.

Basilica of St. George and Convent—The first Bohemian convent was established here near the palace in 973. Today the convent houses the Czech Gallery (best Czech paintings from Gothic, Renaissance, and Baroque periods). The beautifully lit basilica is Prague's best-preserved Romanesque church. St. Ludmila was buried here in 973. Continue walking downhill through the castle grounds. Turn left on the first street, which leads into a cute lane.

Golden Lane—This street of old buildings, which originally housed goldsmiths, is now jammed with tourists and lined with expensive gift shops, boutiques, galleries, and cafés. The Czech writer Franz Kafka lived at #22. There's a deli/bistro at the top and a convenient public WC at the bottom. Beyond that, at the end of the castle, are fortifications beefed up in anticipation of the Turkish attack—the cause for most medieval arms buildups in Europe—and steps funneling the mobs of tourists back into town. At the bottom of the castle, follow its walls around to the right and pay (40 kč, 10:00–18:00) to shortcut through the "Garden on the Ramparts" back down to the Little Quarter (Malá Strana).

Sights—Prague's Jewish Quarter

▲▲▲**Jewish Quarter (Josefov)**—The Jewish people were dispersed by the Romans 2,000 years ago. Over the centuries, their culture survived in enclaves throughout the Western world: "Time was their sanctuary which no army could destroy." Jews first came to Prague in the 10th century. The main intersection of Josefov (Maiselova and Siroka Streets) was the meeting point of two medieval trade routes. Jewish traders settled here in the 13th century and built a synagogue.

When the pope declared Jews and Christians should not live together, Jews had to wear yellow badges, and their quarter was walled in so that it became a ghetto. In the 16th and 17th centuries Prague had the biggest ghetto in Europe with 11,000 inhabitants—nearly half the population of Prague. Within its six gates, Prague's Jewish Quarter was a gaggle of two hundred wooden buildings. Someone wrote: "Jews nested rather than dwelled."

The "outcasts" of Christianity relied on profits from money lending (forbidden to Christians) and community solidarity to survive. While their money protected them, it was also a curse. Throughout Europe, when times got tough and Christian debts to the Jewish community mounted, entire Jewish communities were evicted or killed.

Prague's Jewish Quarter

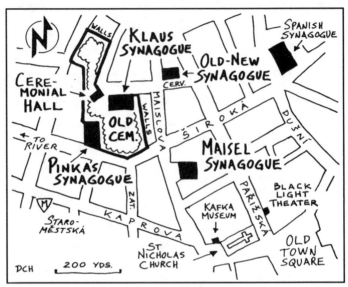

In the 1780s Emperor Joseph II eased much of the discrimination against Jews. In 1848 the walls were torn down and the neighborhood, named Josefov in honor of the emperor who was less anti-Semitic than the norm, was incorporated as a district of Prague.

In 1897, ramshackle Josefov was razed and replaced with a new modern town—the original 31 streets and 220 buildings became 10 streets and 83 buildings. This is what you'll see today: an attractive neighborhood of fine, mostly Art Nouveau buildings, with a few surviving historic Jewish buildings. In the 1930s some 50,000 Jews lived in Josefov. Today only a couple of thousand remain.

Strangely, the museums of the Jewish Quarter are, in part, the work of Hitler. He preserved Josefov to be his museum of the "exterminated race." Seven sites scattered over a three-block area make the tourists' Jewish Quarter. Six, called "the Museum," are treated as one admission. Your ticket comes with a map locating the sights and admission appointments: times you'll be let in if it's very crowded. (Without crowds, ignore the times.)

For all seven sights you'll pay 480 kč (280 kč for the "Museum" and 200 kč for the Old-New Synagogue). The sites are open from Sunday to Friday 9:00 to 17:30, and closed on Saturday (the Jewish Sabbath). There are occasional guided walks in English (often at 14:00, 40 kč, 2.5 hrs, starts at Maisel Synagogue, tel. 02/231-7191). Most stops are well described in English. These museums are well presented and profoundly moving: For me, this is the most interesting Jewish site in Europe.

Maisel Synagogue—This shows a thousand years of Jewish history in Bohemia and Moravia. Ironically, the collection was assembled from synagogues throughout the region by Nazis planning to archive the "extinct Jewish culture" here in Josefov with a huge museum. Exhibits include topics such as the origin of the Star of David, Jewish mysticism, discrimination, and the creation of the Prague Ghetto.

Spanish Synagogue—This 19th-century, ornate, Moorish-style synagogue continues the history the Maisel Synagogue started, covering the 18th, 19th, and tumultuous 20th centuries. The upstairs is particularly interesting (with c. 1900 photos of Josefov).

Pinkas Synagogue—A site of Jewish worship for 400 years, today this is a poignant memorial to the victims of the Nazis. Of the 120,000 Jews living around here in 1939, only 15,000 lived to see liberation in 1945. The walls are covered with the handwritten names of 77,297 local Jews who were sent from here to the gas chambers of Auschwitz. Family names are in gold, followed by the individuals' first names in black, with birthdays and the last date known to be alive (usually the date of transport—to one of the camps listed by the altar). Notice that families generally perished together. Climb six steps into the women's gallery. The names near the ceiling in poor condition are from 1953. When the Communists moved in, they closed the synagogue and erased everything. With freedom, in 1989, the Pinkas Synagogue was reopened and all the names rewritten.

Upstairs is the Terezin Children's Art Exhibit. Terezin, near Prague, was a fortified town of 7,000 Czechs. The Nazis moved these people out and moved in 60,000 Jews, creating their model "Jewish town," a concentration camp dolled up for propaganda purposes. The town's medieval walls, originally to keep people from getting in, were used by Nazis to prevent people from getting out. Jewish culture seemed to thrive in Terezin as "citizens" put on plays and concerts, published a magazine, and raised their families in ways impressive to Red Cross inspectors. But virtually all of the Jews ended up dying at concentration camps in the East such as Auschwitz. The art of the children of Terezin survives as a striking testimony to the horror of the Holocaust. While the Communists kept the art away from the public, today it's well displayed and described in English.

Terezin is a powerful day trip from Prague for those interested in touring the concentration camp memorial/museum; you can either take a public bus (6/day, 60 min, leaves from Prague's Florenc bus station) or a tour bus (see "Tours of Prague," above).

Old Jewish Cemetery—As you wander among 12,000 evocative tombstones, remember that from 1439 until 1787 this was the only burial ground allowed for the Jews of Prague. With limited space and over 100,000 graves, tombs were piled atop each other. With as many as 12 layers, the cemetery became a small plateau. The Jewish word for cemetery means "House of Life"; like Christians, Jews believe that death is the gateway into the next world. Pebbles on the tombstones are "flowers of the desert," reminiscent of the old days when a rock was placed upon the sand gravesite to keep the body covered. Often a scrap of paper with a prayer on it is under a pebble.

Ceremonial Hall—Leaving the cemetery you'll find a neo-Romanesque mortuary house built in 1911 for the purification of the dead (on left). It's filled with an interesting and well-described exhibition on Jewish burial traditions with historic paintings of the cemetery.

Klaus Synagogue—This 17th-century synagogue (also at the exit of the cemetery) is the final wing of this museum, devoted to Jewish religious practices. On the ground floor, exhibits explain the festive Jewish calendar. Upstairs features the ritual stages of Jewish life.

Old-New Synagogue—For over 700 years this has been the most important synagogue and central building in Josefov. Standing like a bomb-hardened bunker, it feels like it's survived plenty of hard times. Stairs take you down to the street level of the 13th century and into the Gothic interior. Built in 1270, it's the oldest synagogue in Europe. Originally called the "New Synagogue," it was renamed "Old-New" as other synagogues were built. The Shrine of the Arc in front is the focus of worship. It holds the sacred scrolls of the Torah, the holiest place in the synagogue. The old rabbi's chair to the right remains empty out of respect. Twelve is a popular number (e.g., windows) because it symbolizes the 12 tribes of Israel. The slitlike windows on the left are an 18th-century addition allowing women to view the men-only services (separate 200 kč admission, open 9:30–18:00).

Art Nouveau

Prague is the best Art Nouveau town in Europe with fun-loving facades gracing streets all over town. The streets of Josefov, the Mucha window in the St. Vitus Cathedral, and Hotel Europa and its sisters on Wenceslas Square are just a few highlights. The top two places for Art Nouveau fans are the Mucha Museum and the Municipal House.

▲▲**Mucha Museum**—This is one of Europe's most enjoyable little museums. I find the art of Alfons Mucha (moo-kah, 1860–1939) insistently likeable. Read how this popular Czech artist's posters were patriotic banners in disguise, see the crucifixion scene he painted as an eight-year-old, and check out the photographs of his models. Prague isn't much on museums, but if you're into Art Nouveau, this one is great. Run by Mucha's grandson, it's two blocks off Wenceslas Square and wonderfully described and displayed on one comfortable floor (120 kč, daily 10:00–18:00, Panska 7, tel. 02/628-4162, www.mucha.cz). While the exhibit is well described in English, the 30-kč English brochure on the art is a good supplement. The video is also worthwhile (30 min, hrly in English, ask upon entry).

Municipal House—The Municipal House (Obecní Dum, built 1905–1911, near Powder Tower) features Prague's largest concert hall, a great Art Nouveau café with handy cyber access, and two other restaurants. Look for the *Homage to Prague* mosaic—with a goddesslike Praha presiding over a land of peace and high culture—on the building's striking facade; it stoked cultural pride and nationalist sentiment. Then choose your place for a meal or drink (described below in "Eating").

Entertainment

Prague booms with live (and inexpensive) theater, opera, classical, jazz, and pop entertainment. Everything's listed in Prague's monthly cultural events program (free at TI).

Black Light Theater, a kind of mime/modern dance variety show, has no language barrier and is, for many, more entertaining than a classical concert.

Six or eight classical "tourist" concerts a day resound throughout the famous Old Town halls and churches generally within a three-minute walk of the Old Town Square or bridge. The music is of the crowd-pleasing sort: Vivaldi, Best of Mozart, Most Famous Arias, and works by local boy Anton Dvořák. Leafleteers are everywhere announcing the evening's events. Concerts typically cost 400 to 1000 kč, start anywhere from 17:00 to 20:00, last one hour, and are usually quartets (e.g., flute, French horn, cello, violin).

Common venues are in the Little Quarter Square—Malostranské Náměstí (at the Church of St. Nicholas and the Prague Academy of Music in Lichtenstein Palace), at the city end of Charles Bridge (St. Francis Church), and on the Old Town Square (another St. Nicholas Church).

To really understand all your options (the street Mozarts are pushing only their concert), drop by the box office at the Tyn Church. The wall display clearly shows what's playing today and tomorrow (concerts, Black Light Theater, marionette shows, photos of each venue, and a map locating everything, daily 10:00–18:00, tel. 02/231-4936).

Shopping

Moser's Bohemian Crystal shop offers a top-end look at this local specialty. Climb the stairs into the elegant showrooms, housed in the 19th-century mansion of a local Jewish family that's sold crystal

since 1925. It's like a museum (Mon–Fri 9:00–20:00, Sat–Sun
10:00–18:00, midway between bottom of Wenceslas Square and
Powder Tower at Na Příkope 12, tel. 02/2421-1293).

The huge Kotva department store (the name means "anchor")
on the edge of the Old Town is a fun opportunity to see work-a-
day Czech consumerism. Since cosmetics were scarce in the
Communist days, that's the big draw even today; cosmetics and
perfume routinely are placed by the front door of department
stores (latest Czech fashions, cheap manicures, sprawling grocery
store in basement, Mon–Fri 9:00–20:00, Sat–Sun 10:00–18:00,
few minutes' walk from Old Town Square on Kraládvorská).

Sleeping in Prague
(38 kč = about $1, country code: 420, area code: 02)
Sleep Code: **S** = Single, **D** = Double/Twin, **T** = Triple, **Q** = Quad,
b = bathroom, **t** = toilet only, **s** = shower only, **CC** = Credit Card
(**V**isa, **M**asterCard, **A**mex).

Finding a bed in Prague worries Western tourists. It shouldn't.
You have several options. Capitalism is working as Adam Smith
promised: With a huge demand, the supply is increasing and the
price is going up. Peak time is May, June, September, October,
Christmas, and Easter. July and August are not too bad. Expect
crowds on weekends. I've listed peak time prices. If you're traveling
in July or August, you'll save about 20 percent. English is generally
spoken. Reserve by phone or e-mail. Generally you simply promise
to come and need no deposit.

Room-Booking Services
The city is awash with fancy rooms on the push list, private, small-
time operators with rooms to rent in their apartments, and roving
agents eager to book you a bed and win a commission. You can
save about 30 percent by showing up in Prague without a reservation and finding accommodations upon arrival.

AVE, at the main train station (Hlavní Nádraží), is a helpful
and well-organized booking service (daily 6:00–23:00, tel.
02/2422-3226, fax 02/2423-0783, e-mail: ave@avetravel.cz). With
the tracks at your back, walk down to the orange ceiling—their
office is in the left corner by the exit to the rip-off taxis. Another
AVE office is at Holešovice station. Their display board shows
discounted hotels. They have a slew of private rooms and small pensions available ($50 pension doubles in the old center, $35 doubles a
metro ride away). You can reserve by e-mail (using your credit card
as a deposit) or just show up at the office and request a room.

Athos Travel, run by Filip Antos, is basically a Web site
designed to set you up with budget beds in Prague. It's a work
in progress, but log onto www.athos.cz and see what happens
(e-mail: filip@antos.cz).

For a more personal touch, contact Lida at **Magic Praha** for help with accommodations (tel. 02/302-5170, e-mail: mp .ludmila@post.cz, see "Helpful Hints," above).

Three-Star Hotels

Prague's three-star hotels—each plenty professional and comfortable—are often beholden to agencies that have a lock on rooms (generally until 6 weeks in advance). Agencies get a 30 percent discount and can sell the rooms at whatever price they like between that and the "rack rate." Consequently, Prague has a reputation of being perpetually booked up. But as the agencies rarely use up their allotment, the "crowds" are only an illusion. You need to make reservations either long in advance, when the few rooms not reserved for agencies are still available, or a few weeks in advance, after the agencies have released their rooms.

Hotel Julian—an oasis of professional, predictable decency in a quiet, untouristy neighborhood—is a five-minute taxi or tram ride from the action on the castle side of the river. Its 29 spacious, fresh, well-furnished rooms and big, homey public spaces hide behind a noble neoclassical facade. The staff is friendly and helpful (Sb-3,080 kč, Db-3,380 kč, suite Db-4,180 kč, extra bed-900 kč, family room, CC:VMA, 5 percent discount off best quoted rate with this book, parking lot, elevator, Internet services, Elisky Peskove 11, Prague 5, tel. 02/5731-1150, reception tel. 02/5731-1144, fax 02/5731-1149, www.julian.cz, e-mail: casjul@vol.cz,). Free lockers and a shower are available for those needing to check out early but stay until late (e.g., for an overnight train). Mike's Chauffeur Service based here is reliable and affordable (see "Transportation Connections," below).

Hotel Central is as likeable as an old horse. I stayed there in the Communist days, and—while the rooms are modestly renovated—it hasn't changed a lot since. Even Charlie is still at the reception desk. The 68 rooms are proletarian plain, but the place is well run and the location, three blocks east of the old square, is excellent (Sb-3,000 kč, Db-3,500 kč, Tb-4,000 kč, CC:VMA, elevator, Rybna 8, Praha 1, metro: Náměstí Republiky, tel. 02/2481-2041, fax 02/232-8404, e-mail: what's that?).

Betlem Club is a shiny jewel of comfort on a pleasant medieval square in the heart of the Old Town across from the Betlem Chapel where Jan Hus preached his trouble-making sermons. Its 22 modern and comfy rooms face a quiet inner courtyard, and breakfast is served in a Gothic cellar (Sb-2,500 kč, Db-3,600 kč, extra bed-900 kč, elevator, Betlémské Náměstí 9, Praha 1, tel. 02/2222-1575, fax 02/2222-0580, e-mail: betlem.club@login.cz).

Hotel U Klenotnika, with 10 modern and comfortable rooms in a plain building, is three blocks off the old square

(Sb-2,500 kč, Db-3,800 kč, Tb-4,500 kč, 10 percent off when booking direct with this book, CC:VMA, no elevator, Rytirska 3, Praha 1, tel. 02/2421-1699, fax 02/2422-1025).

Hotel Lunik is a stately no-nonsense place out of the medieval faux-rustic world and in a normal, pleasant business district two metro stops from the main station (metro: Pavlova) or a 10-minute walk from Wenceslas Square. It's friendly, spacious, and rents 35 pleasant rooms (Db-2,500 kč, Tb-2,900 kč, CC:VMA, elevator, no reservations more than 6 weeks in advance, Londynska 50, Praha 2, tel. 02/2425-3974, fax 02/2425-3986, e-mail: hotel.lunik@email.cz).

Hotel Union is a grand 1906 Art Nouveau building filling its street corner. Like Hotel Lunik, it's away from the touristic center in a more laid-back neighborhood a direct 10-minute ride to the station on tram #24 or to Charles Bridge on tram #18 (57 rooms, Sb-2,815 kč, Db-3,380 kč, Db deluxe-3,580 kč, extra bed-865 kč, CC:VMA, elevator, Nusle Ostrcilovo Náměstí 1, Praha 2, tel. 02/6121-4812, fax 02/6121-4820, e-mail: hotel.union@telecom.cz).

Hotel 16, a stately little place with an intriguing Art Nouveau facade, a garden, high ceilings, and a clean, sleek interior, rents 13 fine rooms (Sb-2,300 kč, Db-3,100 kč, Tb-3,500 kč, CC:VM, elevator, a 10-minute walk south of Wenceslas Square, metro: Pavlova, Katerinska 16, 12800 Praha 2, tel. 02/2492-0636, fax 02/2492-0626, www.hotel16.cz).

Hotel Adria, with a prime Wenceslas Square location, cool Art Nouveau facade, and completely modern and business-class interior, is your big-time central splurge (88 air-con rooms, Db-$185, CC:VMA, elevator, minibars . . . the works, Václavske Náměstí 26, tel. 02/2108-1111, fax 02/2108-1300, www.hoteladria.cz, e-mail: mailbox@hoteladria.cz).

Cloister Inn is a modern, three-star place with 70 rooms and more concrete than charm but plenty comfortable and well located (Db-3,800 kč, Konviktska 14, 11000 Praha 1, tel. 02/2421-1020, fax 02/2421-0800, www.cloister-inn.cz).

Three-Star Hotels near the Castle in the Little Quarter (Malá Strana)

Hotel Sax, on a quiet corner a block below the action, will delight the artsy yuppie with its airy atrium and modern, stylish decor (22 rooms, Sb-3,700 kč, Db-4,400 kč, Db suite-5,100 kč, CC:VMA, elevator, near St. Nicholas church, 1 block below Nerudova at Jansky Vrsek 3, tel. 02/5753-1268, fax 02/5753-4101, e-mail: hotelsax@bon.cz).

Domus Henrici, just above the castle square, is a quiet retreat that charges—and gets—top kroner for its smartly appointed rooms, some of which include good views (Db-$150/$170/$180 depending on size, extra bed-$40, pleasant breakfast terrace, Loretanska 11, tel. 02/2051-1369, fax 02/2051-1502, www.domus-henrici.cz). This is a five-minute walk above the castle gate in a stately and quiet area.

Pensions

With the rush of tourists into Prague, small 6- to 15-room pensions are popping up everywhere. Most have small, spartan rooms—often with no plumbing at all; sinks, showers, and toilets are down the hall. Breakfast is included in the price. Some of these places take bookings no more than a month in advance. All are in the Old Town, close to the Můstek metro station.

The **Laundromat** nearest most recommended hotels is at Karoliny Svetle 10, Praha 1 (200 kč/load, 200 meters from the bridge, Mon–Sat 7:30–19:00, closed Sun).

Pension Unitas rents 34 small and tidy youth hostel–type rooms with plain, minimalist furnishings and no sinks (S-1,020 kč, D-1,200 kč, T-1,650 kč, Q-2,000 kč, T and Q are cramped with bunks in D-sized rooms, Bartolomejska 9, 11000 Praha 1, tel. 02/2421-1020, fax 02/2421-0800, www.cloister-inn.cz/unitas).

Hotel Europa is in a class by itself. This landmark place, famous for its wonderful 1903 Art Nouveau facade, is the center-piece of Wenceslas Square. But someone pulled the plug on the hotel about 50 years ago, and it's a mess. It offers haunting beauty in all the public spaces with 90 dreary, ramshackle rooms and a weary staff (S-1,300 kč, Sb-2,700 kč, D-2,600 kč, Db-4,000 kč, T-3,100 kč, Tb-5,000 kč, CC:VMA, elevator, Václavské Náměstí 25, Praha 1, tel. 02/2422-8117, fax 02/2422-4544).

Express Pension rents 24 simple rooms and serves a lousy continental breakfast (Sb-2,400 kč, D-1,800 kč, Db-2,600 kč, Tb-3,000 kč, no elevator and lots of stairs, Skorepka 5, Praha 1, tel. 02/2421-1801, fax 02/2422-3309, e-mail: express@zero.cz).

Pension U Medvidku has 22 comfortably renovated rooms in a big, rustic, medieval shell (Sb-2,265 kč, Db-3,000 kč, Tb-4,000 kč, CC:VMA, Na Perstyne 7, Praha 1, tel. 02/2421-1916, fax 02/2422-0930, www.umedvidu.cz). The pension runs a popular restaurant that has live music nightly until 23:00.

Guest House Lida, with homey and spacious rooms, fills a big house in a quiet residential area that's a 10-minute walk or five-minute tram ride from the center. Jan and Jiri Prouza, who run the place, are a wealth of information and know how to make people feel at home (Db-$55, 10 percent off Nov–March, family rooms, metro: Prazskeho Povstani, Lopatecka 26, 14700 Praha 4, tel. & fax 02/6121-4766, e-mail: lida@login.cz).

Eating in Prague

The beauty of Prague is wandering aimlessly through the winding old quarters marveling at the architecture, people watching, and

sniffing out restaurants. You can eat well and for very little
money. What you'd pay for a basic meal in Vienna or Munich
will get you an elegant meal in Prague. Choose between traditional, dark Czech beer hall–type ambience, elegant Jugendstil
turn-of-the-century atmosphere, or a hip, modern place. For
traditional cuisine, wander the Old Town (Staré Město).

Traditional Czech Beer Halls near the Old Town Square

Plzenska Restaurace U Dvou Kocek is a typical Czech pub
with cheap, local, no-nonsense, hearty Czech food, great beer,
and a local crowd (150 kč for 3 courses and beer, serving original
Pilsner Urquell with accordion music nightly until 23:00, under
an arcade, facing the tiny square between Perlova and Skorepka
Streets, tel. 02/267-729).

    U Vejvodu is a rollicking place with great Czech beer,
raditional grub, and lots of brass and wood. The deeper you go,
the more smoky and atmospheric it gets (150 kč dinners, 2 blocks
off the Old Town Square at Jilska 4).

    Restaurace U Rotta is a new pub, bright and classy but low-
key traditional with good beer on tap and music nightly at 20:00
under medieval arches (daily 11:00–24:00, a block toward the bridge
from Old Town Square at Male Náměstí 3, tel. 02/269-537).

Art Nouveau Restaurants

The sumptuous Art Nouveau concert hall—**Municipal House**—
has three special restaurants: a café, a French restaurant, and a
beer cellar (Náměstí Republiky 5). The dressy cafe, **Kavarna
Obecní Dům**, is drenched in chandeliered Art Nouveau elegance
(light meals, 1 hot meal special daily—200 kč, live piano 16:30–
20:30; cybercafé: 40 kč/10 min). **Krancouzska Restaurant**,
the fine French restaurant, is in the next wing (500-kč meals).
Plzenska Restaurant, downstairs, brags it's the most beautiful
Art Nouveau pub in Europe (cheap meals, great atmosphere,
12:00–23:00 daily).

    Restaurant Mucha is touristy with decent Czech food in a
formal Art Nouveau dining room (300-kč meals, daily until 24:00,
Melantrichova 5, tel. 02/263-586).

Uniquely Czech Places near the Old Town Square

Prices go way down when you get away from the tourist areas.
At least once, eat in a restaurant with no English menu.

    Restaurant U Plebana is a quiet little place with good
service, Czech cuisine, and a modern yet elegant setting (daily
until 24:00, Betlémské Náměstí 10, tel. 02/2222-1568).

    Country Life Vegetarian Restaurant is a bright and easy
cafeteria that has a well-displayed buffet of salads and veggie hot

dishes in a smoke-free restaurant midway between the Old Town Square and the bottom of Wenceslas Square. They are serious about their vegetarianism, serving only plant-based, unprocessed, and unrefined food (Sun–Thu 11:00–20:30, Fri 11:00–18:00, closed Sat, through courtyard at Melantrichova 15/Michalska 18, tel. 02/2421-3366).

Czech Kitchen (Ceska Kuchyne) is a new blue-collar cafeteria serving steamy old Czech cuisine to a local clientele market. There's no English. Just pick up your tally sheet at the door, grab a tray, and point liberally to whatever you'd like. It's extremely cheap (daily 9:30–17:00, across from Havelská market at Havelská 23).

37 Patro Fast Food is another super-cheap cafeteria catering to locals. This one's actually in the Můstek metro station (downstairs under Jungmannovo Náměstí).

Czech Beer

For many, *pivo* (beer) is the top Czech tourist attraction. After all, the Czechs invented lager in nearby Pilsen. This is the famous Pilsner Urquell, a great lager on tap everywhere. Budvar is the local Budweiser, but it's not related to the American brew. Czechs are among the world's biggest beer drinkers—adults drink about 80 gallons a year. The big degree symbol on bottles and menus marks the beer's heaviness, not its alcohol content (12 degrees is darker, 10 degrees lighter). The smaller figure shows alcohol content. Order beer from the tap (*sudove pivo*) in either small (.3 liter, *male pivo*) or large (.5 liter, *pivo*). In many restaurants a beer hits your table like a glass of water in the United States. *Pivo* for lunch has me sightseeing for the rest of the day on Czech knees. Be sure to venture beyond the Pilsner Urquell. There are plenty of other good Czech beers.

Transportation Connections—Prague

Getting to Prague: Those with railpasses need to purchase tickets to cover the portion of their journey from the border of the Czech Republic to Prague (buy at station before you board train for Prague). Or supplement your pass with a "Prague Excursion" pass, giving you passage from any Czech border station into Prague and back to any border station within seven days. Ask about this pass (and get reservations) at the EurAide offices in Munich or Berlin (90 DM first class, 60 DM second class, 45 DM for youths under 26, tel. 089/593-889). EurAide's U.S. office sells these passes for a bit less (U.S. tel. 941/480-1555, fax 941/480-1522). Direct trains leave Munich for Prague daily around 7:00, 14:00, and 23:00, (5–6 hr trip). Tickets cost about 100 DM from Munich or, if you have a railpass covering Germany, 30 DM from the border.

By train to: Český Krumlov (8/day, 4 hrs, verify departing station), **Berlin** (5/day, 5 hrs), **Munich** (3/day, 5 hrs), **Frankfurt**

(3/day, 6 hrs), **Vienna** (3/day, 5 hrs), **Budapest** (6/day, 9 hrs). Train info: tel. 02/2422-4200. Czech Rail Agency: tel. 02/800-805.

By bus to: Český Krumlov (6/day, 3.5 hrs, 120 miles, take metro to Florence station; an easy direct bus leaves at about 9:00).

By car with a driver: Mike's Chauffeur Service is a reliable little company with fair and fixed rates around town and beyond (round-trip fares with waiting time included: Český Krumlov-3,500 kč, Terezin-1,700 kč, Karlštejn-1,500 kč; up to 4 people, tel. 02/5156-5161, e-mail: mike.chauffeur@cmail.cz). On the way to Český, Mike will stop at no extra charge at Hluboka castle or Český Budijovice, where the original Bud beer is made.

ČESKÝ KRUMLOV

Český Krumlov means "Czech bend in the river." Lassoed by its river and dominated by its castle, this simple, enchanting town feels lost in a time warp. Český Krumlov is the Czech Republic's answer to Germany's Rothenburg, but 40 years ago. Its buildings are slowly being restored; for every tired building with peeling paint there's one just renovated. And while popular with Czech and German tourists, few Americans find Český. The town attracts a young, Bohemian crowd, drawn here for its simple beauty and cheap living. Hostels cost $6, comfortable pensions with private baths run $30 for a double, and a good dinner will set you back $3 to $5.

Orientation (area code: 0337)

This place is initially confusing, thanks to the snaking Vltava River, which makes a perfect "S" through the town. Use the pink castle tower and the soaring spire of the Church of St. Vitus to stay oriented. With only three bridges (one is a foot bridge) and one square, you'll get your bearings quickly enough. Most hotels and restaurants are in the island center, within a few blocks of the main square, Náměstí Svornosti. The TI, banks, ATMs, a few hotels, and taxis are on the square. Banks close at 17:00, stores at 18:00.

Tourist Information: The eager-to-please TI is on the main square (Mon–Sat 9:00–20:00 in summer, Sept 9:00–19:00, other months 9:00–18:00, closed Sun, tel. 0337/711-183). Pick up the free city map. The 99-kč *City Guide* has a great 3-D map on one side with key sights and many hotels identified, and gives you a basic but helpful English background on the city and key sights. The TI can check train, bus, and flight schedules, and change traveler's checks (fair rate). Ask about concerts, city walking tours in English, car rentals, and canoe trips on the river (400–900 kč). The TI can reserve a room, but they'll take a 10 percent deposit that will be deducted from your hotel bill. Save your host's money and go direct.

Internet Access: Try South Bohemian University, just off the main square (Mon–Fri 9:00–18:00, Horni 155, tel. 0337/913-075).

Český Krumlov

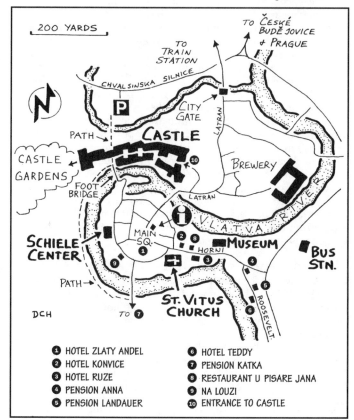

200 YARDS

TO ČESKÉ
BUDĚJOVICE
& PRAGUE

TO
TRAIN
STATION

CHVALSINSKA SILNICE

CITY
GATE

LATRAN

PATH

CASTLE

BREWERY

CASTLE
GARDENS

FOOT
BRIDGE

LATRAN

VLATVA RIVER

SCHIELE
CENTER

MAIN
SQ.

HORNI

MUSEUM

BUS
STN.

PATH

ROOSEVELT

DCH

TO ⑦

ST. VITUS
CHURCH

① HOTEL ZLATY ANDEL
② HOTEL KONVICE
③ HOTEL RUZE
④ PENSION ANNA
⑤ PENSION LANDAUER

⑥ HOTEL TEDDY
⑦ PENSION KATKA
⑧ RESTAURANT U PISARE JANA
⑨ NA LOUZI
⑩ ENTRANCE TO CASTLE

Arrival in Český Krumlov

By Train and Bus: The train station is a 20-minute walk from town (turn right out of the station, walk downhill onto a steep cobbled path leading to an overpass into town center), while the bus station is just three blocks away from the center (from the bus station, drop down to main road and turn left, then turn right at Potraving grocery store to reach center). Taxis are cheap; don't hesitate to take one from the train station (about 140 kč).

Sights—Český Krumlov

The main square, **Náměstí Svornosti**, will seduce you rather than bowl you over. Best at twilight, this colorful huddle of Renaissance and Baroque facades surrounds a simple, unpretentious square. The local economy can't support more than the two small cafés. Enjoy people watching from its benches. The white Venetian-looking town hall (housing the TI) seems strangely out of place. On the hill, that looming castle, or **"Mansion"** as locals call it, is Český's key sight. You'll find a live bear pit below the entry and, high above, a cylindrical castle tower looking more like a beer stein just begging to be climbed (30 kč, June–Aug 9:00–17:00, Sept–May 10:00–16:00, great view, 162 steps). If you want to tour the surprisingly opulent and impressive castle interior, hold off on the tower and continue uphill through the courtyard to the ticket room. Admission is by one-hour guided tour only (50 kč, 9:00–17:00, ask for next tour in English, then kill time at tower or in gardens). The upper castle gardens are modest but pleasant.

Back in the center, Český's small **District Museum of Natural History** offers a quick look at regional costumes, tools, and traditions; ask for the simple English translation that also gives a lengthy history of Český (30 kč, 10:00–12:30, 13:00–18:00, across from Hotel Ruze at Horni 152). Český is best at night—save energy for a romantic post-dinner stroll.

Sleeping and Eating in Český Krumlov
(38 kč = about $1, country code: 420, area code: 0337)
Český is filled with small, good, family-run pensions offering doubles with baths from 900 to 1,000 kč and hostel beds for 200 kč (buyer beware). Summer weekends and festivals are busiest; reserve ahead when possible. Unless otherwise noted, all prices include breakfast. Hotels speak some English and accept credit cards; pensions rarely do either.

Hotel Zlaty Andel has its reception right on the main square, though most of its comfortable and thoughtfully appointed rooms are tucked behind (Sb-1,190 kč, Db-1,690–2,290 kč, Tb-2,690 kč, Qb-3,290 kč, CC:M, satellite TV, minibar, Náměstí Svornosti 10, tel. 0337/7123-1015, fax 0337/71235).

Leaving the main square via the central, uphill street (Horni), you'll find the next five places in this order:

Hotel Konvice is popular with Germans, offering polished, almost elegant rooms (Sb-1,150 kč, Db-1,400 kč, extra bed-500 kč, Qb apartment-2,600 kč, Horni Ulice 144, tel. 0337/711-611, fax 0337/711-327).

Hotel Ruze, from its red-carpeted halls to its elegant, wood-furnished rooms, feels like a Spanish parador. Český's affordable four-star splurge, located in a beautifully renovated historic building, has grand public spaces, a brilliant backyard terrace overlooking the river, rooms with all the comforts and then some, and the slickest kids' beds in town (Sb-2,790 kč, Db-3,420 kč, deluxe Db-3,870 kč, apartment-4,320 kč, extra bed-540 kč, CC:VMA, Horni 154, tel. 0337/772-100, fax 0337/713-146, e-mail: hotelruze@ck.ipex.cz).

Just after the Horni bridge you'll see the pretty gray Baroque **Pension Anna**, a well-run little pension with comfortable, just-renovated rooms (Db-1,100 kč, Tb-1,700 kč, Rooseveltova 41, tel. 0337/711-692). **Pension Landauer**, with small and simple but comfortable rooms and a good restaurant, is a fair value—unless it's hot (Sb-600 kč, Db-1,000 kč, Rooseveltova 32, tel. & fax 0337/711-790). The little **Hotel Teddy** has several river-view rooms sharing a common balcony (Db-1,100 kč, Rooseveltova 38, tel. 0337/711-595).

Pension Katka, on the opposite, lower side of town, across the bridge below the island, is well run and comfortable (Sb-600 kč, Db-1,000 kč, Tb-1,400 kč, Linecka 51, tel. 0337/711-902).

For a good, reasonably priced meal with views over Český, try **Restaurant U Pisare Jana** (Horni 151, tel. 0337/712-401). **Na Louzi**, a block below the main square on Kajovska 66, is popular with locals and very cheap.

Transportation Connections—Český Krumlov
By train to: Prague (7/day, 2.5 hrs), **Vienna** (4/day, 7 hrs), **Budapest** (4/day, 11 hrs). Virtually all train rides to/from Český require a transfer in Český Budějovice.

By bus to: Prague (6/day, 3.5 hrs).

AUSTRIA
(ÖSTERREICH, THE KINGDOM OF THE EAST)

- 32,000 square miles (the size of South Carolina, or two Switzerlands)
- 7.6 million people (235 per square mile and holding, 85 percent Catholic)
- 15 Austrian schillings (AS) = about $1 (figure 7 cents each)

During the grand old Hapsburg days, Austria was Europe's most powerful empire. Its royalty built a giant kingdom of more than 50 million people by making love, not war (having lots of children and marrying them into the other royal houses of Europe).

Today this small, landlocked country does more to cling to its elegant past than any other nation in Europe. The waltz is still the rage. Austrians are very sociable; it's important to greet people in the breakfast room and those you pass on the streets or meet in shops. The Austrian's version of "Hi" is a cheerful "*Grüss Gott*" ("May God greet you"). You'll get the correct pronunciation after the first volley—listen and copy.

While they speak German and talked about unity with Germany long before Hitler ever said "*Anschluss*," the Austrians cherish their distinct cultural and historical traditions. They are not Germans. Austria is mellow and relaxed compared to Deutschland. *Gemütlichkeit* is the local word for this special Austrian cozy-and-easy approach to life. It's good living—whether engulfed in mountain beauty or bathed in lavish high culture.

The people stroll as if every day were Sunday, topping things off with a cheerful visit to a coffee shop or pastry shop.

It must be nice to be past your prime—no longer troubled by being powerful, able to kick back and celebrate life in the clean, untroubled mountain air. While the Austrians make less money than their neighbors, they enjoy a short work week and a long life span.

The Austrian schilling (S or AS) is divided into 100 groschen. To convert prices into dollars, drop the last zero and subtract one-third (e.g., 450 AS = about $30, actually $31.50). About seven Austrian schillings equal one Deutsche Mark (DM). While merchants and waiters near the border are happy to accept DM, you'll save money if you use schillings. Prices in Austria are lower than in Germany and much lower than in Switzerland. Shops are open from 8:00 to 17:00 or 18:00.

Austrians eat on about the same schedule we do. Treats include *Wiener Schnitzel* (breaded veal cutlet), *Knödel* (dumplings), *Apfelstrudel*, and fancy desserts like the *Sachertorte*, Vienna's famous chocolate cake. Bread on the table sometimes costs extra (if you eat it). Service is included in restaurant bills, but it's polite to leave a little extra (less than 5 percent).

"Die Vignette" Motorway Toll Stickers: In Austria, all cars must have a "Die Vignette" toll label stuck to the inside of their windshield. These are sold at all border crossings (24 hours a day) and at big gas stations near borders. Stickers cost 105 AS for 10 days (300 AS for 2 months). Not having one earns you a stiff fine.

Most major train stations rent bikes (70 AS/half day, 120 AS/full day, 50 percent more without a train ticket) and allow you to drop them at other stations for a 45-AS fee.

In this section of the book, I'll cover Austria's top cities *except* for Reutte in Tirol. For this book, Reutte was annexed by Germany. You'll find it in the Bavaria and Tirol chapter.

VIENNA
(WIEN)

Vienna is a head without a body. For 640 years the capital of the once-grand Hapsburg Empire, she started and lost World War I and, with it, her far-flung holdings. Today you'll find an elegant capital of 1.6 million people (20 percent of Austria's population) ruling a small, relatively insignificant country. Culturally, histori-cally, and from a sightseeing point of view, this city is the sum of its illustrious past. The city of Freud, Brahms, a gaggle of Strausses, Maria Theresa's many children, and a dynasty of Holy Roman Emperors is right up there with Paris, London, and Rome.

Vienna has always been the easternmost city of the West. In Roman times it was Vindobona, on the Danube facing the Germanic barbarians. In medieval times Vienna was Europe's bastion against the Ottoman Turks (a "horde" of 300,000 was repelled in 1683). While the ancient walls held out the Turks, World War II bombs destroyed nearly a quarter of the city's buildings. In modern times Vienna took a big bite out of the USSR's Warsaw Pact buffer zone.

The truly Viennese person is not Austrian but a second-generation Hapsburg cocktail, with grandparents from the distant corners of the old empire—Polish, Serbian, Hungar-ian, Romanian, Czech, or Italian. Vienna is the melting-pot capital of an empire of 60 million—of which only 8 million were Austrian.

In 1900, Vienna's 2.2 million inhabitants made it the world's fifth-largest city (after New York, London, Paris, and Berlin). But the average Viennese mother has 1.3 children, and the popu-lation is down to 1.6 million. (Dogs are the preferred "child.")

Some ad agency has convinced Vienna to make Elisabeth, wife of Emperor Franz Josef, with her narcissism and difficulties with

Vienna Overview

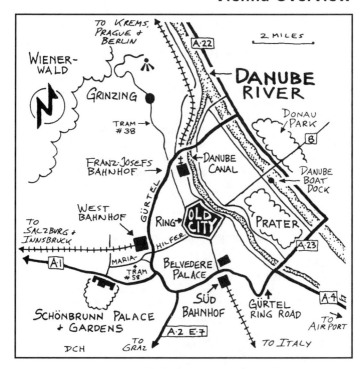

royal life, the darling of the local tourist scene. You'll see "Sissy" all over town. But stay focused on the Hapsburgs who mattered.

Of the Hapsburgs who ruled Austria from 1273 to 1918, Maria Theresa (ruled 1740–1765) and Franz Josef (ruled 1848–1916) are the most famous. People are quick to remember Maria Theresa as the mother of 16 children (12 survived). This was actually no big deal back then (one of her daughters had 18 kids, and a son fathered 16). Maria Theresa's reign followed the Austrian defeat of the Turks, when Europe recognized Austria as a great power. She was a strong and effective queen. (Her rival, the Prussian emperor, said, "When at last the Hapsburgs get a great man, it's a woman.")

Maria Theresa was a great social reformer. During her reign she avoided wars and expanded her empire by skillfully marrying her children into the right families. With daughter Marie Antoinette's marriage into the French Bourbon family (to Louis XVI), for instance, a country that had been an enemy became an ally. (Unfortunately for Marie, she arrived in time for the Revolution, and she lost her head.)

In tune with her age and as a great reformer, Maria Theresa's "Robin Hood" policies helped Austria glide through the "age of revolution" without turmoil. She taxed the church and the nobility and provided six years of obligatory education to all children and free health care to all in her realm. And she welcomed the boy genius Mozart into her court.

As far back as the 12th century, Vienna was a mecca for musicians—both sacred and secular (troubadours). The Hapsburg emperors of the 17th and 18th centuries were not only generous supporters of music but fine musicians and composers themselves. (Maria Theresa played a mean double bass.) Composers like Haydn, Mozart, Beethoven, Schubert, Brahms, and Mahler gravitated to this music-friendly environment. They taught each other, jammed together, and spent a lot of time in Hapsburg palaces. Beethoven was a famous figure, walking—lost in musical thought—through Vienna's woods.

After the defeat of Napoleon and the Congress of Vienna in 1815 (which shaped 19th-century Europe), Vienna enjoyed its violin-filled belle epoque, which shaped our romantic image of the city—fine wine, chocolates, cafés, and waltzes. "Waltz King" Johann Strauss and his brothers kept Vienna's 300 ballrooms spinning.

This musical tradition continues in our century leaving some prestigious Viennese institutions for today's tourists to enjoy: the Opera, the Boys' Choir, and the great Baroque halls and churches, all busy with classical and waltz concerts.

Planning Your Time

For a big city, Vienna is pleasant and laid-back. Vienna is worth two days and two nights on the speediest trip. Not only is it packed with great sights, but it's also a joy to simply spend time in. It seems like Vienna was designed to help people just meander through a day. To be grand-tour efficient, you could sleep in and sleep out on the train (Berlin, Venice, Rome, the Swiss Alps, Paris, and the Rhine are each handy night trains away). But then you'd miss the Danube and Melk. I'd come in from Salzburg via Hallstatt, Melk, and the Danube and spend two days this way:

Day 1: 9:00–Circle the "Ring" by tram, following the self-guided tour (see "Do-It-Yourself Bus Orientation Tour," below), 10:00–Tour Opera (take care of any TI and ticket needs), 11:00–Horse lovers tour the Lipizzaner Museum and see the horses practicing; art fans can visit the Academy of Fine Arts; people watchers and picnic gatherers wander Naschmarkt, 12:00–Lunch at Buffet Trzesniewski or Rosenberger Markt Restaurant, 13:00–Tour Hofburg, visiting royal apartments, treasury, and Kaisergruft, 16:30–Stroll Kärntner Strasse, tour St. Stephan's cathedral, and stroll Graben and Kohlmarkt, 19:00–Choose classical music (concert or opera), House of Music museum, or Heurige wine garden.

Day 2: 9:00–Schönbrunn Palace (drivers: this is conveniently on
the way out of town toward Salzburg), 13:00–Kunsthistorisches
Museum after lunch, 15:00–Your choice of the many sights left
to see in Vienna, Evening–See Day 1 evening options.

Orientation (area code: 01)

Vienna, or Wien (veen) in German, is bordered on three sides by
the Vienna Woods (Wienerwald) and on one side by the Danube
(Donau). To the southeast is industrial sprawl. The Alps, which
arc across Europe from Marseilles, end at Vienna's wooded hills.
These provide a popular playground for walking and new-wine
drinking. This greenery's momentum carries on into the city.
You'll notice more than half of Vienna is parkland, filled with
ponds, gardens, trees, and statue memories of Austria's glory days.

Think of the city map as a target. The bull's-eye is the cathedral, the first circle is the Ring, and the second is the Gürtel. The
old town snuggles around towering St. Stephan's Cathedral south
of the Donau, and is bound tightly by the Ringstrasse. The Ring,
marking what was the city wall, circles the first district (or *Bezirk*).
The Gürtel, a broader ring road, contains the rest of downtown
(*Bezirkes* 2–9).

Addresses start with the *Bezirk*, followed by street and building number. Any address higher than the ninth *Bezirk* is beyond
the Gürtel, far from the center. The middle two digits of Vienna's
postal codes show the district, or *Bezirk*. The address "7, Lindengasse 4" is in the seventh district, #4 on Linden Street. Its postal
code would be 1070. Nearly all your sightseeing will be done
in the core first district or along the Ringstrasse. As a tourist,
concern yourself only with this compact old center. When you
do, sprawling Vienna suddenly becomes manageable.

Tourist Information

Vienna has one real tourist office (near the Opera in the old
center). Hotel and ticket booking agencies answer questions and
give out maps and brochures at the train stations and airport.

The main Vienna tourist office is at a slick and spacious
location a block behind the Opera House at Albertinaplatz (daily
9:00–19:00, tel. 01/211-140, www.info.wien.at). Confirm your
sightseeing plans and pick up the free and essential city map
(also available at most hotels), the museum brochure (listing
hours), the monthly program of concerts (called "Programm"),
the fact-filled *Vienna Scene* magazine, and the youth guide ("Ten
Good Reasons For Vienna").

Consider the TI's handy 50-AS *Vienna from A to Z* booklet.
Every important building sports a numbered flag banner that keys
into this guidebook. A to Z numbers are keyed into the TI's city
map. When lost, find one of the "famous-building flags" and

match its number to your map. If you're at a "famous building," check the map to see what other key numbers are nearby, then check the A to Z book description to see if you want to go in. This system is especially helpful for those just wandering aimlessly among Vienna's historic charms.

Skip the much promoted 210-AS "Vienna Card." It gives you a 72-hour transit pass (worth 150 AS) and insignificant discounts at museums on the push list.

Arrival in Vienna

By Train at the West Station (Westbahnhof): Train travelers arriving from Munich, Salzburg, and Melk land at the Westbahnhof. The Reisebüro am Bahnhof books hotels (for a fee), has free maps, and answers questions (daily 7:00–22:00). To get to the city center (and most likely, your hotel), catch the U-3 metro (buy the 60-AS 24-hr pass from a *Tabak* shop in the station or from a machine—good on all city transit). U-3 signs lead down to the metro tracks. Catch a train in the direction of U-3 Erdberg. If your hotel is along Mariahilfer Strasse, your stop is on this line (see "Sleeping," below). If you're sleeping in the center or just sightseeing, ride five stops to Stephansplatz, escalate in the exit direction "Stephansplatz," and you'll hit the cathedral. The TI is a five-minute stroll down the busy Kärntner Strasse pedestrian street.

The Westbahnhof has a grocery store (daily 5:30–23:00), change offices (station ticket windows offer better rates and shorter lines than change offices), storage facilities, and rental bikes (see "Getting around Vienna," below). Airport buses and taxis await in front of the station.

By Train at the South Station (Südbahnhof): Those arriving from Italy and Prague land here. The Sudbahnhof has all the services, including bike rental, left luggage, and a TI (9:00–19:00). To reach Vienna's center, follow the "S" (Schnellbahn) signs to the right and down the stairs, and take any train in the direction "Floridsdorf"; transfer in two stops (at Landsstrasse/Wien Mitte) to the U3 (yellow) line, direction "Ottakring" which goes directly to Stephansplatz and Mariahilfer Strasse hotels. Also, tram D goes to the Ring and bus #13A goes to Mariahilfer Strasse.

By Plane: The airport (10 miles from town, tel. 01/7007-22233) is connected by 70 AS shuttle buses (2/hrly) to either the Westbahnhof (35 min) or the City Air Terminal (20 min) near the river in the old center. Taxis into town cost about 400 AS. Hotels arrange for fixed-rate car service to the airport (30-minute ride, 400 AS).

Getting around Vienna

By Bus, Tram, and Metro: Take full advantage of Vienna's simple, cheap, and super-efficient transit system. Buses, trams, and the metro all use the same tickets. Buy your tickets from *Tabak*

shops, station machines, or Vorverkauf offices in the station.
You have lots of choices:

- single tickets (19 AS, 22 AS if bought on tram—exact change only, good for 1 journey with necessary transfers)
- 24-hour pass (60 AS)
- 72-hour pass (150 AS)
- 7-day pass (155 AS, Mon–Sun)
- 8 Tage Umwelt Streifennetzkarte: eight all-day strips for 300 AS (can be shared, e.g., 4 people for 2 days each). Per person cost: 38 AS/day (compared to 60 AS/day for a 24-hour pass—a big savings for groups).

Take a moment to study the eye-friendly city center map on metro station walls to internalize how the metro and tram system can help you (metro routes are signed by the end-of-the-line stop). I use it mostly to zip along the Ring (tram #1 or #2), and take the metro to more outlying sights or hotels. The 30-AS transit map is overkill. All necessary routes are listed on the free tourist city map. Numbered lines (e.g., #38) are trams, numbers followed by an "A" (e.g., #38A) are buses.

Stamp a time on your ticket or transit pass as you enter the system or tram (stiff 600-AS fine if caught without a validated ticket—then they make you buy a ticket). Rookies miss stops because they fail to open the door. Push buttons, pull latches—do whatever it takes. Study your street map before you exit the metro. Choosing the right exit—signposted from the moment you step off the train—saves lots of walking (for information call 01/790-9105).

By Taxi: Vienna's comfortable, civilized, and easy-to-flag-down taxis start at 27 AS. You'll pay 90 AS to go from the Opera to the South or West Train Station.

By Bike: Good as the city's transit system is, you may want to rent a bike and follow one of the routes recommended in the TI's biking brochure. Bikes are available at any train station (daily 04:00–24:00, 100 AS/day with railpass or train ticket, 150 AS without; rent early in morning before supply runs out, tel. 01/5800-32985). Pedal Power offers rental bikes (300 AS/half day, 395 AS/24 hrs, includes delivery and pick up from your hotel) and 3.5-hour, two-language city tours (daily at 10:00, 280 AS includes bike, Austellungsstrasse 3, U-1 to Praterstern and 5-minute walk, tel. 01/729-7234, www.pedalpower.co.at).

By Buggy: Rich romantics get around by traditional horse and buggy. You'll see the horse buggies, called Fiakers, clip-clopping tourists on tours lasting 20 minutes (500 AS), 40 minutes (800 AS), or one hour (1,300 AS).

Helpful Hints

Bank Alert: Abundant ATMs are the smart way to change money. Banking is expensive in Vienna. Save three percent by comparing rates. (Warning: "Rieger Bank" is an expensive exchange bureau in disguise.) Banks are open weekdays roughly from 8:00 to 15:00 and until 17:30 on Tuesday and Thursday. After hours you can change money at train stations, the airport, or post offices. Commissions of 100 AS are sadly normal (American Express charges no commissions on its checks, Mon–Fri 9:00–17:30, Sat 9:00–12:00, Kärntner Strasse 21–23, tel. 01/5154-0456).

Post Offices: Choose from the main post office (Postgasse in center, open 24 hrs daily, handy metered phones), West and South Train Stations (open 04:00–24:00), and one near the Opera (Mon–Fri 7:00–19:00, Krugerstrasse 13).

English Bookstores: Consider the British Bookshop (at the corner of Weihburggasse and Seilerstätte) or Shakespeare & Co. (Sterngasse 2, north of Höher Markt square, tel. 01/535-5053).

Internet Access: The TI has an updated list. Amadeus in Steffl is central (Mon–Fri 9:30–19:00, Sat–Sun 9:30–17:00, Kärntner Strasse 19, tel. 01/513-1450) and Internet Aktiv is near the Mariahilfer Strasse hotels (Zieglergasse 29, tel. 01/526-7389). Coffeeshop Company (a Starbucks-like place just off Kärntner Strasse at Krugerstrasse 6) gives free Internet access to customers.

Laundry: These are few and far between; ask at your hotel. Gottshalks will do your laundry in a day (50 AS/1 kilo, Mon–Fri 8:00–18:00, Sat 9:00–12:00, near St. Stephan's at Singerstrasse 22). Launderette, near Mariahilfer Strasse, is handy (Mon–Fri 8:00–18:00, closed Sat–Sun, Siebensternstrasse 52, walk 4 blocks up Zollergasse from Mariahilfer Strasse).

City Tours

Walks: The *Walks in Vienna* brochure at the TI describes Vienna's guided walks in English (basic 90-minute intro, 140 AS, daily at 14:00 from TI and other locations, tel. 01/876-7111, www.wienguide.at). Monika Tentschert, a local teacher and private guide who knows her stuff, charges 1,500 AS for a half-day tour (tel. 01/212-0640).

Bus Tours: Vienna Line offers hop-on hop-off tours covering the 14 predictable sightseeing stops. Given Vienna's excellent public transportation and this outfit's meager one-bus-per-hour frequency, I'd take this not to hop on and off, but only to get the narrated orientation drive through town (in German and English, 250 AS, good for 2 days, or 140 AS if you stay on for 1 ride). The basic Vienna city sights tour includes a visit to the Schönnbrùn Palace and a bus tour around town (3.5 hrs, 400 AS, 3/day from Opera, to book this or get info on other tours, call 01/712-46830).

Do-It-Yourself Bus Orientation Tour

▲▲**Ringstrasse Tram #2 Tour**—In the 1860s Emperor Franz Josef had the city's ingrown medieval wall torn down and replaced

Vienna

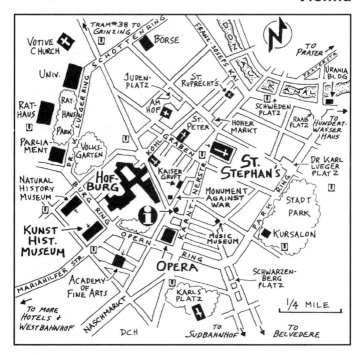

with a grand boulevard 190 feet wide. The road, arcing nearly three miles around the city's core, predates all the buildings that line it. So what you'll see is neo-Gothic, neoclassical, and neo-Renaissance. One of Europe's great streets, it's lined with many of the city's top sights. Trams #1 and #2 and a great bike path circle the whole route and so should you.

This self-service tram tour gives you a fun orientation and a ridiculously quick glimpse of the major sights as you glide by (19 AS, 30-minute circular tour). For an actual look at these sights, consider biking or hiking most of the route. Tram #1 goes clockwise; tram #2, counterclockwise. Most sights are on the outside, so tram #2 is best (sit on right—ideally in the front of the front car). Start at the Opera House. You can jump on and off as you go—trams come every five minutes. Read ahead and pay attention, these sights can fly by. Let's go:

☛ Immediately on the left: The city's main pedestrian drag, Kärntner Strasse, leads to the zigzag roof of **St. Stephan's Cathedral**. This tram tour makes a 360-degree circle around the cathedral, staying about this same distance from it.

☞ At first bend (before first stop): Look right toward the tall fountain and the guy on a horse. Schwartzenberg Platz shows off its **equestrian statue** of Prince Charles Schwartzenberg, who fought Napoleon. Behind that is the Russian monument (behind the fountain), which was built in 1945 as a forced thanks to the Soviets for liberating Austria from the Nazis. Formerly a sore point, now it's just ignored.

☞ Going down Schubertring, you reach the huge *Stadtpark* (city park) on the right, which honors 20 great Viennese musicians and composers with statues. At the beginning of the park, the white-and-yellow concert hall behind the trees is the **Kursalon**, opened in 1867 by the Strauss brothers, who directed many waltzes here (closed in 2001 for restoration, normally site of great waltz concerts, may reopen late in 2001, more likely in 2002).

☞ Immediately after next stop: In the same park, the gilded statue of Waltz King **Johann Strauss** holds his violin as he did when he conducted his orchestra.

☞ While at next stop at end of park: On the left, a green statue of Dr. Karl Lueger honors the popular man who was mayor of Vienna until 1910.

☞ At next bend: On the right, the quaint white building with military helmets decorating the windows was the Austrian ministry of war—back when that was a serious operation. Field Marshal Radetzky, a military big shot in the 19th century under Franz Josef, still sits on his high horse. He's pointing towards the post office, the only Art Nouveau building on the Ring. Locals call the architecture along the Ring **"historicism"** because it's all neo-this and neo-that—generally fitting the purpose of the building (farther along the Ring, we'll see: a neo-Gothic city hall—recalling when medieval burgers ran the city government in Gothic days; a neoclassical parliament building—celebrating ancient Greek notions of democracy; and a neo-Renaissance opera house—venerating the high culture filling it).

☞ At next corner: The white-domed building over your right shoulder as you turn is the Urania, Franz Josef's 1910 **observatory**. Lean forward and look behind it for a peek at the huge red cars of the giant 100-year-old Ferris wheel in Vienna's Prater Park (fun for families, described in "Top People-Watching and Strolling Sights," below).

☞ Now you're rolling along the **Danube Canal**. This "Baby Danube" is one of the many small arms of the river that once made up the Danube at this location. The rest have been gathered together in a mightier modern-day Danube, farther away. This was the site of the original Roman town, Vindobona. In three long blocks, on the left (opposite BP station, be ready—it passes fast), you'll see the ivy-covered walls and round Romanesque arches of St. Ruprechts, the oldest church in Vienna (built in the

11th century on a bit of Roman ruins). By about 1200, Vienna had grown to fill the area within this ring road.

☞ Leaving the canal, turning up Schottenring, at first stop: On the left, the orange-and-white, neo-Renaissance temple of money, the **Börse**, is Vienna's stock exchange.

☞ Next stop, at corner: The huge, frilly, neo-Gothic church on the right is a "votive church," built as a thanks to God when an 1853 assassination attempt on Emperor Franz Josef failed. Ahead on the right (in front of tram stop) is the Vienna University building (established in 1365, it has no real campus as the buildings are scattered around town). It faces (on the left, behind gilded angel) a chunk of the old city wall.

☞ At next stop on right: The neo-Gothic city hall, flying the flag of Europe, towers over **Rathaus Platz**, a festive site in summer with a huge screen showing outdoor movies, opera, and concerts. Immediately across the street (on left) is the **Hofburg Theater**, Austria's national theater.

☞ At next stop on right: The neo-Greek temple of democracy houses the **Austrian Parliament**. The lady with the golden helmet is Athena, goddess of wisdom. Across the street (on left) is the royal park called the "Volksgarten."

☞ After next stop on the right is the **Natural History Museum**, the first of Vienna's huge twin museums. It faces the **Kunsthistorisches Museum**, containing the city's greatest collection of paintings. A hefty statue of Empress Maria Theresa sits between the museums, facing the grand gate to the **Hofburg**, the emperor's palace (on left). Of the five arches, only the center one was used by the emperor.

☞ Fifty meters after the next stop, on the left through a gate in the black iron fence is the statue of Mozart. It's one of many charms in the **Burggarten**, which until 1880 was the private garden of the emperor. Vienna had more than its share of intellectual and creative geniuses. A hundred meters farther (on left, just out of the park), Goethe sits in a big, thought-provoking chair playing trivia with Schiller (across the street on your right). Behind the statue of Schiller is the Academy of Fine Arts.

☞ Hey, there's the **Opera** again. Jump off the bus and see the rest of the city.

Sights—Vienna's Old Center
Sights are listed in a logical walking order.

▲▲▲**Opera (Staatsoper)**—The Opera, facing the Ring and near the TI, is a central point for any visitor. While the critical reception of the building 130 years ago led the architect to commit suicide, and though it's been rebuilt since the World War II bombings, it's still a dazzling place (65 AS, by guided 35-minute tour only, daily in English, July–Aug at 11:00, 13:00, 14:00, 15:00, and often at 10:00 and 16:00; Sept–June afternoons only). Tours are often canceled for rehearsals and shows, so check the posted schedule or call 01/514-442-959.

The Vienna State Opera is one of the world's top opera houses, even though the Vienna Philharmonic Orchestra doesn't perform here. Instead its farm team plays in the pit (you can't get into the best orchestra in town without doing time here first). There are 300 performances a year—nearly nightly, except in July and August when the singers rest their voices. Expensive seats are normally sold out.

Tickets for seats: For ticket information call 01/513-1513 (phone answered daily 10:00–21:00, www.culturall.com, e-mail: tickets@volksoper.at). Last-minute tickets are sold for 400 AS from 9:00 to 12:00 the day before.

Standing room: Unless Pavarotti is in town, it's easy to get one of 567 *Stehplatz* (standing-room spots, 30–50 AS at the very top or—better—downstairs). The *Stehplatz* ticket window in the front lobby opens 80 minutes before each performance (tel. 01/5144-42419). If fewer than 567 people are in line, there's no need to line up early. Dress is casual (but do your best) at the standing-room bar.

Rick's crude tip: For me, three hours is a lot of opera. But just to see and hear the Opera House in action for half an hour is a treat. You can buy a standing room spot intending to just drop in for part of the show. Ushers don't mind letting tourists with standing-room tickets in for a short look. Ending time is posted in the lobby—you could drop in for just the finale. If you go for the start or finish you'll see Vienna dressed up. With all the time you save, consider stopping by...

Sacher Café, home of every chocoholic's fantasy, the *Sachertorte*, faces the rear of the Opera (on Philharmoniker Strasse). While locals complain that the cakes have gone down-hill, a coffee and slice of cake here is 100 AS well invested.

▲**Monument against War and Fascism**—A powerful four-part statue stands behind the Opera House, on Albertinaplatz. The split white statue, "The Gates of Violence," remembers the victims of the 1938 to 1945 Nazi rule of Austria. A montage of wartime images—clubs and gas masks, a dying woman birthing a future soldier, slave laborers—sits on a pedestal of granite cut from the infamous quarry at Mathausen, a nearby concentration camp. The hunched-over figure on the ground behind is a Jew forced to wash anti-Nazi graffiti off a street with a toothbrush. The statue with its head buried in the stone reminds Austrians of the consequences of not keeping their government on track. The 1945 declaration of Austria's second republic is cut into the stone behind that. The monument stands over the spot where a hundred people were buried alive while hiding in the cellar of a fancy building, demolished in a WWII bombing attack.

Austria was pulled into WWII by Germany, who annexed the country in 1938, saying Austrians were wannabe Germans anyway. But Austrians are not Germans—never were, never will be. They're quick to tell you that, while Austria was founded in 976, Germany wasn't born until 1870. For seven years during WWII (1938–1945), there was no Austria. In 1955, after 10 years of joint occupation by the victorious Allies, Austria regained her independence.

▲**Kärntner Strasse**—This grand mall (traffic free since 1974) is the people-watching delight of this in-love-with-life city. It points south in the direction of the southern Austrian state of Kärnten (for which it's named). Starting from the Opera, you'll find lots of action—shops, street music, the city casino (at #41), American Express (#21–23), and then, finally, the cathedral.

▲▲**Haus der Musik**—Vienna's newest museum is long overdue—the House of Music. While it has a floor devoted to the Vienna Philharmonic and fine audio-visual exhibits on each of the famous hometown boys (Haydn, Mozart, Beethoven, Strauss, and Mahler), this museum is unique for its effective use of interactive touch-screen computers and headphones to literally put you in the musical driving seat. You can twist, dissect, and bend sounds to make your own musical language, merge your voice with a duck's quack or a city's traffic roar. Wander through the "sonosphere" and marvel at the amazing acoustics—I could actually hear what I thought only a piano tuner can hear. Pick up a virtual baton to conduct the Vienna Philharmonic Orchestra (each time you screw up, the orchestra stops and ridicules you). Really seeing the place takes time. It's open late and makes a good evening activity (110 AS, daily 10:00–22:00, 2 blocks from Opera at Seilerstatte 30, tel. 01/51648).

▲▲**St. Stephan's Cathedral**—Stephansdom is the Gothic needle around which Vienna spins. It's survived Vienna's many wars and symbolizes the city's freedom (daily 6:00–22:00, entertaining English tours daily April–Oct at 15:45, information board inside entry has tour schedules and time of impressive 50-minute daily Mass).

This is the third church to stand on this spot. (In fact, an older Romanesque chapel—the Virgilkapelle—is on display in the adjacent metro station.) The last bit of the 11th-century Romanesque church can be seen on the west end (above the entry): the portal and the round windows of the towers. The church survived the bombs of World War II, but, in the last days of the war, fires from the street fighting between Russian and Nazi troops leapt to the rooftop; the original timbered Gothic rooftop burned, and the cathedral's huge bell crashed to the ground. With a financial out-pouring of civic pride, the roof of this symbol of Austria was rebuilt in its original splendor by 1952. The ceramic tiles are purely decorative (locals each "own" one for the many small post-war donations made to finance the rebuilding).

Inside, find the Gothic sandstone **pulpit** in the middle of the

nave (on left). A spiral stairway winds up to the lectern, surrounded and supported by the four Latin Church fathers: Saints
Ambrose, Jerome, Gregory, and Augustine. The railing leading
up swarms with symbolism: lizards (animals of light), battle toads
(animals of darkness), and the "Dog of the Lord" standing at the
top to be sure none of those toads pollute the sermon. Below the
toads, wheels with three parts (the Trinity) roll up while wheels
with four parts (standing for the four seasons, symbolizing mortal
life) roll down. This work, by Anton Pilgram, has all the elements
of flamboyant Gothic in miniature. But this was around 1500, and
the Italian Renaissance was going strong in Italy. While Gothic
persisted in the north, the Renaissance spirit had already arrived.
Pilgram included a rare self-portrait bust in his work (the guy
"with sculptor's tools, looking out a window under the stairs").
Gothic art was to the glory of God. Artists were anonymous. In
the more humanist Renaissance, man was allowed to shine—and
artists became famous.

St. Stephan's is draped in history—carved in its walls and
buried in its **crypt** (left transept, 40 AS, open at odd times, tel.
01/5155-23526). You can ascend both towers, the north (via
crowded elevator inside on the left) and the south (outside right
transept, by spiral staircase). The north shows you a big bell (the
21-ton Pummerin, cast from the cannon captured from the Turks
in 1683, supposedly the second biggest bell in the world that rings
by swinging) but a mediocre view (50 AS, Mon–Sat 9:00–18:00,
Sun 13:00–17:00). The 450-foot-high **south tower**, called St.
Stephan's Tower, offers a great view—343 tightly wound steps
up the spiral staircase (30 AS, daily 9:00–17:30, this hike burns
about one *Sachertorte* of calories). From the top, use your *Vienna
from A to Z* to locate the famous sights.

The peaceful Cathedral Museum (Dom Museum, outside left
transept past horses) gives a close-up look at piles of religious paintings, statues, and a treasury (50 AS, Tue–Sat 10:00–17:00, closed
Mon, behind church and past buggy stand, Stephansplatz 6).

▲▲**Stephansplatz, Graben, and Kohlmarkt**—The atmosphere
of the church square, Stephansplatz, is colorful and lively. At
nearby Graben Street (which was once a *Graben* or "ditch"),
top-notch street entertainment dances around an exotic plague
monument (at Brauner Strass). In medieval times people did not
understand the causes of plagues and figured they were a punishment from God. It was common for survivors to thank God with
a monument like this one from the 1600s. Find Emperor Leopold,
who ruled during the plague and made this statue in gratitude.
(Hint: The typical inbreeding of royal families left him with a
gaping underbite.) Below Leopold, "Faith" (with the help of a
disgusting little cupid) tosses old naked women—symbolizing the
plague—into the abyss.

Just beyond the monument is a fine set of Jugendstil public toilets (5.50 AS). St. Peter's Church faces the toilets. Step into this festival of Baroque (from 1708) and check out the jeweled skeletons (flanking the altar)—anonymous martyrs donated by the pope.

At the end of Graben, turn left on **Kohlmarkt**, Vienna's most elegant shopping street (except for "American Catalog Shopping," at #5, second floor). Kohlmarkt leads to the palace. En route, check out the edible window displays at Demel (Kohlmarkt 14). Then drool through the interior (coffee and cake for 100 AS). Shops like this boast "K. u. K." This means a shop considered good enough for the *König und Kaiser* (king and emperor—same guy).

Kohlmarkt ends at Michaelerplatz. The stables of the Spanish Riding School face this square a block to the left. Notice the Roman excavation in the center. Enter the Hofburg Palace by walking through the gate, under the dome, and into the first square (In der Burg).

Sights—Vienna's Hofburg Palace

▲▲**Hofburg**—The complex, confusing, and imposing Imperial Palace, with 640 years of architecture, demands your attention. This first Hapsburg residence grew with the family empire from the 13th century until 1913, when the new wing was opened. The winter residence of the Hapsburg rulers until 1918, it's still the home of the Spanish Riding School, the Vienna Boys' Choir, the Austrian president's office, 5,000 government workers, and several important museums.

Rather than lose yourself in its myriad halls and courtyards, focus on three things: the Imperial Apartments, Treasury, and Neue Burg (New Palace).

Orient from **In der Burg Square**. The statue is of Emperor Franz II, grandson of Maria Theresa, grandfather of Franz Josef, and father-in-law of Napoleon. Behind him is a tower with three kinds of clocks (the yellow disc shows the stage of the moon tonight). On the right, a door leads to the Imperial Apartments and Hofburg model. Franz II faces the oldest part of the palace. The colorful gate, which used to have a drawbridge, leads to the 13th-century Swiss Court (named for the Swiss mercenary guards once stationed here), the Schatzkammer (treasury), and the Hof-burgkappelle (palace chapel, where the Boys' Choir sings the Mass). For the Hero's Square and the New Palace, continue opposite the way you entered In der Burg, passing through the left-most tunnel (with a tiny but handy sandwich bar—Hofburg Stüberl).

Tour the Imperial Apartments first.

▲▲**Imperial Apartments (Kaiserappartements)**—These lavish, Versailles-type "wish-I-were-God" royal rooms are a small, downtown version of the grander Schönbrunn Palace. If rushed

Vienna's Hofburg Palace

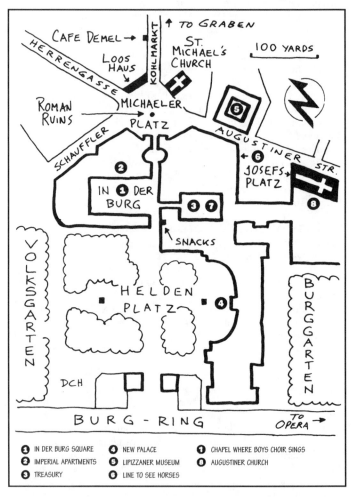

❶	IN DER BURG SQUARE	❹	NEW PALACE	❼	CHAPEL WHERE BOYS CHOIR SINGS
❷	IMPERIAL APARTMENTS	❺	LIPIZZANER MUSEUM	❽	AUGUSTINER CHURCH
❸	TREASURY	❻	LINE TO SEE HORSES		

and you have time for only one, these suffice (95 AS, daily 9:00–17:00, from courtyard through St. Michael's Gate, just off Michaelerplatz, tel. 01/533-7570). Study the great Hofburg model outside near the ticket line. Palace visits are a one-way romp through 20 rooms. You'll find some helpful English information within, and, together with the following description, you won't need the 95-AS Hofburg guidebook. Tickets include the royal silver and porcelain collection near the turnstile.

Get your ticket and climb two flights. The first two rooms give an overview (in English) of Empress Elisabeth's assortment of luxury homes, including the Hofburg.

Amble through the first several furnished rooms to the ...

Audience chamber: Every citizen had the right to meet privately with the emperor. Three huge paintings would entertain guests while they waited. They were propaganda, showing crowds of commoners enthusiastic about their Hapsburg royalty. On the right: The emperor returning to Vienna celebrating news that Napoleon had begun his retreat in 1809. Left: The return of the emperor from the 1814 Peace of Paris, the treaty that ended the Napoleonic wars. (The 1815 Congress of Vienna that followed was the greatest assembly of diplomats in European history. Its goal: to establish peace through a "balance of power" among nations. While rulers ignored nationalism in favor of continued dynastic rule, this worked for about 100 years, when a colossal war—WWI—wiped out Europe's royal families.) Center: Less important, the emperor makes his first public appearance to adoring crowds after recovering from a life-threatening illness (1826). The chandelier—considered the best in the palace—is Baroque of Bohemian crystal.

Audience room: Suddenly you were face-to-face with the emp. The portrait on the easel shows Franz Josef (who gets my vote for the greatest Hapsburg emperor) in 1915 when he was over 80 years old. Famously energetic, he lived a spartan life dedicated to duty. He'd stand at the high table here to meet with commoners who came to show gratitude or make a request. (Standing kept things moving.) On the table you see a partial list of 56 appointments he had on January 3, 1910.

Conference room: The emperor presided here over the equivalent of cabinet meetings. Remember, after 1867, he ruled the Austro-Hungarian Empire and Hungarians sat at these meetings. The paintings on the wall show the military defeat of a popular Hungarian uprising ... subtle.

Emperor Franz Josef's study: The desk was originally between the windows. Franz Josef could look up from his work and see his lovely empress Elisabeth's reflection in the mirror. Notice the trompe l'oeil paintings above each door giving the believable illusion of marble relief.

The walls between the rooms are wide enough to hide servants' corridors (the door to his valet's room is open). The emperor lived with a personal staff of 14: "3 valets, 4 lackeys, 2 doormen, 2 manservants, and 3 chambermaids."

Emperor's bedroom: This features his famous spartan iron bed and portable washstand (necessary until 1880 when the palace got running water). A small painted porcelain portrait of the newlywed royal couple sits on the dresser. Franz Josef lived

Sissy

Empress Elisabeth, Emperor Franz Joseph's mysterious, narcissistic, and beautiful wife, is in vogue. She was mostly silent, worked out frantically to maintain her Barbie Doll figure, and spent hours each day tending to her ankle-length hair. "Sissy's" main purpose in life seemed to be to preserve her reputation as a beautiful empress and maintain her fairy-tale hair. In spite of severe dieting and fanatic exercise, age took its toll. After turning 30, she allowed no more portraits painted and was seen in public generally with a delicate fan covering her face. Complex and influential, she was adored by Franz Joseph whom she respected. Her political cause was promoting Hungary's bid for nationalism, her tragedy was the death of her son Rudolf, the crown prince, by suicide. Hating Vienna and the confines of the court, she traveled more and more frequently. Over the years, the restless Sissy and her hardworking husband became estranged. In 1898, while visiting Geneva, Switzerland, she was murdered by an Italian anarchist. Sissy has been compared to Princess Diana because of her beauty, bittersweet life, and tragic death.

here after his estrangement from Sissy. An etching shows the empress—an avid hunter—riding sidesaddle while jumping a hedge. The big ornate stove in the corner was fed from behind. Through the 19th century, this was a standard form of heating.

Great salon: See the paintings of the emperor and empress in grand gala ballroom outfits from 1865. Look for window shades with English descriptions of royal life in the next several rooms.

Emperor's smoking room: This is dedicated to the memory of the assassinated Emperor Maximillian of Mexico (bearded portrait, killed in 1867). A smoking room was necessary in the early 19th century, when smoking was newly fashionable but only for men and then not in the presence of women.

Empress' bedroom and drawing room: This was Sissy's, refurbished neo-rococo in 1854. She lived here—the bed was rolled in and out daily—until her death in 1898.

Sissy's dressing/gymnastic room: This was the marital bedroom of the newlywed couple. The open bathroom door shows her huge copper tub. Servants worked two hours a day on Sissy's famous hair here. She'd exercise on the wooden structure. While she had a tough time with people, she did fine with animals. Her favorite circus horses, Flick and Flock, prance on the wall.

Empress' great salon: The room is painted with

Mediterranean escapes, the 19th-century equivalent of travel posters. The statue is of Elisa, Napoleon's oldest sister (by the neoclassical master Canova). At the end of the hall admire the Empress' hard-earned thin waist. Turn the corner and pass through the anterooms of Alexander's apartments.

Reception room: The Gobelin wall hangings were a 1776 gift from Marie Antoinette and Louis XVI in Paris to their Viennese counterparts.

Dining room: It's dinner time, and Franz Josef has called his large family together. The settings are modest...just silver. Gold was saved for formal state dinners. Next to each name card was a menu with the chef responsible for each dish. (Talk about pressure.) While the Hofburg had tableware for 4,000, feeding 3,000 was a typical day. The cellar was stocked with 60,000 bottles of wine. The kitchen was huge—50 birds could be roasted on the hand-driven spits at once.

Small salon: The last room is dedicated to Franz Josef's first two heirs: Rudolf (his troubled son, who committed suicide in 1889) and Franz Ferdinand (his liberal nephew, assassinated in Sarajevo in 1914). Back on the street, two quick lefts take you back to the palace square (In der Burg) and the treasury.

▲▲▲**Treasury (Weltliche und Geistliche Schatzkammer)**— This Secular and Religious Treasure Room contains the best jewels on the Continent. Slip through the vault doors and reflect on the glitter of 21 rooms filled with scepters, swords, crowns, orbs, weighty robes, double-headed eagles, gowns, gem-studded bangles, and a 2.5-meter-tall, 500-year-old unicorn horn (or maybe the tusk of a narwhal)—which was incredibly powerful in the old days, giving its owner the grace of God. Remember that these were owned by the Holy Roman Emperor—a divine monarch (100 AS, Wed–Mon 10:00–18:00, closed Tue, follow "Schatzkammer" signs through the black, red, and gold arch leading from the main courtyard into Schweizerhof, tel. 01/533-7931). Take advantage of the ingenious and extremely helpful Art-Guide mini-video (free, deposit: passport or 100 AS). Point this infrared computer at display cases to get information.

Room 2: The personal crown of Rudolf II survived since 1602 because it was considered too well crafted to cannibalize for other crowns. This crown is a big deal because it's the adopted crown of the Austrian Empire, established in 1806 after Napoleon dissolved the Holy Roman Empire (so named because it had tried to be the grand continuation of the Roman Empire). Pressured by Napoleon, the Austrian Francis II—who'd been Holy Roman Emperor—became Francis I, Emperor of Austria. Francis I/II (the stern guy on the wall) ruled from 1792 to 1835. Look at the crown. Its design merges the typical medieval king's crown and a bishop's miter.

Rooms 3 and 4: These contain some of the coronation vestments and regalia needed for the new Austrian emperor.

Room 5: Ponder the Throne Cradle. Napoleon's son was born in 1811 and made king of Rome. The little eagle at the foot is symbolically not yet able to fly but glory bound. Glory is symbolized by the star with dad's big "N" raised high.

Room 11: The collection's highlight is the 10th-century crown of the Holy Roman Emperor. The imperial crown swirls with symbolism "proving" that the emperor is both holy and Roman. The jeweled arch over the top is reminiscent of the parade helmet of ancient Roman emperors whose successors the HRE claimed to be. The cross on top says that the HRE rules as Christ's representative on earth. King Solomon's portrait (right of cross) is Old Testament proof that kings can be wise and good. King David (next panel) is similar proof that they can be just. The crown's eight sides represent the celestial city of Jerusalem's eight gates. The jewels on the front panel symbolize the Twelve Apostles. The nearby 11th-century Imperial Cross preceded the emperor in ceremonies. Crusted with jewels, it carried a substantial chunk of *the* cross (see it below).

Two cases in this room have jewels from the reign of Karl der Grosse (Charlemagne), the greatest ruler of medieval Europe. Notice Charlemagne modeling the crown in the tall painting adjacent.

Room 12: This features a painting of the coronation of Josef II in 1764, wearing the crown and royal garb you've just seen.

Room 16: Most tourists walk right by perhaps the most exquisite workmanship in the entire treasury, the royal vestments (15th century). Look closely—they are painted with gold and silver threads.

▲**Hero's Square and the New Palace (Heldenplatz and the Neue Burg)**—This last grand addition to the palace, from just before World War I, was built for Franz Ferdinand but never used. (It was tradition for rulers not to move into their predecessor's quarters.) Its grand facade arches around Heldenplatz, or Hero's Square. Notice statues of the two great Austrian heroes on horseback: Prince Eugene of Savoy (who saved the city from the Turks) and Archduke Charles (first to beat Napoleon in a battle, breaking Nappy's image of invincibility and heralding the end of the Napoleonic age). The frilly spires of Vienna's neo-Gothic city hall break the horizon and a line of horse-drawn carriages await their customers.

▲**New Palace Museums: Armor, Music, and Ancient Greek Statues**—The Neue Burg—labeled "Kunsthistorisches Museum" because it contains one wing from the main museum across the way—houses three small but fine museums (same ticket): an armory, historical musical instruments, and classical statuary from ancient

Ephesus. The musical instruments are particularly entertaining. Free radio headsets—when they work—play appropriate music in each room. Wait for the brief German description to finish, and you might hear the instruments you're seeing. Stay tuned in, as graceful period music accompanies your wander through the neighboring halls of medieval weaponry—a killer collection of crossbows, swords, and armor. An added bonus is the chance to wander all alone among those royal Hapsburg halls, stairways, and painted ceilings (60 AS, Wed–Mon 10:00–18:00, closed Tue, almost no tourists, not a word of English—and proud of it).

More Hofburg Sights

These sights are near—and associated with—the palace.

▲**Lipizzaner Museum**—A must for horse lovers, this tidy museum in the Renaissance Stallburg Palace shows (and tells in English) the 400-year history of the famous riding school. Videos show the horses in action (on TVs throughout and in the basement theater—45-minute movie in German, but great horse footage). A highlight for many is the opportunity to view the stable from a museum window and actually see the famous white horses just sitting there looking common (70 AS, daily 9:00–18:00, Reitschulgasse 2 between Josefsplatz and Michaelerplatz, tel. 01/533-7811). Part of the exhibit explains how, at the end of World War II, U.S. General Patton—knowing that the Soviets were about to take control of Vienna—ordered a raid on the stable to save the horses and insure the survival of their fine old bloodlines.

    Seeing the Lipizzaner Stallions: Seats for performances by Vienna's prestigious Spanish Riding School book up long in advance, but standing room is usually available the same day (tickets-250–900 AS, standing room-200 AS, 1 or 2 shows/week May–June and Sept–Dec). Lucky for the masses, training sessions in a chandeliered Baroque hall are open to the public (100 AS at the door, Tue–Fri 10:00–12:00 roughly Feb–June and Sept–Dec; occasional rehearsals with music on Sat are more entertaining than the generally low-energy training sessions). The gang lines up early at Josefsplatz, gate 2. Save money and avoid the wait by buying the 140-AS combo ticket covering both the museum and the training session. Or, better yet, simply show up late. Tourists line up for hours to get in at 10:00. Since almost no one stays for the full two hours—except for the horses—you can just waltz in with no wait at all after 11:00.

▲**Augustinian Church**—Step into the nearby Augustinerkirche (on Josefsplatz), the Gothic and neo-Gothic church where the Hapsburgs latched, then buried, their hearts (weddings took place here and the royal hearts are in the vault). Don't miss the exquisite Canova tomb (neoclassical, 1805) of Maria Theresa's favorite daughter, Maria Christina, with its incredibly sad white-marble procession. The church's 11:00 Sunday Mass is a hit with music lovers (pipe organ and choral, especially outside of summer).

▲▲**Kaisergruft, the Remains of the Hapsburgs**—Visiting the imperial remains is not as easy as you might imagine. These original organ donors left their bodies—147 in all—in the Kaisergruft (Capuchin Crypt), their hearts in the Augustinian Church (church open daily, but to see the goods you'll have to talk to a priest; Augustinerstrasse 3), and their entrails in the crypt below St. Stephan's Cathedral. Don't tripe.

Upon entering the Kaisergruft (40 AS, daily 9:30–16:00, behind Opera on Neuer Markt), see the Capuchin brother at the door and buy the 5-AS map with a Hapsburg family tree and a chart locating each coffin. The double coffin of Maria Theresa and her husband is worth a close look for its artwork. Don't miss the tombs of Franz Josef, Sissy (always with fresh flowers), and— the latest addition—Empress Zita, buried in 1989. Her burial procession was probably the last such Old Regime event in European history. The monarchy died hard in Austria. Take a whiff. The crypt is smelling funny and will probably be closed sometime in the near future for restoration and freshening up.

Rather than chasing down all these body parts, remember that the magnificence of this city is the real remains of the Hapsburgs. Pan up. Watch the clouds glide by the ornate gables of Vienna.

Sights—Schönbrunn Palace

▲▲▲**Schönbrunn Palace**—Among Europe's palaces, only Schloss Schönbrunn rivals Versailles. Located four miles from the center, it was the Hapsburgs' summer residence. It's big— 1,441 rooms—but don't worry, only 40 rooms are shown to the public. (The families of 260 civil servants actually rent simple apartments in the rest of the palace.)

While the exterior is Baroque, the interior was finished under Maria Theresa in let-them-eat-cake rococo. The chandeliers are either of hand-carved wood with gold-leaf gilding or of Bohemian crystal. Thick walls hid the servants as they ran around stoking the ceramic stoves from the back, and so on. Most of the public rooms are decorated in neo-Baroque as they were under Franz Josef (ruled 1848–1916). When World War II bombs rained on the city and the palace grounds, the palace itself took only one direct hit. Thankfully, that bomb, which crashed through three floors, including the sumptuous central ballroom, was a dud.

Reservations, Hours: Schönbrunn suffers from crowds. To avoid the long delays, make a reservation by telephone (01/ 8111-3239, they answer daily 8:00–17:00). You'll get an appointment time and ticket number. Check in at least 30 minutes early. Upon arrival, go to the first desk for group leaders, give your number, pick up your ticket, and jump in ahead of the masses. If you show up without calling first, you deserve the frustration. Wait in line, buy your ticket, and wait until the listed time to enter (which could be tomorrow). Kill time in the gardens or coach museum (palace open daily 8:30–17:45, last entry 17:00, off-season until 17:15, last entry 16:30). Crowds are worst from 9:30 to 11:30 and on weekends; it's least crowded from 12:00 to 14:00 and after 16:00.

Cost, Tours: The admission price is the price of the tour you select. Choose among two recorded audioguide tours (Imperial Tour or the bigger Grand Tour) or a live tour. The Imperial Tour covers 22 rooms (95 AS, 35 min, Grand Palace rooms plus apartments of Franz Josef and Elisabeth). I'd recommend the Grand Tour, which covers those 22 rooms plus 18 more (125 AS, 75 min, adds apartments of Maria Theresa). While there are occasional live guided tours doing all 40 rooms (150 AS, call day before your visit to ask if English tour is scheduled), I prefer the headphones.

Getting to Palace: Take tram #58 from Westbahnhof directly to the palace or ride U-4 to Schönbrunn and walk 300 meters. The main entrance is in the left side of the palace (as you face it).

Coach Museum Wagenburg—The Schönbrunn coach museum is a 19th-century traffic jam of 50 impressive royal carriages and sleighs. Highlights include silly sedan chairs, the death-black hearse carriage (used for Franz Josef in 1916 and most recently for Empress Zita in 1989), and an extravagantly gilded imperial carriage pulled by eight Cinderella horses (60 AS, daily 9:00–18:00, off-season 10:00–16:00 and closed on winter Mon, 200 meters from palace, walk through right arch as you face palace).

Palace Gardens—After strolling through all the Hapsburgs tucked neatly into their crypts, a stroll through the emperor's garden with countless commoners is a celebration of the natural (and necessary) evolution of civilization from autocracy into real democracy. As a civilization, we're doing well. The sculpted gardens (with a palm house, 60 AS, 9:30–18:00) lead past Europe's oldest zoo (Tiergarten, 120 AS, built by Maria Theresa's husband for the entertainment and education of the court in 1752) up to the Gloriette, a purely decorative monument celebrating an obscure Austrian military victory and offering a fine city view (and an expensive cup of coffee). The park is free (daily 6:00–20:30, entrance on either side of the palace).

Vienna's Other Top Sights

▲▲▲**Kunsthistorisches Museum**—This exciting museum across the Ring from the Hofburg Palace showcases the great Hapsburg art collection—masterpieces by Dürer, Rubens, Titian, Raphael, and especially Brueghel. There's also a fine display of Egyptian, classical, and applied arts, including a divine golden salt bowl by

Cellini. The paintings are hung on one glorious floor (100 AS, higher depending on special exhibitions, Tue–Sun 10:00–18:00, Thu until 21:00, closed Mon, sporadic 90-minute English tours April–Oct Tue–Sun, could be at 11:00 and 15:00, tel. 01/525-240).

▲**Natural History Museum**—In the twin building facing the art museum, you'll find moon rocks, dinosaur stuff, and the fist-sized *Venus of Willendorf*—at 30,000 years old, the world's oldest sex symbol, found in the Danube Valley (30 AS, Wed–Mon 9:00–18:30, Wed until 21:00, closed Tue, off-season 9:00–15:00, tel. 01/521-770).

▲**Academy of Fine Arts**—This small but exciting collection includes works by Bosch, Botticelli, and Rubens; a Venice series by Guardi; and a self-portrait by 15-year-old Van Dyck (50 AS, Tue–Sun 10:00–16:00, closed Mon, 3 blocks from Opera at Schillerplatz 3, tel. 01/5881-6225). As you wander the halls of this academy, ponder how history might have been different if Hitler—who applied to study architecture here but was rejected—would have been accepted.

KunstHausWien—This "make yourself at home" modern-art museum is a hit with lovers of modern art. It features the work of local painter/environmentalist Hundertwasser (95 AS, 48 AS on Mon, daily 10:00–19:00; Weissgerberstrasse 13, metro: U-3 Landstrasse, tel. 01/712-0491).

Nearby, the one-with-nature **Hundertwasserhaus** (at Löwengasse and Kegelgasse) is a complex of 50 lived-in apartments. This was built in the 1980s as a breath of architectural fresh air in a city of boring blocky apartment complexes. It's not open to visitors but is worth visiting for its fun-loving and colorful patchwork exterior, the Hundertwasser festival of shops across the street, and for the pleasure of annoying its neighbors. People wait for years to get an apartment here.

▲**Belvedere Palace**—The elegant palace of Prince Eugene of Savoy (the still-much-appreciated conqueror of the Turks), and later home of Franz Ferdinand, houses the Austrian Gallery of 19th- and 20th-century art. Skip the lower palace and focus on the garden and the top floor of the upper palace (Oberes Belvedere) for a winning view of the city and a fine collection of Jugendstil art, Klimt, and Kokoschka (80 AS, Tue–Sun 10:00–17:00, closed Mon, entrance at Prinz Eugen Strasse 27, tel. 01/7955-7134). Your ticket includes the Austrian Baroque and Gothic art in the Lower Palace.

Honorable Mention—There's much, much more. The city museum brochure lists everything. If you're into butterflies, Esperanto, undertakers, tobacco, clowns, fire fighting, Freud, or the homes of dead composers, you'll find them all in Vienna. Several good museums that try very hard but are submerged in the greatness of Vienna include: **Historical Museum of the**

Jugendstil

Vienna gave birth to its own curvaceous brand of Art Nouveau around the early 1900s: Jugendstil. The TI has a brochure laying out Vienna's 20th-century architecture. The best of Vienna's scattered Jugendstil sights: the Belvedere Palace collection, the clock on Höher Markt (which does a musical act at noon), and the Karlsplatz metro stop, where you'll find the gilded-cabbage-domed gallery with the movement's slogan: "To each century its art and to art its liberty." Klimt, Wagner, and friends (who called themselves the Vienna Succession) first exhibited their "liberty style" art here in 1897.

City of Vienna (Tue–Sun 9:00–16:30, Karlsplatz), **Folkloric Museum of Austria** (Laudongasse 15, tel. 01/406-8905), and **Museum of Military History**, one of Europe's best if you like swords and shields (Heeresgeschichtliches Museum, Sat–Thu 9:00–17:00, closed Fri, Arsenal district, Objekt 18, tel. 01/795-610). The **Albertina Museum**, with its superb collection of sketches and graphic art, is closed until 2002.

For a walk in the **Vienna Woods**, catch the U-4 metro to Heiligenstadt, then bus #38A to Kahlenberg, for great views and a café overlooking the city. From there it's a peaceful 45-minute downhill hike to the *Heurigen* of Nussdorf or Grinzing to enjoy some wine (see "Vienna's Wine Gardens," below).

Top People-Watching and Strolling Sights

▲**City Park**—Vienna's Stadtpark is a waltzing world of gardens, memorials to local musicians, ponds, peacocks, music in bandstands, and locals escaping the city. Notice the Jugendstil entry at the Stadtpark metro station. The Kursalon is where Strauss was the violin-toting master of waltzing ceremonies.

▲**Prater**—Vienna's sprawling amusement park tempts many visitors with its huge 220-foot-high, famous, and lazy Ferris wheel (*Riesenrad*), roller coaster, bumper cars, Lilliputian railroad, and endless eateries. Especially if you're traveling with kids, this is a fun, goofy place to share the evening with thousands of Viennese (daily 9:00–24:00 in summer, metro: Praterstern). For a local-style family dinner, eat at Schweizerhaus (good food, great beer) or Wieselburger Bierinsel.

Sunbathing—Like most Europeans, the Austrians worship the sun. Their lavish swimming centers are as much for tanning as for swimming. For the best man-made island beach, head for the "Danube Sea," Vienna's 30-kilometer beach along Danube Island (metro: Donauinsel).

▲**Naschmarkt**—Vienna's ye olde produce market bustles daily, near the Opera along Wienzeile Street. It's likably seedy and surrounded by sausage stands, Turkish *döner kebab* stalls, cafés, and theaters. Each Saturday it's infested by a huge flea market where, in olden days, locals would come to hire a monkey to pick little critters out of their hair (Mon–Fri 7:00–18:00, Sat 6:00–13:00, metro: Kettenbruckengasse). For a picnic park, walk a block down Schleifmuhlgasse.

Summer Music Scene

Vienna is Europe's music capital. It's music *con brio* from October through June, reaching a symphonic climax during the Vienna Festival each May and June. Sadly, in July and August, the Boys' Choir, the Opera, and many more music companies are—like you—on vacation. But Vienna hums year-round with live classical music. In the summer, you have these basic choices:

Touristy Mozart and Strauss Concerts—If the music comes to you, it's touristy—designed for flash-in-the-pan Mozart fans. Powdered-wig orchestra performances are given almost nightly in grand traditional settings (400–700 AS). Pesky wigged and powdered Mozarts peddle tickets in the streets with slick sales pitches about the magic of the venue and the quality of the musicians. Second-rate orchestras, clad in historic costumes, perform the greatest hits of Mozart and Strauss. While there's not a local person in the audience, the tourists generally enjoy the evening. To sort through all your options, check with the ticket office in the TI (same price as on the street but with all venues to choose from).

Strauss in the Palais Borse—For years Strauss concerts have been held in the Kursalon, where the Waltz King himself directed wildly popular concerts 100 years ago. Until 2002, while the Kursalon is renovated, concerts are in the less exciting but still classy Palais Borse (north end of the Ring, daily July–Sept at 20:00, 390–590 AS, tel. 01/718-9666). Shows are a touristy mix of ballet, waltzes, 15-piece orchestra in wigs and old outfits, and a chance for anyone in the audience to get on the floor and waltz.

Serious Concerts—These events, including the Opera, are listed in the monthly *Programm* (available at the TI). Tickets run from 300 to 1000 AS (plus a stiff 22 percent booking fee when booked in advance or through a box office like the one at the TI). If you call a concert hall directly, they can advise you on the availability of (cheaper) tickets at the door. Vienna takes care of its starving artists (and tourists) by offering cheap standing-room tickets to top-notch music and opera (1 hr before show time).

Vienna's **Summer of Music Festival** assures that even from June through September you'll find lots of great concerts, choirs, and symphonies (special *Klang Bogen* brochure at TI; get tickets at

Wien Ticket pavilion off Kärntner Strasse next to Opera House,
or go directly to location of particular event, tel. 01/4000-8410
for information).

▲▲**Vienna Boys' Choir**—The boys sing (heard but not seen,
from a high balcony) at Mass in the Imperial Chapel (Hofburg-
kapelle) of the Hofburg (entrance at Schweizerhof) at 9:15 on
Sundays, except in July and August. While seats must be reserved
two months in advance (70–380 AS), standing room inside is free
and open to the first 60 who line up. Rather than line up early,
you can simply swing by and stand in the narthex just outside,
from where you can hear the boys and see the Mass on a TV
monitor. Boys' Choir concerts (on stage in the Konzerthaus) are
also given Fridays at 15:30 in May, June, September, and October
(390–430 AS, tel. 01/5880-4141 or 01/533-9927, fax 011-431-
533-992-775 from the U.S., or write Hofmusikkapelle, Hofburg,
A-1010 Wien). They're nice kids, but, for my taste, not worth all
the commotion.

Vienna's Cafés and Wine Gardens

▲**Viennese Coffeehouses**—In Vienna the living room is down
the street at the neighborhood coffeehouse. This tradition is just
another example of the Viennese expertise in good living. Each of
Vienna's many long-established (and sometimes even legendary)
coffeehouses has its individual character (and characters). They
offer newspapers, pastries, sofas, elegance, a smoky ambience,
and a "take all the time you want" charm for the price of a cup
of coffee. Order it *malange* (with a little milk) or *schwarzer* (black).
Rather than buy the *Herald Tribune* ahead of time, buy a cup of
coffee and read it for free Vienna-style.

My favorites are: **Café Hawelka**, with a dark, "brooding
Trotsky" atmosphere, paintings on the walls by struggling artists
who couldn't pay, a saloon-wood flavor, chalkboard menu, smoked
velvet couches, an international selection of newspapers, and a
phone that rings for regulars (8:00–02:00, Sun from 16:00, closed
Tue, Dorotheergasse 6, just off Graben); **Café Central**, with
Jugendstil decor and great *Apfelstrudel* (high prices and rude staff,
Mon–Sat 8:00–20:00, closed Sun, Herrengasse 14); the **Jugendstil
Café Sperl**, dating from 1880 (Mon–Sat 7:00–23:00, closed Sun in
summer, Gumpendorfer 11, just off Naschmarkt near Mariahilfer
Strasse); and the basic, untouristy **Café Ritter** (daily 8:00–20:00,
Mariahilfer Strasse 73, at Neubaugasse metro stop near several
recommended hotels).

▲**Wine Gardens**—The *Heurige* is a uniquely Viennese institution
celebrating the *Heurige*, or new wine. When the Hapsburgs let
Vienna's vintners sell their own wine tax free for 300 days a year,
several hundred families opened *Heurigen* (wine-garden restaurants
clustered around the edge of Vienna), and a tradition was born.

Today they do their best to maintain their old-village atmosphere, serving the homemade new wine (the last vintage, until November 11) with light meals and strolling musicians. For a *Heurige* evening, rather than go to a particular place, tram to the wine-garden district of your choice and wander around, choosing the place with the best ambience. Here are some options:

Grinzing: Of the many *Heurige* suburbs, Grinzing (tram #38 or bus #38A) is the most famous, lively…and touristy—with lots of tour buses. Many people precede their Grinzing meal and drinking by riding bus #38A to its end, high up at Kahlenberg for a grand Vienna view and then ride 20 minutes back into the *Heurige* action. Away from the commotion, consider **Heuriger am Oberen** at Reisenbergweg 15 (tram #38 to end, hike 200 meters uphill, through gate, 400 meters through vineyard to restaurant).

Nussdorf: Less touristy but still characteristic and popular with locals, Nussdorf has plenty of *Heurige* ambience. Two fine places are right at the end of tram D.

Bus #38A connects Grinzing and Nussdorf. Midway, Pfarr-platz has many decent spots including the famous and touristy **Beethoven's home** (Heiligenstadt, with live music, 10-minute walk from bus stop, tel. 01/370-3361). Beethoven lived—and composed his Sixth Symphony—here in 1817. (He hoped the local spa would cure his worsening deafness.)

Neustift am Walde: This neighborhood has lots of *Heuri-gen*, plenty of charm, and the fewest tourists of all (metro: U-6 Nussdorferstrasse, then bus #35A).

Gumpoldskirchen: This small medieval village farther outside of Vienna has more *Heurige* ambience than tourists. Ride the commuter train from the Opera to Gumpoldskirchen, and you'll find plenty of places to choose from.

At any *Heurige*, fill your plate at a self-serve cold-cut buffet (75–125 AS for dinner). Dishes to look out for: *Stelze* (grilled knuckle of pork), *Fleischlaberln* (fried ground meat patties), *Schinkenfleckerln* (pasta with cheese and ham), *Blunzen* (black pudding…sausage made from blood), *Presskopf* (jellied brains and innards), *Liptauer* (spicy cheese spread), *Kornspitz* (wholemeal bread roll), and *Kummelbraten* (crispy roast pork with caraway). Waitresses will then take your wine order (30 AS per quarter liter). Many locals claim it takes several years of practice to distinguish between *Heurige* and vinegar. For a near-*Heurige* experience right downtown, drop by Gigerl Stadtheuriger (see "Eating," below).

Shopping

The best-value shopping street, with more than 2,000 shops, is Mariahilfer Strasse. For an aristocrat's flea market, drop by Austria's answer to Sotheby's, the **Dorotheum**—five floors of

antique furniture and fancy knickknacks put up either for immediate sale or auction (often by people who inherited old things they
don't have room for, Mon–Fri 10:00–18:00, Sat 9:00–17:00, closed
Sun, between Graben and the Hofburg at Dorotheergasse 17).

Nightlife

If old music or new wine isn't your thing, Vienna has plenty of
alternatives. For an up-to-date rundown on fun after dark, get
the TI's free *Ten Reasons for Vienna* booklet. An area known as the
"Bermuda Dreieck" (Triangle), north of the cathedral between
Rotenturmstrasse and Judengasse, is the hot local nightspot, with
lots of classy pubs, or *Beisl* (such as Krah Krah, Salzamt, Slammer,
and Bermuda Brau), and music spots. On balmy summer evenings
the liveliest scene is at Danube Island. If you're just want a good
movie, the English Cinema Haydn plays English movies nightly
(Mariahilfer Strasse 57, tel. 01/587-2262).

Sleeping in Vienna
(15 AS = about $1, country code: 43, area code: 01)

Sleep Code: **S** = Single, **D** = Double/Twin, **T** = Triple, **Q** = Quad,
b = bathroom, **t** = toilet only, **s** = shower only, **CC** = Credit Card
(**V**isa, **M**asterCard, **A**mex). English is spoken at each place.

Book accommodations by phone a few days in advance. Most
places will hold a room without a deposit if you promise to arrive
before 17:00. My recommendations stretch mainly along the likeable Mariahilfer Strasse from the Westbahnhof (West Station) to
the town center. These hotels are listed starting from the not-so-
appealing Westbahnhof and working toward the city center. Unless
otherwise noted, prices include a continental breakfast. Postal code
is 1XX0, with XX being the district.

Sleeping near the Westbahnhof Train Station

Pension Funfhaus is big, clean, stark, and quiet. Although the
neighborhood is run-down, this place is a good value (S-395 AS,
Sb-480 AS, D-570 AS, Db-650 AS, T-850 AS, Tb-930 AS, 2-
bedroom apartments for 4 people-1,140 AS, closed mid-Nov–Feb,
Sperrgasse 12, 1150 Wien, tel. 01/892-3545 or 01/892-0286, fax
01/892-0460, Frau Susi Tersch). Half the rooms are in the fine
main building and half are in the annex, which has good rooms
but is near the train tracks and a bit scary on the street at night.
From the station, ride tram #52 or #58 two stops down Mariahilfer Strasse to Sperrgasse.

Hotel Ibis Wien, a modern high-rise hotel with American
charm, is ideal for anyone tired of quaint old Europe. Its 340
cookie-cutter rooms are bright, comfortable, modern, and have
all the conveniences (Sb-890 AS, Db-1,090 AS, Tb-1,290 AS,
breakfast-125 AS, CC:VMA, elevator, smoke-free rooms,

air-con, 400 meters to the right leaving Westbahnhof, Mariahilfer Gürtel 22–24, A-1060 Wien, tel. 01/59998, fax 01/597-9090, e-mail: resamariahilf@hotel-ibis.co.at).

Hotel Furstenhof, right across from the station, charges top schilling for its Old World, red-floral, spacious rooms and Internet access (S-560 AS, Sb-880–1,220 AS, D-890 AS, Db-1,390 AS, Tb-1,440 AS, Qb-1,480 AS, CC:VMA, Europlatz 4, tel. 01/523-3267, fax 01/523-326-726, www.hotelfuerstenhof.com).

Hotels along Mariahilfer Strasse
Lively Mariahilfer Strasse connects the West Station with the center. The U-3 metro line, starting at the Westbahnhof, goes down Mariahilfer Strasse to the cathedral. This very Viennese street is a comfortable and vibrant area filled with local shops and cafés. Most hotels are within a few steps of a metro stop, just one or two stops from the West Train Station.

Pension Hargita, with 19 generally small, bright, and tidy rooms (mostly twins), is right at the U-3 Zieglergasse stop (S-400 AS, Ss-450 AS, D-600 AS, Ds-700 AS, Db-800–900 AS, Ts-850 AS, Tb-1,050 AS, Qb-1,100 AS, CC:VM, breakfast-40 AS, cheaper off-season, corner of Mariahilfer Strasse and Andreas-gasse, Andreasgasse 1, 1070 Wien, tel. 01/526-1928, fax 01/526-0492, www.hargita.at, e-mail: pension@hargita.at).

Astron Suite Hotel Wien is two stern, business hotels a few blocks apart on Mariahilfer Strasse. Both rent ideal-for-families suites, each with a living room, two TVs, bathroom, desk, and kitchenette (Db suite-1,980 AS, apartment for 2–3 adults-2,880 AS, kids under 12 free, kids over 12-490 AS each, CC:VMA, non-smoking rooms, elevator, www.astron-hotels.de). One is at Mariahilfer Strasse 78 (at U-3 Zieglergasse metro stop, tel. 01/5245-6000, fax 01/524-560-015), the other is at Mariahilfer Strasse 32 (metro: U-3 Neubaugasse, tel. 01/521-720, fax 01/521-7215).

Pension Corvinus is small, bright, modern, and warmly run. Its comfortable rooms have small bathrooms (Sb-750 AS, Db-1,150 AS, Tb-1,350 AS, prices promised through 2001 with this book, extra bed-350 AS, CC:VM, elevator, air-con available, garage-150 AS, Mariahilfer Strasse 57, tel. 01/587-7239, fax 01/587-723-920, e-mail: hotel@corvinus.at). In the same building, **Haydn Hotel** is a big, hotelesque place with spacious rooms (Sb-890 AS, Db-1,290 AS, extra bed-400 AS, garage-150 AS, CC:VM, Mariahilfer Strasse 57, tel. 01/587-4414, fax 01/586-1950, e-mail: info@haydn-hotel.at).

Pension Mariahilf is a four-star place offering a clean aristo-cratic air in an affordable and cozy pension package. Its 12 rooms are spacious and feel new, but with an art deco flair. With four stars, everything's done right. You'll find the latest American magazines and even free Mozart balls at the reception desk

Vienna: Hotels Outside the Ring

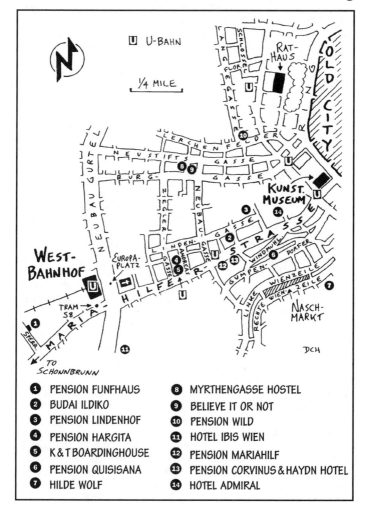

❶	PENSION FUNFHAUS	❽	MYRTHENGASSE HOSTEL
❷	BUDAI ILDIKO	❾	BELIEVE IT OR NOT
❸	PENSION LINDENHOF	❿	PENSION WILD
❹	PENSION HARGITA	⓫	HOTEL IBIS WIEN
❺	K & T BOARDINGHOUSE	⓬	PENSION MARIAHILF
❻	PENSION QUISISANA	⓭	PENSION CORVINUS & HAYDN HOTEL
❼	HILDE WOLF	⓮	HOTEL ADMIRAL

(Sb-800 AS, Db-1,300 AS, Tb-1,700 AS, at U-3 Neubaugasse metro stop, Mariahilfer Strasse 49, tel. 01/586-1781, fax 01/586-178-122, e-mail: penma@atnet.at, warmly run by Frau and Herr Ender).

Beyond its plain lobby, **Hotel Admiral** is a huge, quiet, family-run hotel that has large, comfortable rooms. Alexandra works hard to keep her guests happy (Sb-750–860 AS, Db-1,000

AS, special price with this book through 2001, extra bed-310 AS, free parking, metro: U-2 or U-3 Volkstheater, a block off Mariahilfer Strasse at Karl Schweighofer Gasse 7, tel. 01/521-410, fax 01/521-4116, e-mail: hoteladmiralwien@aon.at).

At **K&T Boardinghouse**, Tina and Fred Kaled rent four big, comfortable rooms (3 with full bathrooms) with the comforts you'd pay lots for in a hotel. This place—with the best cheap doubles in town—is homey with accommodating hosts (D-600 AS, Db-700 AS, Tb-950 AS, Qb-1,200 AS, no breakfast, Internet access, laundry, nonsmoking, 3 flights up, no elevator, Mariahilfer Strasse #72, tel. 01/523-2989, fax 01/522-0345, http://members .chello.at/timea.fetoui/, e-mail: kaled@chello.at).

Two women rent rooms out of their dark and homey apartments in the same building at Lindengasse 39 (1070 Wien). Each have high ceilings and Old World furnishings with two cavernous rooms sleeping two to four and a skinny twin room, all sharing one bathroom. These places are great if you're on a tight budget and wish you had a grandmother to visit in Vienna: **Maria Pribojszki** (S-400 AS, D-550 AS, T-800 AS, Q-1,000 AS, breakfast-50 AS, free laundry service for 4-night stays, tel. 01/523-9006, e-mail: e.boehm@xpoint.at) or **Budai Ildiko** (S-390 AS, D-600 AS, T-870 AS, Q-1,120 AS, no breakfast but free coffee, laundry-40 AS, tel. 01/523-1058, tel. & fax 01/526-2595, e-mail: budai@hotmail.com).

Pension Lindenhof is worn but clean, filled with plants, and run with Bulgarian and Armenian warmth (S-380 AS, Sb-480 AS, D-640 AS, Db-860 AS, cheaper in winter, hall showers-20 AS, metro: U-3 Neubaugasse, Lindengasse 4, 1070 Wien, tel. 01/523-0498, fax 01/523-7362).

Pension Quisisana—a tired and ramshackle time warp—is cheap and sleep-worthy for vagabonds (S-340 AS, Ss-390 AS, D-540 AS, Ds-610–650 AS, Db-710–750 AS, third person-260 AS, Windmuhlgasse 6, 1060 Wien, tel. 01/587-7155, fax 01/587-715-633).

Hilde Wolf shares her homey apartment with travelers (7 blocks off Mariahilfer Strasse and 3 blocks below Naschmarkt). Her four huge but stuffy rooms are like old libraries. Hilde won't overwhelm you with friendliness but she may do your laundry if you stay two nights (S-450 AS, D-650 AS, T-955 AS, Q-1,225 AS, prices good through 2001, reserve with CC but pay in cash, small breakfast, elevator, metro: U-2 Karlsplatz, Schleifmühlgasse 7, 1040 Vienna, tel. 01/586-5103).

Dorms and Hostels near Mariahilfer Strasse

Jugendherbergen Myrthengasse is a well-run youth hostel (185–215-AS beds, nonmembers-40 AS extra, includes sheets and breakfast, 3- to 6-bed rooms, some private rooms for couples and families, Myrthengasse 7, 1070 Wien, tel. 01/523-6316, fax 01/523-5849, e-mail: hostel@chello.at). Other hostels near

Mariahilfer Strasse are **Wombats City Hostel** (Grangasse 6, tel. 01/897-2336, e-mail: wombats@chello.at) and **Hostel Ruthensteiner** (Robert-Hamerling-Gasse 24, tel. 01/893-4202, e-mail: hostel.ruthensteiner@telecom.at).

Believe It or Not is a friendly and basic place with two coed rooms for up to 10 travelers under age 30. It's locked up from 10:30 to 12:30, has kitchen facilities, and no curfew (160 AS per bed, 110 AS Nov–Easter, Myrthengasse 10, ring Apt. #14, tel. 01/526-4658, run by Gosha).

Sleeping within the Ring, in the Old City Center

You'll pay extra to sleep in the old center. The first two are in the shadow of St. Stephan's Cathedral, on or near the Graben, where the elegance of Old Vienna strums happily over the cobbles. The next two are near the Opera and TI, five minutes from the cathedral. If you can afford it, staying here gives you the best classy Vienna experience.

At **Pension Nossek**, an elevator takes you above any street noise into Frau Bernad's and Frau Gundolf's world, where the children seem to be placed among the lace and flowers by an interior designer. Right on the wonderful Graben, this is particularly good value (Ss-700 AS, Sb-800–1,100 AS, Db-1,300 AS, Tb-1,700 AS, 300 AS extra for sprawling suites, Graben 17, tel. 01/5337-0410, fax 01/535-3646, e-mail: pension.nossek@faxvia.net).

Pension Pertschy circles an old courtyard and is bigger and more hotelesque than the others. The rooms are huge but musty. Those on the courtyard are quietest (Sb-940 AS, Db-1,460–1,660 AS depending on size, cheaper off-season, extra person-380 AS, CC:VM, Hapsburgergasse 5, tel. 01/534-490, fax 01/534-4949, www.pertschy.com, e-mail: pertschy@pertschy.com).

Baroque and doily as you'll find in this price range, **Pension Suzanne** is wonderfully located a few meters from the Opera. It's quiet and simple but run with the class of a bigger hotel (Sb-950 AS, Db-1,150–1,450 AS depending on size, third person-500 AS, huge discounts in winter, reserve with CC but pay cash, a block from Opera, at metro: Karlsplatz take Opera exit, Walfischgasse 4, 1010 Wien, tel. 01/513-2507, fax 01/513-2500, www.pension-suzanne.at, e-mail: info@pension-suzanne.at).

Hotel zur Wiener Staatsoper is quiet, rich, and hotelesque. Its rooms come with high ceilings, chandeliers, and fancy carpets on parquet floors—a good value for this locale and ideal for people whose hotel tastes are a cut above mine (Sb-1,200 AS, Db-1,500–1,750 AS, depending on season, summer is cheaper, extra bed-300 AS, family deals, CC:VMA, a block from Opera at Krugerstrasse 11, 1010 Wien, tel. 01/513-1274, fax 01/5131-27415, e-mail: office@zurwienerstaatsoper.at).

Schweizer Pension Solderer, family owned for three

Hotels in Central Vienna

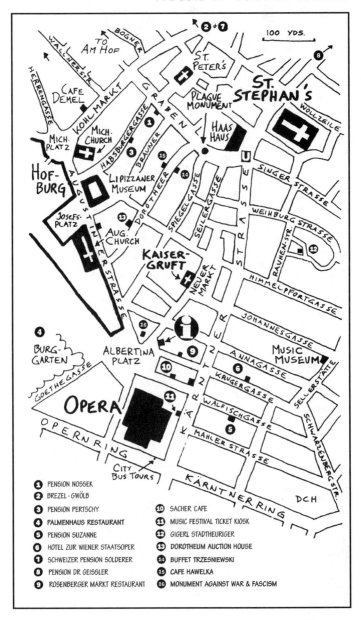

① PENSION NOSSEK
② BREZEL - GWÖLB
③ PENSION PERTSCHY
④ PALMENHAUS RESTAURANT
⑤ PENSION SUZANNE
⑥ HOTEL ZUR WIENER STAATSOPER
⑦ SCHWEIZER PENSION SOLDERER
⑧ PENSION DR GEISSLER
⑨ ROSENBERGER MARKT RESTAURANT
⑩ SACHER CAFE
⑪ MUSIC FESTIVAL TICKET KIOSK
⑫ GIGERL STADTHEURIGER
⑬ DOROTHEUM AUCTION HOUSE
⑭ BUFFET TRZESNIEWSKI
⑮ CAFE HAWELKA
⑯ MONUMENT AGAINST WAR & FASCISM

generations, is warmly run by two friendly sisters, Monica and Anita. Enjoy the homey feel, 11 big, comfortable rooms, parquet floors, and lots of tourist info (S-490 AS, Ss-700–800 AS, D-780 AS, Ds-980 AS, Db-1,050–1,100 AS, elevator, laundry-150 AS, nonsmoking, metro: U-2 Schottenring, Heinrichsgasse 2, 1010 Wien, tel. 01/533-8156, fax 01/535-6469, e-mail: schweizer .pension@chello.at).

Pension Dr. Geissler has comfortable rooms on the eighth floor of a modern building about 10 blocks northeast of St. Stephan's, just below the canal (S-580 AS, Sb-800–900 AS, D-800 AS, Ds-980 AS, Db-1000–1,200 AS, prices vary with season, CC:VMA, metro: Schwedenplatz, Postgasse 14, 1010 Wien, tel. 01/533-2803, fax 01/533-2635).

Pension Wild is outside of the old center, behind the City Hall. But with 20 delightful, just-renovated rooms, two family apartments, and a good, keep-it-simple-and-affordable attitude, it's one of Vienna's top values (S-490 AS, Sb-690 AS, D-590 AS, Db-990 AS, reserve with CC but pay cash, elevator, metro: U-2 Rathaus, Langegasse 10, 1080 Vienna, tel. 01/406-5174, fax 01/ 402-2168, www.pension-wild.com).

Eating in Vienna

The Viennese appreciate the fine points of life, and right up there with waltzing is eating. The city has many atmospheric restaurants. As you ponder the Slavic and eastern European specialties on menus, remember that Vienna's diverse empire may be gone, but its flavor lingers.

While cuisines are routinely named for countries, Vienna claims to be the only city with a cuisine of its own: Vienna soups come with fillings (semolina dumpling, liver dumpling, or pancake slices). *Gulasch* is a beef ragout of Hungarian origin (spiced with onion and paprika). Of course, Vienna Schnitzel (*Wiener Schnitzel*) is a breaded and fried veal cutlet. Another meat specialty is boiled beef (*Tafelspitz*). While you're sure to have *Apfelstrudel*, try the sweet cheese strudel, too (*Topfenstrudel*, wafer-thin strudel pastry filled with sweet cheese and raisins).

On nearly every corner you can find a colorful *Beisl* (Viennese tavern) filled with poetry teachers and their students, couples loving without touching, housewives on their way home from cello lessons, and waiters who enjoy serving hearty food and good drink at an affordable price. Ask at your hotel for a good *Beisl*.

Wherever you're eating, some vocabulary will help. Try the *grüner Veltliner* (dry white wine, any time), *Traubenmost* (a heavenly grape juice on the verge of wine, autumn only, sometimes just called *Most*), and *Sturm* (barely fermented *Most*, autumn only). The local red wine (called *Portuguese*) is pretty good. Since the Austrian wine is often very sweet, remember the word *Trocken* (dry). You can order your wine by the *Viertel* (quarter liter) or *Achtel* (eighth liter). Beer comes in a *Krugel* (half liter) or *Seidel* (.3 liter).

Eating in the City Center

These eateries are within a five-minute walk of the cathedral.

Gigerl Stadtheuriger offers a near-*Heurige* experience (à la Grinzing, see "Vienna's Cafes and Wine Gardens," above) without leaving the center. Just point to what looks good. Food is sold by the weight (cheese and cold meats cost about 35 AS/100 grams, salads are about 15 AS/100 grams; price sheet is posted, 10 dag equals 100 grams). They also have menu entrées, along with spinach strudel, quiche, *Apfelstrudel*, and, of course, casks of new and local wines. Meals run from 100 AS to 150 AS (daily 11:00–24:00, indoor/outdoor seating, behind cathedral, a block off Kärntner Strasse, a few cobbles off Rauhensteingasse on Blumenstock, tel. 01/513-4431).

The next five places are within a block of Am Hof square (metro: U-3 Herrengasse). **Restaurant Ofenloch** serves good old-fashioned Viennese cuisine with friendly service both indoors and out. This 300-year-old eatery, with great traditional ambience, is very central but not overrun with tourists (150–200 AS meals, daily 10:00–24:00, Kurrentgasse 8, tel. 01/533-8844). **Brezel-Gwölb**, a wonderfully atmospheric wine cellar with outdoor dining on a quiet square, serves delicious light meals, fine *Krautsuppe*, and old-fashioned local dishes. It's ideal for a romantic late-night glass of wine (daily 11:30–01:00, take Drahtgasse 20 meters off Am Hof, Ledererhof 9, tel. 01/533-8811). Around the corner, **Zum Scherer Sitz u. Stehbeisl** is just as untouristy, with indoor or outdoor seating, a soothing woody atmosphere, intriguing decor, and local specialties (Mon–Sat 11:00–01:00, Sun 17:00–24:00, Judenplatz 7, near Am Hof). Just below Am Hof, **Stadtbeisl** offers a good mix of value, local cuisine, and atmosphere (nightly, Naglergasse 21, tel. 01/533-3507). Around the corner, the ancient and popular **Esterhazykeller** has traditional fare deep underground or outside on a delightful square (daily, self-service buffet in lowest cellar or from menu, Haarhof 1, tel. 01/533-9340).

These wine cellars are fun and touristic but typical, in the old center of town, with reasonable prices and plenty of smoke: **Melker Stiftskeller**, less touristy, is a *Stadtheurige* in a deep and rustic cellar with hearty, inexpensive meals and new wine (Tue–Sat 17:00–24:00, closed Sun–Mon, between Am Hof and the Schottentor metro stop at Schottengasse 3, tel. 01/533-5530). **Zu den Drei Hacken** is famous for its local specialties (Mon–Fri 9:00–24:00, Sat 10:00–24:00, closed Sun, indoor/outdoor seating, CC:VA, Singerstrasse 28).

Cafe Restaurant Palmenhaus, overlooking the palace garden (*Burggarten*), tucked away in a green and peaceful corner two blocks behind the Opera in the Hofburg's backyard, is a world apart. If you want to eat modern Austrian cuisine with palm trees rather than tourists, this is it. And at the edge of a huge park, it's great for families (150-AS lunches, 200-AS dinners, serious vegetarian dishes and good wine, daily 10:00–24:00, indoors in greenhouse or outdoors, cool parkside outdoor pub just below, at Burggarten, tel. 01/533-1033).

Rosenberger Markt Restaurant is my favorite for a fast, light, and central lunch. Just a block toward the cathedral from the Opera, this place—while not cheap—is brilliant. Friendly and efficient, with special theme rooms for dining, it offers a fresh, smoke-free, and healthy cornucopia of food and drink (daily 10:30–23:00, lots of fruits, veggies, fresh-squeezed juices, addictive banana milk, ride the glass elevator downstairs, Mayseder-gasse 2). You can stack a small salad or veggie plate into a tower of gobble for 35 AS.

Buffet Trzesniewski is an institution—justly famous for its elegant and cheap finger sandwiches and small beers (10 AS each). Three different sandwiches and a *kleines Bier* (*Pfiff*) make a fun, light lunch. Point to whichever delights look tasty and pay for them and a drink. Take your drink tokens to the lady on the right. Sit on the bench and scoot over to a tiny table when a spot opens up (Mon–Fri 8:30–19:30, Sat 9:00–17:00, closed Sun, 50 meters off Graben, nearly across from brooding Café Hawelka, on Dorotheergasse 2).

Akakiko Sushi: If you're just schnitzeled out, a small chain of Japanese restaurants with an easy sushi menu may suit you (next to downtown recommended eateries in the heart of old center at Heidenschuss 3 or at Mariahilfer Strasse 40, tel. 01/533-8514).

Eating near Mariahilfer Strasse

Mariahilfer Strasse is filled with reasonable cafés serving all types of cuisine. A few blocks away, on the romantic streets just north of Siebensterngasse (take Stiftgasse from Mariahilfer Strasse), several cobbled alleys open their sidewalks and courtyards to appreciative locals (ideal for dinner or a relaxing drink). Stroll Spitellberggasse, Schrankgasse, and Gutenberggassse and pick your favorite place. Check out the courtyard inside Spittelberggasse 3, and don't miss the vine-strewn wine garden inside Schrankgasse 1. For traditional Viennese cuisine, consider **Witwe Bolte** (Gutenberggasse 13, daily 11:30–24:00, tel. 01/523-1450).

Restaurant Beim Novak serves good local cuisine away from the modern rush (Mon–Sat 18:00–24:00, closed Sun, a block down Andreasgasse from Mariahilfer Strasse at Richtergasse 12, tel. 01/523-3244).

Naschmarkt is Vienna's best Old World market, with plenty of fresh produce, cheap local-style eateries, cafés, and *döner kebab* and sausage stands (Mon–Fri 7:00–18:00, Sat until 12:00, closed Sun).

Transportation Connections—Vienna

Vienna has two main train stations: the Westbahnhof (West Train Station), serving Munich, Salzburg, Melk, and Budapest; and the Südbahnhof (South Train Station), serving Italy, Budapest, and Prague. A third station, Franz Josefs, serves Krems and the Danube Valley (but Melk is served by the Westbahnhof). Metro line U-3 connects the Westbahnhof with the center, tram D takes you from the Südbahnhof and the Franz Josefs to downtown, and tram #18 connects West and South Stations. Train info: tel. 051717 (wait through long German recording for operator).

By train to: Melk (hrly, 75 min), **Krems** (hrly, 1 hr), **Salzburg** (hrly, 3 hrs), **Innsbruck** (3/day, 5.5 hrs), **Budapest** (3/day, 3 hrs), **Prague** (4/day, 5.5 hrs), **Munich** (10/day, 4.5 hrs), **Berlin** (2/day 14 hrs), **Zurich** (4/day, 9 hrs), **Rome** (3/day, 14 hrs), **Venice** (6/day, 9 hrs), **Frankfurt** (7/day, 7.5 hrs), **Amsterdam** (2/day, 14 hrs).

To Eastern Europe: Vienna is the springboard for a quick trip to Prague and Budapest—three hours by train from Budapest (370 AS, 740 AS round-trip, free with Eurail) and 5.5 hours from Prague (486 AS one-way, 1,030 AS round-trip, 710 AS round-trip with Eurail). Visas are not required. Purchase tickets at most travel agencies. Eurail passholders bound for Prague must pay to ride the rails in the Czech Republic; for details, see "Transportation Connections" in the Berlin chapter.

Route Tips for Drivers

Driving in and out of Vienna: Navigating in Vienna isn't bad. Study the map. As you approach from Krems, you'll cross the North Bridge and land on the Gürtel, or outer ring. You can continue along the Danube canal to the inner ring, called the Ringstrasse (clockwise traffic only). Circle around either thoroughfare until you reach the "spoke" street you need.

Vienna west to Hall in Tirol (280 miles): To leave Vienna, follow the signs past the Westbahnhof to Schloss Schönbrunn (Schönbrunn Palace), which is directly on the way to the West A-1 Autobahn to Linz. Leave the palace by 15:00, beating rush hour, and follow autobahn signs to West A-1, passing Linz and Salzburg, nipping through Germany, and turning right onto Route 93 in the direction of Kufstein, Innsbruck, and Austria at the Dreieck Inntal (autobahn intersection). Crossing back into Austria, you'll follow the scenic Inn River valley until you stop five miles east of Innsbruck at Hall in Tirol. There's an autobahn tourist information station just before Hall (in season daily 10:00–22:00, working for the town's hotels but still helpful).

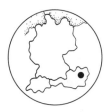

DANUBE VALLEY

The Danube is at its romantic best just west of Vienna. Mix a cruise with a bike ride through the Danube's Wachau Valley, lined with ruined castles, beautiful abbeys, small towns, and vineyard upon vineyard. After touring the glorious abbey of Melk, douse your warm, fairy-tale glow with a bucket of Hitler at the Mauthausen concentration camp.

Planning Your Time

For a day trip from Vienna, catch the early train to Melk, tour the abbey, eat lunch, and take an afternoon trip along the river from Melk to Krems (try a boat/bike combination). Note that the boat goes much faster downstream (east) (from Melk to Krems) than vice-versa. From Krems, catch the train back to Vienna. While this region is a logical day trip from Vienna, with good train connections to both Krems and Melk, spending a night in Melk is a winning idea. Melk is on the main Munich/Salzburg/Vienna train line. Mauthausen, farther away, should be seen en route to or from Vienna. On a three-week trip through Germany, Austria, and Switzerland, I'd see only one concentration camp. Mauthausen is more powerful than the more convenient Dachau and worthwhile if you have a car.

Cruising the Danube

By car, bike, or boat, the 38-kilometer stretch of the Danube between Krems and Melk is as pretty as they come. You'll cruise the Danube's wine road, passing wine gardens all along the river. Those hanging out a wreath of straw or greenery are inviting you in to taste. In local slang, someone who's feeling his wine is "blue." Blue Danube? Note that in German, Danube is Donau, as you'll see by the signs.

Danube Valley

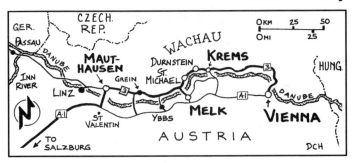

By Boat: Boats run between Krems and Melk three times a day in each direction (April–Oct, 200-AS one-way, 270-AS round-trip ticket allowing stopovers, bikes free). Boats depart from Melk at 11:00, 13:50, and 16:15 (90-minute ride downstream). Boats depart from Krems at 10:15, 13:00, and 15:45 (because of the 6-knot flow of the Danube, the same ride upstream takes 3 hrs). The 16:15 departure from Melk and the 15:45 departure from Krems require an easy transfer in Spitz; the rest are direct. To confirm these times, call the DDSG boat company (tel. 01/588-800 in Vienna), the Melk TI (tel. 02752/523-07410), or the Krems TI (tel. 02732/82676). If you'd like a longer cruise, ask which boats start or end in Vienna.

By Bike: See the Melk–Krems bike ride described in "Sights," below.

By Bus: The bus between Melk and Krems is a good budget or rainy-day alternative to the boat (75 AS, 60 min, 3/day, catch bus at train station, buy ticket on bus; for best views sit on the driver's side from Melk to Krems or the nondriver's side from Krems to Melk).

By Train: Regular trains connect Vienna with Krems and Melk, tiny one-car milk-run trains chug along from village to village up the river (but they don't stop at Melk—see bike ride in "Sights," below). Trains for Krems depart about hourly from Vienna's Franz Josef Bahnhof. For an easier departure (or return), consider starting (or ending) your train ride at Vienna's Spittelau (the train's first stop after the Franz Josef Bahnhof) instead of the Bahnhof. Spittelau has a U-Bahn station and Franz Josef Bahnhof does not. Melk is accessed from Vienna's West-bahnhof (Melk train info: tel. 02572/5232-1350).

MELK

Sleepy and elegant under its huge abbey that seems to police the Danube, the town of Melk offers a pleasant stop.

Tourist Information: The TI is a block off the upper end of the main square (look for green signs) and has info on nearby castles, bike rides along the river, and a list of *Zimmer* (Mon–Sat 9:00–19:00, plus Sun 10:00–14:00 July–Aug; off-season Mon–Fri 9:00–12:00, 14:00–18:00, Sat 9:00–12:00, good picnic garden with WC behind TI, tel. 02752/5230-7410). For accommodations, see "Sleeping," below.

Arrival in Melk: Walk straight out of the station (lockers available) for several blocks; at the curve, keep straight, following the cobbled alley that dumps you into the center of the village. The abbey access is up on your right and the TI is a block off the end of the square to your right. If you're coming from the boat dock, turn right at the BP gas station and follow the road along the river, walking below the abbey into the village (5-minute walk).

Sights—Melk

▲▲**Melk Abbey (Benediktinerstift)**—Melk's newly restored abbey, beaming proudly over the Danube Valley, is one of Europe's great sights. Established as a fortified Benedictine abbey in the 11th century, it was destroyed by fire. What you see today is 18th-century Baroque. Architect Jakob Prandtauer made the building one with nature. The Abbey Church, with its 200-foot-tall dome and symmetrical towers, dominates the complex—emphasizing its sacred purpose.

Freshly painted and gilded throughout, it's a Baroque dream, a lily alone. The grand restoration project—financed in part by the sale of the abbey's Gutenberg Bible to Harvard—was completed by 1996 to celebrate the 1,000th anniversary of the first reference to a country named Österreich (Austria).

Here's a quick tour.

East Facade: Approaching the grand entry, imagine the abbot on the balcony greeting you as he used to greet important guests. Flanking him are statues of Peter and Paul (leaders of the apostles and patron saints of the abbey church) and the monastery's coat of arms (crossed keys). High above are the Latin words "Glory only in the cross" and a huge copy of the Melk Cross (one of the monastery's treasures).

Prelate's Courtyard: Pass into the main courtyard. This is more than a museum. For 900 years monks of St. Benedict have lived and worked here. Their task: bringing and maintaining Christianity and culture to the region. (Many of the monks live outside the abbey in the community.) They run a high school with about 800 students, a small boarding school, and a busy retreat center.

There have been low points. During the Reformation (1500s), only eight monks "held down the theological fort." Napoleon made his headquarters here in 1805 and 1809. And in 1938, when Hitler annexed Austria, the monastery was squeezed into one end of the complex and nearly dissolved. But today the institution survives—

that's the point of the four modern frescoes gracing the courtyard, funded by agriculture (historically, monasteries are big landowners) and your visit. In the far left-hand corner, climb the stairs to...

Imperial Corridor: This 640-foot-long corridor, lined with paintings of Austrian royalty, is the spine of the permanent exhibition, *Melk Abbey, Past and Present*. Art treasures (including the 11th-century Melk Cross) fill several rooms.

Marble Hall: While the door frames are real marble, most of this large dining room/ballroom is stucco. The treasure here is the ceiling fresco (by Tyrolian Paul Troger, 1731). Notice three themes: 1) The Hapsburgs liked to be portrayed like Hercules; 2) Athena, the goddess of wisdom, is included, because the Hapsburgs were smart as well as strong; and 3) The Hapsburgs were into art and culture. This is symbolized by angels figuratively reining in the forces of evil, darkness, and brutality so—through this wise moderation—goodness, beauty, art, and science can rule.

Balcony: Here we enjoy dramatic views of the Danube Valley, the town of Melk, and the facade of the monastery church. The huge statue above everything shows the risen Christ, cross in hand and victorious over death—the central message of the entire place.

Library: The inlaid bookshelves, matching bindings, and another fine Troger fresco combine harmoniously to provide for the Marble Hall's thematic counterpart. This room celebrates not wise politics, but faith. The ceiling shows a woman surrounded by the four cardinal virtues (wisdom, justice, fortitude, and recycling)—natural virtues that lead to a supernatural faith. The statues flanking the doors represent the four traditional university faculties (law, medicine, philosophy, and theology). The globes show a 17th-century view of the earth and heavens. Many of the monastery's 100,000 volumes fill the shelves (some of the oldest and most precious are in the glass display case).

Church: The finale is the church with its architecture, ceiling frescos, stucco marble, grand pipe organ, and sumptuous chapels combining in full Baroque style to make the theological point: a just battle leads to victory. The ceiling shows St. Benedict's triumphant entry into heaven (on a fancy carpet). In the front, above the huge papal crown, saints Peter and Paul shake hands before departing for their final battles and ultimate victory. And high above, the painting in the dome shows that victory: the Holy Trinity, surrounded by saints of particular importance to Melk, happily in heaven.

Tours, Cost, Hours: While English tours of the abbey are offered daily (May–Sept at 14:55), it's easiest to just wander through on your own—perhaps with the help of a rentable, 40-AS audioguide (abbey-70 AS, with tour-90 AS, private guide-600 AS, daily 9:00–18:00, last entry 17:00, in winter the abbey is open only for bilingual tours at 11:00 and 14:00, tel. 02752/555-232). The abbey has a fine garden, café, and a restaurant in its orangerie.

Sights—The Danube Valley

▲▲Melk-to-Krems Danube Valley Bike Ride—The three-hour pedal from Melk to Krems takes you through the Wachau Valley—steeped in tradition, blanketed with vineyards, and ornamented with cute villages. Bikers rule here, and you'll find all the amenities that make this valley so popular with Austrians on two wheels.

The route is clearly marked with green "Donau-Radwander-weg" signs. The local TIs give out a free "Donau Radweg" brochure with a helpful if basic route map. As you study it, note the north bank has the best and most popular trail; it's paved all the way, winds through picturesque villages, and runs near though not on the river. But consider the south bank, which has less car traffic; although the bike trail merges with the actual road about half the time, it comes with better river views. (Note: The bike-in-a-red-border signs mean "no biking.")

Pedal downstream toward Krems to enjoy a gradual slope in your favor. While catching the boat back makes for a much longer day (it's slow upstream), cute one-car milk-run trains rattle up the valley stopping at most towns along the way (about hrly, 60 min from Krems to Emmersdorf opposite Melk, bike rack at rear of train—carry bike up the stairs). If you prefer, you can go half-and-half by cruising to Spitz—a good midway point—and then hopping on a bike (or vice versa). Spitz has a boat station and train station with bike rentals (the bike path between Spitz and Krems is more interesting than between Melk and Spitz). Little ferries shuttle vacation-goers regularly across the river at three points.

A good day plan from Melk: depart Melk at 8:00, bike the valley, lunch in Krems or picnic on train, and catch the 13:00 train from Krems back to Emmersdorf (across the river, 5 km from Melk). If you run out of steam or time, you can catch a rain at most towns en route.

Rent a bike at the Melk, Spitz, or Krems train stations (120 AS with a railpass or train ticket, otherwise 180 AS, 50 AS extra to drop bike at a different station, fine 21-speeds, no helmets, each open daily 7:00–20:00).

Krems—This is a gem of a town. From the boat dock, walk a few blocks to the TI (pick up a town map). Then stroll the traffic-free, shopper's-wonderland old town. If nothing else, it's a pleas-ant 30-minute walk from the dock to the train station (Krems–Vienna trains: hrly, 60 min). The local TI can find you a bed in a private home (D-450 AS, Db-600 AS) if you decide to side-trip into Vienna from this small-town alternative (TI open Mon–Fri 9:00–19:00, Sat–Sun 10:00–12:00, 13:00–19:00, less off-season, tel. 02732/82676).

Melanie Stasny's Gästezimmer is a super place to stay (300 AS/person in Db, Tb, or Qb, friendly with a proud vineyard and wine cellar, 300 meters from dock at Steiner Landstrasse 22, tel.

02732/82843); when they're booked they send travelers to their son's place down the street.

Durnstein—This touristic flypaper lures hordes of visitors with its traffic-free quaintness and its one claim to fame (and fortune): Richard the Lion-Hearted was imprisoned here in 1193. You can probably sleep in his bedroom. The ruined castle above can be reached via a good hike with great river views.

Willendorf—This is known among art buffs as the town where the oldest piece of European art was found. There's a tiny museum in the village center (free, limited hrs). A block farther uphill (follow the signs to "Venus," just under tracks follow stairs to right) you can see the monument where the well-endowed, 30,000-year-old fertility symbol, the Venus of Willendorf, was discovered. (The fist-sized original is now in Vienna's Natural History Museum.)

Sleeping in Melk
(15 AS = about $1, country code: 43, area code: 02752, zip code: 3390)

Sleep Code: **S** = Single, **D** = Double/Twin, **T** = Triple, **Q** = Quad, **b** = bathroom, **t** = toilet only, **s** = shower only, **CC** = Credit Card (Visa, MasterCard, Amex). Breakfast is included, many places take cash only, and at least some English is spoken.

Melk makes a fine overnight stop. Except during August, you shouldn't have any trouble finding a good room at a reasonable rate. The TI has a long list of people renting rooms for about 220 AS per person. Most of these are a few kilometers from the center.

Hotel Fürst (look for Café zum Fursten) is a clean and creaky old place with 15 rooms. Run by the Madar family, it's right on the traffic-free main square. A fountain is just outside the door and the abbey hovers overhead (Sb-480 AS, Db-800–900 AS, Tb-980–1,080 AS, Rathausplatz 3–5, tel. 02752/52343, fax 02752/523-434, e-mail: cafe.madar@netway.at).

The lively **Gasthof Goldener Stern** is a quiet, cozy, and time-lapse place with barn-flavored elegance. It's on the small alley that veers right off the main square with the abbey to your right (D-530 AS, cheaper 3- to 5-bed rooms, free showers, Sterngasse 17, tel. 02752/52214, fax 02752/522-144).

The small **Gasthof Weisses Lamm** is a decent value with Old World hallways but modern rooms (Db-550 AS, Linzer Strasse 7, tel. 02752/54085).

Hotel zur Post feels the most like a modern hotel with a good restaurant and the only elevator I saw in town. It has 27 comfy if nondescript rooms and modern baths (Sb-700 AS, Db-1,020–1,160 AS depending on size, Tb-1,430–1,530 AS, CC:V, 10 percent discount with cash and this book, Linzer Strasse 1, tel. 02752/52345, fax 02752/234-550, e-mail: ebner.post@netway.at, family Ebner).

Hotel Stadt Melk, a block below the main square, is comfortable but stiff and heavy on concrete (Sb-680 AS, Db-860–980, CC:VM, Hauptplatz 1, tel. 02752/52475, fax 02752/524-7519, e-mail: hotel.stadtmelk@netway.at).

Hotel Wachau is a big, clean, and well-run modern place with a residential elegance in a modern suburb ideal for drivers. Half of the 24 rooms are nonsmoking (Sb-620 AS, small Db-790 AS, big Db-890 AS, bike rental-100 AS/day, near autobahn exit, just off Wiener Strasse at Wachberg 157, tel. 02752/52531, fax 02572/525-3113, e-mail: hotel.wachau@netway.at, Hipfinger family).

The modern **youth hostel** is a 10-minute walk from the station; turn right at the post office (beds in quads-180 AS, nonmembers-40 AS extra, includes sheets and breakfast, 25 rooms, closed 10:00–17:00, Abt-Karl-Strasse 42, tel. 02752/52681, fax 02752/54257).

Eating in Melk

While several restaurants serve decent food on the main square, **Hotel Restaurant zur Post** is worth the few extra schillings (good local dishes, muggy courtyard but fine street-side seating with an abbey view, CC:V, Linzer Strasse 1, tel. 02752/52345). The most elegant meals in town are served at **Hotel Restaurant Stadt Melk** (600-AS menu or 300-AS entree, terrace seating, reservations smart, tel. 02752/52475). In season, look for *Marillen Knodel*, the local apricot dumpling—a dessert the Viennese come to Melk for in July and August (out of season, they're likely frozen and take 20 min to cook, so order early).

Transportation Connections—Melk

Melk is on the autobahn and the Salzburg–Vienna train line.

By train to: Vienna's Westbahnhof (hrly, 1–2 hrs), **Salzburg** (hrly, 2 hrs), **Mauthausen** (nearly hrly, 75 min, with a transfer at St. Valentin).

MAUTHAUSEN CONCENTRATION CAMP

More powerful and less tourist-oriented than Dachau, this slave-labor and death camp functioned from 1938 to 1945 for the exploitation and extermination of Hitler's opponents. More than half of its 206,000 quarry-working prisoners died here, mostly from starvation or exhaustion. Mauthausen has a strangely serene setting next to the Danube above an overgrown quarry (25 AS, daily 8:00–18:00, last entry at 17:00, closes mid-Dec–Jan and at 16:00 off-season, tel. 07238/2269 or 07238/3696, TI tel. 07238/3860). While you can borrow a free, tape-recorded 20-minute tour, the excellent 35-AS English guidebook covers the site very well (bookshop just inside entrance, closed 12:30–13:00). Allow two hours to tour the camp completely.

The camp barracks house a worthwhile museum at the far

end of the camp on the right (no English). See the graphic 45-minute movie shown at the top of each hour. There are several film rooms. Find one marked English. If it's running, you can just slip in.

The most emotionally moving rooms and the gas chamber are downstairs. The spirits of the victims of these horrors can still be felt. Back outside the camp, each victim's country has erected a gripping memorial. Many yellowed photos have fresh flowers. Find the barbed-wire memorial overlooking the quarry and the "stairway of death" (*Todesstiege*) and walk at least halfway down (very uneven path). Return to the parking lot via the upper wall for a good perspective over the camp.

By visiting a concentration camp and putting ourselves through this emotional wringer, we heed and respect the fervent wish of the victims of this fascism—that we "never forget." Many people forget by choosing not to know.

Near Mauthausen
Moststub 'n Frellerhof, a farmhouse 50 meters below the Mauthausen parking lot, offers a refreshing, peaceful break after your visit. They serve *Most* (grape juice ready to become wine but not yet alcoholic), homemade schnapps, and light farm-fresh meals (open daily from 13:00, playground with zip cord—swing that rolls down a line—for kids, tel. 07238/2789).

Sleeping in Enns, near Mauthausen: Just off the autobahn six kilometers southwest of Mauthausen and 100 kilometers west of Vienna, Enns calls itself Austria's oldest town. **Hotel Zum Goldenen Schiff**, facing Enns' delightful main square, is a decent value with 25 comfy rooms and a great location (Sb-550 AS, old Db-700 AS, new Db-900 AS, family rooms, free parking, Hauptplatz 23, tel. 07223/86086, fax 07223/860-8615, e-mail: wolfgang.brunner@liwest.at).

Transportation Connections—Mauthausen
Most trains stop at St. Valentin, midway between Salzburg and Vienna, where sporadic trains make the 15-minute ride to the Mauthausen station (get map from station attendant, camp is #9 on map, baggage check-30 AS).

Getting to Mauthausen Camp from Mauthausen Station: To cover the five kilometers between the camp and station, you can hike (1 hr), bike (90-AS rental at station with railpass or ticket, 150 AS without), or taxi (minibus taxis available, about 120 AS one-way; ask the taxi to pick you up in 2 hrs; share the cost with other tourists, tel. 07238/2439). Train info: tel. 07238/2207.

Vienna by train to Mauthausen: You can reach Mauthausen direct from Vienna's Franz Josef Bahnhof or faster from the Westbahnhof with a transfer in St. Valentin.

St. Valentin by train to: Salzburg (hrly, 2 hrs), **Vienna** (hrly, 2 hrs).

Route Tips for Drivers

Hallstatt to Vienna, via Mauthausen, Melk, and Wachau Valley (210 miles): Leave Hallstatt early. Follow the scenic Route 145 through Gmunden to the autobahn and head east. After Linz, take exit #155, Enns, and follow the signs for Mauthausen (8 km from freeway). Go through Mauthausen town and follow the signs to "Ehemaliges KZ-Gedenkstatte Lager." From Mauthausen, it's a speedy 60 minutes to Melk via the autobahn, but the curvy and scenic Route 3 along the river is worth the nausea. At Melk, signs to "Stift Melk" lead to the Benediktinerstift (Benedictine Abbey). Other Melk signs lead into the town.

The most scenic stretch of the Donau is the Wachau Valley between Melk and Krems. From Melk (get a Vienna map at the TI), cross the river again (signs to Donaubrucke) and stay on Route 3. After Krems it hits the autobahn (A-22), and you'll barrel right into Vienna's traffic. (See "Route Tips for Drivers" in the Vienna chapter for details.)

SALZBURG, SALZKAMMERGUT, AND WEST AUSTRIA

Enjoy the sights, sounds, and splendor of Mozart's hometown, Salzburg, then commune with nature in the Salzkammergut, Austria's *Sound of Music* country. Amid hills alive with the S.O.M., you'll find the tiny town of Hallstatt, as pretty as a postcard (and not much bigger). Farther west, the Golden Roof of Innsbruck glitters—but you'll strike it rich in neighboring Hall, which has twice the charm and none of the tourist crowds.

SALZBURG

Salzburg is forever smiling to the tunes of Mozart and *The Sound of Music*. Thanks to its charmingly preserved old town, splendid gardens, Baroque churches, and Europe's largest intact medieval castle, Salzburg feels made for tourism.

But even without Mozart and the von Trapps, Salzburg is steeped in history. In about A.D. 700, Bavaria gave Salzburg to Bishop Rupert for his promise to Christianize the area. Salzburg remained an independent state until Napoleon came (around 1800). Salzburg managed to avoid the ravages of war for 1,200 years...until World War II. Half the town was destroyed by WWII bombs, but the historic old town survived.

Eight million tourists crawl its cobbles each year. That's a lot of Mozart balls—and all that popularity has led to a glut of businesses hoping to catch the tourist dollar. Still, Salzburg makes for a pleasant visit.

Planning Your Time

While Vienna measures much higher on the Richter scale of sightseeing thrills, Salzburg is simply a stroller's delight—a touristy delight. If you're going into the nearby Salzkammergut lake country,

Salzburg

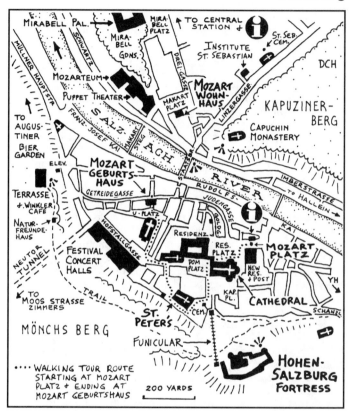

MIRABELL PAL.
MIRA-BELL PLATZ
TO CENTRAL STATION
ST. SEB. CEM.
INSTITUTE ST. SEBASTIAN
DCH
MIRA-BELL GDNS.
MOZARTEUM
PUPPET THEATER
MOZART WOHN-HAUS
KAPUZINER-BERG
CAPUCHIN MONASTERY
TO AUGUS-TINER BIER GARDEN
ELEV.
MOZART GEBURTS-HAUS
GETREIDEGASSE
RIVER
TO HALLEIN
IMBERSTRASSE
TERRASSE & WINKLER CAFE
NATUR-FREUNDE-HAUS
U-PLATZ
RESIDENZ
RES. PLATZ
MOZART PLATZ
FESTIVAL CONCERT HALLS
HOFSTALLGASSE
DOM PLATZ
NEW RES. & POST
YH
TO MOOS STRASSE ZIMMERS
TRAIL
KAP. PL.
CEM.
CATHEDRAL
SCHANZ
MÖNCHS BERG
ST. PETER'S
FUNICULAR
HOHEN-SALZBURG FORTRESS
•••• WALKING TOUR ROUTE STARTING AT MOZART PLATZ & ENDING AT MOZART GEBURTSHAUS
200 YARDS

skip the *Sound of Music* tour—if not, allow half a day for it. The
S.O.M. tour kills a nest of sightseeing birds with one ticket (city
overview, S.O.M. sights, a luge ride, and a fine drive through the
lakes). You'll probably need two nights for Salzburg; nights are
important for swilling beer in atmospheric local gardens and attend-
ing concerts in Baroque halls and chapels. Seriously consider one of
Salzburg's many evening musical events (about 350–400 AS). While
the sights are mediocre, the town is an enjoyable Baroque museum
of cobbled streets and elegant buildings. And to get away from it all,
bike down the river or hike across the Mönchsberg.

Orientation (area code: 0662)
Salzburg, a city of 150,000 (Austria's fourth largest), is divided into
old and new. The old town, sitting between the Salzach River and

the 1,600-foot-high hill called Mönchsberg, holds nearly all the charm and most of the tourists.

Tourist Information: Salzburg's many TIs are helpful (at the train station—daily 8:15–21:00; on Mozartplatz in the old center—daily 9:00–20:00 in summer, closes at 19:00 off-season; on freeway exits; and at the airport, tel. 0662/8898-7330, www.salzburginfo .or.at). You can pick up a city map (10 AS, free at most hotels), a list of sights with current hours, and a schedule of events. The TI sells a "Salzburg Card" which covers all your bus transportation and admission to all the city sights (225 AS/24 hrs, 320 AS/48 hrs); it pays for itself after two admissions and one bus ride. The new "Salzburg Plus Light" adds 150 AS to the Salzburg Card for a dinner and two drinks at your choice of the city's big hotels. Book a concert upon arrival. The TIs also book rooms (30-AS fee, or 60 AS for 3 people or more).

Arrival in Salzburg

By Train: The little Salzburg station makes it easy. The TI is at track 2A. Downstairs, at street level, you'll find a place to store your luggage, rent bikes, buy tickets, and get train information. The bus station is across the street (where buses #1, #5, #6, #51, and #55 go to the old center; get off at the first stop after you cross the river for most sights and city center hotels, or just before the bridge for Linzergasse hotels). Figure 90 AS for a taxi to the center. To walk downtown (15 min), leave the station ticket hall to the left near the Bankomat and walk straight down Rainerstrasse, which leads under the tracks past Mirabellplatz, turning into Dreitaltigkeitsgasse. From here you can turn left onto Paris-Lodron Strasse or Linzergasse for many hotels listed in this book or cross the *Staatsbrücke* (bridge) for the old town (and more hotels). For a more dramatic approach, leave the station the same way but follow the tracks to the river, turn left, and walk the riverside path toward the castle.

By Car: Follow Zentrum signs to the center and park short-term on the street or longer under Mirabellplatz. Ask at your hotel for suggestions.

Getting around Salzburg

By Bus: Single-ride tickets are sold on the bus for 20 AS. Daily passes called *Tageskarte* cost 40 AS (good for 1 calendar day only). Bus info: tel. 0662/4480-6262.

By Bike: Salzburg is bike friendly. From 7:00 until midnight, the train station rents good road bikes for 100 AS and mountain bikes for 175 AS; if you don't have a railpass or train ticket, you'll pay 25 to 50 AS more (no deposit required, pay at counter #3, pick bike up at "left luggage"). Velo-Active rents bikes on Residenzplatz under the Glockenspiel in the old town (60 AS/hr, 190

AS/24 hrs, 150 AS/24 hrs with this book, daily 9:00–19:00 but hours unreliable, less off-season and in bad weather, passport number for security, extra charge for mountain bikes, tel. 0662/435-5950).

By Funicular and Elevator: The old town is connected to Mönchsberg (and great views) via funicular and elevator. The funicular whisks you up to the imposing Hohensalzburg fortress (76-AS round-trip includes fortress admission; 34 AS for ride and grounds only; last ride up at 21:30, last down at 22:00). The elevator on the east side of the old town propels you to Café Winkler, the recommended Naturfreundehaus (see "Sleeping in the Old Town," below), and lots of wooded paths (16 AS one-way, 27 AS round-trip).

By Taxi: Salzburg is a fine taxi town. Meters start at 33 AS. A ride from the station to the old town runs about 90 AS.

Helpful Hints

Guide Association: Salzburg's many guides can give you a good three-hour walk through town for 1,600 AS (tel. 0662/840-406). Barbel Boxrainer packs in the information and enjoys leaving the touristy places (tel. 0662/632-225).

Laundromat: You'll find it near recommended Linzergasse hotels at the corner of Paris-Lodron Strasse and Wolf-Dietrich Strasse (Mon–Fri 7:30–18:00, Sat 8:00–12:00, self-serve or drop-off service, tel. 0662/876-381).

Internet Access: The Internet Cafe on Mozartplatz is fast and handy, right next to the TI (20 AS/10 min, 120 AS/hr, daily 10:00–24:00, 12 stations, Mozartplatz 5, tel. 0662/844-822). Another cybercafé is at Gstattengasse 27; turn right where Griesgasse meets the hill (80 AS/hr, daily 14:00–20:00, tel. 0662/8426-1622).

American Express: Amex charges no commission to cash Amex checks (Mon–Fri 9:00–17:30, Sat 9:00–12:00, Mozartplatz 5, A-5010 Salzburg, tel. 0662/8080).

City View: For a painless, grand view, ride Hotel Stein's elevator to the seventh floor (near where Linzergasse meets the main bridge).

Old Town Walking Tour

The two-language, one-hour guided walks of the old town are informative and worthwhile if you don't mind listening to a half hour of German (100 AS, daily at 12:15, not on winter Sun, start at TI on Mozartplatz, tel. 0662/88987), but you can easily do it on your own.

Here's a basic old-town orientation walk (start on Mozart-platz in the old town):

Mozartplatz: This square features a statue of Mozart erected in 1842. Mozart spent most of his first 20 years (1756–1777) in

Salzburg, the greatest Baroque city north of the Alps. But the city's much older. The Mozart statue actually sits on bits of Roman Salzburg. And the pink church of St. Michael overlooking the square is from A.D. 800. Surrounding you are Café Glockenspiel, an Internet café, the American Express office, and the tourist information office with a concert box office. Just around the corner is a pedestrian bridge leading over the Salzach River to the quiet, most medieval street in town, Steingasse (see "Sights—Across the River," below). Walk toward the cathedral into the big square with the huge fountain.

Residenz Platz: Salzburg's energetic Prince-Archbishop Wolf Dietrich (who ruled from 1587–1612) was raised in Rome, counted the Medicis as his buddies, and had grand Renaissance ambitions for Salzburg. After a convenient fire destroyed much of the old town, he set about building "the Rome of the North." This square, with his new cathedral and palace, was the centerpiece of his Baroque dream city. A series of interconnecting squares lead from here through the old town.

For centuries, Salzburg's leaders were both important church officials and princes of the Holy Roman Empire, hence their title—mixing sacred and secular authority. Wolf Dietrich abused his power and spent his last five years imprisoned in the Salzburg castle.

The fountain is as Italian as can be, with a Triton matching Bernini's famous *Triton Fountain* in Rome. As the north became aware of the exciting things going on in Italy, things Italian were respected. (You know, when a bumpkin in a faraway land "stuck a feather in his cap and called it macaroni.") Local architects even Italianized their names in order to raise their rates.

Near the fountain is a picnic-friendly grocery with an orange awning (Mon–Fri 8:30–18:00, Sat 8:00–17:00).

Residenz: Dietrich's palace is connected to the cathedral by a skyway. A series of ornately decorated rooms and an art gallery are open to visitors with time to kill (90 AS includes audioguide, daily 10:00–17:00, tel. 0662/8042-2690).

Opposite the old Residenz is the new Residenz, which has long been a government administration building with the central post office and the Hiematwerk, a shop showing off all the best local handicrafts (Mon–Fri 9:00–18:00, Sat 9:00–13:00). Atop the new Residenz is the famous...

Glockenspiel: This bell tower has a carillon of 35 17th-century bells (cast in Antwerp) that chimes throughout the day and plays tunes (appropriate to the month) at 7:00, 11:00, and 18:00. There was a time when Salzburg could afford to take tourists to the top of the tower to actually see the big adjustable barrel turn... pulling the right bells in the right rhythm—a fascinating show. Notice the ornamental top: an upside-down heart in flames surrounding the solar system (symbolizing that God loves all).

Look back past Mozart's statue to the 4,220-foot-tall Gais-
berg (the forested hill with the television tower). A road leads
to the top for a commanding view. It's a favorite destination for
local bikers. Walking under the Prince-Archbishop's skyway, step
into Domplatz, the cathedral square.

Salzburg Cathedral: Built in the 17th century, this was
one of the first Baroque buildings north of the Alps (free, daily
10:00–18:30). The dates on the iron gates refer to milestones in
the church's history: In 774 the previous church (long since
destroyed) was founded by St. Virgil, to be replaced in 1628 by
the church you see today. In 1959 the reconstruction was completed after a WWII bomb blew through the dome.

Wander inside. Built in just 14 years (1614–1628), the architecture is harmonious. When the pope visited in 1998, 5,000 people
filled the cathedral (dimensions: 110 meters long, 70 meters tall).
The baptismal font, left of the entry, is from the previous cathedral.
Mozart was baptized here (Amadeus means "beloved by God").
Gape up. The interior is marvelous. Concert and Mass schedules
are posted at the entrance; the Sunday Mass at 10:00 is famous for
its music. (The 11:30 Mass also has music. Acoustics are best in
pews immediately under the dome.)

Under the skyway, a stairway leads down to the excavation
site under the church with a few second-century Christian Roman
mosaics and the foundation stones of the previous Romanesque and
Gothic churches (20 AS, Wed–Sun 9:00–17:00). The Cathedral (or
Dom) Museum has a rich collection of church art (entry at portico).

From Cathedral Square to St. Peter's: The cathedral square
is surrounded by "ecclesiastical palaces." The statue of Mary (1771)
is looking away from the church, but if you stand in the rear of the
square immediately under the middle arch, you'll see how she's
positioned to be crowned by the two angels on the church facade.

From the arch, walk back across the square to the front
of the cathedral and turn right (going past the underground public toilets) into the next square. Walk past the giant chessboard
to the pond. This was a horse bath, the 18th-century equivalent
of a car wash. Notice the puzzle above it—the artist wove the
date of the structure into a phrase. It says, "Leopold the Ruler
Built Me," using the letters LLDVICMXVXI, which totals
1732—the year it was built. A small road leads up to the castle
(and castle lift). Leave the square through a gate on the right
(past the souvenir stalls) which reads "St. Peter." It leads to a
waterfall and St. Peter's Cemetery.

The waterfall is part of a canal system that has brought water
into Salzburg from Berchtesgaden, 25 kilometers away, since 1150.
The busy water used to flush out the streets (Saturday morning was
flood-the-streets day) and power factories (over 100 firms as late as
the 19th century). Drop into the traditional bakery at the waterfall

(hard to beat their rocklike *Roggenbrot*, sold 7:00–17:30) and then step into the cemetery.

St. Peter's Cemetery: This collection of lovingly tended mini-gardens is butted up against the Mönchberg's rock wall. The graves are cared for by relatives. (In Austria, grave sites are rented not owned. Rent bills are sent out every 10 years. If no one cares enough to make the payment, you're gone.) Look up the cliff. Medieval hermit monks lived in the hillside. You can climb up to see their chapel (12 AS, Tue–Sun 10:30–17:00, closed Mon). While the cemetery the von Trapp family hid out in was actually in Hollywood, it was inspired by this one. Walk through the cemetery (silence is requested) and out the opposite end. Drop into St. Peter's Church, a Romanesque basilica done up beautifully Baroque. Continue (through arch opposite hillside, left at church, take the second right, pass the public WC, another square, and church) to . . .

Universitätsplatz: This square comes with a busy open-air produce market—Salzburg's liveliest (mornings Mon–Sat, best on Sat when the farmers are in town—60 percent of Austria's produce is now grown organically). You can see the market stall numbers in the pavement. Exit through the covered arcade at #10 to Getreidegasse. Several of these characteristic and nicely arcaded medieval tunnel passages connect Salzburg's streets.

Getreidegasse: This street was old Salzburg's busy, colorful main drag. Famous for its old wrought-iron signs, it still looks much as it did in Mozart's day. (The Nordsee Restaurant was even more of a scandal than the coming of McDonald's—notice the medieval golden arches street sign.) *Schmuck* means jewelry. Wolfgang was born on this street. Find his very gold house.

Mozart's Birthplace (Geburtshaus): Mozart was born here in 1756. It was in this building that he composed most of his boy-genius works. This is the most popular Mozart sight in town. Filled with scores of scores, portraits, old keyboard instruments and violins, and a furnished middle class apartment from Mozart's time (all well-described in English), it's almost a pilgrimage. If you're a fan, you'll have to check it out (70 AS, or 110 AS for combined ticket to Mozart's *Wohnhaus*—see "Sights—Across the River," below, daily 9:00–18:00, shorter hours off-season, Getreidegasse 9). Note that Mozart's *Wohnhaus* provides a more informative visit than this more visited site.

Sights—Above the Old Town

▲Hohensalzburg Fortress—Built on a rock 400 feet above the Salzach River, this castle is a testament to the importance of the salt trade. One of Europe's mightiest, it dominates Salzburg's skyline and offers incredible views. You can hike up or ride the *Festungsbahn* (funicular, 76-AS round-trip includes fortress courtyard, 66 AS one-way, pleasant to walk down). The castle visit has two parts—a relatively dull courtyard with some fine views (42 AS or included in 76-AS funicular fare) and the palatial interior (worth the 42-AS extra admission). The included audio-guide gives a 40-minute room-by-room narration—good information but makes a short story long (feel free to skip rooms). The highlight is the commanding city view from the top of a tower. It ends at the museum showing the fortress through its battle-torn years including World War II (fortress open daily 8:00–19:00, off-season 9:00–17:00, tel. 0662/842-430). Kids may enjoy the marionette exhibit in the fortress courtyard (adults-35 AS, kids-20 AS, daily 10:00–17:00).

▲**The Hills Are Alive Walk**—For a most enjoyable approach to the castle, consider riding the elevator to Café Winkler and walking 20 minutes across Salzburg's little mountain, Mönchsberg. A trail goes through the woods high above the city to Festung Hohensalzburg (stay on the high paved paths, or you'll have a needless climb back up to the castle).

In 1669, a huge Mönchsberg landslide killed over 200 towns-people. Since then the cliffs have been carefully checked each spring and fall. Even today, you'll see crews of three on the cliff monitoring its stability.

Sights—Across the River

Salzach River—Cross the river (ideally on a pedestrian bridge—the one farthest upstream, built in 1903, is just a block off Mozartplatz). It's called "salt river" not because it's salty but because the important salt mines of Hallein are just 15 kilo-meters upstream. Salt could be transported from here all the way to the Danube and on to Russia. The riverbanks and roads were built in 1860. Before that, the Salzach was much wider and slower moving. Houses opposite the old town fronted the river with docks and garages for boats.

▲**Steingasse**—This street, a block in from the river, was the only street in the Middle Ages going south to Hallein. Today it's won-derfully peaceful and free of Salzburg's touristy crush. Wander down Steingasse (from Mozartplatz, cross the pedestrian bridge, go a block inland, and turn left).

There's a great castle viewpoint midway up Steingasse. Notice the oldest nunnery in the German-speaking world (estab-lished in 712) under the castle and to the left. Maria from *The Sound of Music* taught in this nunnery's school. In 1927, she and Herr von Trapp were married in the church you see here (not the church filmed in the movie). He was 47. She was 22. Hmmmm.

At #19 find the carvings on the old door. Look for the notices from beggars to the begging community (more numerous after the economic dislocation caused by the wars over religion following the Reformation) indicating whether the residents would give or not. The four ringers indicate four families lived at this address.

Across the street, the wall is gouged out. This was left even after the building was restored so locals could remember the American GI who tried to get a tank down this road during a visit to the Steingasse brothel.

At #9 a plaque shows where Joseph Mohr, who wrote the words to *Silent Night*, was born, poor and illegitimate, in 1792.

▲St. Sebastian Cemetery—Wander through this peaceful place— so Baroque and so Italian (daily 9:00–19:00, Linzergasse 43). Mozart's father and most of his family are buried here (near entry on left). When Prince-Archbishop Wolf Dietrich had the cemetery moved from around the cathedral and put here, across the river, people didn't like it. To help popularize it, he had his mausoleum built as its centerpiece. Step into his dome, read the legalistic epitaph (posted in English), and look at the tomb through the grate in the floor. To get to the cemetery (Friedhof St. Sebastian), take Linzergasse, the best shopping street in Salzburg.

▲▲Mozart's Wohnhaus—This reconstruction of Mozart's second home (his family moved here when he was 17) is the most informative Mozart sight in town. The English-language audio-guides (free with admission, keep it carefully pointed at the trans-mitters and don't move while listening) provide a fascinating insight into Mozart's life and music. Along with the usual scores and old pianos, the highlight is an intriguing film (30 min, runs continu-ously, in English) that leaves you wanting to know more about Mozart and his remarkable family (65 AS, or 110 AS for combined ticket to birthplace, guidebook-59 AS, daily 9:00–18:00, until 19:00 July–Aug, allow 1 hr for visit, just over the river at Marktplatz 8, tel. 0662/8742-2740). The gift shop here sells unique CDs featuring Mozart's music performed on Mozart's piano.

▲Mirabell Gardens and Palace (Schloss)—The bubbly gardens, laid out in 1730, are always open and free. You may recognize the statues and the arbor featured in *The S.O.M.* A brass band plays free park concerts twice weekly (Sun 10:30, Wed 20:30). To properly enjoy the lavish Mirabell Palace—once Wolf Dietrich's summer palace and now the seat of the mayor—get a ticket to a *Schlosskonzert* (my favorite venue for a classical concert). Baroque music flying around a Baroque hall is a happy bird in the right cage. Tickets are around 400 AS (student-250 AS) and are rarely sold out (tel. 0662/ 848-586). The Café Bazar, nearby and overlooking the river, is a great place for a classy drink with an old town and castle view.

More Sights—Salzburg

▲▲Riverside Bike Ride—The Salzach River has smooth, flat, and scenic bike paths along each side. On a sunny day I can think of no more shout-worthy escape from the city. Hallein is a

Sound of Music Debunked

Rather than visit the real-life sights from the life of Maria von Trapp and family, most tourists want to see the places Hollywood chose to film this fanciful story. Local guides are happy not to burst any *S.O.M* pilgrim's bubble, but keep these points in mind:

- "Edelweiss" is not a cherished Austrian folk tune or national anthem. It was composed by Rodgers and Hammerstein for the movie.
- Maria was never a nun. She taught at the nunnery school.
- The colonel didn't run a tight domestic ship. In fact, his seven children were as unruly as most. He did use a whistle to call them. Each kid was trained to respond to a certain pitch.
- The family never escaped to Switzerland (which is a five-hour drive away). Rather, they went, legally, on a singing tour of the USA. The scene showing them climbing into Switzerland is actually near Berchtesgaden...home to Hitler's Eagle's Nest, and certainly not a smart place to flee.
- The actual von Trapp family house exists...but it's not the one you see in the film. In fact, the mansion in the movie is actually two different buildings (one used for the exterior and the other for the interior).
- Maria was given the choice: royalties or $8,000 for her story. She didn't think her story would sell so she traded all the rights for $8,000.

pleasant destination (with a salt mine tour, 9:00–17:00, 15 kilometers away, the north or "new town" side of river is most scenic). Even a quickie ride from one end of town to the other is a great Salzburg experience. In the evening, the riverbanks are a hand-in-hand, floodlit-spires world.

▲▲*Sound of Music* **Tour**—I took this tour skeptically (as part of my research chores) and liked it. It includes a quick but good general city tour, stops for a luge ride (45 AS extra, in season, fair weather), hits some *S.O.M.* spots (including the stately home, gazebo, and wedding church), and shows you a lovely stretch of the Salzkammergut. The Salzburg Panorama Tours Company charges 400 AS for the four-hour, English-only tour (from Mirabellplatz daily at 9:30 and 14:00, ask for a reservation and a free hotel pickup; travelers with this book who buy their tickets with cash at the Mirabellplatz ticket booth get a 10 percent discount on this and any other tour they do; tel. 0662/874-029,

Greater Salzburg

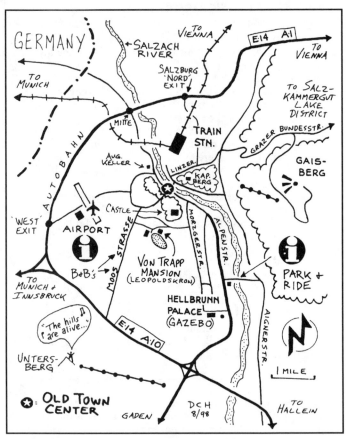

www.panoramatours.at). This is worthwhile for *S.O.M.* fans and those who won't otherwise be going into the Salzkammergut. Warning: Many think rolling through the Austrian countryside with 30 Americans singing "Doe, a deer" is pretty schmaltzy. Local Austrians don't understand all the commotion.

Several similar and very competitive tour companies offer every conceivable tour of and from Salzburg (Mozart sights, Berchtesgaden, salt mines, Salzkammergut lakes and mountains). Some hotels have their brochures and get a healthy commission. Bob's Special Tours uses a minibus (several different tours, Kaigasse 10, tel. 0662/849-511, www.austria.at/bob/, e-mail: bobs-special-tours@net4you.co.at).

▲**Hellbrunn Castle**—The attractions here are a garden full of clever trick fountains and the sadistic joy the tour guide gets from soaking tourists. The Baroque garden, one of the oldest in Europe, is pretty enough and now features the "I am 16, going on 17" gazebo (80 AS for 35-minute tour and admission, daily 9:00–17:30, until 22:00 July–Aug, until 16:30 in April and Oct, closed Nov–March, tel. 0662/820-372). The archbishop's mediocre 17th-century palace, in the courtyard, is open by tour only (40 AS, 2/hrly, 20 min). Hellbrunn is three miles south of Salzburg (bus #55 from station or downtown, 2/hrly, 20 min). It's most fun on a sunny day or with kids, but, for many, it's a lot of trouble for a few water tricks.

Music Scene
▲▲**Salzburg Festival**—Each summer, from late July to the end of August, Salzburg hosts its famous Salzburger Festspiele, founded in 1920 partly to employ Vienna's musicians in the summer. This fun and festive time is crowded, but there are plenty of beds (except for a few August weekends). Tickets are normally available the day of the concert unless it's a really big show (the ticket office on Mozartplatz, in the TI, prints a daily list of concerts). You can contact the Austrian National Tourist Office in the United States for specifics on this year's festival schedule and tickets (Box 1142, New York, NY 10108-1142, tel. 212/944-6880, fax 212/730-4568, www.experienceaustria.com, e-mail: info@oewnyc.com), but I've never planned in advance and have enjoyed great concerts with every visit.

▲▲**Musical Events outside of Festival Time**—Salzburg is busy throughout the year with 2,000 classical performances in its palaces and churches annually. Pick up the events calendar at the TI (free, comes out monthly). Whenever you visit, you'll have a number of concerts to choose from. There are nearly nightly concerts at the Mirabell Palace and up in the fortress (both with open seating and 400-AS tickets, concerts at 19:30 or 20:30, doors open 30 min early). The *Schlosskonzerte* at the Mirabell Palace offer a fine Baroque setting for your Mozart (tel. 0662/848-586). The fortress concerts, called *Festungskonzerte*, are held in the "prince's chamber" (usually chamber music—a string quartet, tel. 0662/825-858 to reserve, you can pick up tickets at the door). This medieval-feeling room atop the castle has windows overlooking the city and the concert gives you a chance to enjoy a stroll through the castle courtyard and the grand city view (76-AS funicular, round-trip; only 34 AS if you have a concert ticket).

The almost daily "5:00 Concert" next to St. Peter's is cheaper, since it features young artists (120 AS, daily except Wed, 45 min, tel. 0662/8445-7619). While the series is named after the brother of Joseph Haydn, it features music from various masters.

Salzburg's impressive Marionette Theater performs operas with remarkable marionettes and recorded music (350–480 AS, nearly nightly May–Sept, tel. 0662/872-406, www.marionetten.at).

For those who'd like some classical music but would rather not sit through a concert, Stiftskeller St. Peter offers a **Mozart Dinner Concert** with a traditional candlelit three-course meal mixed with Mozart performed in historic costumes in an elegant Baroque setting (560 AS, nightly at 20:00, see "Eating," below, call to reserve at 0662/828-6950).

The *S.O.M.* musical at the Sternbrau restaurant (see "Eating," below) gets good reviews from couples and families.

Sights—Near Salzburg

▲**Bad Dürnberg Salzbergwerke**—Like its salty neighbors, this salt mine tour and cable-car ride above the town of Hallein (15 kilometers from Salzburg) is a fun experience while wearing white overalls, sliding down the sleek wooden chutes, and crossing underground from Austria into Germany (200 AS, daily 9:00–17:00, English-speaking guides and information sheets, easy bus and train connections from Salzburg, tel. 06245/852-8515). A convenient "Salt Ticket" from Salzburg's train station covers admission, train, and cable-car fees for 289 AS.

▲**Berchtesgaden**—This Alpine resort just across the German border (20 km from Salzburg) flaunts its attractions, and you may find yourself in a traffic jam of desperate tourists trying to turn their money into fun. During peak season, it's not worth the headaches for the speedy tourist. Berchtesgaden caters to long-term German guests.

From the station and TI (tel. 08652/9670), buses go to the salt mines (a 15-minute walk otherwise) and the idyllic Königsee (24 DM, 2-hr scenic cruises, 2/hrly, stopovers anywhere, tel. 08652/963-618).

At the **salt mines**, you put on traditional miners' outfits, get on funny little trains, and zip deep into the mountain. For one hour you'll cruise subterranean lakes; slide speedily down two long, slick, wooden banisters; and learn how they mined salt so long ago. Call for crowd-avoidance advice. You can buy a ticket early and browse through the town until your appointed tour time (21 DM, daily 9:00–17:00, winter Mon–Sat 12:00–16:00, tel. 08652/60020).

Hitler's famous (but overrated) **Eagle's Nest** towers high above Obersalzberg near Berchtesgaden. The site is open to visitors, but little remains of the Alpine retreat Hitler visited only five times. The bus ride up the private road and the lift to the top (a 2,000-foot altitude gain) cost 28.50 DM from the station, 22 DM from the parking lot. If the weather's cloudy, as it often is, you'll Nazi a thing.

Berchtesgaden is a train ride from Munich (hrly, 2.5 hrs, with 1 change). From Salzburg, take the bus (2/hrly, 30 min); it's more scenic and direct than the train.

Sleeping in Salzburg
(15 AS = about $1, country code: 43, area code: 0662, zip code: 5020)
Sleep Code: **S** = Single, **D** = Double/Twin, **T** = Triple, **Q** = Quad, **b** = bathroom, **t** = toilet only, **s** = shower only, **CC** = Credit Card (**V**isa, **M**asterCard, **A**mex), **SE**=Speaks English, **NSE**= No English.

Finding a room in Salzburg, even during the music festival, is usually easy. Unless otherwise noted, all my listings come with breakfast and at least some English is spoken. Rates rise significantly during the music festival (late July and Aug).

Sleeping in (or above) the Old Town
Gasthaus zur Goldenen Ente, run by the family Steinwender, is a good splurge if you'd like to sleep in a 600-year-old building above a fine restaurant as central as you can be on a pedestrian street in old Salzburg. Somehow the 15 modern and comfortable doubles fit into this building's medieval-style stone arches and narrow stairs (Sb-720–820 AS, Db-1,080–1,280 AS with this book, extra person-400 AS, the higher prices occur July–Aug, CC:VMA, elevator, parking-80 AS/day, Goldgasse 10, tel. 0662/845-622, fax 0662/845-6229, www.ente.at, e-mail: ente@eunet.at). The breakfast is buffet-big and their restaurant is a treat (see "Eating," below).

Hotel Restaurant Weisses Kreuz is a classy, comfy, family-run place on a cobbled back street under the castle away from the crowds with a fine restaurant (Sb-800 AS, Db-1,200 AS, Tb-1,600 AS, CC:VMA, peaceful roof garden, garage, Bierjodlgasse 6, tel. 0662/845-641, fax 0662/845-6419, e-mail: weisseskreuz@eunet.at).

Gasthof Hinterbrühl is a smoky, ramshackle old place with a handy location, minimal plumbing, and not a tourist in sight (S-450 AS, D-570 AS, T-600 AS, optional breakfast-60 AS, above a bar that can be noisy, workable parking, on a villagelike square under the castle's river end at Schanzlgasse 12, tel. 0662/846-798, fax 0662/841-859, e-mail: hinterbruhl@kronline.at).

Naturfreundehaus, also called "Gasthaus Bürgerwehr," is a local version of a mountaineer's hut. It's a great budget alternative in a forest guarded by singing birds and snuggled in the remains of a 15th-century castle wall overlooking Salzburg, with magnificent town and mountain views (D-280 AS, 120 AS/person in 4- to 6-bed dorms, breakfast-30 AS, dinner-68–108 AS, 01:00 curfew, open May–Sept, 2 min from the top of the 27-AS round-trip Mönchsberg elevator, Mönchsberg 19, tel. 0662/841-729). High above the old town, it's the stone house to the left of the glass Café Winkler.

Salzburg Hotels

1. GASTHAUS GOLDENEN ENTE
2. HOTEL WEISSES KREUZ
3. GASTHOF HINTERBRÜHL
4. HOTEL TRUMER STUBE
5. HOTEL GOLDENE KRONE
6. INTSTITUTE ST. SEBASTIAN
7. HOTEL JUNGEN FUCHS
8. HOTEL WOLF DIETRICH
9. PENSION BERGLAND, JEDERMANN & GANSLHOF
10. GASTHOF WILDER MANN
11. STIFTSKELLER ST. PETER
12. STIEGLKELLER
13. STERNBRAU INN

Sleeping on Linzergasse and Rupertgasse

These listings are between the train station and the old city in a pleasant neighborhood (with easy parking), a 15-minute walk from the train station (for directions, see "Arrival In Salzburg/By Train," above) and 10 to 15 minutes to the old city. If you're coming from the old city, simply cross the main bridge (Staatsbrücke) to nearly traffic-free Linzergasse. The first listings are on or very near Linzergasse, across the bridge from Mozartville. The last ones are farther out with easier parking.

Hotel Trumer Stube, a comfy little hotel-pension a few blocks from the river just off Linzergasse, has clean new rooms and a friendly can-do owner (Sb-780 AS, Db-1,320 AS, Tb-1,490 AS, Qb-1,826 AS, higher in Aug, lower in winter, CC to reserve but pay cash, elevator, parking-100 AS, Bergstrasse 6, tel. 0662/874-776, fax 0662/874-326, www.members.eunet.at/hotel.trumer-stube.sbg, e-mail: hotel.trumer-stube.sbg@eunet.at, Sylvia SE).

Hotel Goldene Krone, about five blocks from the river, is big, quiet, and creaky-traditional but modern, with comforts rare in this price range (Sb-500–570 AS, D-750–800 AS, Db-850–970 AS, Tb-1,000–1,300 AS, elevator, Linzergasse 48, tel. 0662/872-300, fax 0662/8723-0066).

Institute St. Sebastian—a somewhat sterile but very clean, historic building—has spacious public areas, a roof garden, and rents some of the best rooms and dorm beds in town for the money. The doubles come with modern baths and head-to-toe twin beds (Sb-400 AS, Db-700 AS, Tb-900 AS, elevator, reception closes at 21:00, Linzergasse 41, enter through arch at #37, tel. 0662/871-386, fax 0662/8713-8685). Students like the 210-AS bunks in 10-bed dorms (30 AS less if you have sheets, no lockout time, lockers, free showers). Self-service kitchens on each floor (fridge space is free; just request a key). Ask about their washer and dryer.

Hotel zum Jungen Fuchs turns on troglodytes. It's plain but clean and wonderfully located in a funky, dumpy old building (S-300 AS, D-400 AS, T-500 AS, no breakfast, just up from Hotel Krone at Linzergasse 54, tel. 0662/875-496).

Rudolf Schneider Zimmer—a basic, no breakfast, no-speak-English place perfectly located on Linzergasse—rents six fine rooms at a great price (Sb-350 AS, Db-600–700 AS, Linzergasse 70, tel. & fax 0662/876-327).

Altstadthotel Wolf Dietrich, one block above Hotel zum Jungen Fuchs, around the corner on Wolf-Dietrich Strasse, is well located and a reasonable option if you want a formal hotel (Sb-1,000 AS, Db-1,460–1,860 AS, prices go up 500 AS in Aug, CC:VMA, Wolf-Dietrich Strasse 7, tel. 0662/871-275, fax 0662/882-320, e-mail: office@salzburg-hotel.at).

These three hotels are about five blocks farther from the river up Paris-Lodron Strasse to Rupertgasse, a breeze for drivers.

Pension Bergland is a charming, classy oasis of calm with rustic rooms and musical evenings (Sb-590 AS, Db-970 AS, Tb-1,100 AS, music room open 17:00–21:30, Internet access, bike rental, English library, Rupertgasse 15, tel. 0662/872-318, fax 0662/872-3188, www.sol.at/bergland, e-mail: pkuhn@sol.at).

The similar boutiquelike **Hotel Jedermann**, a few doors down, is tastefully done and comfortable with friendly owners, a cheery breakfast room, and a bird-chirping backyard garden (Sb-690–790 AS, Db-920–1,250 AS, Qb-1,700–1,840 AS, CC:VMA, cable TV, Internet access, Rupertgasse 25, tel. 0662/873-241, fax 0662/873-2419, e-mail: jedermann@salzburginfo.at, Walter SE).

Gasthaus Ganslhof, around the corner to the right, facing a hill of trees, is decent and clean with Motel 6 ambience, a parking lot, and 25 surprisingly comfortable rooms (Db-850–1,100 AS, CC:VMA, elevator, TV, phone, Vogelweiderstrasse 6, tel. 0662/873-853, fax 0662/8738-5323, e-mail: office.ganslhof@aon.at).

Zimmer

These are generally roomy and comfortable and come with a good breakfast, easy parking, and tourist information. Off-season, competition softens prices. They are a bus ride from town, but, with a day pass and the frequent service, this shouldn't keep you away. Unsavory *Zimmer* skimmers lurk at the station. Ignore them.

Brigitte Lenglachner fills her big, traditional home with a warm welcome (S-290 AS, D-480 AS, bunk bed D-390 AS, Db-550 AS, T-690 AS, Tb-830 AS, Qb-1,100 AS, fifth person-280 AS, apartment with kitchen available: Sb-500, Db-800, Scheibenweg 8, tel. & fax 0662/438-044). It's a 10-minute walk northeast of the station (cross pedestrian Pioneer bridge, turn right, walk along the river 300 meters, cross canal, left on linke Glanzeile for 3 min, right onto Wachtelgasse).

Trude Poppenberger's three pleasant rooms offer a mountain-view balcony (S-280 AS, D-480 AS, T-720 AS; stay 2 nights she'll do your laundry for 100 AS; Wachtelgasse 9, tel. & fax 0662/430-094, e-mail: trudeshome@yline.com). She offers free pick up at the station. Or it's a 30-minute walk northwest of the station (cross pedestrian Pioneer bridge, turn right, walk along river 300 meters, cross canal, left on Linke Glanzeile for 3 min, right onto Wachtelgasse).

Zimmers on Moosstrasse: The street called Moosstrasse, southwest of Mönchsberg, is lined with *Zimmer*. Those farther out are farmhouses. From the station, catch bus #1 and change to bus #60 immediately after crossing the river. From the old town, ride bus #60. If you're driving from the center, go through the tunnel, straight on Neutorstrasse, and take the fourth left onto Moosstrasse.

Maria Gassner rents 10 sparkling clean, comfortable rooms in her modern house (St-300 AS, Sb-400 AS, D-450 AS, Db-500

AS, big Db-600 AS, 10 percent more for 1-night stays, family deals, CC:VM, 60-AS coin-op laundry, Moosstrasse 126-B, tel. 0662/824-990, fax 0662/822-075).

Frau Ballwein offers cozy, charming rooms in an old farm-house (S-220 AS, Ss-260 AS, D-420 AS, Db-500 AS, farm-fresh breakfasts, Moosstrasse 69A, tel. & fax 0662/824-029).

Haus Reichl also has good rooms (Db-600 AS, Tb-850 AS, Qb-1,000 AS, family deals, Q rooms have balcony and view, between Ballwein and Bankhammer B&Bs at Reiterweg 52, tel. & fax 0662/826-248, www.privatzimmer.at, e-mail: haus.reichl@telering.at).

Helga Bankhammer rents recently renovated, pleasant rooms in a farmhouse with farm animals nearby (D-450 AS, Db-520 AS, Moosstrasse 77, tel. & fax 0662/830-067, e-mail: helga.bankhammer@telering.at).

Gästehaus Blobergerhof is rural and comfortable (Sb-350–400 AS, Db-550–650 AS, 10 percent more for 1-night stays, CC:VM; breakfast buffet, free bike usage, laundry service, will pick up at station, Hammerauerstrasse 4, Querstrasse zur Moos-strasse, tel. 0662/830-227, fax 0662/827-061, www.privatzimmer .at, e-mail: keuschnigg@eunet.at).

Sleeping near the Train Station

Pension Adlerhof, a plain and decent old place, is two blocks in front of the train station (left off Kaiserschutzenstrasse), but a 15-minute walk from the sightseeing action. It has a quirky staff and well-maintained rooms (S-420–440 AS, Sb-650 AS, D-670 AS, Db-850 AS, Elisabethstrasse 25, tel. 0662/875-236, fax 0662/873-6636, e-mail: adlerhof@pension-adlerhof.at).

Gottfried's International Youth Hotel, a.k.a. the "Yo-Ho," is the most fun, handy, and American of Salzburg's many hostels (150 AS in 6- to 8-bed dorms, D-200 AS/person, T or Q-170 AS/person, sheets-20 AS, 6 blocks from station toward Linzergasse and 6 blocks from river at Paracelsusstrasse 9, tel. 0662/879-649, www.yoho.at). This easygoing place speaks English first; has cheap meals, 400 beds, lockers, a laundry, tour discounts, and a soft 01:00 curfew; plays *The Sound of Music* free daily about noon; runs a lively bar; and welcomes anyone of any age. The fun, noisy atmosphere can make it hard to sleep.

Eating in Salzburg

Salzburg boasts many inexpensive, fun, and atmospheric places to eat. I'm a sucker for big cellars with their smoky, Old World atmosphere, heavy medieval arches, time-darkened paintings, antlers, hearty meals, and plump patrons. These places are famous with visitors but are also enjoyed by the locals. All but the last two places are central in the old city.

Gasthaus zum Wilder Mann is the place if the weather's bad and you're in the mood for Hofbräu atmosphere and a hearty, cheap meal at a shared table in one small, well-antlered room (Mon–Sat 11:00–21:00, closed Sun, smoky, 2 min from Mozart's birthplace, enter from Getreidegasse 20 or Griesgasse 17, tel. 0662/841-787). For a quick lunch, get the *Bauernschmaus*, a mountain of dumplings, kraut, and peasant's meats.

Stiftskeller St. Peter has been in business for more than 1,000 years—it was mentioned in the biography of Charlemagne. It's classy (with strolling musicians), more central, and a good splurge for traditional Austrian cuisine in medieval sauce (meals 100–200 AS, daily 11:00–24:00, indoor/outdoor seating, hosts Mozart Dinner Concert mentioned in "Music Scene," above: 560 AS, nightly at 20:00, call to reserve, CC:VMA, next to St. Peter's church at foot of Mönchsberg, tel. 0662/841-268).

Gasthaus zur Goldenen Ente (see "Sleeping," above) serves great food in a classy, subdued hotel dining room. The chef, Robert, specializes in roast duck (*Ente*) and seafood, along with "Salzburger *Nockerl*," the mountainous sweet soufflé served all over town. It's big enough for four (Mon–Fri 11:00–21:00, closed Sat–Sun, Goldgasse 10, tel. 0662/845-622).

Stieglkeller is a huge, atmospheric institution that has several rustic rooms and outdoor garden seating with a great rooftop view of the old town (daily 10:00–23:00, 50 meters uphill from the lift to the castle, Festungsgasse 10, tel. 0662/842-681).

Sternbrau Inn is a sprawling complex of popular eateries (traditional and vegetarian). One elegant room hosts the *Sound of Music* dinner show. A piano player and a hard-working quartet of singers perform an entertaining mix of *Sound of Music* hits and traditional folk songs (570 AS includes a schnitzel and crisp apple strudel dinner at 19:30, 370 AS for 20:30 show only, ideal for families, daily May–Sept, Griesgasse 23, tel. 0662/826-617).

Resch & Lieblich Bierhaus, wedged between the cliff side and the back of the big concert hall, is a rough and characteristic place popular with locals for salads, goulash, and light meals (indoor/outdoor seating: in rustic little cellar or under umbrellas on square, Toscaninihof, tel. 0662/843-675).

Café Glockenspiel, on Mozartplatz 2, is the place to see and be seen (daily 9:00–24:00).

Nestled behind the cathedral and under the castle, **Restaurant Weisses Kreuz** serves fine Balkan cuisine in a pleasant dining room (nightly, Bierjodlgasse 6, tel. 0662/845-641).

Picnickers will appreciate the bustling morning produce market (daily except Sun) on Universitätsplatz, just behind Mozart's house. **Restaurant Zipfer Bierhaus**, facing Universitätsplatz, serves good salads and traditional meals at a decent price (closed Sun).

Sausage stands serve the local fast food. The best places (such as the one on the side of the Collegiate Church just off Universitätsplatz) use the same boiling water all day, which fills the wienies with more flavor. Key wienie words: *bratwurst:* boiled white sausage, *bosna:* with onions and curry, *kas krainer:* with melted cheese inside, and *senf:* mustard (ask for sweet: *süss* or sharp: *scharf*). Only a tourist puts the sausage in a bun like a hot dog. Munch alternately between the meat and the bread (that's why you have two hands), and you'll look like a local.

The next two places are on the old-town side of the river, about a 10-minute walk along the river (river on your right) from the Staatsbrücke bridge.

Krimplestätter employs 450 years of experience serving authentic old-Salzburger food in its authentic old-Austrian interior or its cheery garden (Tue–Sun 10:00–24:00, closed Mon all year and Sun in winter, Müllner Hauptstrasse 31). For fine food with a wild finale, eat here and drink at the nearby Augustiner Bräustübl.

Augustiner Bräustübl, a monk-run brewery, is rustic and crude. On busy nights it's like a Munich beer hall with no music but the volume turned up. When it's cool you'll enjoy a historic setting with beer-sloshed and smoke-stained halls. On balmy evenings it's a Monet painting with beer breath under chestnut trees in the garden. Local students mix with tourists eating hearty slabs of schnitzel with their fingers or cold meals from the self-serve picnic counter while children frolic on the playground kegs. Waiters only bring drinks. For food, go up the stairs, survey the hallway of deli counters, and assemble your meal (or, as long as you buy a drink, you can bring in your picnic, open daily 15:00–23:00, Augustinergasse 4, head up Müllner Hauptstrasse northwest along the river, and ask for "Müllnerbräu," its local nickname). Don't be fooled by second-rate gardens serving the same beer nearby. Augustiner Bräustübl is a huge, 1,000-seat place within the Augustiner brewery. For your beer: Pick up a half-liter or full-liter mug (*"shank"* means self-serve price, *"bedienung"* is the price with waiter service), pay the lady, wash your mug, and give Mr. Keg your receipt and empty mug to be filled. For dessert—after a visit to the strudel kiosk—enjoy the incomparable floodlit view of old Salzburg from the nearby pedestrian bridge and a riverside stroll home.

Eating on or near Linzergasse

These cheaper places are near the recommended hotels on Linzergasse. **Frauenberger** is friendly, picnic-ready, and inexpensive, with indoor or outdoor seating (Mon–Fri 8:00–14:00, across from Linzergasse 16). **Spicy Spices** is a vegetarian-Indian lunch take-out restaurant (with a few tables) serving tasty curry and rice boxes, *samosas*, organic salads, and fresh juices (Mon–Sat 10:00–22:00, closed Sun, Wolf-Dietrich Strasse 1, tel. 0662/870-712). Nearby, **Restaurant Ahrlich** offers a delicious variety of organic meals (Mon–Sat 18:00–22:00, also 12:00–14:00 July–Aug, closed Sun, Wolf-Dietrich Strasse 7, tel. 0662/8712-7539). **Mensa Aicherpassage** serves some of Salzburg's cheapest meals in the basement (Mon–Fri 11:30–14:30, near Mirabellplatz, walk into Aicherpassage, go under arch, enter metal door to "Mozarteum," and go down 1 floor). Closer to the hotels on Rupertgasse and away from the tourists is the very local **Biergarten Weisse** (daily 11:00–24:00, on Rupertgasse east of Bayerhamerstrasse).

Transportation Connections—Salzburg
By train to: Innsbruck (every 2 hrs, 2 hrs), **Vienna** (2/hrly, 3.5 hrs), **Hallstatt** (hrly, 50 min to Attnang Puchheim, 20-minute wait, 90 min to Hallstatt), **Reutte** (every 2 hrs, 4 hrs, transfer to a bus in Innsbruck), **Munich** (hrly, 90 min). Train info: tel. 051717 (wait through long German recording for operator).

   By car: To leave town driving west, go under the Mönchsberg tunnel and follow blue A1 signs to Munich. It's 90 minutes from Salzburg to Innsbruck.

SALZKAMMERGUT LAKE DISTRICT AND HALLSTATT
Commune with nature in Austria's Lake District. "The hills are alive," and you're surrounded by the loveliness that has turned on everyone from Emperor Franz Josef to Julie Andrews. This is *The Sound of Music* country. Idyllic and majestic, but not rugged, it's a gentle land of lakes, forested mountains, and storybook villages, rich in hiking opportunities and inexpensive lodging. Settle down in the postcard-pretty, fjord-cuddling town of Hallstatt.

Planning Your Time
While there are plenty of lakes and charming villages, Hallstatt is really the only one that matters. One night and a few hours to browse are all you'll need to fall in love. To relax or take a hike in the surroundings, give it two nights and a day. It's a relaxing break between Salzburg and Vienna. My best Austrian week: the two big cities—Salzburg and Vienna, a bike ride along the Danube, and a stay in Hallstatt.

Orientation (area code: 06134)
Lovable Hallstatt is a tiny town bullied onto a ledge between a selfish mountain and a swan-ruled lake, with a waterfall ripping furiously through its middle. It can be toured on foot in about 15 minutes. The town is one of Europe's oldest, going back centuries before Christ. The charm of Hallstatt is the village and its lakeside setting. Go there to relax, nibble, wander, and paddle. While tourist crowds can trample much of Hallstatt's charm in August,

Hallstatt

NOT TO SCALE—
BUS STOP TO MARKTPLATZ IS A 10 MINUTE WALK

SALT MINE

TO ECHERNTAL VALLEY

FUNICULAR ROAD

GROC ROAD

SMALL UPPER PARKING LOT #1 IN TUNNEL

CATHOLIC CHURCH

TO BAD ISCHL & SALZBURG

TUNNEL

MAIN ROAD

DR. MORTON WEG

MUSEUM

MARKT PLATZ

GOSAUMUHL

MAIN

BUS STOP W.C. & PARKING LOT #2

BOAT RENTAL

PROT. CHURCH

MARKT DOCK

BOAT RENTAL

TO OBERTRAUN

LAHN DOCK

POST

HALLSTATTERSEE

TO HALLSTATT TRAIN STATION

① GASTHOF SIMONY
② GASTHOF ZAUNER
③ GASTHAUS ZUR MÜHLE
④ PENSION SEETHALER
⑤ HELGA LENZ ZIMMER
⑥ FRAU ZIMMERMAN ZIMMER
⑦ PENSION SARSTEIN

the place is almost dead in the off-season. The lake is famous for its good fishing and pure water.

Tourist Information: The TI, on the main drag, can explain hikes and excursions, arrange private tours of Hallstatt (600 AS), and find you a room (Mon–Fri 9:00–17:00, Sat–Sun 10:00–14:00, less off-season, a block from Marktplatz toward the lakefront parking, above post office, Seestrasse 169, tel. 06134/8208, www.tiscover .com/hallstatt, e-mail: hallstatt-info@eunet.at). Hallstatt gives any-one spending the night a "guest card" allowing free parking and discounts to local attractions (free, from your hotel, ask for it).

Arrival in Hallstatt

By Train: Hallstatt's train station is a wide spot on the tracks across the lake. *Stefanie* (a boat) meets you at the station and glides scenically across the lake into town (25 AS, meets each train until 18:40—don't arrive after that). Last departing boat-train connec-tion leaves Hallstatt at 18:15. Walk left from the boat dock for the TI and most hotels. Since there's no train station in town, the TI provides schedule information (10 AS).

By Car: The main road skirts Hallstatt via a long tunnel above the town. Parking is tight mid-June through mid-October.

Hallstatt has several numbered parking areas outside the town center. Parking lot #1 is in the tunnel above the town (swing through to check for a spot, free with guest card). Otherwise several numbered lots are just after the tunnel. If you have a hotel reservation, the guard will let you drive into town to drop your bags (ask if your hotel has any in-town parking). It's a lovely 10- to 20-minute lakeside walk to the center of town from the lots. Without a guest card, you'll pay 50 AS per day for parking. Off-season parking in town is easy and free.

Helpful Hints

Laundromat: A small full-service Laundromat is at the campground near the island of Bade-Insel (100 AS per load, based on weight). In the center, Hotel Gruner Baum also does laundry for nonguests (more expensive) and rents bikes (80 AS/half day, 120 AS/day, facing market square).

Parks and Swimming: Green and peaceful lakeside parks line the south end of Lake Hallstatt. If you walk 10 minutes south of town to Hallstatt-Lahn, you'll find a grassy public park, playground, and swimming area with a fun man-made play island (Badestrand and Bade-Insel).

Views: For a great view over Hallstatt, hike above Helga Lenz's *Zimmer* as far as you like (see "Sleeping," below), or climb any path leading up the hill. The 40-minute steep hike down from the salt mine tour gives the best views (see "Sights," below).

Hallstatt Historic Town Walk

This short walk starts at the dock.

Boat Landing: There was a Hallstatt before there was a Rome. In fact, because of the importance of salt mining here, an entire epoch—the Hallstatt era from 800 to 400 B.C.—is named for this important spot. Through the centuries, salt was traded and people came and went by boat. You'll still see the traditional "Fuhr" boats, designed to carry heavy loads in shallow water.

Towering above the town is the Catholic church. Its faded St. Christopher—patron saint of travelers with his cane and baby Jesus on his shoulder—watched over those sailing in and out. Until 1875, the only way into town was by boat. Then came the train and the road. The good ship *Stefanie* shuttles travelers back and forth from here to the Hallstatt train station immediately across the lake. The *Bootverleih* sign advertises boat rentals (see "Lake Trip," below).

Notice the one-lane road out of town (with the waiting time, width, and height posted). Until 1966, when a bigger tunnel was built above Hallstatt, all the traffic crept single file right through the town.

Look down the shore at the huge homes. Housing several

families back when Hallstatt's population was about double its present 1,000, many of these rent rooms to visitors today.

Parking is tight here in the tourist season. Locals and hotels have cards getting them into the prime town center lot. From October through May, the barricade is lifted and anyone can park here. Hallstatt is snowbound for about three months each winter. But the lake hasn't frozen over since 1981.

See any swans? They've patrolled the lake like they own it since the 1860s when Emperor Franz Josef and Empress Sissy—the Lady Diana of her day—made this region their annual holiday retreat. Sissy loved swans, so locals made sure she'd see them here. During this period, the Romantics discovered Hallstatt, many top painters worked here, and the town got its first hotel.

Tiny Hallstatt has two big churches—Protestant (step into its cemetery, which is actually a grassy lakeside playground) and Catholic up above (described below with its fascinating bone chapel). After the Reformation, most of Hallstatt was Protestant. Then, under Hapsburg rule, it was mostly Catholic. Today, 60 percent of the town is Catholic. Walk over the town's stream, past the Protestant church one block to...

Market Square: In 1750, a fire leveled this part of town. The buildings you see now are all late 18th century and built of stone rather than burnable wood. Take a close look at the two-dimensional, up-against-the-wall pear tree (it likes the sun-warmed wall). The statue features the Holy Trinity. At #58 study the painting of Hallstatt in 1750. Continue a block past Hotel Simony to the pair of phone booths and step into the...

City Museum Square: Because 20th-century Hallstatt was of no industrial importance, it was untouched by World War II. But once upon a time its salt was worth defending. High above, peeking out of the trees, is Rudolf's Tower (*Rudolfsturm*). Originally a 13th-century watchtower protecting the salt mines and later the mansion of a salt mine boss, today it's a restaurant with a great view. A zigzag trail connects the town with *Rudolfsturm* and the salt mines just beyond. The big white houses by the waterfall were water-powered mills that once ground Hallstatt's grain. If you hike up a few blocks, you'll see the river raging through town. Around you are the town's TI, post office, two museums, city hall, and the Janu Sport shop (with its prehistoric basement—described below). The statue on the square is of the mine manager who excavated prehistoric graves around 1850. Much of the *Schmuck* (jewelry) sold locally is inspired by the jewelry found in the area's Bronze Age tombs.

For thousands of years people have been leaching salt out of this mountain. A brine spring sprung here, attracting Bronze Age people around 1500 B.C. Later, they dug tunnels to mine the rock, which was 70 percent salt, dissolved it into a brine, and distilled out salt—precious for preserving meat (and making French fries so tasty). For a look at early salt mining implements, visit the museum.

Sights—Hallstatt

Prehistory Museum—The humble Prehistory Museum adjacent to the TI is interesting because little Hallstatt was the important salt-mining hub of a culture that spread from France to the Balkans during the "Hallstatt Period" (800–400 B.C.). Back then, Celtic tribes dug for precious salt, and Hallstatt was, as its name means, the "place of salt." Your 50-AS Prehistory Museum ticket also gets you into the cute Heimatmuseum of folk culture (both open daily 10:00–18:00 in summer, tel. 06134/8398). Historians like the English booklet that covers both museums (25 AS). The Janu Sport shop across from the TI dug into a prehistoric site, and now its basement is another small museum (free).

▲▲**Hallstatt's Catholic Church and Bone Chapel**—The Catholic church overlooks the town from above. From near the boat dock, hike up the covered wooden stairway to the church. The lovely church has 500-year-old altars and frescoes dedicated to St. Barbara (patron of miners) and St. Catherine (patron of foresters—lots of wood was needed to fortify the miles of tunnels and boil the brine to distill out the salt).

Behind the church, in the well-tended graveyard, is the 12th-century Chapel of St. Michael (even older than the church). Its bone chapel—or charnel house—contains over 600 painted skulls. Each skull has been lovingly named, dated, and decorated (skulls with dark, thick garlands are oldest—18th century, flowers indicate more recent—19th century). Space was so limited in this cemetery that bones had only 12 peaceful, buried years here before making way for the freshly dead. Many of the dug-up bones and skulls ended up in this chapel. They stopped this practice in the 1960s, about the same time the Catholic Church began permitting cremation (Beinhaus, 10 AS, daily 10:00–18:00).

▲**Lake Trip**—While there are full lake tours, you can ride *Stefanie* across the lake and back for 50 AS. It stops at the tiny Hallstatt train station for 30 minutes giving you time to walk to a hanging bridge and enjoy the peaceful, deep part of the lake. Those into relaxation can rent a sleepy electric motorboat to enjoy town views from the water (75 AS/30 min, 120 AS/60 min, until 19:00; boats have 2 speeds: slow and stop; spend 20 AS more for faster 500-watt boats, rental place next to ferry dock).

▲▲**Salt Mine Tour**—If you have yet to do a salt mine, Hallstatt's—which claims to be the oldest in the world—is a good one. You'll ride a steep funicular high above the town (105 AS round-trip, 65 AS one-way, May–Sept 9:00–18:00, until 16:30 in Oct, tel. 06134/8400), take a 10-minute hike, check your bag and put on old miners' clothes, hike 200 meters higher in your funny outfit

Salzkammergut Lakes

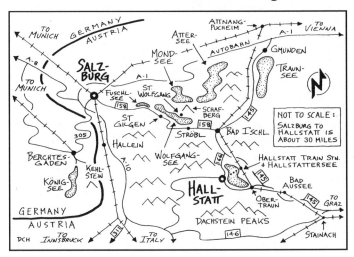

to meet your guide, load onto the train, and ride into the mountain through a tunnel actually made by prehistoric miners. Inside, you'll listen to a great video (English headsets), slide down two banisters, and follow your guide. While the tour is mostly in German, the guide is required to speak English if you ask—so ask (140 AS, May–Oct daily 9:30–16:30, the 16:00 funicular departure catches the last tour at 16:30, no children under age 4, rarely a long wait but arrive after 15:00 and you'll find no lines and a smaller group, tel. 06134/8400). The well-publicized ancient Celtic graveyard excavation sites nearby are really dead (precious little to see). If you skip the funicular, the scenic 40-minute hike back into town is (with strong knees) a joy.

At the base of the funicular, notice train tracks leading to the Erbstollen tunnel entrance. This lowest of the salt tunnels goes miles into the mountain where a shaft connects it to the tunnels you just explored. Today the salty brine from these tunnels flows 25 miles through the world's oldest pipeline to the huge modern salt works (next to the highway) at Ebensee. You'll pass a stack of the original 120-year-old wooden pipes between the lift and the mine.

▲**Local Hikes**—Mountain lovers, hikers, and spelunkers keep busy for days using Hallstatt as their home base (ask the TI for ideas). Local hikes are well described in the TI's *Dachstein Hiking Guide* (80 AS, English). A good, short, and easy walk is the two-hour round-trip up the Echerntal Valley to the Waldbachstrub waterfall and back. With a car, consider hiking around nearby Altaussee (flat, 3-hour hike) or along Grundlsee to Tolpitzsee.

Regular buses connect Hallstatt with Gosausee for a pleasant hour-long walk around that lake. The TI can recommend a great two-day hike with an overnight in a nearby mountain hut.

Sights—Near Hallstatt

▲▲**Dachstein Mountain Cable Car and Caves**—For a refreshing activity, ride a scenic cable car up a mountain to visit huge, chilly caves.

Dachstein Cable Car: From Obertraun, five kilometers beyond Hallstatt, a mighty gondola goes in three stages high up the Dachstein Plateau—crowned by Dachstein, the highest mountain in the Salzkammergut (over 9,000 feet). The first segment stops at Schonbergalm (4,500 feet) with a mountain restaurant and two huge caves (described below). The second segment goes to Krippenstein, a 6,600-foot summit with a classy hotel/restaurant and a rustic chalet restaurant. The third segment descends a bit to Gjaidalm (5,800 feet) from which several hikes begin. For a quick high-country experience, Krippenstein is better than Gjaidalm. From Krippenstein you'll survey a scrubby limestone "karst" landscape (which absorbs rainfall through its many cracks and ultimately carves all those caves) with 360-degree views of the surrounding mountains (cable car ride to the caves-170 AS, to Krippenstein-260 AS, tel. 06131/273).

Giant Ice Caves (Riesen-Eishohle, 4,500 feet): These were discovered in 1910. Today, guides lead tours in German and English on an hour-long, one-kilometer hike through an eerie, icy, subterranean world, passing limestone canyons the size of subway stations. The limestone caverns, carved by rushing water, are named for scenes from Wagner operas—the favorite of the mountaineers who first came here. If you're nervous, note that the iron oxide covering the ceiling takes 5,000 years to form. Things are very stable.

At the lift station, report to the ticket window to get your cave appointment. While the temperature is just above freezing and the 600 steps help keep you warm, bring a sweater. Allow 90 minutes, including the 10-minute hike from the station (90 AS, or 150-AS combo ticket with Mammoth Caves, open mid-May–mid-Oct, hour-long tours from 9:00–16:00, stay in front and assert yourself for English information, tel. 06134/8400).

Drop by the little free museum near the lift station—in a local-style wood cabin designed to support 200 tons of snow—to see the huge cave system model, exhibits about its exploration, and life in the caves.

Mammoth Caves: While huge and well promoted, these are much less interesting than the Ice Caves and—for most—not worth the time. Of the 30-mile limestone labyrinth excavated so far, you'll walk a kilometer with a German-speaking guide (90 AS, or 150-AS combo ticket with Ice Caves, hour-long tours 10:00–15:00, entrance a 10-minute hike from lift station).

Luge Rides on the Hallstatt–Salzburg Road—If you're driving between Salzburg and Hallstatt, you'll pass two luge rides. Each is a ski lift which drags you backwards up the hill as you sit on your go-cart. At the top you ride the cart down the winding metal course. Operating the sled is simple. Push to go, pull to stop, take your hands off your stick and you get hurt.

Each course is just off the road with easy parking. The ride up and down takes about 15 minutes. Look for "*Riesen-Rutschbahn*" or "*Sommerrodelbahn*" signs. The one near Fuschlsee (closest to Salzburg) is half as long and half the price (45 AS/ride, 320 AS/10 rides, 600 meters). The one near Walfgangsee is a double course, more fun and scenic with grand lake views (70 AS/ride, 480 AS/10 rides, 1,300 meters, each track is the same speed). Courses are open April through October from 10:00 to 18:00 (July–Aug 9:30–19:00, tel. 06235/7297). While these are fun, the concrete courses near Reutte are better.

Sleeping in Hallstatt
(15 AS = about $1, country code: 43, area code: 06134, zip code: 4830)
Sleep Code: **S** = Single, **D** = Double/Twin, **T** = Triple, **Q** = Quad, **b** = bathroom, **t** = toilet only, **s** = shower only, **CC** = Credit Card (**V**isa, **M**asterCard, **A**mex), **SE** = Speaks English, **NSE** = No English.

Hallstatt's TI can almost always find you a room (either in town or at B&Bs and small hotels outside of town—which are more likely to have rooms available and come with easy parking). Mid-July and August can be tight. Early August is worst. A bed in a private home costs about 200 AS with breakfast. It's hard to get a one-night advance reservation. But if you drop in and they have a spot, one-nighters are welcome. Prices include breakfast, lots of stairs, and a silent night. "*Zimmer mit Aussicht?*" means "Room with view?"—worth asking for. Only two of my listings accept plastic, which goes for most businesses here.

Gasthof Simony is my stocking-feet-tidy, 500-year-old favorite. It's right on the square with a lake view, balconies, creaky wood floors, slippery rag rugs, antique furniture, a lakefront garden, and a huge breakfast. Reserve in advance. For safety, reconfirm a day or two before you arrive and call again if arriving late (S-380 AS, Sb-650 AS, D-550 AS, Db-900–950 AS, third person-350–450 AS, Markt 105, tel. & fax 06134/8231, Susan Scheutz SE). Downstairs and in the lakefront garden, Frau Zopf runs a traditional Austrian restaurant—try her delicious homemade desserts. Grab a lakeside table.

Braugasthof Hallstatt is another creaky old place—a former brewery—with eight mostly lake-view rooms near the town center

(Db-920 AS, less off-season, CC:VM, Seestrasse 120, tel. 06134/8221, fax 06134/82214, Lobisser family).

Gasthof Zauner, at the opposite end of the square from the Simony, is my second listing that accepts credit cards. It's a business machine offering modern pine-flavored rooms with all the comforts on the main square, and a restaurant specializing in grilled meat and fish (12 rooms, Db-1,230 AS, CC:VM, Marktplatz 51, tel. 06134/8246, fax 06134/82468, e-mail: zauner@hallstatt.at).

Gasthaus zur Mühle Jugendherberge, below the waterfall with the best cheap beds in town, is popular for its great pizzas and cheap grub (bed in 3- to 20-bed coed dorms-120 AS, D-270 AS, sheets-40 AS extra, family quads, breakfast-40 AS, big lockers, closed Nov, below tunnel car park, Kirchenweg 36, tel. & fax 06134/8318, e-mail: toeroe.f@magnet.at, run by Ferdinand Törö).

Pension Seethaler is a homey old lodge with 45 beds and a breakfast room mossy with antlers, perched above the lake. The place is very simple with coin-op showers downstairs (215 AS/person in S, D, T, or Q, 280 AS/person in rooms with private bath, multinight stays-20 AS less; from the Boote paddleboats between the lake parking lot and Marktplatz, find and climb the steps then turn right, Dr. Morton Weg 22, tel. 06134/8421, fax 06134/84214, Frau Seethaler).

Helga Lenz is a five-minute climb above the Seethaler (look for the green *Zimmer* sign). This big, sprawling, woodsy house has a nifty garden perch, wins the best-view award, and is ideal for those who sleep well in tree houses (D-400 AS, T-570 AS, 1-night stays-20 AS extra, family room, Hallberg 17, tel. 06134/8508, e-mail: haus-lenz@aon.at).

These two listings are 200 meters to the right of the ferry boat dock, with your back to the lake: **Frau Zimmermann** runs a three-room *Zimmer* (as her name implies) in a 500-year-old ramshackle house with low beams, time-polished wood, and fine lake views (S-210 AS, D-420 AS, can be musty, Gosaumühlstrasse 69, tel. 06134/86853). She speaks little English, but you'll find yourself caught up in her charm and laughing together like old friends. A block away, **Pension Sarstein** has 25 beds in basic, dusty rooms with flower-bedecked, lake-view balconies, in a charming building run by friendly Frau Fisher. You can swim from her lakeside garden (D-440 AS, Ds-640 AS with this book, 1-night stays-20 AS per person extra, Gosaumühlstrasse 83, tel. 06134/8217).

Gasthof Pension Gruner Anger is a practical and modern place away from the medieval town center. It's big, quiet, with a normal parking lot, well situated a block from the base of the salt mine lift, and a 10-minute walk from the town center (12 rooms, Sb-450 AS, Db-740 AS, 780 AS in July–Aug, 1-night stays-820 AS, third person-200 AS, CC:VM, Lahn 10, tel. 06134/8397, fax 06134/83974, e-mail: anger@aon.at, Sulzbacher family).

Eating in Hallstatt

You can enjoy good food inexpensively with delightful lakeside settings. While everyone cooks the typical Austrian fare, your best bet here is trout. Reinanke trout is from Lake Hallstatt. Grab a front table at **Gasthof Simony's** garden restaurant (see "Sleeping," above). **Hotel Gruner Baum's** romantic restaurant is fancier and also good. Or feed the swans while your trout cooks at **Restaurant Braugasthof** (they have a fun menu, tel. 06134/20012). While it lacks a lakeside setting, **Gasthof Zauner's** restaurant is well respected for its grilled meat and fish (see "Sleeping," above). For the best pizza in town with a fun-loving local crowd, chow down cheap and hearty at **Gasthaus zur Mühle** (see "Sleeping," above). And every local's favorite place for a good dinner is a 10-minute lakeside hike away near the town beach at the **Strand Café** (great garden setting on the lake, Seelande 102, tel. 06134/8234). For your late-night drink, savor the Market Square from the trendy little pub called the **Ruth Zimmermann**.

Transportation Connections—Hallstatt

By train to: Salzburg (hrly, 90 min to Attnang Puchheim, short wait, 50 min to Salzburg), **Vienna** (hrly, 90 min to Attnang Puchheim, short wait, 2.5 hrs to Vienna). Day-trippers to Hallstatt can check bags at the Attnang Puchheim station. (Note: Connections there and back can be very fast—about 5 minutes. Have three 10-AS coins ready for the lockers.)

INNSBRUCK

Innsbruck is world famous as a resort for skiers and a haven for hikers. But when compared to Salzburg and Vienna, it's stale strudel. Still, a quick look is easy and interesting.

Innsbruck was the Hapsburgs' capital of the Tirol. Its medieval center, now a glitzy, tourist-filled pedestrian zone, still gives you the feel of a provincial medieval capital. The much-ogled Golden Roof (*Goldenes Dach*) is the centerpiece. Built by Emperor Maximilian in 1494, this balcony (with 2,657 gilded copper tiles) offered an impressive spot from which to view his medieval spectacles.

From this square you'll see the Golden Roof, the Baroque-style Helblinghaus, and the city tower (climb it for a great view, 30 AS). Nearby are the palace (Hofburg), church (Hofkirche), and Folklife Museum.

Orientation (area code: 0512)

Tourist Information: Innsbruck has a TI downtown (daily 9:00–18:00, on Burggraben, 3 blocks in front of Golden Roof, tel. 0512/5356) and a hotel room-finding service at the train station, which can be helpful (open until 22:00). The 230-AS, 24-hour Innsbruck Card pays for itself only if you take the Mountain

Lift (also covers Igls Lift, as well as the buses, trams, museums, zoo, and castle). The TI offers two tours daily—combining bus travel and walking—for 160 AS (in English and German, at 12:00 and 14:00, 12:00 only in winter, 2 hrs).

Arrival in Innsbruck: From the train station, it's a 10-minute walk to the old-town center. Leave by veering right to Brixner-strasse. Follow it past the fountain at Boznerplatz and straight until it dead-ends into Maria-Theresa Strasse. Turn right and go 250 meters into the old town (you'll pass the TI on Burggraben on your right), where you'll see the Golden Roof and Hotel Weisses Kreuz. Tram #3 does the same trip in two stops (pay the driver 22 AS or buy a 40-AS all-day pass from a tobacco shop).

Sights—Innsbruck

▲▲Folklife Museum (Tiroler Volkskunst Museum)—This offers the best look anywhere at traditional Tirolean lifestyles. Fascinating exhibits range from wedding dresses and gaily painted cribs and nativity scenes, to maternity clothes and babies' trousers. The upper floors show Tirolean homes through the ages (60 AS, Mon–Sat 9:00–17:00 in summer, Sun 9:00–12:00, hard to appreciate without the English guidebook).

Maria-Theresa Strasse—From the medieval center stretches the fine Baroque Maria-Theresa Strasse. St. Anne's Column marks the center of the old marketplace. At the far end, the Triumphal Arch is a gate Maria Theresa built to celebrate the marriage of her son, Leopold II.

▲Ski Jump View—The great ski jump of the 1964 and 1976 Olympics is an inviting side trip with a superb view, overlooking the city just off the Brenner Pass road on the south side of town (drivers follow signs to "Bergisel" or take tram #1). For the best view, hike to the Olympic rings under the dish that held the Olympic flame, where Dorothy Hamill and a host of others who brought home the gold are honored. Near the car park is a memorial to Andreas Hofer, the hero of the Tirolean battles against Napoleon.

Mountain Lifts and Hiking—A popular mountain-sports center and home of the 1964 and 1976 Winter Olympics, Innsbruck is surrounded by 150 mountain lifts, 1,250 miles of trails, and 250 hikers' huts. If it's sunny, consider riding the lift right out of the city to the mountaintops above (230 AS). Ask your hotel or hostel for an Innsbruck Club card, which offers overnight guests various discounts, bike tours, and free guided hikes in summer. Hikers meet in front of Congress Innsbruck daily at 8:30; each day it's a different hike in the surrounding mountains and valleys (bring only lunch and water; boots, rucksack, and transport are provided; confirm with TI).

Alpenzoo—This zoo is one of Innsbruck's most popular attractions (understandable when the competition is the Golden Roof).

Innsbruck and Hall

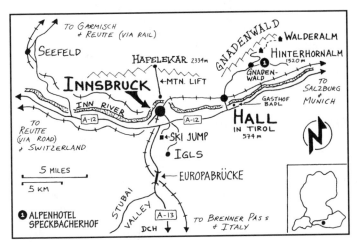

You can ride the funicular up to the zoo (free if you buy your zoo ticket before boarding) and get a look at all the animals that hide out in the Alps: wildcats, owls, elk, vultures, and more (70 AS, cheaper tickets at TI, daily 9:00–18:00).

▲**Slap Dancing**—For your Tirolean folk fun, Innsbruck hotels offer an entertaining evening of slap dancing and yodeling nearly nightly April through October (230 AS includes a drink with 2-hour show, 20:30, tickets at TI). And every summer Thursday, the town puts on a free outdoor folk show under the Golden Roof.

Sights—Near Innsbruck

▲▲**Alpine Side Trip by Car to Hinterhornalm**—In Gnaden-wald, a village sandwiched between Hall and its Alps, pay a 60-AS toll, pick up a brochure, then corkscrew your way up the mountain. Marveling at the crazy amount of energy put into such a remote road project, you'll finally end up at the rustic Hinterhornalm Berg restaurant (crude rooms, often closed, tel. 06641/211-2745). Hinterhornalm is a hang-gliding springboard. On good days, it's a butterfly nest. From there it's a level 20-minute walk to Walderalm, a cluster of three dairy farms with 70 cows that share their meadow with the clouds. The cows—cameras dangling from their thick necks—ramble along ridge-top lanes surrounded by cut-glass peaks. The ladies of the farms serve soup, sandwiches, and drinks (very fresh milk in the afternoon) on rough plank tables. Below you spreads the Inn River Valley and, in the distance, tourist-filled Innsbruck.

Sleeping in Gnadenwald: Alpenhotel Speckbacherhof

is a grand rustic hotel set between a peaceful forest and a meadow with all the comforts, bike rental, mini-golf, laundry, and so on (D-800 AS, Ds & Db-900–1,240 AS, 2 apartments-1,450–2,440 AS, half-board 180 AS/person extra, ask for 10 percent discount with this book, CC:VMA, includes breakfast, closed Nov, Sankt Martin 2, A-6060 Gnadenwald/Tirol, tel. 05223/52511, fax 05223/525-1155, family Mayr). Drive 10 minutes uphill from Hall to the village of Gnadenwald. It's across the street from the Hinterhornalm toll road.

Sleeping in Innsbruck
(15 AS = about $1, country code: 43, area code: 0512)
Hotel Weisses Kreuz, near the Golden Roof, has been housing visitors for 500 years. While it still feels like an old inn, rooms are newly renovated and comfortable (S-470–510 AS, Sb-790–890 AS, D-870 AS, small Db-1,200 AS, the big Db at 1,260 AS is a better value, CC:VMA, includes breakfast, elevator, nonsmoking rooms, 50 meters from Golden Roof, as central as can be in the old town at Herzog-Friedrichstrasse 31, A-6020 Innsbruck, tel. 0512/594-790, fax 0512/594-7990, e-mail: hotel.weisses.kreuz@eunet.at).

Pension Stoi, which rents pleasant rooms, is a very basic place hiding behind a dumpy exterior 200 meters from the train station (S-480 AS, Sb-530 AS, D-700 AS, Db-800 AS, T-840 AS, Tb-940 AS, no breakfast, free parking in alleyway behind #5 at Salurnerstrasse 7, 6020 Innsbruck, tel. 0512/585-434).

Transportation Connections—Innsbruck
To: Hall (4 buses/hrly, 30 min; hrly trains, 15 min), **Salzburg** (trains every 2 hrs, 2 hrs), **Vienna** (trains every 2 hrs, 5 hrs), **Reutte** (trains every 2 hrs, 2.5 hrs with 1 change; or by bus: 4/day, 2.5 hrs), **Bregenz** (every 2 hours, 2.5 hrs), **Zurich** (every 2 hours, 4 hrs), **Munich** (every 2 hours, 2 hrs), **Paris** (2 trains/day, 11 hrs), **Milan** (every 2 hours, 5.5 hrs), **Venice** (5 trains/day, 5.5 hrs). Night trains run to Paris, Milan, and Venice. Train info: tel. 051717 (wait through long German recording for operator).

HALL IN TIROL
Hall was a rich salt-mining center when Innsbruck was just a humble bridge (*Brücke*) town on the Inn River. Hall actually has a larger old town than does its sprawling neighbor, Innsbruck. Hall hosts a colorful morning scene before the daily tour buses arrive, closes down tight for its daily siesta, and sleeps on Sunday. There's a brisk farmers' market on Saturday mornings. (For drivers, Hall is a convenient overnight stop on the long drive from Vienna to Switzerland.)

Tourist Information: Hall's TI is just off the main square (Mon–Fri 9:00–18:00, Sat 9:00–12:00, closed Sun, Wallpachgasse 5, tel. 05223/56269).

Bike Rental: You can rent bikes at the campground (tel. 05223/454-6475). The riverside bike path (11 kilometers from Hall to Volders) is a treat.

Sights—Hall

Hasegg Castle—This was the town mint. As you walk over the old pedestrian bridge from Gasthof Badl (see "Sleeping," below), it's the first old building you'll see. You can pick up a town map and a list of sights here.

Parish Church—Facing the town square, this much-appended Gothic church is decorated Baroque, with fine altars, a twisted apse, and a north wall lined with bony relics.

Salt Museum (Bergbaumuseum)—Back when salt was money, Hall was loaded. Try catching a tour at this museum, where the town has reconstructed one of its original salt mines, complete with pits, shafts, drills, tools, and a slippery but tiny wooden slide (40 AS, April–Oct Mon–Sat, closed Sun, by guided tour only, 30-minute tours depart on the hour from 13:00–17:00 if there are at least 5 people, English spoken, tel. 05223/56269).

Walking Tours—The TI organizes town walks in English (400 AS including admissions, 2 hrs, by reservation only, tel. 05223/ 56269).

Swimming—If you want to make a splash, check out Hall's magnificent *Freischwimmbad*, a huge outdoor pool complex with four diving boards, a giant lap pool, a big slide, and a kiddies' pool, all surrounded by a lush garden, sauna, mini-golf, and lounging locals (38 AS, opens at 9:00, follow signs from downtown, tel. 05223/45464).

Sleeping and Eating in Hall
(15 AS = about $1, country code: 43, area code: 05223)

Lovable towns that specialize in lowering the pulse of local vacationers line the Inn Valley. Hall, while the best town, has the shortest list of accommodations. Up the hill on either side of the river are towns strewn with fine farmhouse hotels and pensions. Most *Zimmer* charge about 200 AS per person but don't accept one-night stays.

Gasthof Badl is a big, comfortable, friendly place run by sunny Frau Steiner and her daughter, Sonja. I like its convenience, peace, big breakfast, easy telephone reservations, and warm welcome (Sb-475 AS, Db-770 AS, Tb-1,080 AS, Qb-1,400 AS, CC:VM, elevator, rental bikes for guests for fine riverside path, Innbrücke 4, A-6060 Hall in Tirol, tel. 05223/56784, fax 05223/567-843, www.netwing.at/tirol/hall/badl, e-mail: badl@tirol .com). Hall's kitchens close early, but Gasthof Badl's restaurant serves excellent dinners until 21:30 (around 120 AS, closed Tue). They stock the essential TI brochures and maps of Hall and

Innsbruck in English. It's easy to find: From the east it's immediately off the Hall-Mitte freeway exit; you'll see the orange-lit "Bed" sign. From Innsbruck, take the Hall-Mitte exit and, rather than turning left over the big bridge into town, go straight.

For a cheaper room in a private home, **Frieda Tollinger** rents out three rooms and accepts one-nighters (220 AS/person with breakfast, across the river from Badl and downstream about a kilometer, follow Untere Lend, which becomes Schopperweg, to Schopperweg 8, tel. 05223/41366, no English spoken).

Transportation Connections—Hall
Innsbruck is the nearest major train station. Hall and Innsbruck are connected by train and bus. Trains do the trip faster but leave only hourly, and Hall's train station is a 10-minute walk from the town center. The white bus #4 takes a bit longer (30 min, 30 AS) but leaves four times per hour and drops you at the edge of town at the wooden bridge by the Billa Supermarket or the Kurhaus at the top of Hall. Buses go to and from the Innsbruck train station, a 10-minute walk from the old-town center. Drivers staying in freeway-handy Hall can side-trip into Innsbruck using bus #4. Immediately over the bridge entering Hall (on right) is a convenient parking lot (90 min free with cardboard clock under windshield, 5-minute walk to old center).

Route Tips for Drivers
Into Salzburg from Munich: After crossing the border, stay on the autobahn, taking the Süd Salzburg exit in the direction of Anif. First you'll pass Schloss Hellbrunn (and zoo), then the TI and a great park-and-ride service. Get sightseeing information and a daylong bus pass from the TI (daily 9:00–20:00), park your car (free), and catch the shuttle bus (20 AS, every 5 min) into town. Mozart never drove in the old town, and neither should you. If you don't believe in park-and-rides, the easiest, cheapest, most central parking lot is the 1,500-car Altstadt lot in the tunnel under the Mönchsberg (160 AS/day; note your slot number and which of the twin lots you're in). Your hotel may provide discounted parking passes.

From Salzburg to Hallstatt (50 miles): Get on the Munich–Wien autobahn (blue signs), head for Vienna, exit at Thalgau, and follow signs to Hof, Fuschl, and St. Gilgen. The Salzburg-to-Hallstatt road passes two luge rides (see "Sights—Near Hallstatt," above), St. Gilgen (pleasant but touristy), and Bad Ischl (the center of the Salzkammergut with a spa, salt mine tour, casino, the emperor's villa if you need a Hapsburg history fix, and a good TI—tel. 06132/277-570).

Hallstatt is basically traffic free. To park, try parking lot #1 in the tunnel above the town (free with guest card). Otherwise try the lakeside lots (a pleasant 10- to 20-minute walk from the town center) after the tunnel on the far side of town. If you're traveling off-season and staying downtown, you can drive in and park by the boat dock. (For more on parking in Hallstatt, see "Arrival in Hallstatt," above.)

From Hall into Innsbruck and on to Switzerland: For Old Innsbruck, take the autobahn from Hall to the Innsbruck Ost exit and follow the signs to "Zentrum," then "Kongresshaus," and park as close as you can to the old center on the river (Hofgarden).

Just south of Innsbruck is the Olympic ski jump (from the autobahn take the Innsbruck Süd exit and follow signs to "Bergisel"). Park at the end of the road near the Andreas Hofer Memorial, and climb to the empty, grassy stands for a picnic.

Leaving Innsbruck for Switzerland (from ski jump, go down into town along huge cemetery—thoughtfully placed just beyond the jump landing—and follow blue A12, Garmisch, Arlberg signs), head west on the autobahn (direction: Bregenz). The 8-mile-long Arlberg tunnel saves you 30 minutes but costs you lots of scenery and 130 AS (Swiss francs and credit cards accepted). For a joyride and to save a few bucks, skip the tunnel, exit at St. Anton, and go via Stuben.

After the speedy Arlberg tunnel, you're 30 minutes from Switzerland. Bludenz, with its characteristic medieval quarter, makes a good rest stop. Pass Feldkirch (and another long tunnel) and exit the autobahn at Rankweil/Feldkirch Nord, following signs for Altstätten and Meiningen (CH). Crossing the baby Rhine River, leave Austria.

To side-trip to Liechtenstein, follow FL signs at Feldkirch (see "Side Trip Through Liechtenstein" in the Appenzell chapter).

Leaving Hall or Innsbruck for Reutte, go west (as above, direction Switzerland) and leave the freeway at Telfs where signs direct you to Reutte (a 90-minute drive).

Side Trip over Brenner Pass into Italy: A short swing into Italy is fast and easy from Innsbruck or Hall (45-minute drive, easy border crossing, Austrian schillings accepted in border towns). To get to Italy, take the great Europa Bridge over Brenner Pass. It costs about $10, but in 30 minutes you'll be at the border. (Note: Traffic can be heavy on summer weekends.) In Italy drive to the colorful market town of Vipiteno/Sterzing. **Reifenstein Castle** is a unique and wonderfully preserved medieval castle, just south of town on the west side of the valley, down a small road next to the autobahn. The lady who lives at the castle gives tours in German, Italian, and a little English (open Easter–Oct, entry by tour only, 6,000 lire or 45 AS, tours on Mon at 14:00 and 15:00, Tue–Thu and Sat–Sun at 9:30, 10:30, 14:00, and 15:00, closed Fri and Nov–Easter, tel. from Austria 00-39-0472-647-196, in Italy: tel. 0472-647-196).

SWITZERLAND
(SCHWEIZ, SUISSE, SVIZZERA)

- 16,000 square miles (half the size of Ireland, or 13 Rhode Islands)
- About 6 million people (400 people per square mile, declining slightly)
- 1 Swiss franc (SF) = about 60 cents, 1.70 SF = about $1

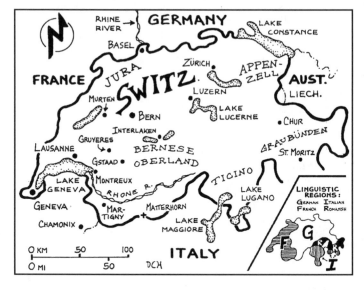

Switzerland is one of Europe's richest, best-organized, and most expensive countries. Like Boy Scouts, the Swiss count cleanliness, neatness, punctuality, tolerance, independence, thrift, and hard work as virtues, and they love pocketknives. Their high income, a great social security system, and the Alps give the Swiss plenty to be thankful for.

Switzerland is Europe's most mountainous country. Forty percent of the country consists of uninhabitable rocks, lakes, and rugged Alps. Its geography has given it distinct cultural regions. Two-thirds of the people speak German, 20 percent French, 10 percent Italian, and a small group in the southeast speak Romansch, a descendant of ancient Latin. The singsongy Swiss German, the spoken dialect, is quite different from the written High German. Most Swiss are multilingual, and English is widely spoken.

Historically, Switzerland is one of the oldest democracies

(yet women didn't get the vote until 1971). Born when three states, or cantons, united in 1291, the Confederation Helvetica, as it was called in Roman times (the "CH" decal on cars doesn't stand for chocolate), grew to the 23 cantons of today. The government is decentralized, and cantonal loyalty is very strong.

Fiercely independent, Switzerland loves its neutrality and stayed out of both world wars. But it's far from lax defensively. Every fit man serves in the army and stays in the reserve. Each house has a gun and a bomb shelter. Switzerland bristles with 600,000 rifles in homes and 12,000 heavy guns in place. Swiss vacuum-packed emergency army bread, which lasts two years, is also said to function as a weapon. Airstrips hide inside mountains behind Batmobile doors. With the push of a button, all road, rail, and bridge entries to the country can be destroyed, changing Switzerland into a formidable mountain fortress. Notice the innocent-looking but explosive patches checkerboarding the roads at key points like tunnel entrances and mountain summits (and hope no one invades until you get past). Sentiments are changing, and Switzerland has come close to voting away its entire military.

Prices are high. More and more locals call sitting on the pavement around a bottle of wine "going out." Hotels with double rooms under $80 are rare. Even dormitory beds cost $15. If your budget is tight, be sure to chase down hostels (many have family rooms) and keep your eyes peeled for *Matratzenlagers* (literally, "mattress dorms"). Hiking is free, though major Alpine lifts run $20 to $40.

The Swiss eat when we do and enjoy a straightforward, no-nonsense cuisine. Specialties include delicious fondue, rich chocolates, a melted cheese dish called raclette, fresh dairy products (try muesli yogurt), 100 varieties of cheese, and *Fendant*, a good, crisp, local white wine. The Co-op and Migros grocery stores are the hungry hiker's best budget bet; groceries charge only 50 percent more than U.S. prices.

You can get anywhere quickly on Switzerland's scenic and efficient trains or its fine road system (the world's most expensive per mile to build). Drivers pay a one-time, 40-SF fee for a permit to use Swiss autobahns—check to see if your rental car already has one; if not, buy it at the border, gas station, or rental agency. Anyone caught driving on a Swiss autobahn without this tax sticker is likely to be cop-stopped and fined.

While Switzerland's booming big cities are cosmopolitan, traditional culture survives in the Alpine villages. Spend most of your time getting high in the Alps. On Sunday you're most likely to enjoy traditional music, clothing, and culture. August 1 is the festive Swiss national holiday.

GIMMELWALD
AND THE BERNER
OBERLAND

Frolic and hike high above the stress and clouds of the real world. Take a vacation from your busy vacation. Recharge your touristic batteries up here in the Alps, where distant avalanches, cowbells, the fluff of a down comforter, and the crunchy footsteps of happy hikers are the dominant sounds. If the weather's good (and your budget's healthy), ride a gondola from the traffic-free village of Gimmelwald to a hearty breakfast at Schilthorn's 10,000-foot revolving Piz Gloria restaurant. Linger among Alpine whitecaps before riding, hiking, or parasailing down (5,000 feet) to Mürren and home to Gimmelwald.

Your gateway to the rugged Berner Oberland is the grand old resort town of Interlaken. Near Interlaken is Switzerland's open-air folk museum, Ballenberg, where you can climb through traditional houses from every corner of this diverse country.

Ah, but the weather's fine and the Alps beckon. Head deep into the heart of the Alps and ride the gondola to the stop just this side of heaven—Gimmelwald.

Planning Your Time

Rather than tackling a checklist of famous Swiss mountains and resorts, choose one region to savor—the Berner Oberland. Interlaken is the administrative headquarters and a fine transportation hub. Use it for business (banking, post office, laundry, shopping) and as a springboard for Alpine thrills. With decent weather, explore the two areas (south of Interlaken) that tower above either side of the Lauterbrunnen Valley: Kleine Scheidegg/Jungfrau and Schilthorn/Mürren. Ideally, home-base three nights in the village of Gimmelwald and spend a day on each side of the valley. On a speedy train trip you can overnight into and out of Interlaken.

For the fastest look, consider a night in Gimmelwald, breakfast at the Schilthorn, an afternoon doing the Männlichen-to-Wengen hike, and an evening or night train out. What? A nature lover not spending the night high in the Alps? Alpus-interruptus.

Getting around the Berner Oberland
For more than 100 years, this has been the target of nature-worshiping pilgrims. And Swiss engineers and visionaries have made the most exciting Alpine perches accessible by lift or train. Part of the fun (and most of the expense) here is riding the many lifts. Generally, scenic trains and lifts are not covered on train passes, but a Eurail, Europass, or Eurail Selectpass gets you a 25 percent discount on even the highest lifts (without the loss of a flexi-day). Ask about discounts for early (and late) trips, youths, seniors, families, groups, and those staying awhile. The Junior Card pays for itself on the first hour of trains and lifts: children under 16 travel free with parents (20 SF for 1 child, 40 SF for 2 or more; available at Swiss train stations but not at gondola stations). Get a list of discounts and the free fare and time schedule at any train station. Study the "Alpine Lifts in the Berner Oberland" chart in this chapter. Lifts generally go at least twice hourly, from about 7:00 until about 20:00 (sneak preview: www.jungfrau.ch). Drivers can park at the gondola station in Stechelberg for the lift to Gimmelwald, Mürren, and the Schilthorn (5 SF/day), or at the train station in Lauterbrunnen for trains to Wengen and Kleine Scheidegg.

INTERLAKEN
When the 19th-century Romantics redefined mountains as something more than cold and troublesome obstacles, Interlaken became the original Alpine resort. Ever since then, tourists have flocked to the Alps because they're there. Interlaken's glory days are long gone, its elegant old hotels eclipsed by the new, more jet-setty Alpine resorts. Today its shops are filled with chocolate bars, Swiss Army knives, and sunburned backpackers.

Orientation (area code: 033)
Efficient Interlaken is a good administrative and shopping center. Take care of business, give the town a quick look, and view the live TV coverage of the Jungfrau and Schilthorn weather in the window of the Schilthornbahn office on the main street (at Höheweg 2, also on TV in most hotel lobbies). Then head for the hills. Stay in Interlaken only if you suffer from alptitude sickness (see "Sleeping in Interlaken," at the end of this chapter).

Tourist Information: The TI has good information for the region, advice on Alpine lift discounts, and a room-finding service (July–Sept Mon–Fri 8:00–18:30, Sat 8:00–17:00, Sun 10:00–12:00, 16:00–18:00; Oct–June Mon–Fri 8:00–12:00, 14:00–18:00,

Interlaken

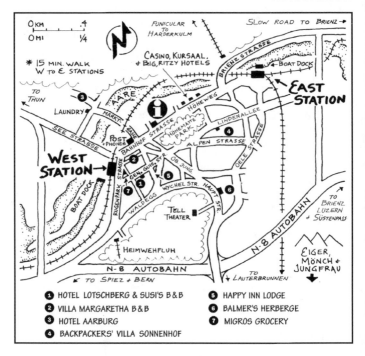

●1 HOTEL LOTSCHBERG & SUSI'S B & B

●2 VILLA MARGARETHA B & B

●3 HOTEL AARBURG

●4 BACKPACKERS' VILLA SONNENHOF

●5 HAPPY INN LODGE

●6 BALMER'S HERBERGE

●7 MIGROS GROCERY

Sat 9:00–12:00, closed Sun, tel. 033/826-5300, on main street, 5-minute walk from West station). While the Jungfrau region map costs 2 SF, a good mini-version is included in the free Jungfrau region train timetable. Pick up a Bern map if that's your next destination. The TI organizes town walks in English in summer (10 SF, June–Sept daily at 18:00, 60 min, depart from TI).

Arrival in Interlaken: Interlaken has two train stations: East and West. Most major trains stop at the Interlaken-West station. This station's train information desk answers tourists' questions (Mon–Fri 7:00–20:00, Sat–Sun 8:00–12:00, 14:00–18:00, tel. 033/826-4750), and there's a fair exchange booth next to the ticket windows. Ask at the station about discount passes, special fares, railpass discounts, and schedules for the scenic mountain trains (tel. 033/826-4750).

It's a pleasant 15-minute walk between the West and East stations, or an easy, frequent train connection. From the Interlaken-East station, private trains take you deep into the mountainous Jungfrau region (see "Transportation Connections," at the end of this chapter).

Helpful Hints

Telephone: Phone booths cluster outside the post office near the West station. For efficiency, buy a phone card from a newsstand. (There's a card phone in Gimmelwald that doesn't take coins.)

Laundry: Helen Schmocker's *Wäscherei* (laundry) has a change machine, soap, English instructions, and a pleasant riverside locale (daily, 24 hrs for self-service, or Mon–Sat 8:00–12:00, 13:30–18:00 for full service: drop off 10 pounds in the morning and pick up clean clothes that afternoon, from post office, follow Marktgasse over 2 bridges to Beatenbergstrasse; tel. 033/822-1566).

Grocery: A Migros supermarket is across the street from the train station (Mon–Thu 8:00–18:30, Fri 8:00–21:00, Sat 7:30–16:00, closed Sun).

Sights—Interlaken

Boat Trips—*Interlaken* means "between the lakes." Lazy boat trips explore these lakes (8/day, fewer off-season, free with Eurail/Euro/Eurail Selectpass, schedules at TI). The boats on **Lake Thun** stop at Beatushöhlen (interesting caves, 30 min from Interlaken, cave entry-14 SF, mid-April–mid-Oct, daily 10:30–17:00) and two visit-worthy towns: Spiez (1 hr from Interlaken) and Thun (1.75 hrs away). The boats on **Lake Brienz** stop at the super-cute and quiet village of Iseltwald (45 min away), and Brienz (1.25 hrs away, near Ballenberg Open-Air Folk Museum).

Adventure Trips—For the adventurer with money and little concern for personal safety, several companies offer high-adrenaline trips such as rafting, canyoning (rappelling down watery gorges), bungee jumping, and paragliding. Most adventure trips cost from 90 to 180 SF. Interlaken companies include: Alpin Raft (Postfach 78, tel. 033/823-4100, www.alpinraft.ch), Alpin Center (near East station, tel. 033/823-5523, www.alpincenter.ch), and Swiss Adventures (tel. 033/773-7373, www.swissadventures.ch).

Recent fatal accidents have understandably hurt the adventure-sport business in the Berner Oberland. In the summer of 1999, 22 tourists died canyoning on the Saxetenbach River, 10 miles from Interlaken (a flash flood pummeled the entire tour group with debris). In the spring of 2000, an American died bungee jumping from the Stechelberg-Mürren gondola (the operator used a 180-meter rope for a 100-meter jump). Also in 2000, a landslide killed several hikers. Enjoying nature up close comes with risks. Adventure sports increase those risks dramatically. Use good judgment.

GIMMELWALD

Saved from developers by its "avalanche zone" classification, Gimmelwald was (before tourism) one of the poorest places in Switzerland. Its traditional economy was stuck in the hay, and its farmers, unable to make it in their disadvantaged trade, survived only by

Gimmelwald

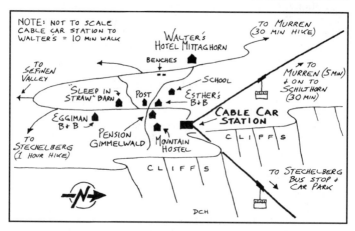

Swiss government subsidies (and working the ski lifts in the winter). For some travelers there's little to see in the village. Others enjoy a fascinating day sitting on a bench and learning why they say, "If heaven isn't what it's cracked up to be, send me back to Gimmelwald." Gimmelwald is my home base in the Berner Oberland (see "Sleeping in Gimmelwald," below).

Take a walk through the town. This place is for real. Most of the 130 residents have the same last name—von Allmen. They are tough and proud. Raising hay in this rugged terrain is labor intensive. One family harvests enough to feed only 15 or 20 cows. But they'd have it no other way and, unlike the absentee landlord town of Mürren, Gimmelwald is locally owned. (When word got out that urban planners wished to develop Gimmelwald into a town of 1,000, locals pulled some strings to secure the town's bogus avalanche-zone building code.)

Do not confuse obscure Gimmelwald with touristy and commercialized Grindelwald just over the Kleine Scheidegg ridge.

A Walk through Gimmelwald

Gimmelwald, while tiny with one zigzag street, gives a fine look at a traditional mountain Swiss community. Here's a quick walking tour.

Gondola Station: When the lift came in the 1960s, this village's back end became Gimmelwald's front door. This was and still is a farm village. Stepping off the gondola you see a sweet little hut. Set on stilts to keep out mice, the hut was used for storing cheese (the rocks on the rooftop keep the shingles on through wild winter winds). Notice the yellow Alpine "street sign" showing where you are, the altitude (1,363 meters), and how many hours and minutes it takes to walk to nearby points. Behind the cheese hut stands the village schoolhouse. In Catholic-Swiss towns, the biggest building is the church. In Protestant towns, it's the school. Gimmelwald's biggest building is the school (2 teachers, 19 students, and a room that doubles as a chapel when the Protestant pastor makes his monthly visit).

In the opposite direction, just beyond the little playground, is Gimmelwald's "Mountain Hostel."

Walk up the lane 50 meters, past the shower in the phone booth, to Gimmelwald's . . . .

"Times Square": From this tiny intersection, we'll follow the only paved road in town. Most of the buildings housed two families and are divided vertically right down the middle. The writing on the post office building is a folksy blessing: "Summer brings green, winter brings snow. The sun greets the day, the stars greet the night. This house will keep you warm. May God give us his blessings." The date indicates when it was built or rebuilt (1911).

Main Street: Walk up Main Street. Notice the town announcement board: one side tourist news, the other for local news. Cross the street and peek into the big new barn dated 1995. This is part of the "Sleep in Straw" association which rents out barn spots to travelers when the cows are in the high country (see "Sleeping," below). To the left of the door is a cow scratcher. Swiss cows have legal rights (e.g., in the winter they must be taken out for exercise at least three times a week). This big barn is built in a modern style. Traditionally, barns were small (like those on the hillside high above) and closer to the hay. But with trucks and paved roads, hay can be moved easier and farther and farms need more cows to be viable. Still, even a well-run big farm hopes just to break even. The industry survives only with government subsidies.

Water Fountain/Trough: This is the site of the town's historic water supply. Local kids love to bathe in this when the cows aren't drinking from it. From here, detour left down a lane about 50 meters (along a wooden fence and past pea-patch gardens) to the next trough and the oldest building in town, "Husmattli," from 1658. Study the log-cabin construction. Many are built without nails.

Back on the paved road, continue uphill. Gimmelwald has a strict building code. For instance, shutters can only be natural, green, or white. Notice the cute cheese hut on the right (with stones on the shingles and Alp cheese for sale). It's full of strong cheese— up to three years old. On the left (at B&B sign) is the home of Olle and Maria (the village school teachers). Gimmelwald heats with wood and, since the wood needs to age a couple of years to burn well, it's stacked everywhere. Fifty meters farther is . . .

Alpenrose: At the old schoolhouse, big ceremonial cowbells under its uphill eave. These swing from the necks of cows during the Alpine procession from the town to the high Alps (mid-June) and back down (around Sept 20). At the end of town notice the dramatic Sefinen valley. The road switches back at the...

Gimmelwald Fire Station: Check out the notices on the fire station building. Every Swiss male does a year in the military and then a few days a year in the reserves until about age 40. The 2001 Swiss Army calendar tells the reserves when and where to go. The Schiessubungen poster details the shooting exercises required this year. Keeping with the William Tell heritage, each Swiss man does shooting practice annually for the military (or spends 3 days in jail).

High Road: Follow the high road to Hotel Mittaghorn. The resort of Mürren hangs high above in the distance. And high on the left, notice the hay field with terraces. These are from WWII days when Switzerland, wanting self-sufficiency, required all farmers to grow potatoes. From Hotel Mittaghorn, you can return to Gimmelwald's "Times Square" via the stepped path. (For a map and photos of this walk, visit www.gimmelwald-news.ch.)

Gimmelwald After Dark—Evening fun in Gimmelwald is found at the youth hostel (offering a pool table, Internet access, lots of young Alp-aholics, and a good chance to share information on the surrounding mountains) or at Pension Gimmelwald's terrace restaurant next door. Walter's bar is a local farmers' hangout. When they've made their hay, they come here to play. They look like what we'd call hicks, but they speak some English and can be fun to get to know. Sit outside (benches just below the rails, 100 meters down the lane from Walter's) and watch the sun tuck the mountaintops into bed as the moon rises over the Jungfrau.

Alpine Excursions

There are days of possible hikes from Gimmelwald. Many are a fun combination of trails, mountain trains, and gondola rides. Don't mind the fences (but wires can be electrified—solar powered); a hiker has the right-of-way in Switzerland. However, as late as early June, snow can curtail your hiking plans (the Männlichen lift doesn't even open until June 6). Before setting out on any hike, get advice from a knowledgeable local to confirm that it is safe and accessible. Clouds can roll in anytime, but skies are usually clearest in the morning. Refer to maps (within this chapter) as you read about the following hikes.

▲▲▲**The Schilthorn: Hikes, Lifts, and a 10,000-Foot Breakfast**—The Schilthornbahn carries skiers, hikers, and sightseers effortlessly to the 10,000-foot summit of the Schilthorn where the Piz Gloria station (of James Bond movie fame) awaits with a revolving restaurant, shop, and panorama terrace. Linger on top. Piz Gloria has a "touristorama" film room showing a multiscreen slide show and explosive highlights from the James Bond thriller that featured the Schilthorn (free).

Lauterbrunnen Valley: West Side Story

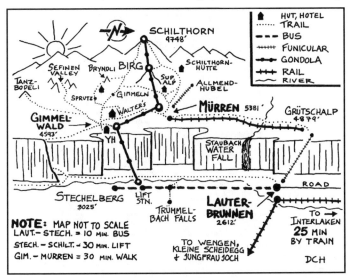

Watch hang gliders set up, psych up, and take off, flying 30 minutes with the birds to distant Interlaken. Walk along the ridge out back. This is a great place for a photo of the "mountain-climber you." For another cheap thrill, ask the gondola attendant to crank down the window (easiest on the Mürren-Birg section). Then stick your head out the window...and you're hang gliding.

The early-bird and afternoon-special gondola tickets (about 69 SF, before 9:00 or after 15:30) take you from Gimmelwald to the Schilthorn and back at a discount (normal rate-75 SF, or 90 SF from Stechelberg car park, parking-5 SF/day). Ask the Schilthorn station for a gondola souvenir decal (Schilthornbahn, in Stechelberg, tel. 033/823-1444 or 033/555-2141). For breakfast at 10,000 feet, there's no à la carte, only a 15-SF and a 22.50-SF meal. Ask for more hot drinks if necessary. If you're not revolving, ask them to turn it on.

Lifts go twice hourly, and the ride (including 2 transfers) to the Schilthorn takes 30 minutes. Watch the altitude meter in the gondola. (The Gimmelwald–Schilthorn hike is free if you don't mind a 5,000-foot altitude gain.) You can ride up to the Schilthorn and hike down, but it's tough (weather can change; wear good shoes). Youth hostelers scream down the ice fields on plastic-bag sleds from the Schilthorn mountaintop. (English-speaking doctor in Mürren.) For an easier hike, go halfway down by cable car and walk down from the Birg station (steep and gravelly). Buy the

Berner Oberland

NOTE:
THIS BIRD'S EYE
VIEW LOOKS
SOUTH...

EIGER 13026' MONCH 13449' JUNGFRAU 13642' SCHILT-HORN 9748'

JUNG-FRAU-JOCH

GIMMEL-WALD 4593'

BIRG 8784'

TUNNEL

KLEINE SCHEIDEGG 6762'

W. ALP

MÜRREN 5381'

GRINDEL-WALD 3393'

MÄNN-LICHEN 7317'

STECHEL-BERG 3025'

NICE WALK

GRUND

GRÜTSCHALP 4879'

TO FIRST

WENGEN 4180'

LAUTERBRUNNEN 2612'

ISENFLUH

WILDERSWIL 1916'

ISELT-WALD

SCHYNIGE PLATTE 6454'

SPIEZ

TO LUZERN

E.

W.

LAKE

BRIENZ

LAKE BRIENZ

INTER-LAKEN 1860'

LAKE THUN

TO BERN

BALLENBERG

┿┿ PRIVATE RAIL - EURAIL NOT VALID
┿┿ OTHER RAIL - EURAIL VALID
○─○ MTN. LIFTS

--- BUS
•••• BOAT
····· TRAIL

NOT TO SCALE!

DCH

round-trip excursion early-bird fare (cheaper than the Gimmel-wald-Schilthorn-Birg ticket) and decide at Birg if you want to hike or ride down.

Just below Birg is Schilthorn-Hutte. Drop in for soup, cocoa, or a coffee schnapps. You can spend the night in the hut's crude loft (bed-20 SF, plus 45 SF if you want breakfast and dinner, open July–Sept, tel. 033/855-5053).

The most interesting trail from Birg to Gimmelwald is the high one via Grauseewli Lake and Wasenegg Ridge to Brünli, then down to Spielbodenalp and the Sprutz waterfall. From the Birg lift, hike toward the Schilthorn, taking your first left down to the little, newly made Grauseewli Lake. From the lake a gravelly trail leads down rough switchbacks until it levels out. When you see a rock painted with arrows pointing to "Mürren" and "Rot-stockhütte," follow the path to Rotstockhütte, traversing the cow-grazed mountainside. Follow Wasenegg Ridge left and down along the barbed-wire fence to Brünli. (For maximum thrills, stay on the ridge and climb all the way to the knobby little summit

Alpine Lifts in the Berner Oberland

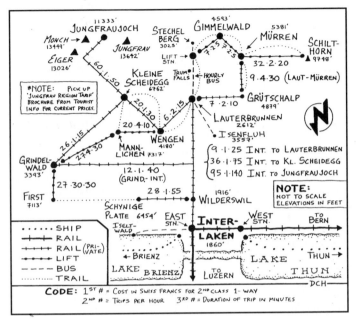

where you'll enjoy an incredible 360-degree view and a chance to sign your name on the register stored in the little wooden box.) A steep trail winds directly down from Brünli toward Gimmelwald and soon hits a bigger, easy trail. The trail bends right (just before the popular restaurant/mountain hut at Spielbodenalp), leading to Sprutz. Walk under the Sprutz waterfall, then follow a steep, wooded trail that will deposit you in a meadow of flowers at the top side of Gimmelwald.

▲▲**North Face Trail from Mürren**—For a pleasant two-hour hike (6 km, 1,946 meters–1,638 meters), ride the Allmendhubel funicular up from Mürren (cheaper than Schilthorn, good restaurant at top). From there, follow the well-promoted and described route circling around to Mürren (or cut off near the end down to Gimmelwald). You'll enjoy great views, flowery meadows, mountain huts, and a dozen information boards along the way describing the climbing history of the great peaks around you.

▲▲▲**The Männlichen–Kleine Scheidegg Hike**—This is my favorite easy Alpine hike. It's entertaining all the way with glorious Jungfrau, Eiger, and Mönch views. (That's the Young Maiden being protected from the Ogre by the Monk.)

If the weather's good, descend from Gimmelwald bright and

early to Stechelberg. From here, get to the Lauterbrunnen train station by post bus (3.60 SF, bus is synchronized to depart with the arrival of each lift) or by car (parking at the large multistoried pay lot behind the Lauterbrunnen station). At Lauterbrunnen, buy a train ticket to Männlichen. Ride past great valley views to Wengen, where you'll walk across town (buy a picnic but don't waste time here if it's sunny) and catch the Männlichen lift (departing every 15 min, from June 6) to the top of the ridge high above you. (Trails may be snowbound into early June. Ask about conditions at the lift stations or local TI. If the Männlichen lift is closed, take the train straight from Lauterbrunnen to Kleine Scheidegg.)

From the tip of the Männlichen lift, hike 20 minutes north to the little peak for that king- or queen-of-the-mountain feeling. From Männlichen, its an easy hour's walk—facing the Alpine panorama views of the north faces of the Eiger, Jungfrau, and Mönch—to Kleine Scheidegg for a picnic or restaurant lunch.

From Kleine Scheidegg you can catch the train to "the top of Europe" (see "Jungfraujoch," below). Or head downhill, riding the train or hiking (30 gorgeous min to Wengeralp station; 90 more steep minutes from there into the town of Wengen). The Alpine views might be accompanied by the valley-filling mellow sound of Alp horns and distant avalanches.

If the weather turns bad or you run out of steam, catch the train early at the little Wengeralp station along the way. After Wengeralp, the trail to Wengen is steep and, while not dangerous, requires a good set of knees. Wengen is a good shopping town. (For accommodations, see "Sleeping in Wengen," below.) The boring final descent from Wengen to Lauterbrunnen is knee-killer steep—catch the train.

▲▲▲**Jungfraujoch**—The literal high point of any trip to the Swiss Alps is a train ride through the Eiger to the Jungfraujoch. At 11,333 feet, it's Europe's highest train station. The ride from Kleine Scheidegg takes about an hour, including two five-minute stops at stations actually halfway up the notorious North Face of the Eiger. You have time to look out windows and marvel at how people could climb the Eiger and how the Swiss built this train over a hundred years ago. Once you reach the top, study the Jungfraujoch chart to see your options. There's a restaurant, history exhibit, ice palace (a cavern with a gallery of ice statues), and a 20-minute video (continuous). A tunnel leads outside where you can ski (30 SF for gear and lift ticket), sled (free loaner discs), ride in a dog sled (morning only), or hike 45 minutes across the ice to Mönchsjochhutte (a mountain hut with a small restaurant). An elevator leads to the Sphinx observatory for the highest viewing point from which you can see Aletsch Glacier—Europe's longest at 11 miles—stretch to the south. The first trip of the day to Jungfraujoch is discounted; ask for a Good Morning Ticket and return from the top by noon (runs all year, round-trip fares to Jungfrau-joch: from Kleine Scheidegg-normally about 100 SF, 60 SF for first trip of day—about 8:00 in summer; from Lauterbrunnen-about 145 SF, 105 SF for first trip—about 7:00 in summer, con-firm times and prices, get leaflet on lifts at a local TI or call 033/826-4750, www.jungfrau.ch, discounts for Eurail/Euro/Eurail Selectpass and Swiss railpass holders, trilingual weather info: tel. 033/855-1022, if it's cloudy—skip the trip).

▲▲**Hike from Schynige Platte to First**—The best day I've had hiking in the Berner Oberland was when I made the demanding six-hour ridge walk high above Lake Brienz on one side with all that Jungfrau beauty on the other. Start at Wilderswil train station (just above Interlaken) and catch the little train up to Schynige Platte (2,000 meters). Walk through the Alpine flower display gar-den and into the wild Alpine yonder. The high point is Faulhorn (2,680 meters, with its famous mountaintop hotel). Hike to a small gondola called "First" (2,168 meters), then descend to Grindel-wald and catch a train back to your starting point, Wilderswil. Or, if you have a regional train pass or no car but endless money, return to Gimmelwald via Lauterbrunnen from Grindelwald over Kleine Scheidegg. For an abbreviated ridge walk, consider the Panoramaweg, a short loop from Schynige Platte to Daub Peak.

▲**Mountain Biking**—Mountain biking is popular and accepted (as long as you stay on the clearly marked mountain-bike paths). A popular ride is the round-trip "Mürren Loop" that runs from Mürren-Gimmelwald-Stechelberg-Lauterbrunnen-Grütschalp (by funicular, bike costs same as person-7 SF)-Mürren. You can rent bikes in Mürren (Salomon Sports, 25 SF/half day, 35 SF/24 hrs, 10 SF extra for full suspension, daily 8:30–17:00, at gondola station, tel. 033/855-2330, www.staegersport.ch) or in Lauter-brunnen (Imboden Bike, 25 SF/4 hrs, 35 SF/day, Mon–Sat 8:00–12:00, 13:30–18:00, Sun 9:00–17:30, tel. 033/855-2114).

You can also bike the Lauterbrunnen Valley from Lauterbrun-nen to Interlaken. It's a gentle downhill ride via a peaceful bike path over the river from the road. Rent a bike at Lauterbrunnen (see above), bike to Interlaken, and then return to Lauterbrunnen by train (pay 5 SF extra to take bike on train). Or rent a bike at either Interlaken station and take the train to Lauterbrunnen.

▲**More Hikes near Gimmelwald**—For a not-too-tough, three-hour walk (but there's a scary 20-minute stretch) with great Jungfrau views and some mountain farm action, ride the funicular from Mür-ren to Allmendhubel (1,934 meters) and walk to Marchegg, Saustal, and Grütschalp (a drop of about 500 meters), where you can catch the panorama train back to Mürren. An easier version is the lower Bergweg from Allmenhubel to Grütschalp via Winteregg. For an easy family stroll with grand views, walk from Mürren just above the train tracks to either Winteregg (40 min, restaurant, playground, train station) or Grütschalp (60 min, train station) and catch the panorama train back to Mürren. An easy, go-as-far-as-you-like trail from Gimmelwald is up the Sefinen Valley. Or you can wind from Gimmelwald down to Stechelberg (60 min).

You can get specifics at the Mürren TI. For a description of six diverse hikes on the west side of Lauterbrunnen, pick up the fine and free *Mürren-Schilthorn Hikes* brochure (at stations, hotels, and TIs). The 3-D map of the Mürren mountainside, which includes hiking trails, makes a useful and attractive souvenir (2 SF at TI and lift station). For an extensive rundown on the region, get Don Chmura's fine 8-SF Lauterbrunnen Valley guidebook (includes info on hikes, flora, fauna, culture, and travel tips; available at Mountain Hostel in Gimmelwald).

Rainy-Day Options

If clouds roll in, don't despair. They can roll out just as quickly, and there are some good bad-weather options.

▲▲**Cloudy Day Lauterbrunnen Valley Walk**—There are easy trails and pleasant walks along the floor of the Lauterbrunnen Valley. For a smell-the-cows-and-flowers lowland walk—ideal for a cloudy day, weary body, or tight budget—follow the riverside trail from Stechelberg's Schilthornbahn station for five kilometers to Lauterbrunnen's Staubach Falls, near the town church (you can reverse the route, but it's a gradual uphill to Stechelberg). Detour to Trümmelbach Falls en route (below). There's a fine paved car-free and riverside path all the way.

If you're staying in Gimmelwald: Take the lift down to Stechelberg (5 min), then walk to Lauterbrunnen, detouring to Trümmelbach Falls shortly after Stechelberg. From Lauterbrunnen, take the funicular up to Grütschalp (10 min), then either walk (60 minutes) or take the panorama train (15 min) to Mürren. From Mürren it's a downhill walk (30 min) to Gimmelwald. (This loop trip can be reversed.)

▲**Trümmelbach Falls**—If all the waterfalls have you intrigued, sneak a behind-the-scenes look at the valley's most powerful one, Trümmelbach Falls (10 SF, April–June and Sept–Nov daily 9:00–17:00, July–Aug daily 8:00–18:00, on Lauterbrunnen-Stechelberg road, tel. 033/855-3232). You'll ride an elevator up through the mountain and climb through several caves to see the melt from the Eiger, Mönch, and Jungfrau grinding like God's band saw through the mountain at the rate of up to 20,000 liters a second (nearly double the beer consumption at Oktoberfest). The upper area is the best, so if your legs ache you can skip the lower ones and ride the lift down.

Lauterbrunnen Folk Museum—The Heimatmuseum in Lauterbrunnen shows off the local folk culture (3 SF, mid-June–Sept Tue, Thu, and Sat–Sun 14:00–17:30, just over bridge).

Mürren Activities—This low-key Alpine resort town offers a variety of rainy-day activities, from its shops to its slick Sportzentrum (sports center) with pools, steam baths, squash, and a fitness center (for details, see "Sleeping in Mürren," below).

Interlaken Boat Trips—Consider taking a boat trip from Interlaken (see "Sights—Interlaken," above).

▲▲**Swiss Open-Air Folk Museum at Ballenberg**—Near Interlaken, the Swiss Open-Air Museum of Vernacular Architecture, Country Life, and Crafts in the Bernese Oberland is a rich collection of traditional and historic farmhouses from every region of the country. Each house is carefully furnished, and many feature traditional craftspeople at work. The sprawling 50-acre park, laid out roughly as a huge Swiss map, is a natural preserve providing a wonderful setting for this culture-on-a-lazy-Susan look at Switzerland.

The Thurgau house (#621) has an interesting wattle-and-daub (half-timbered construction) display, and house #331 has a fun bread museum. Use the 2-SF map/guide. The more expensive picture book is a better souvenir than guide. (14-SF entry, half price after 16:00, mid-April–Oct daily 10:00–17:00, houses close at 17:00, park stays open later, craft demonstration schedules are listed just inside the entry, tel. 033/951-1123.) A reasonable outdoor cafeteria is inside the west entrance, and fresh bread, sausage, mountain cheese, and other goodies are on sale in several houses. Picnic tables and grills with free firewood are scattered throughout the park. The little wooden village of Brienzwiler (near the east entrance) is a museum in itself with a lovely little church. Trains run frequently from Interlaken to Brienzwiler, an easy walk from the museum.

Sleeping and Eating in the Berner Oberland
(1.70 SF = about $1, country code: 41, area code: 033)
Sleep Code: **S** = Single, **D** = Double/Twin, **T** = Triple, **Q** = Quad, **b** = bathroom, **t** = toilet only, **s** = shower only, **CC** = Credit Card (**V**isa, **M**asterCard, **A**mex), **SE** = Speaks English, **NSE** = No English. Unless otherwise noted, breakfast is included and credit cards are not accepted.

Sleeping and Eating in Gimmelwald
(4,500 feet, country code: 41, area code: 033,
zip code: 3826)
To inhale the Alps and really hold it in, sleep high in Gimmelwald. Poor but pleasantly stuck in the past, the village has a creaky hotel, happy hostel, decent pension, and a couple of B&Bs. The only bad news is that the lift costs 8 SF each way to get there.

Hotel Mittaghorn, the treasure of Gimmelwald, is run by Walter Mittler, a perfect Swiss gentleman. Walter's hotel is a classic, creaky, Alpine-style place with memorable beds, ancient down comforters (short and fat; wear socks and drape the blanket over your feet), and a million-dollar view of the Jungfrau Alps. The Yodelin' Seniors' loft has a dozen real beds, several sinks, down comforters, and a fire ladder out the back window. The hotel has one shower for 10 rooms (1 SF/5 min). Walter is careful not to let his place get too hectic or big and enjoys sensitive Back Door travelers. He runs the hotel with a little help from Rosemary from the village, and keeps things simple. This is a good place to receive mail from home (check the mail barrel in entry hall).

To some, Hotel Mittaghorn is a fire waiting to happen with a kitchen that would never pass code, lumpy beds, teeny towels, and minimal plumbing, run by an eccentric old grouch. These people enjoy Interlaken, Wengen, or Mürren, and that's where they should sleep. Be warned, you'll see more of my readers than locals here, but it's a fun crowd (D-70–80 SF, T-100 SF, Q-125 SF, Yodelin' Seniors' loft beds-25 SF, all with breakfast, 3-SF surcharge for 1-night stays, cash only, closed Nov–April, CH-3826 Gimmelwald/Bern, tel. 033/855-1658, www.ricksteves .com/mittaghorn). Reserve by telephone only, then reconfirm by telephone the day before your arrival. Walter usually offers his guests a simple 15-SF dinner. Hotel Mittaghorn is at the top of Gimmelwald, a five-minute climb up the steps from the village intersection.

Mountain Hostel is a beehive of activity, simple and as clean as its guests, cheap, and very friendly. Phone ahead (2 days maximum) or, to secure one of its 70 dorm beds the same day, call after 9:30 and leave your name. The hostel has low ceilings, a self-service kitchen, a mini-grocery, and healthy plumbing. While it's mostly a college-age crowd with late night sing-a-longs, families and older travelers are welcome. Internet access is 12 SF per hour. Petra Brunner has filled the place with flowers. This relaxed hostel survives with the help of its guests. Read the signs (please clean the kitchen), respect Petra's rules, and leave it cleaner than you found it. The place is one of those rare spots where a family atmosphere spontaneously combusts, and spaghetti becomes communal as it softens (20 SF per bed in 6- to 15-bed rooms, showers-1 SF, no breakfast and no sheets—bring your own, hostel membership not required, 20 meters from lift station, tel. & fax 033/855-1704, e-mail: mountainhostel@tcnet.ch).

Pension Restaurant Gimmelwald, next door, offers 12 basic rooms under low, creaky ceilings (D-110 SF, Db-130 SF, T-150 SF, Q-180 SF, 5-SF surcharge for 1-night stays). It also has sheetless backpacker beds (25–35 SF in small dorm rooms). Prices include a buffet breakfast. The pension has Gimmelwald's scenic terrace overlooking the Jungfrau and the hostel, and is the village's only restaurant (fine meals—their specialty is *Rösti* and bratwurst). It's great for camaraderie but not for peace (closed Nov and first half of May, CC:VM, nonsmoking, 50 meters from gondola station; reserve by phone, plus obligatory reconfirmation by phone 2 or 3 days in advance of arrival, tel. 033/855-1730, fax 033/855-1925, e-mail: pensiongimmelwald@tcnet.ch, run by Liesi and Männi).

Maria and Olle Eggimann rent two rooms—Gimmelwald's most comfortable—in their Alpine-sleek chalet. Fifteen-year town residents, Maria and Olle, who job-share the village's only teaching position and raise three kids of their own, offer visitors a rare inside peek at this community (D-100 SF, Db with kitchenette-180 SF for 2 or 3 people, optional breakfast-18 SF, no CC, last check-in 18:30, 3-night minimum for advance reservations; from gondola continue straight for 200 meters along the town's only road, B&B on left, CH-3826 Gimmelwald, tel. 033/855-3575, e-mail: oeggimann@bluewin.ch, SE fluently).

Esther's Guesthouse, overlooking the main intersection of the village, is like an upscale, mini-hostel with five clean, basic, but comfortable rooms sharing two bathrooms and a great kitchen (S-30 SF, D-70–85 SF, T-90-110 SF, Q-140 SF, 2-night minimum, make your own breakfast, no smoking, tel. 033/855-5488, fax 033/855-5492, e-mail: evallmen@bluewin.ch, some English spoken).

Schlaf im Stroh ("Sleep in Straw") offers exactly that in an actual barn. After the cows head for higher ground in the summer, the friendly von Allmen family hoses out their barn and fills it with straw and budget travelers. Blankets are free, but bring your own sheet, sleep sack, or sleeping bag. No beds, no bunks, no mattresses, no kidding (20 SF, 12 SF for kids under 12, includes breakfast and a modern bathroom, showers-2 SF, open mid-June–mid-Oct, depending on grass and snow levels, almost never full; from lift, continue straight through intersection, barn marked "1995" on right, tel. 033/855-5488, fax 033/855-5492, e-mail: evallmen@bluewin.ch).

Eating in Gimmelwald: Pension Gimmelwald, the only restaurant in town, serves a hearty breakfast buffet for 13.50 SF, fine lunches, and good 15-SF dinners featuring a fine *Rösti* and a sampling of organic produce from the local farmers. The hostel has a decent members' kitchen and a small grocery but serves no food. Hotel Mittaghorn serves dinner only to its guests (15 SF); follow dinner with a Heidi Cocoa (cocoa *mit* peppermint schnapps) or a Virgin Heidi. Consider packing in a picnic meal from the larger towns.

The local farmers sell their produce. Esther (at the main intersection of the village) sells cheese, sausage, and Gimmelwald's best yogurt—but only until the cows go up in June.

Sleeping and Eating in Mürren
(5,500 feet, country code: 41, area code: 033, zip code: 3825)

Mürren—pleasant as an Alpine resort can be—is traffic free, filled with bakeries, cafés, souvenirs, old-timers with walking sticks, GE employees enjoying incentive trips, and Japanese making movies of each other with a Fujichrome backdrop. Its chalets are prefab-rustic. Sitting on a ledge 2,000 feet above the Lauterbrunnen Valley, surrounded by a fortissimo chorus of mountains, it has all the comforts of home (for a price) without the pretentiousness of more famous resorts. With a gondola, train, and funicular, hiking options are endless from Mürren. Mürren has an ATM (by the Co-op grocery), and there are lockers at both the train and gondola stations (located a 10-minute walk apart, on opposite ends of town).

Mürren's helpful **TI** can find you a room, give hiking advice, and change money (mid-July–mid-Sept Mon–Wed 9:00–12:00, 13:00–18:30, Thu until 20:00, Sat 13:00–18:00, Sun 13:00–17:30, less off-season, above the village, follow signs to Sportzentrum, tel. 033/856-8686, www.muerren.ch). The slick **Sportzentrum** (sports center) that houses the TI offers a world of indoor activities (13 SF to use pool and whirlpool, 8 SF for Mürren and Gimmelwald hotel guests, mid-June–Oct Mon–Sat afternoon).

Salomon Sports, right at the gondola station, rents mountain bikes (35 SF/half day, 45 SF/full day), hiking boots (12 SF/day), and is the village Internet station (12 SF/hr, daily 8:30–17:00, tel. 033/855-2330, www.staegersport.ch). **Top Apartments** will do your **laundry** by request (14:00–17:30, across from Hotel Belle-vue's backside, look for blue triangle, please call first, tel. 033/855-3706). They also have a few cheap rooms (30–40 SF per person).

Prices for accommodations are often higher during the ski season and from July 15 to August 15.

Guesthouse Eiger offers good budget rooms. This is a friendly, creaky, very wooden home away from home (S-60 SF, D-100 SF, Db-130 SF, 39-SF beds in 2-, 4-, and 6-bunk rooms, with sheets and breakfast, CC:VMA, closed Nov, across from train station, tel. 033/856-5460, fax 033/856-5461, e-mail: eigerguesthouse@muerren.ch, well run by Alan and Veronique). The restaurant serves good, reasonably priced dinners, and its poolroom is a popular local hangout.

Hotel Alpina is a simple, modern place with 24 comfortable rooms and a concrete feeling—a good thing, given its cliff-edge position (Sb-75–85 SF, Db-130–170 SF, Tb-180 SF, Qb-200 SF with awesome Jungfrau views and balconies, CC:VMA, exit left from station, walk 2 min gradually downhill, tel. 033/855-1361, fax 033/855-1049, www.muerren.ch/alpina, Frau and Herr Taugwalder).

Mürren

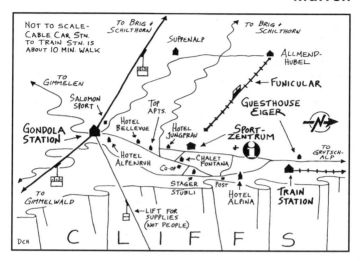

Chalet Fontana, run by a charming Englishwoman, Denise Fussell, is a rare budget option in Mürren with simple, crispy-clean, and comfortable rooms (35–45 SF per person in small doubles or triples with breakfast, 5 SF cheaper without breakfast, 1 apartment with kitchenette-50 SF per person, third and fourth person-10 SF each, closed Nov–April, across street from Stäger-stübli restaurant in town center, tel. 033/855-2686, fax 033/856-8696, cellular 078/642-3485, e-mail: chaletfontana@compuserve.com). If no one's home, check at the Ed Abegglen shop next door (tel. 033/855-1245, off-season only).

Hotel Jungfrau offers two options: a hotel with pricey, modern, and comfortable rooms and an elevator (Db-170–200 SF with view, 150–180 SF without); and a lodge in a basic, blocky, 20-room annex with well-worn but fine rooms and better Jungfrau views (Db-120–190 SF, Tb-156–210 SF, family apartments-280 SF, CC:VMA, near TI and Sportzentrum, tel. 033/855-4545, fax 033/855-4549, www.muerren.ch/jungfrau). All rooms include the same fancy buffet breakfast and free entrance to the Sportzentrum's pools. Without breakfast, deduct 10 SF per person.

Hotel Alpenruh, expensive and yuppie-rustic, is about the only hotel in Mürren open year-round. The comfortable rooms come with views and some balconies (Sb-95–125 SF, Db-180–260 SF depending on season, CC:VMA, elevator, attached restaurant, sauna, free vouchers for breakfast atop Schilthorn, 10 meters from gondola station, tel. 033/856-8800, fax 033/856-8888, e-mail: alpruh@schilthorn.ch).

Hotel Bellevue-Crystal has a homey lounge, great view terrace, and 27 good rooms at fair rates, most with balconies and views. The more expensive rooms are newly renovated and larger (Db-130–200 SF, a few family apartments-225–345 SF, tel. 033/855-1401, fax 033/855-1490, www.muerren.ch/bellevue).

Eating in Mürren: For a rare bit of ruggedness, eat at the **Stägerstübli** (10–30-SF lunches and dinners, closed Tue off-season). The **Kandhar Snack Bar** at the Sportzentrum has fun, creative, and inexpensive light meals, a good selection of teas and pastries, and impressive views. The **Edelweiss** self-serve restaurant is reasonable and wins the best view award (next to Hotel Alpina). Mürren's bakery is excellent. For picnic fixings, shop at the Co-op (normally Mon and Wed–Fri 8:00–12:00, 14:00–18:30, Tue and Sat 8:00–12:00 only, closed Sun).

Sleeping in Wengen
(4,200 feet, country code: 41, area code: 033, zip code: 3823)

Wengen, a bigger, fancier Mürren on the other side of the valley, has mostly grand hotels, many shops, tennis courts, mini-golf, and terrific views. This traffic-free resort is an easy train ride above Lauterbrunnen and halfway up to Kleine Scheidegg and Männlichen, and offers more activities for those needing distraction from the scenery. Hiking is better from Mürren and Gimmelwald. The TI is next to the PTT (post office) one block from the station (Mon–Sat 8:30–12:00, 14:00–18:00, closed Sun, tel. 033/855-1414).

Several hotels offer reasonable accommodations in this otherwise upscale place. Turn left from the station along the main shopping drag to find these places: **Hot Chili Peppers** is *the* youth hangout in town, offering cheery and comfortable private rooms and dorm rooms, lockers, a common kitchen, a view deck, and a relaxed bar (35–45 SF per person in private rooms, 26–38 SF for dorm beds, includes breakfast, CC:VM, tel. & fax 033/855-5020, www.wengen.com/chilis). A few doors up, the low-key **Hotel Bernerhof** is clean and a good value (S-35–45 SF, D-70–90 SF, Sb-55–65 SF, Db-100–130 SF, dorm bed-17 SF, includes breakfast, tel. 033/855-2721, fax 033/855-3358, e-mail: bernerhof@wengen.com). **Chalet Bergheim** has some doubles and six 26-SF dorm beds with sheets (Db-76–86 SF, CC:VM, includes breakfast, opens in June, check in at the well-signed Hotel Jungfraublick, tel. 033/855-2755, fax 033/855-2726, e-mail: jungfraublick@wengen.com).

Turn right out of the station for these places: For top views and absentee management, try the tricky-to-find **Hotel Schweizerheim Garni**'s simple but adequately comfortable rooms (Db-120–150 SF, CC:VM, buffet breakfast, closed Nov–May, great garden terrace; walk under train tracks, then down, turn right at Family Hotel; tel. 033/855-1581, fax 033/855-2327, e-mail: schweizerheim@wengen.com). Follow the tracks uphill three minutes to **Hotel Eden**—spotless, homey, and warmly run by Kerstin Bucher (S-65 SF, D-130 SF, Sb-72 SF, Db-144 SF, CC: VMA, 18 rooms without baths have killer balcony views, tel. 033/855-1634, fax 033/855-3950, SE). The same hotel runs **Eddy's Hostel**, a block away, with 26-SF dorm beds in one 20-bed room. Consider **Clare and Andy's Chalet** (one Db-68–80 SF, one Qb-148–168 SF, breakfast-10 SF, dinner by request-25 SF, 4-night minimum preferred, tel. & fax 033/855-1712, http://home.sunrise.ch/aregez, Clare's English, Andy's Swiss).

Sleeping in Kleine Scheidegg
(6,762 feet, country code: 41, area code: 033, zip code: 3801)
Sleep face to face with the Eiger at Kleine Scheidegg's **Bahnhof Buffet** (dorm bed-60 SF, D-150 SF, prices include breakfast and dinner, CC:VMA, tel. 033/855-1151, fax 033/855-1152, www .bahnhof-scheidegg.ch) or at **Restaurant Grindelwaldblick** (35 SF for bed in 12-bed room, no sheets, closed Nov–May, tel. 033/855-1374, fax 033/855-4205). Confirm price and availability before ascending.

Sleeping near the Stechelberg Lift
(2,800 feet, country code: 41, area code: 033, zip code: 3824)
Stechelberg is a hamlet at the end of the valley. **Nelli Beer**, renting three rooms in a quiet, scenic, and folksy setting, is your best Stechelberg option (S-27 SF, D-50 SF, 2-night minimum, over river behind Stechelberg post office at big "Zimmer" sign, get off post bus at post office, tel. 033/855-3930, some English spoken).

Hotel Stechelberg, at road's end, is surrounded by waterfalls and vertical rock with 20 comfortable, spacious, and quiet rooms and a lovely garden terrace (D-78–96 SF, Db-118–138 SF, Tb-126–174 SF, Qb-152–188 SF, CC:VMA, post bus stops here, tel. 033/855-2921, fax 033/855-4438, www.stechelberg.ch). **Naturfreundehaus Alpenhof** is a rugged Alpine lodge for hikers (60 coed beds, 4–8 per room, 20.70 SF per bed, breakfast-8 SF, dinner-15 SF, no sheets, tel. 033/855-1202).

Here's a wild idea: **Mountain Hotel Obersteinberg** is a working Alpine farm with cheese, cows, a mule shuttling up food once a day, and an American (Vickie) who fell in love with a mountain man. It's a 2.5-hour hike either from Stechelberg or from Gimmelwald. They rent 12 primitive rooms and a bunch of loft beds. There's no shower, no hot water, and only meager solar-panel electricity. Candles light up the night, and you can take a hot-water bottle to bed if necessary (S-79 SF, D-158 SF, includes linen, breakfast, and dinner, sheetless dorm beds-62 SF with dinner and breakfast, closed Oct–May, tel. 033/855-2033). The place is filled with locals and Germans on weekends but is all yours on weekdays. Why not hike there from Gimmelwald and leave the Alps a day later?

Sleeping in Lauterbrunnen
(2,600 feet, country code: 41, area code: 033, zip code: 3822)
Lauterbrunnen—with a train station, funicular, TI (1 block up from station, tel. 033/855-1955), bank, shops, and lots of hotels—is the valley's commercial center. This is the jumping-off point for Jungfrau and Schilthorn adventures. It's idyllic in spite of the busy road and big buildings. You can rent a bike at Imboden Bike on the main street (25 SF/4 hrs, 35 SF/day, Mon–Sat 8:00–12:00, 13:30–18:00, Sun 9:00–17:30, tel. 033/855-2114).

Hotel Staubbach, a cavernous Old World place—one of the first hotels in the valley—is being lovingly restored by hardworking American Craig and his Swiss wife, Corinne. Its 30 plain, comfortable rooms are family friendly, there's a kids' play area, and the parking is free. Many rooms have great views. They keep their prices down by providing room-cleaning every third day (Db-100–110 SF, figure 40 SF per person in family rooms sleeping up to 6, CC:VM, includes buffet breakfast, elevator, 4 blocks up from station on the left, tel. 033/855-5454, fax 033/855-5484, www.staubbach.ch).

Valley Hostel is practical and comfortable, offering inexpensive beds for quieter travelers of all ages, with a pleasant garden and welcoming owners Martha and Alfred Abegglen (D-50–60 SF, beds in larger family-friendly rooms-22 SF each, ask about their new rooms with balcony, breakfast extra, nonsmoking, Internet access, laundry service, 2 blocks up from train station, tel. & fax 033/855-2008, www.valleyhostel.ch).

Chalet im Rohr, a creaky, old, fire-waiting-to-happen place, has oodles of character and 26-SF beds in big one- to four-bed rooms (no breakfast, common kitchen, below church on main drag, tel. 033/855-2182).

Masenlager Stocki is rustic and humble with the cheapest beds in town (13 SF with sheets in easygoing little 30-bed coed dorm with kitchen, closed Nov–Dec; below the church, take the second road under the train viaduct and walk 200 meters; tel. 033/855-1754).

Two campgrounds just south of town provide 15- to 25-SF beds (in dorms and 2-, 4-, and 6-bed bungalows, no sheets, kitchen facilities, big English-speaking tour groups). **Mountain Holiday Park-Camping Jungfrau**, romantically situated beyond Staubach

Falls, is huge and well organized by Hans (tel. 033/856-2010, fax 033/856-2020, www.camping-jungfrau.ch). It also has fancier cabins (20 SF per person). **Schützenbach Campground**, on the left just past Lauterbrunnen toward Stechelberg, is simpler (tel. 033/855-1268).

Sleeping in Interlaken
(country code: 41, area code: 033, zip code: 3800)
I'd head for Gimmelwald or at least Lauterbrunnen (20 min by train or car). Interlaken is not the Alps. But if you must stay…

Hotel Lotschberg, with a sun terrace and wonderful rooms, is run by English-speaking Susi and Fritz and is the best real hotel value in town. Information abounds, and Fritz organizes guided adventures (Sb-100 SF, Db-145 SF, big Db-180 SF, extra bed-20–25 SF, family deals, cheaper Nov–May, CC:VMA, elevator, bar, nonsmoking, laundry service-8 SF, bike rental, cheap e-mail access, discounted parasailing if you "Fly with Fritz," 3-minute walk from station, exit right from West Station, then take a left at traffic circle to General Guisanstrasse 31, tel. 033/822-2545, fax 033/822-2579, www.lotschberg.ch, e-mail: hotel@lotschberg.ch).

Guest House Susi's B&B is Hotel Lotschberg's no-frills, cash-only annex, run by the same people (same address and phone number). It has simple, cozy, cheaper rooms (Db-119 SF, apartments with kitchenettes for 2 people-100 SF; for 4–5 people-175 SF, cheaper Nov–May).

Villa Margaretha B&B, run by English-speaking Frau Kunz-Joerin, offers the best cheap beds in town. It's a big Victorian house with a garden on a quiet residential street three blocks directly in front of the West Station (D-80 SF, T-120 SF, 3 rooms share a big bathroom, kitchenette, 2-night minimum, lots of rules to abide by, Aarmühlestrasse 13, tel. 033/822-1813).

Hotel Aarburg offers 13 plain, peaceful rooms in a beautifully located but run-down old building five minutes' walk from the West Station (D-100 SF, Db-120 SF, next to Laundromat at Beatenbergstrasse 1, tel. 033/822-2615, fax 033/822-6397).

Backpackers' Villa Sonnenhof is a creative guesthouse run by a Methodist Church group. It's fun and youthful but without the frat-party ambience of Balmer's (below). Rooms are comfortable, and half come with Jungfrau-view balconies (D-74–86 SF, dorm beds in 4- to 6-bed rooms with lockers and sheets-29–32 SF each, cheaper if you BYO sheets, includes breakfast, kitchen, garden, Internet access, game room, no curfew, open all day, check-in from 16:00–21:00, 10-minute walk from either station across grassy field from TI, Alpenstrasse 16, tel. 033/826-7171, fax 033/826-7172, www.villa.ch).

Happy Inn Lodge has cheap rooms a five-minute walk

from the West Station (D-60–70 SF, dorm beds-19–28 SF, breakfast-7 SF, Rosenstrasse 17, tel. 033/822-3225, fax 033/822-3268, e-mail: happyinn@tcnet.ch).

For many, **Balmer's Herberge** is backpacker heaven. This Interlaken institution comes with movies, Ping-Pong, a Laundromat, bar, restaurant, swapping library, Internet stations, tiny grocery, bike rental, currency exchange, rafting excursions, a shuttle-bus service (which meets every arriving train), and a friendly, hardworking staff. This little Nebraska is home for those who miss their fraternity. Particularly on summer weekends, it's a mob scene (dorm beds-24–26 SF, S-40 SF; D, T, or Q-28–34 SF per person, includes sheets and breakfast, CC:VMA, nonsmoking, open year-round, recommend reservations 5 days in advance, Hauptstrasse 23, in Matten, 15-minute walk from either Interlaken station, tel. 033/822-1961, fax 033/823-3261, www.balmers.com, e-mail: balmers@tcnet.ch).

Transportation Connections—Interlaken
By train to: Spiez (2/hrly, 15 min), **Brienz** (hrly, 20 min), **Bern** (hrly, 1 hr). While there are a few long trains from Interlaken, you'll generally connect from Bern.

By train from Bern to: Lausanne (hrly, 70 min), **Zurich** (hrly, 70 min), **Salzburg** (4/day, 8 hrs, transfers include Zurich), **Munich** (4/day, 5.5 hrs), **Frankfurt** (hrly, 4.5 hrs, transfers in Basel and Mannheim), **Paris** (4/day, 4.5 hrs).

Interlaken to Gimmelwald: Take the train from the Interlaken East (Ost) Station to Lauterbrunnen, then cross the street to catch the funicular to Mürren. Ride up to Grütschalp, where a special scenic train (Panorama Fahrt) will roll you along the cliff into Mürren. From there, either walk an easy, paved 30 minutes downhill to Gimmelwald, or walk 10 minutes across Mürren to catch the gondola (costs 8 SF and once in Gimmelwald, you'll have a 5-minute uphill hike to reach accommodations). A good bad-weather option (or vice versa) is to ride the post bus from Lauterbrunnen station (hrly bus departure coordinated with arrival of train) to Stechelberg and the base of the Schilthornbahn gondola station (tel. 033/823-1444 or 033/555-2141), which will whisk you in five thrilling minutes up to Gimmelwald.

By car it's a 30-minute drive from Interlaken to Stechelberg. The pay parking lot (5 SF/day) at the gondola station is safe. Gimmelwald is the first stop above Stechelberg on the Schilthorn gondola (8 SF, 2 trips/hrly at :25 and :55, get off at first stop). Note that for a week in early May and from mid-November through early December, the Schilthornbahn is closed for servicing.

APPENZELL

Welcome to cowbell country. In moo-mellow and storybook-friendly Appenzell, you'll find the warm, intimate side of the land of staggering icy Alps. Savor Appenzell's cozy small-town ambience.

Appenzell is Switzerland's most traditional region and the butt of humor because of it. Entire villages used to meet in town squares to vote (an event featured on most postcard racks). Until 1991 the women of Appenzell couldn't vote on local issues. (But lately the region has become more progressive. In 2000 its schools were the first to make English mandatory—rather than French.)

A gentle beauty blankets the region overlooked by the 8,200-foot peak Säntis. As you travel, you'll enjoy an ever-changing parade of finely carved chalets, traditional villages, and cows moaning "milk me." While farmers' bikini-clad daughters make hay, old ladies walk the steep roads with scythes, looking as if they just pushed the Grim Reaper down the hill. When locals are asked about Appenzell cheese, they clench their fists as they answer, "It's the best." (It is, without any doubt, the smelliest.)

If you're here in late August or early September, there's a good chance you'll get in on or at least have your road blocked by the ceremonial procession of flower-bedecked cows and whistling herders in traditional, formal outfits. The festive march down from the high pastures is a spontaneous move by the herding families, and when they finally do burst into town (a slow-motion Swiss Pamplona), the people become children again, running into the streets.

Planning Your Time

Appenzell's charms are subtle, prices are high, and the public transportation is disappointing. For many on a fast trip with no car, the area is not worth the trouble. But by car it's a joy.

Appenzell Region

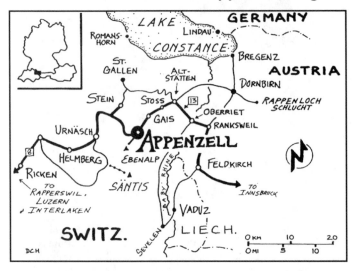

Ideally it's an interesting way for drivers to connect Austria and Bavaria with the Berner Oberland (Switzerland's Jungfrau region). Drive in from Tirol in time to get up the lift to Ebenalp (for the most memorable overnight), descend the next morning and spend the day sampling the charms of Appenzell town, and get to the Interlaken area that night.

Getting around Appenzell

Those with a car have the region by the tail. Those without wheels will need more time and patience. The center of the Appenzell region is Appenzell town. An hourly train connects Appenzell with Wasserauen (20 min) and Herisau (40 min), from which bigger trains depart hourly for St. Gallen (20 min) and Luzern (2 hrs). Regional buses connect all towns several times a day.

Sights—Appenzell Region

Appenzell Town—In this traditional town, kids play "barn" instead of "house" while mom and dad watch yodeling on TV. The town center is a painfully cute pedestrian zone which delights tourists born to shop. The TI is on the main street (Hauptgasse, Mon–Fri 9:00–12:00, 13:30–18:00, Sat 10:00–12:00, 14:00–17:00, tel. 071/788-9641). The post office is in front of the train station. Don't bother looking for a Laundromat. Bikes can be rented at the train station. For accommodations, see "Sleeping in the Town of Appenzell," below.

▲**Folk Music**—Local restaurants host folk-music concerts about twice a week (June–Oct, most Wed and Sat nights, dinner sometimes required but often free). A big-tent music show is staged about 10 nights during the summer. Get specifics at the TI.

Ebenalp

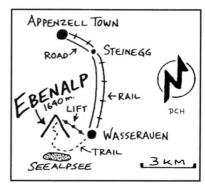

▲▲**Appenzeller Folk Museum**—The folk museum next to the TI provides an excellent look at the local cow culture. Ride the elevator to the sixth floor and work your way down through traditional costumes, living rooms, art, and crafts (5 SF, daily in summer 10:00–12:00, 14:00–17:00, less in winter, ask for free loaner book in English).

Bike to the Rhine—To experience this area on two wheels, rent a bike at the station and glide about two hours down into the Rhine valley to the town of Alstatten. From there, take the single-car train back up the hill to Appenzell (details at TI or station, tel. 071/354-5060).

▲▲**Ebenalp**—This cliff-hanging hut is a thin-air alternative to Appenzell town. Ride the lift from Wasserauen, eight kilometers south of Appenzell town, to Ebenalp (5,000 feet). On the way up (left side) you'll get a sneak preview of Ebenalp's cave church and the cliffside boardwalk that leads to the guest house. From the top you'll enjoy a sweeping view all the way to Lake Constance (Bodensee).

Leaving the lift, take a 12-minute hike through a prehistoric cave (slippery and dimly lit—hold the railing and you'll come to daylight), past a hermit's home (a tiny museum, always open) and the 400-year-old Wildkirchi cave church (hermit monks lived there from 1658 to 1853), to a 170-year-old guest house built precariously into the cliff. Originally housing farmers, goats, and cows, the hut evolved into a guest house for pilgrims coming to the monk for spiritual guidance. Today, Berggasthaus Aescher welcomes tourists with hot and hearty plates of *Rösti* (traditional hash browns with Alp cheese, see "Sleeping in Ebenalp," below).

The region is a hit with hikers who make the circuit of mountain hotels. There are 24, each a day's hike apart. All originated as Alpine farms. Of these, Berggasthaus Aescher is the oldest and smallest.

From Ebenalp's sunny cliff perch you can almost hear the cows munching on the far side of the valley. Only the parasailors, like neon jellyfish, tag your world "21st century." In the distance, nestled below Säntis Peak, is the Seealpsee (lake). The one-hour hike down to the lake is steep but pleasurable (take left at first fork below guest house).

The Ebenalp lift runs at least twice hourly until 19:00 in July and August, 18:00 in June and September, and 17:00 in spring and fall (17.50 SF up, 23 SF round-trip, if sleeping there, claim your 5-SF ticket discount, free and reportedly safe parking at lift, free hiking brochure, tel. 071/799-1212, www.ebenalp.ch).

▲**Stein**—The town of Stein has the Appenzell Showcase Cheese Dairy (*Schaukäserei*, daily 9:00–19:00, cheese-making normally 9:00–14:00). It's fast, free, smelly, and well explained in a 15-minute English video and the free English brochure (with cheese recipes). The lady at the cheese counter loves to cut it so you can sample it. They also have yogurt and cheap boxes of cold iced tea for sale. The restaurant serves powerful cheese specialties. Stein's TI and a great folk moo-seum (*Volkskunde*) are next door. This cow-culture museum, with old-fashioned cheese-making demonstrations, peasant houses, fascinating embroidering machinery, cow art, and folk-craft demonstrations, is not worth the 7 SF if you've seen the similar museum in Appenzell (Mon 13:30–17:00, Tue–Sat 10:00–12:00, 13:30–17:00, Sun 10:00–18:00, may open early if you ask nicely, closed in winter, tel. 071/368-5056).

▲**Urnäsch**—This appealing one-street town has Europe's cutest museum. The Appenzeller Museum, on the town square, brings this region's folk customs to life. Warm and homey, it's a happy little honeycomb of Appenzeller culture (4 SF, daily in summer 13:30–17:00, less in spring and fall, closed in winter, good English description brochure, will open for groups of 5 or more if you call the director at 071/364-1487 or 071/364-2322). **Gasthaus Ochsen** is a fine traditional hotel with good food, low ceilings, and wonderful atmosphere (D-90 SF, 3 doors down from the museum, tel. 071/364-1117). Peek into its old restaurant.

Sleeping in the Appenzell Region
(1.70 SF = about $1, country code: 41, area code: 071, zip code: 9050)
Sleep Code: **S** = Single, **D** = Double/Twin, **T** = Triple, **Q** = Quad, **b** = bathroom, **t** = toilet only, **s** = shower only, **CC** = Credit Card (Visa, MasterCard, Amex), **SE** = Speaks English, **NSE** = No English.

Sleeping High in Ebenalp
There's no reason to sleep in Appenzell town. The Ebenalp lift, across from the tiny Wasserauen train station, is a few minutes' drive (or a 20-minute bus ride) south. For a memorable experience, sleep in **Berggasthaus Aescher**. The 170-year-old house

has only rainwater and no shower. Friday and Saturday nights often have great live music but can be crowded with groups and noisy with up to 40 people and parties going into the wee hours. Monday through Thursday you'll normally get a small woody dorm to yourself. The hut is actually built into the cliff side; its back wall is the rock. From the toilet you can study this Alpine architecture. Sip your coffee on the deck, sheltered from drips from the gnarly overhang 30 meters above. The guest book goes back to 1940, there's a fun drawer filled with an Alpine percussion section, and the piano in the comfortable dining/living room was brought in by helicopter. For a great 45-minute pre-dinner hike, check out the goats. Take the high trail toward the lake and circle clockwise back up the peak to the lift and down the way you originally came. Claudia can show you the rock-climbing charts (dorm beds-15 SF, blankets but no sheets required or provided, no towels or showers available, breakfast-10 SF, dinner-14–22 SF, closed Nov–April, 12 min by steep trail below top of lift, 9057 Weissbad, tel. 071/799-1142, www.aescher-ai.ch, e-mail: info@aescher-ai.ch, run by Claudia and Bennie Knechtle-Wyss, their 5 children: Bernhardt-age 16, Reto-15, Lukas-12, Lilian-11, Dominik-9, 3 pigs, 4 goats, 2 donkeys, 6 rabbits, 2 dogs, and 40 sheep).

The less atmospheric and more normal **Berg Gasthaus Ebenalp** sits atop the mountains just above the lift. It's booked long in advance on Saturdays but is wide open otherwise (dorm beds with blankets but no sheets-30 SF, D-90 SF, includes breakfast, coin-op shower, tel. 071/799-1194, Sutter family).

From Wasserauen you can hike up the private road to **Berggasthaus Seealpsee**, on the idyllic Alpine lake, Seealpsee (loft dorm beds with sheets-25 SF, D-90 SF, includes breakfast, CC:VMA, 9057 Weissbad, tel. 071/799-1140, fax 071/799-1820, Dörig family).

Sleeping and Eating in the Town of Appenzell

The town is small but touristy. Hotels are good and central. The *Zimmer* are six blocks from the center.

Hotel Adler, above a delicious café/bakery in a fine location, offers two kinds of rooms: modern or newly refurbished, traditional Appenzeller (Db-150–170 SF, Qb-240 SF, CC:VMA, elevator, between TI and bridge, tel. 071/787-1389, fax 071/787-1365, e-mail: info@adlerhotel.ch, helpful Franz Leu).

Hotel Traube (not Hotel Taube), two blocks from the TI, is another comfortable hotel with six tastefully decorated rooms above a fine restaurant (Db-150–160 SF, CC:VMA, Marktgasse 7, tel. 071/787-1407, fax 071/787-2419, e-mail: info@hotel-traube.ch).

To experience a pleasant Swiss suburban neighborhood, try one of these *Zimmer*: **Haus Lydia**, a six-room Appenzell-style home filled with tourist information and a woodsy folk atmosphere, is on the edge of town and includes a garden and a powerful mountain view. It's run by friendly Frau Mock-Inauen (D-80 SF, great breakfast; east of town over bridge, past Mercedes-Esso station, take next right and go 600 meters, Eggerstanden Strasse 53, CH 9050 Appenzell, tel. 071/787-4233, fax 071/367-2170, www.hauslydia.ch, SE). **Gästezimmer Koller-Rempfler** is a family-friendly, traditional place several blocks before Haus Lydia (D-80 SF, Db-85 SF, 5 SF less for 2-night stays, Eggerstandenstrasse 9, tel. 071/787-2117, NSE).

Eating in Appenzell: The Appenzeller beer is famous, good, and about the only thing cheap in the region. Ideally, eat dinner up in Ebenalp at **Berggasthaus Ascher**, even if you're staying in Appenzell town (see "Sleeping in Ebenalp," above; last lift down at 19:00 in summer, earlier off-season).

In Appenzell, locals like **Restaurant Marktplatz** or **Hotel Traube**. For less refinement, consider **Gasthaus Hof. Hotel Appenzell** is good for vegetarian meals. If the weather's nice or you just feel like a walk, try **Gasthaus Freudenberg** for its reasonable meals and great views over Appenzell from outdoor tables (about a 15-minute walk south from center across tracks, Postfach, tel. 071/787-1240).

Route Tips for Drivers

Hall to Appenzell (130 miles): From the Austria/Switzerland border town of Feldkirch, it's an easy, scenic drive through Altstätten and Gais to Appenzell. At the Swiss border you must buy an annual road-use permit for 40 SF (or the AS or DM equivalent) to drive on the Swiss autobahn system (anyone without this tax sticker is likely to be fined).

From picturesque Altstätten, wind up a steep mountain pass and your world becomes a miniature train set. The Stoss railroad station, straddling the summit of the pass, has glorious views. Park here, cross to the chapel, and walk through the meadow—past munching cows, to the monument that celebrates an Appenzeller victory over Hapsburg Austria. From this spectacular spot, you can see the Rhine Valley, Liechtenstein, and Austrian Alps—and feast on a memorable picnic.

Side Trip through Liechtenstein: If you must see the tiny and touristy country of Liechtenstein, take this 30-minute detour: From Feldkirch drive south on E77 (follow "FL" signs) and go through Schaan to Vaduz, the capital. Park near the city hall, post office, and TI. Passports can be stamped (for 2.50 SF) in the TI. Liechtenstein's banks (open until 16:30) sell Swiss francs at uniform and acceptable rates. The prince looks down on his 7-by-20-kilometer country from his castle, a 20-minute hike above Vaduz (castle closed but offers a fine view; catch trail from Café Berg). To leave, cross the Rhine at Rotenboden, immediately get on the autobahn and drive north from Sevelen to the Oberriet exit, and check another country off your list.

Appenzell to Interlaken/Gimmelwald (120 miles): It's a three-hour drive from Appenzell to Ballenberg and another hour from there to the Gimmelwald lift. Head out of Appenzell town following signs to Herisau/Wattwill. A few scenic kilometers out of town, in Stein, "Schaukäserei" signs direct you to the big, modern cheese dairy. From there, head for Wattwil. Drive through Ricken into the town of Rapperswil. Once you're in Rapperswil, follow the green signs to Gotthard/Zurich over the long bridge, then continue southward, following signs to Einsiedeln and Gotthard. You'll go through the town of Schwyz, the historic core of Switzerland that gave its name to the country.

From Brunnen, one of the busiest, most impressive, and expensive-to-build roads in Switzerland wings you along the Urnersee. It's dangerously scenic, so stop at the parking place after the first tunnel (on right, opposite Stoos turnoff) where you can enjoy the view and a rare Turkish toilet. Follow signs to Gotthard through Flüelen, then autobahn for Luzern, vanishing into a long tunnel that should make you feel a little better about your 40-SF autobahn sticker. Exit at the Stans-Nord exit (signs to Interlaken). Go along the Alpnachersee south toward Sarnen. Continue past Sarnensee to Brienzwiler before Brienz. A sign at Brienzwiler will direct you to the Ballenberg Freilicht (Swiss Open-Air Museum)/ Ballenberg Ost. You can park here, but I prefer the west entrance, a few minutes down the road near Brienz.

From Brienzwiler, take the autobahn to Interlaken along the south side of Lake Brienz. Cruise through the old resort town down Interlaken's main street from the Ost Bahnhof, past the cow field with a great Eiger-Jungfrau view on your left and grand old hotels, the TI, post office, and banks on your right, to the West Bahnhof at the opposite end of town. If stopping in Interlaken, park there. Otherwise, follow signs to Lauterbrunnen. Gimmelwald is a 30-minute drive and a five-minute gondola ride away.

WEST SWITZERLAND

Enjoy urban Switzerland at its best in the charming, compact capital of Bern. Ramble the ramparts of Murten, Switzerland's best-preserved medieval town, and resurrect the ruins of an ancient Roman capital in nearby Avenches. The Swiss countryside offers up chocolates, Gruyère cheese, and a fine folk museum. On Lake Geneva, the Swiss Riviera, explore the romantic Château Chillon and stylishly syncopated Montreux. South of Murten, the predominant language is French, *s'il vous plaît*, and, as you'll see, that means more than language.

Planning Your Time

The region doesn't merit a lot of time on a quick trip. Bern, Lake Geneva, and Murten are each worth half a day. Bern is easily seen en route to Murten—"Morat," if you're speaking French. I'd establish a home base in Murten from which to explore the southwest in a day by car. Without a car, use a better transportation hub such as Bern, Lausanne, or Montreux.

For a day by car from Murten: 8:45–Depart, 10:00–Tour Château Chillon, 11:30–Quick visit or drive through Montreux, Vevey, and the Corniche de Lavaux, 14:00–Cheese-making demo in Gruyère or Moleson, 15:30–Gruerien folk museum in Bulle, 18:00–Roman ruins in Avenches, 19:00–Home in Murten for salad by the sea.

BERN

Stately but human, classy but fun, the Swiss capital gives you the most (maybe even the only) enjoyable look at urban Switzerland. User-friendly Bern is packed into a peninsula bounded by the Aare River.

West Switzerland

Tourist Information: Start your visit at the TI inside the train station (daily 9:00–20:30, until 18:30 in winter, watch your bags, tel. 031/328-1212). Pick up a map of Bern (and any other Swiss cities you'll be visiting) and a list of city sights. Sometimes there's a second TI at the Bear Pits (daily 10:00–17:00).

Arrival in Bern: From the train station TI, cross the street, walk 50 meters and turn left at the church onto Spitalgasse. Note the colorful men-without-hats fountains as you go downhill through the heart of town to the bear pits and Rose Garden (30-minute stroll). Catch trolley #12 back to the station (buy cheapest ticket from machine, 1.50 SF).

Bike Rental: Free loaner 21-speed city bikes are available in two locations: Bubenbergplatz, near the train station (straight out of station past church and main street, bikes are outside next to Loeb store) and Casinoplatz (2 blocks south of Clock Tower, in old town). Leave your passport and a 20-SF deposit.

Sights—Bern

▲▲**Old Town**—Window shopping and people watching through dilly-dally arcaded streets and busy market squares are Bern's top attractions. There are over three miles of arcades in this tiny capital of 130,000 people. This is my kind of shopping town: Prices are so high there's no danger of buying (shops open Mon–Fri 9:00–18:30, Thu until 21:00, Sat 8:00–16:00, closed Sun).

Clock Tower (Zytglogge-turm)—The clock performs four minutes before each hour. Apparently this five-minute nonevent was considered entertaining in 1530. To pass the time during the performance, read the TI's brochure explaining what's so interesting about the fancy old clock. Enthusiasts can tour the medieval mechanics daily at 16:30 (6 SF, 45 min, May–Oct).

▲**Cathedral**—The 1421 Swiss late-Gothic *Münster*, or cathedral, is worth a look (Tue–Sun 11:00–17:00, closed Mon; Oct–April Mon–Sat 10:00–12:00, 14:00–16:00, Sun 11:30–14:00). Climb the spiral staircase 100 meters above the town for the view, exercise, and a chance to meet a live church watchman. Elisabeth Bissig lives way up there, watching over the church, answering questions, and charging tourists 3 SF for the view.

Parliament (Bundeshaus)—You can tour Switzerland's imposing Parliament building (free 45-minute tours most days at 9:00, 10:00, 11:00, 14:00, 15:00, and 16:00, fewer on Sun; can watch when in session in March, June, Sept, and Dec, tour canceled if less than 5 people show up, tel. 031/322-8522 to confirm). Don't miss the view from the Bundeshaus terrace. You may see some national legislators, but you wouldn't know it—everything looks very casual for a national capital.

Einstein's House—Einstein did much of his most important thinking while living in this house on the old town's main drag. It was just another house to me, but I guess everything's relative (3 SF, Tue–Fri 10:00–17:00, Sat 10:00–16:00, closed Sun–Mon and Dec–Jan, Kramgasse 49).

▲**Bear Pits and Rose Garden**—The symbol of Bern is the bear, and some lively ones frolic (April–Sept 9:00–18:00, Oct–March 9:00–16:00) to the delight of locals and tourists alike in the big, barren, concrete pits (*Graben*) just over the river. You may see graffiti from the B.L.M. (Bear Liberation Movement) which, through its terrorist means, has forced a reluctant city government to give the bears better living conditions.

Old Tram Depot—This depot, next to the bear pits, hosts a slick new tourist center. Its excellent multimedia show, complete with an animated town model and marching Napoleonic-era soldiers, illustrates the history and wonders of Bern. Worth the time, the show is more interesting than the bears (free, every 20 minutes, May–Sept Wed–Mon 9:00–18:00, Oct–April 10:00–16:00, closed Tue). Up the pathway is the Rosengarten, a restaurant, and a great city view.

Bern

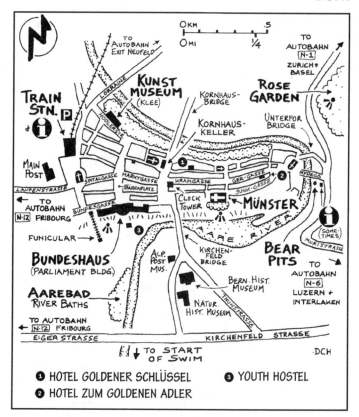

● HOTEL GOLDENER SCHLÜSSEL   ● YOUTH HOSTEL

● HOTEL ZUM GOLDENEN ADLER

▲▲**The Berner Swim**—For something to write home about, join the local merchants, students, and carp in a float down the Aare River. The Bernese, proud of their very clean river and their basic ruddiness, have a tradition—sort of a wet, urban paseo. On summer days they hike upstream five to 30 minutes then float back down to the excellent (and free) riverside baths and pools (*Aarebad*) just below the Parliament building. While the locals make it look easy, this is dangerous—the current is swift. If you miss the last pole, you're history. If the river is a bit much, you're welcome to enjoy just the Aarebad. If the river is not enough, a popular day trip is to raft all the way from Thun to Bern.

▲▲**Museum of Fine Arts (Kunstmuseum)**—While it features 1,000 years of local art and some Impressionism, the real hit is its fabulous collection of Paul Klee's playful paintings. If you don't know Klee, I'd love to introduce you (6 SF, Tue 10:00–21:00, Wed–Sun 10:00–17:00, closed Mon, 4 blocks from station, Holdergasse 12, tel. 031/311-0944).

Other Bern Museums—Across the bridge from the Parliament building on Helvetiaplatz are several museums (Alpine, Berner History, Postal) that sound more interesting than they are (most open Tue–Sun 10:00–17:00, closed Mon).

Sleeping in Bern
(1.70 SF = about $1, country code: 41, area code: 031)

Sleep Code: **S** = Single, **D** = Double/Twin, **T** = Triple, **Q** = Quad, **b** = bathroom, **t** = toilet only, **s** = shower only, **CC** = Credit Card (**V**isa, **M**asterCard, **A**mex), **SE** = Speaks English, **NSE** = No English. These are in the old town, within a 10-minute walk of the station.

Hotel National has bright, well-furnished rooms with big windows and street noise (S-60–80 SF, Sb-85–110 SF, D-100–120 SF, Db-130–150 SF, apartment-170–260 SF, CC:VMA, elevator, Hirschengraben 24, 3011 Bern, tel. 031/381-1988, fax 031/381-6878, www.nationalbern.ch).

Hotel Goldener Schlüssel is an old, basic, comfortable, crank-'em-out hotel in the center (S-80 SF, Sb-104 SF, D-116 SF, Db-148 SF, Tb-185 SF, CC:VMA, elevator, Rathausgasse 72, tel. 031/311-0216, fax 031/311-5688, www.goldener-schluessel.ch).

Hotel zum Goldenen Adler has comfy (but worn and smoky) rooms with all the amenities (Sb-130 SF, Db-170 SF, CC:VMA, elevator, Gerechtigkeitsgasse 7, tel. 031/311-1725, fax 031/311-3761).

Bern's big, sterile, well-run **IYHF youth hostel** has 4- to 26-bed rooms and provides an all-day lounge, laundry machines, and cheap meals (dorm beds-28 SF, nonmembers-33 SF, breakfast-6 SF, CC:VM, office open 7:00–10:30, 15:00–24:00, down the stairs from Parliament building, by the river at Weihergasse 4, tel. 031/311-6316, fax 031/312-5240, www.jugibern.ch).

Transportation Connections—Bern
By train to: Murten (hrly, 30 min, most change in Kerzers), **Lausanne** (2/hrly, 70 min), **Interlaken** (hrly, 1 hr), **Zurich** (2/hrly, 70 min), **Fribourg** in Switzerland (2/hrly, 30 min), **Munich** (4/day, 5.5 hrs), **Frankfurt** (hrly, 4.5 hrs), **Paris** (4/day, 4.5 hrs).

MURTEN

The finest medieval ramparts in Switzerland surround the 5,000 people of Murten. We're on the lingua-cusp of Switzerland: 25 percent of Murten speaks French; a few miles to the south and west, nearly everyone does. Murten is a totally charming mini-Bern with surprisingly lively streets, the middle one nicely arcaded with breezy outdoor cafés and elegant shops (many closed Mon). Its castle is romantically set, overlooking the Murtensee lake and the rolling vineyards of gentle Mount Vully in the distance. Spend a night here and have dinner with a local Vully wine, light white or rose. Murten is touristic but seems to be enjoyed mostly by its own people. Nearby Avenches, with its Roman ruins, glows at sunset.

The only required sightseeing is to do the rampart ramble (free, always open, easy stairway access on east side of town). Notice the old town clock reconstructed in the base of the tower (behind Hotel Ringmauer) and be glad you have a watch. The town history museum in an old mill is boring (closed Mon).

To get down to the lazy lakefront, find the access at Rathaus-strasse 17 (one block from Hotel Murtenhof) and veer right halfway down the steps. The lakefront offers a lovely promenade, mini-golf, swimming, and one-hour lake cruises (free with train passes, 11.20 SF otherwise, departing Murten 7:55, 13:40, 15:45, 18:35, no morning boat on weekends). The scenic trip takes an hour—consider a stop in the small town of Praz on the French-speaking shore. From there you can hike through vineyards up Mount Vully, where a bench and fine lake and Alp views await. Or rent a bike at the train station for a lakeside ride (21 SF/half day, 27 SF/full day).

The Migros and Co-op supermarkets, just outside the town gates, have cafeterias (Mon–Fri 8:00–19:00, Sat 7:30–16:00, closed Sun). A small bank with long hours is in the train station (Mon–Sat 5:00–24:00, closed Sun). The post office is in front of the station. Murten has no Laundromat.

Orientation (area code: 026)

Tourist Information: Murten's TI is just inside the gate at the eastern (lower) end of the town (May–Sept Mon–Fri 9:00–12:00, 14:00–18:00, Sat 9:00–12:00, closed Sun, Franziosische Kirchgasse 6, tel. 026/670-5112). While it tries to be helpful, there's not much to say. They offer free town walks (July–Sept, every second Sat at 10:00).

Arrival in Murten: Exit right from the station, take the first left and walk up Bahnhofstrasse, then turn right through the town gate where you'll run into Hotel Murtenhof and the town (a 5-minute walk).

Sights—Near Murten

Avenches—This town, four miles south of Murten, was once Aventicum, the Roman capital of Helvetica. Back then its population was 50,000. Today it could barely fill the well-worn ruins of its 15,000-seat Roman amphitheater. You can tour the Roman museum (2 SF, Tue–Sun 10:00–12:00, 13:00–17:00, closed Mon, near dinky amphitheater in town center), but the best experience is some quiet time at sunset pondering the evocative Roman amphitheater and sanctuary in the fields, a half-mile walk out of town (free, always open). Avenches, with a pleasant, small-French-town feel, is a quieter, less expensive place to stay than Murten. It also makes an easy day trip. The TI and the town are a seven-minute uphill walk from the station (TI tel. 026/675-1159).

Sleeping in Murten and Avenches
(1.70 SF = about $1, country code: 41, area code: 026)

Sleeping in or near Murten
Hotel Ringmauer (German for "ramparts") is friendly and characteristic, but noise can carry through its thin walls. Showers and toilets are within a dash of all 14 rooms (S-60 SF, D-108 SF, CC:VM, attached restaurant, near wall on the side farthest from lake, 1 block from the center, Deutsche Kirchgasse 2, tel. 026/670-1101, fax 026/672-2083).

Hotel Murtenhof, a worthwhile splurge, has nicely appointed rooms—each unique in design—and a lake view from its fine restaurant (Sb-110–165 SF, Db-140–260 SF, extra person-50 SF, CC:VMA, next to castle on Rathausgasse, tel. 026/672-9030, fax 026/672-9039, www.murtenhof.ch, e-mail: info@murtenhof.ch, SE). I eat on Hotel Murtenhof's terrace for their salad bar (summer only): 7.50 SF for a small plate, 15 SF for the big one; the small one carefully stacked is plenty and comes with wonderful bread and a sunset over the lake. The small plate is meant as a side dish, but, if you can handle the ridicule and don't mind being seated in back or outside, the big boss Theodore assured me you can eat one stacked high, and the waiters will even bring you a piece of bread and free water. The terrace is a good place to try the Vully wine—just point to the vineyards across the lake (restaurant open Tue–Sun 11:00–23:00, closed Mon).

Hotel Bahnhof, just across the street from the Murten train station, is a last resort (S-75 SF, Ss-80 SF, D-105 SF, Ds-125 SF, CC:VM, Bahnhofstrasse 14, tel. 026/670-2256, fax 026/672-1336, NSE).

Hotel Bel Air is across the Murten lake in lazy Praz, where hotel values are better than in ritzy Murten. Bel Air has seven flowery, in-love-with-life rooms and balconies—many with breath-taking lake views (D-90–110 SF, extra person-55 SF, CC:VM, no check-in on Thu, Route Principale 145, 1788 Praz-Vully, tel. 026/673-1414, www.belair-lac.ch). Henry, who speaks English, runs a fine restaurant here specializing in fish. While this is easy for drivers, train travelers will need to catch the boat from Murten (see above). They can depart Praz weekday mornings at 8:15, or get to the Sugiez train station (on the main Bern line), just a kilometer away.

Oasis Neuchatel is a friendly 40-bed hostel just outside the town of Neuchatel (dorm beds-24 SF, D-62 SF, CC:V, includes breakfast, vegetarian meals, small kitchen available, Ping-Pong, nonsmoking, creative and young management, call to reserve, office open 8:00–10:00, 17:00–21:00; catch bus #6 from Neuchatel train station to Place Purry, then take bus #1 from center in direction of "Cormondreche," get off at eighth stop, "Vauseyon," walk up hill to Rue du Suchiez 35, 2000 Neuchatel, tel. 032/731-3190, fax 032/730-3709).

Sleeping in and near Avenches
The Avenches **IYHF hostel**, the only hostel in the area, is a beauty. It's run by the Dhyaf family, with four- to eight-bed rooms, an included breakfast, a homey TV room, Ping-Pong, a big backyard, and a very quiet setting near the Roman theater (24 SF for dorm bed, 31 SF for private room, more for nonmembers, office open 7:00–9:30, 17:00–22:30, no curfew, 3 blocks from center at medieval *lavoir* or laundry, Rue du Lavoir 5, 1580 Avenches, tel. 026/675-2666, fax 026/675-2717).

Friendly **Elisabeth Clement-Arnold** has a room in her house (S-35 SF, D-40 SF, breakfast-5 SF, bathroom is yours alone but down the hall, rue Centrale 5, 1580 Avenches, tel. & fax 026/675-3031).

Auberge de l'Ecusson Vaudois is the only hotel in the small village of Oleyres, three kilometers from Avenches (Sb-60 SF, Db-95 SF, dorm bed-25 SF, all with breakfast, 1580 Oleyres, tel. & fax 026/675-1087, www.aubergeoleyres.com, Madame Sidler SE).

Transportation Connections—Murten
By train to: Avenches (hrly, 10 min), **Bern** (hrly, 30 min, most require a change in Kerzers), **Fribourg** in Switzerland (hrly, 30 min), **Lausanne** (hrly, 90 min, transfer in Fribourg). Train info: tel. 026/670-2646.

SOUTHWEST SWISS COUNTRYSIDE
The sublime French Swiss countryside is sprinkled with crystal-clear lakes, tasty chocolates, smelly cheese, and sleepy cows. If you're traveling between Murten, Montreux, and Interlaken, take time for a few of the countryside's sights, tastes, and smells.

Getting around the Countryside
Cross-country buses use Fribourg and Bulle as hubs: **Bulle–Gruyères** (7/day, 15 min) and **Fribourg–Bulle** (hrly, 30 min).

Sights—Swiss Countryside
Caillers Chocolate Factory—The Caillers factory, churning out chocolate in the town of Broc, welcomes visitors with a hygienic peek through a window, a 15-minute movie, and free

melt-in-your-hands samples (free, Mon 13:30–16:00, Tue–Fri 9:00–11:00, 13:30–16:00, closed Sat–Sun, closed July and off-season, follow signs to "Nestlé" and "Broc Fabrique," even individuals need to call a day in advance to reserve, tel. 026/921-5151). Broc town is just the sleepy, sweet-smelling home of the chocolate makers. It has a small, very typical hotel, Auberge des Montagnards (D-70 SF, great Gruyères view, elegant dining room, tel. 026/921-1526). From Bulle, trains run hourly to Broc (10 min).

▲▲**Musée Gruèrien**—Somehow the unassuming little town of Bulle built a refreshing, cheery folk museum that manages to teach you all about life in these parts and leave you feeling very good (5 SF, free English guidebook, Tue–Sat 10:00–12:00, 14:00–17:00, Sun 14:00–17:00, closed Mon, tel. 026/912-7260). When it's over, the guide reminds you, "The Golden Book of Visitors awaits your signature and comments. Don't you think this museum deserves another visit? Thank you!"

▲**Gruyères**—This ultratouristy town, famous for its cheese, fills its fortified hilltop like a bouquet. Its ramparts are a park, and the ancient buildings serve tourists. The castle is mediocre, but do make a short stop for the setting. Minimize your walk by driving up to the second parking lot. Hotels here are expensive.

▲▲**Gruyères Fromagerie**—There are two very different cheese-making exhibits to choose from. Five miles above Gruyères, a dark and smoky 17th-century farmhouse in Moleson gives a fun look at the old and smelly craft (3 SF, mid-May–Oct Sun–Thu 9:30–19:00, Fri–Sat 9:30–22:00, cheese actually being made 10:00–11:00 and 15:00–16:00, TI tel. 026/921-2434). Closer, slicker, and modern, the cheese-production center at the foot of Gruyères town (follow "Fromagerie" signs) opens its doors to tourists with a continuous English audiovisual presentation (5 SF, daily 8:00–19:00). The cute cheese shop in the modern center has lunches and picnic goodies (closed 12:00–13:30).

Glacier des Diablerets—For a grand Alpine trip to the tip of a 10,000-foot peak, take the three-part lift from Reusch or Col du Pillon. The trip takes about 90 minutes and costs 50 SF. Stay for lunch. From the top you can see the Matterhorn and a bit of Mont Blanc, the Alps' highest peak. This is a good chance to do some summer skiing (normally expensive and a major headache). A lift ticket and rental skis, poles, boots, and coat cost about 65 SF. The slopes close at 14:00 during the summer, and at 17:00 from October through April.

The base of the lift is a two-hour drive from Murten or Gimmelwald. Your best public-transportation bet is to catch an early train to des Diablerets with a transfer in Aigle. Then bus to Col du Pillon (7/day) and take the cable car to the top (last departure at 16:00). For more ski information, call 024/492-3377.

▲▲**Taveyanne**—This remote hamlet is a huddle of log cabins used by cowherds in the summer. The hamlet's old bar is a restaurant serving a tiny community of vacationers and hikers. Taveyanne is two miles off the main road between Col de la Croix and Villars. A small sign points down a tiny road to a jumble of huts and snoozing cows stranded at 5,000 feet. The inn is **Refuge de Taveyanne** (1882 Gryon), where the Seibenthal family serves meals in a prizewinning rustic setting with no electricity, low ceilings, and a huge charred fireplace. Consider sleeping in their primitive loft (10 SF, 5 mattresses, access by a ladder outside, urinate with the cows, closed Tue except July–Aug, closed Nov–April, tel. 024/498-1947). A fine opportunity to really get to know prizewinning cows.

LAKE GENEVA (LAC LEMAN)
This is the Swiss Riviera. Lake Geneva separates France and Switzerland, is surrounded by Alps, and is lined with a collage of castles, museums, spas, resort towns, and vineyards. Its crowds, therefore, are understandable. This area is so beautiful that Charlie Chaplin and Idi Amin both chose it as their second home.

Getting around Lake Geneva
Buses connect towns along Lake Geneva every 15 minutes. Boats carry visitors to all sights of importance. The four daily boat trips from Chateau Chillon stop in Montreux (10 min, 6 SF), Vevey (30 min, 12 SF), and Lausanne (90 min, 20 SF, Eurailers sail free, tel. 021/614-0444). The short Montreux–Château Chillon cruise is fun. The pretty town of Vevey gives you the most scenic 30-minute ride from Chillon and 60-minute ride from Lausanne, and makes an enjoyable destination (take bus back). Hourly trains connect Lausanne, Montreux, and Villeneuve.

Sights—Lake Geneva
▲▲▲**Château Chillon**—This wonderfully preserved 13th-century castle, set wistfully at the edge of Lake Geneva, is a joy. Follow the excellent free English brochure from one fascinating room to the next, enjoying tingly views, the dank prison, battle-scarred weapons, mobile furniture, and 700-year-old toilets. The 130-step climb to the top of the keep (#25 in the brochure) isn't worth the time or sweat. Stroll the patrol ramparts, then curl up on a windowsill to enjoy the lake (7 SF, 2 SF extra to join a tour, daily 9:00–18:00, less off-season, easy parking, call to see if English tour group is scheduled, tel. 021/966-8910). If you come by train, get off at Veytaux-Chillon and walk a few minutes along the lake (ideal for picnicking) to the castle.
Villeneuve—This is a relatively run-down little resort a 30-minute walk beyond Château Chillon. The train station is a block from the beach promenade, main street (Grand-Rue),

and TI (Mon 13:30–18:00, Tue–Fri 9:00–12:30, 13:30–18:00, Sat 9:00–12:30, closed Sun, tel. 021/960-2286). Come here only if you need an affordable place to sleep (see "Sleeping," below).

Montreux—This expensive resort has a famous jazz festival each July. The Montreux TI (tel. 021/962-8484) has a list of moderate rooms in the center, including Hotel-Restaurant du Pont (Db-130 SF, great spaghetti, Rue du Pont 12, tel. 021/963-2249). Near Montreux, Vevey is a smaller and more comfortable resort town.

Corniche de Lavaux—The rugged Swiss Wine Road swerves through picturesque towns and the stingy vineyards that produce most of Switzerland's tasty but expensive *Fendant* wine. Hikers can take the boat to Cully and explore on foot from there. A car tour is quick and frightening (from Montreux, go west along the lake through Vevey, following blue signs to Lausanne along the waterfront and taking the Moudon/Chexbres exit). Explore some of the smaller roads.

Geneva—This big city bores me. It's sterile, cosmopolitan, expensive, and full of executives, diplomats, and tourists.

LAUSANNE

This is the most interesting city on the lake. Amble the serene lakefront promenade, stroll through the three-tiered colorful old town, and consider visiting its remarkable Museum of Art Brut. Take a peek at Switzerland's most important Gothic cathedral and climb its tower for the view.

Orientation (area code: 021)

Tourist Information: Lausanne has two TIs, one in the train station (daily 9:00–19:00) and the other at the Ouchy Metro (Mon–Fri 9:00–20:00, Sat–Sun 9:00–18:00, tel. 021/613-7373). Skip the museum pass. Ask if there are free concerts at the cathedral and any walking tours in English (10 SF, tours offered May–Sept Mon–Sat normally at 10:00 and 15:00, subject to availability of English-speaking guide, tel. 021/321-7766).

    Helpful Hints: The **Laundromat** closest to the train station is Quick-Wash (Mon–Fri 8:30–22:00, Sat–Sun 12:00–22:00, Boulevard de Grancy 44). **In Comm** has Internet access (8 SF/hr, directly under train station at access ramp for track 9, tel. 021/601-5150).

Getting around Lausanne

You'll want a map to navigate this city that is steeper than it is big. A five-stop funicular-metro connects the lakefront (called Ouchy—OO-shee) with the train station (CFF) and the upper part of Lausanne (called *vielle ville*, or *centre ville*). The cost is 2.20 SF (tickets good for 1 hr on buses, too). You can walk, but everyone uses the metro. Buy tickets from the window or at the ticket machines. The metro is across the street from the train station. If you're coming from the dock at Ouchy, angle left from the boats to reach the metro (TI there). Buy bus tickets from the white and yellow machine at the bus stop before boarding (2.20 SF; the cheaper 1.30-SF ticket is good for only 3 bus stops or 2 metro stops). The 24-hour pass, which covers both the metro and the bus, is a good deal if you take three trips or more (6.50 SF).

The train station rents bikes (16 SF/half day, 21 SF/full day, plus 12 SF to take bike on train and drop off at another station, no deposit needed except address and passport number).

Sights—Lausanne

Vielle Ville—The vertical old city is laced with shopping streets, modern structures, and the elegant cathedral. From the top metro stop, walk right under the viaduct, then wander left uphill along pedestrian streets to the cathedral. The cathedral is a purely peaceful place with unusual stained-glass windows and a 230-step tower view (2 SF to climb tower but view from terrace below is free).

Collection de l'Art Brut—This brilliantly displayed, thought-provoking collection was produced by untrained artists, many labeled as criminal or crazy by society. Enjoy the unbridled creativity and read about the artists (6 SF, Tue–Sun 11:00–13:00, 14:00–18:00, closed Mon, bus #3 from station, follow signs to Palais de Beaulieu, Avenue des Bergieres 11, tel. 021/647-5435).

Olympics Museum—This high-tech museum includes an extensive film archive of thrilling moments in the history of the Games (14 SF, daily 9:00–18:00, Thu until 20:00, off-season closed Mon, tel. 021/621-6511).

City History Museum—This museum traces life in Lausanne from Roman times with many fun interactive displays and CD-ROM demos. It's notable for its 1:200-scale model of Lausanne in the 17th century, accompanied by an audiovisual presentation (Tue–Sun 11:00–18:00, Thu until 20:00, closed Mon, English handouts in each room). The museum is right next to the cathedral and viewpoint terrace.

Vineyard Strolls—Picturesque vineyards abound along the lake near Lausanne. Consider a 5- to 10-minute train ride to Chexbres or Grandvaux and walk through the villages toward Lutry for stunning views of Lake Geneva.

Sleeping in Lausanne
(1.70 SF = about $1, country code: 41, area code: 021, zip code: 1007)
Breakfast is included unless otherwise noted.

Hotel Mirabeau Lausanne, part of the Best Western chain, offers spiffy rooms with fine views at a good price (Sb-140–185 SF, Db-190–295 SF, more expensive for view room, sometimes

10 percent off for weekends, buffet breakfast, CC:VM, Avenue de la Gare 31, tel. 021/341-4243, fax 021/341-4242, www.mirabeau.ch).

Hotel Regina, on a pedestrian street in the old town, is newly remodeled with 36 comfy rooms. Energetic Michel and Dora provide loads of information about day trips (Sb-110–120 SF, Db-150–160 SF, third person-40 SF, CC:VMA, free overnight parking, Rue Grand Saint-Jean 18, tel. 021/320-2441, fax 021/320-2529, www.hotel-regina.ch).

Jeunotel, clean and affordable, has concrete walls and cell-block rooms. You know it's not a minimum-security prison because they give you a key (dorm bed-30 SF, S-56 SF, Sb-80 SF, D-84 SF, Db-102 SF, T-99 SF, CC:VMA, any age welcome, easy parking, Chemin du Bois-de-Vaux 36, tel. 021/626-0222, fax 021/626-0226, SE). Take the Metro to Ouchy, then bus #2 to the Bois-de-Vaux stop (you'll see signs for the hotel, a block away).

Hotel du Raisin, with dingy, faded furnishings, has a great but noisy location on a popular square in the old town (S-60 SF, D-120 SF, CC:VMA, attached restaurant with sidewalk café, Place de la Palud 19, tel. & fax 021/312-2756).

Sleeping in Villeneuve, near Montreux and Château Chillon
(1.70 SF = about $1, country code: 41, area code: 021, zip code: 1844)

Villeneuve, three miles east, has Montreux's palmy lakeside setting without the crowds or glitz. Its main drag runs parallel to the shore, a block inland. Stroll 30 minutes along the waterfront promenade to Château Chillon. Don't count on speaking English at these hotels. Leaving the train station, take a left on Main Street to find the TI and the first two hotels, or walk straight ahead to find the lakefront listing.

La Romantica, with 13 dark, narrow, cheap-feeling rooms, is a decent value. It has a frumpy, very French bar scene downstairs and a restaurant that guarantees fresh perch daily (Sb-50 SF, Db-100–120 SF, includes breakfast, CC:VMA, Grand-Rue 34, tel. 021/960-1540, fax 021/960-1766, e-mail: romantica@freesurf.ch).

Hotel du Soleil is expensive but comfortable (Sb-70 SF, Db-100–130 SF, CC:VMA, Grand-Rue 20, tel. 021/960-4206, fax 021/960-4208).

Hotel du Port has 22 rooms on the waterfront (Sb-120–132 SF, Ds-154–184 SF, Db-184–220 SF, family deals, CC:VMA, elevator, Rue du Quai 6, tel. 021/960-4145, fax 021/960-3967, www.duport.ch).

Montreux Youth Hostel is at the edge of Montreux, on the lake, a 10-minute stroll north of the château (dorm bed, sheets, and breakfast for 30 SF, D-76 SF, nonmembers pay 5 SF extra, closed 10:00–16:00, cheap meals served, Passage de l'Auberge 8,

1820 Territet, tel. 021/963-4934, fax 021/963-2729, e-mail: montreux@youthhostel.ch). Train noise can be a problem.

Transportation Connections—Lake Geneva
Lausanne by train to: Montreux (hrly, 20 min), **Geneva** (3/hrly, 40 min), **Bern** (hrly, 70 min), **Basel** (direct every 2 hrs, 2.5 hrs), **Milan** (hrly, 3.5 hrs).

Route Tips for Drivers
Interlaken to Bern to Murten (50 miles): From Interlaken, catch the autobahn (direction: Spiez, Thun, Bern). After Spiez, the autobahn takes you directly to Bern. Circle the city on the autobahn, taking the fourth Bern exit, Neufeld Bern. Signs to "Zentrum" take you to Bern Bahnhof. Turn right just before the station into the Bahnhof Parkplatz (2-hr meter parking outside, all-day lot inside, 3 SF/hr). You're just an escalator ride away from a great TI and Switzerland's compact, user-friendly capital. From the station, drive out of Bern following Lausanne signs, then follow the green signs to Neuchatel and Murten. The autobahn ends 20 miles later in Murten.

Parking in Murten is medieval. Ask about parking at your hotel. If you have a dashboard clock, you can try the blue spots near Hotel Ringmauer, but there are large free lots just outside either gate. Walk into Murten. It's a tiny town.

Murten to Lake Geneva (50 miles): The autobahn from Bern to Lausanne/Lake Geneva makes everything speedy. Murten and Avenches are 10 minutes off the autobahn. Broc, Bulle, and Gruyères are within sight of each other and the autobahn. It takes about an hour to drive from Murten to Montreux. The autobahn (direction: Simplon) takes you high above Montreux (pull off at the great viewpoint rest stop) and Château Chillon. For the castle, take the first exit east of the castle (Villeneuve). Signs direct you along the lake back to the castle.

APPENDIX

Let's Talk Telephones

Dialing Direct
Calling between Countries: First dial the international access code, then the country code, the area code (if it starts with zero, drop the zero), and then the local number.

Calling Long Distance within a Country: First dial the area code (including its zero), then the local number.

Europe's Exceptions: Some countries, such as Italy, Spain, Portugal, France, Norway, and Denmark, do not use area codes. To call these countries, dial the international access code (00 if you're in Europe), the country code (see chart below), then the local number in its entirety (OK, so there's one exception; for France, drop the initial zero of the local number). To make long-distance calls within any of these countries, simply dial the local number.

International Access Codes
When dialing direct, first dial the international access code of the country you're calling from. For the U.S. and Canada, it's 011. Virtually all European countries use "00" as their international access code; the only exceptions are Finland (990), Estonia (800), and Lithuania (810).

Country Codes
After you've dialed the international access code, dial the code of the country you're calling.

Austria—43

Belgium—32	France—33	Portugal—351
Britain—44	Germany—49	Spain—34
Canada—1	Greece—30	Sweden—46
Czech Rep.—420	Ireland—353	Switzerland—41
Denmark—45	Italy—39	United States—1
Estonia—372	Netherlands—31	
Finland—358	Norway—47	

Calling Card Operators
	AT&T	MCI	SPRINT
Austria	022-903-011	0800-200-235	0800-200-236
Germany	0130-00-10	0800-888-8000	0800-888-0013
Switzerland	0800-89-0011	0800-89-0222	0800-89-9777
Czech Rep.	00420-00101	00420-00112	00420-87187

Directory Assistance
Austria: national—16, international—08, train information: 051717

Switzerland: national—111, international—191
Swiss info for Germany/Austria: 192
Germany: national—11833, international—11834
German tourist offices: local code, then 19433
German train information: local code, then 19419

Events in Germany, Austria, and Switzerland

January	Perchtenlaufen (winter festival, parades), Tirol & Salzburg, Austria
Jan–Feb	Fasching (carnival season, balls, parades), Austria, Germany
Easter	Easter Festival, Salzburg
May	May Day (on 1st) with Maypole dances, Austria, Germany
	Vienna Festival of Arts and Music
June	Frankfurt Summertime Festival (arts)
	Master Draught (play, procession, festival), Rothenburg, Germany
Late June	Midsummer Eve Celebrations, Austria
July	Salzburg Festival (music)
	Montreux International Jazz Festival
August	Swiss National Day (on 1st) with parades and fireworks
September	Oktoberfest, Munich (starts third weekend, runs 16 days)
	Berlin Festwochen (arts festival)
	Imperial City Festival (costumes, parade, fireworks on second weekend), Rothenburg, Germany
October	Berlin Jazz Festival
November	St. Martin's Day Celebrations (feasts), Austria, Bavaria
	Onion Market Fair, Bern, Switzerland
December	St. Nicholas Day parades, Austria
	L'Escalade (folk festival, parades), Geneva, Switzerland
	Christmas Fairs, Austria, Germany

For more information on festivals and events in these countries, visit these Web sites: www.whatsgoingon.com and www.festivals.com.

Numbers and Stumblers

- Europeans write a few of their numbers differently than we do: 1 = 1 , 4 = 4 , 7= 7 . Learn the difference or miss your train.
- In Europe, dates appear as day/month/year, so Christmas is 25/12/01.
- Commas are decimal points and decimals commas. A dollar and a half is 1,50 and there are 5.280 feet in a mile.

- When pointing, use your whole hand, palm downward.
- When counting with fingers, start with your thumb. If you hold up your first finger to request one item, you'll get two.
- What we Americans call the second floor of a building is the first floor in Europe.
- Europeans keep the left "lane" open for passing on escalators and moving sidewalks. Keep to the right.

Climate

First line, average daily low; second line, average daily high; third line, days of no rain.

J	F	M	A	M	J	J	A	S	O	N	D
Vienna, AUSTRIA											
25°	28°	30°	42°	50°	56°	60°	59°	53°	44°	37°	30°
34°	38°	47°	58°	67°	73°	76°	75°	68°	56°	45°	37°
16	17	18	17	18	16	18	18	20	18	16	16
Prague, CZECH REPUBLIC											
23°	24°	30°	38°	46°	52°	55°	55°	49°	41°	33°	27°
31°	34°	44°	54°	64°	70°	73°	72°	65°	53°	42°	34°
18	17	21	19	18	18	18	19	20	18	18	18
Berlin, GERMANY											
26°	26°	31°	39°	47°	53°	57°	56°	50°	42°	36°	29°
35°	37°	46°	56°	66°	72°	75°	74°	68°	56°	45°	38°
14	13	19	17	19	17	17	17	18	17	14	16
Munich, GERMANY											
23°	23°	30°	38°	45°	51°	55°	54°	48°	40°	33°	26°
35°	38°	48°	56°	64°	70°	74°	73°	67°	56°	44°	36°
15	12	18	15	16	13	15	15	17	18	15	16
Geneva, SWITZERLAND											
29°	30°	36°	42°	49°	55°	58°	58°	53°	44°	37°	31°
38°	42°	51°	59°	66°	73°	77°	76°	69°	58°	47°	40°
20	19	22	21	20	19	22	20	20	21	19	21

Metric Conversions (approximate)

1 inch = 25 millimeters   32 degrees F = 0 degrees C
1 foot = 0.3 meter   82 degrees F = about 28 degrees C
1 yard = 0.9 meter   1 ounce = 28 grams
1 mile = 1.6 kilometers   1 kilogram = 2.2 pounds
1 centimeter = 0.4 inch   1 quart = 0.95 liter
1 meter = 39.4 inches   1 square yard = 0.8 square meter
1 kilometer = .62 mile   1 acre = 0.4 hectare

German Survival Phrases

Hello (good day).	**Guten Tag.**	**goo**-ten tahg
Do you speak English?	**Sprechen Sie Englisch?**	**shprekh**-en zee **eng**-lish
Yes. / No.	**Ja. / Nein.**	yah / nīn
I'm sorry.	**Entschuldigung.**	ent-**shool**-dee-goong
Please. / Thank you.	**Bitte. / Danke.**	**bit**-teh / **dahng**-keh
Goodbye.	**Auf Wiedersehen.**	owf **vee**-der-zayn
Where is...?	**Wo ist...?**	voh ist
...a hotel	**...ein Hotel**	īn hoh-**tel**
...a youth hostel	**...eine Jugend-herberge**	ī-neh **yoo**-gend-hehr-behr-ge
...a restaurant	**...ein Restaurant**	īn res-tow-**rahnt**
...a supermarket	**...ein Supermarkt**	īn **zoo**-per-markt
...the train station	**...der Bahnhof**	dehr **bahn**-hohf
...the tourist information office	**...das Touristen-informationsbüro**	dahs **too**-ris-ten-in-for-maht-see-**ohns**-bew-rol
...the toilet	**...die Toilette**	dee toh-**leh**-teh
men / women	**Herren / Damen**	**hehr**-ren / **dah**-men
How much is it?	**Wieviel kostet das?**	vee-**feel kos**-tet dahs
Cheap / Cheaper.	**Billig / Billiger.**	**bil**-lig / **bil**-lig-er
Included?	**Eingeschlossen?**	**īn**-geh-shlos-sen
Do you have...?	**Haben Sie...?**	**hah**-ben zee
I would like...	**Ich hätte gern...**	ikh **het**-teh gehrn
...just a little.	**...nur ein bißchen.**	noor īn **bis**-yen
...more.	**...mehr.**	mehr
...a ticket.	**...ein Karte.**	īn **kar**-teh
...a room.	**...ein Zimmer.**	īn **tsim**-mer
...the bill.	**...die Rechnung.**	dee **rekh**-noong
one	**eins**	īns
two	**zwei**	tsvī
three	**drei**	drī
four	**vier**	feer
five	**fünf**	fewnf
six	**sechs**	zex
seven	**sieben**	**zee**-ben
eight	**acht**	ahkht
nine	**neun**	noyn
ten	**zehn**	tsayn
At what time?	**Um wieviel Uhr?**	oom vee-**feel** oor
now / soon / later	**jetzt / bald / später**	yetzt / bahld / **shpay**-ter
today / tomorrow	**heute / morgen**	**hoy**-teh / **mor**-gen

Faxing Your Hotel Reservation

Faxing is more accurate and cheaper than telephoning. Use this handy form for your fax (or find it online at www.ricksteves.com/reservation). Photocopy and fax away.

One-Page Fax

To: _____ @ _____
                    hotel   *fax*

From: _____ @ _____
                    name   *fax*

Today's date: ____ /_____ /____
                     day   *month*   *year*

Dear Hotel _____ ,

Please make this reservation for me:

Name: _____

Total # of people: _____   # of rooms: _____   # of nights: _____

Arriving: ____ /_____ /____   My time of arrival (24-hr clock): _____
              day   *month*   *year*   (I will telephone if I will be late)

Departing: ____ /_____ /____
                day   *month*   *year*

Room(s):   Single___   Double___   Twin___   Triple___   Quad___

With: Toilet___   Shower___   Bath___   Sink only___

Special needs: View___   Quiet___   Cheap___   Ground Floor___

Credit card: Visa___   MasterCard___   American Express___

Card #: _____

Expiration date:_____

Name on card: _____

You may charge me for the first night as a deposit. Please fax, e-mail, or mail me confirmation of my reservation, along with the type of room reserved, the price, and whether the price includes breakfast. Thank you.

_____
Signature

_____
Name

_____
Address

_____
City   *State*   *Zip Code*   *Country*

_____
E-mail Address

Road Scholar Feedback for
GERMANY, AUSTRIA & SWITZERLAND 2001

We're all in the same travelers' school of hard knocks. Your feedback helps us improve this guidebook for future travelers. Please fill this out (or use the on-line version at www.ricksteves.com/feedback), attach more info or any tips/favorite discoveries if you like, and send it to us. As thanks for your help, we'll send you our quarterly travel newsletter free for one year. Thanks! **Rick**

Of the recommended accommodations/restaurants used, which was:

Best _____

      Why? _____

Worst _____

      Why? _____

Of the sights/experiences/destinations recommended by this book, which was:

Most overrated _____

      Why? _____

Most underrated _____

      Why? _____

Best ways to improve this book:

_____

_____

I'd like a free newsletter subscription:

_____ Yes   _____ No   _____ Already on list

_____
Name

_____
Address

_____
City, State, Zip

_____
E-mail Address

Please send to: ETBD, Box 2009, Edmonds, WA 98020

INDEX

AVALON
TRAVEL
publishing

BECAUSE TRAVEL MATTERS.

AVALON TRAVEL PUBLISHING knows that travel is more than coming and going—travel is taking part in new experiences, new ideas, and a new outlook. Our goal is to bring you complete and up-to-date information to help you make informed travel decisions.

AVALON TRAVEL GUIDES feature a combination of practicality and spirit, offering a unique traveler-to-traveler perspective perfect for an afternoon hike, around-the-world journey, or anything in between.

WWW.TRAVELMATTERS.COM

Avalon Travel Publishing guides are available at your favorite book or travel store.

FOR TRAVELERS WITH SPECIAL INTERESTS

GUIDES

The 100 Best Small Art Towns in America • Asia in New York City
The Big Book of Adventure Travel • Cities to Go
Cross-Country Ski Vacations • Gene Kilgore's Ranch Vacations
Great American Motorcycle Tours • Healing Centers and Retreats
Indian America • Into the Heart of Jerusalem
The People's Guide to Mexico • The Practical Nomad
Saddle Up! • Staying Healthy in Asia, Africa, and Latin America
Steppin' Out • Travel Unlimited • Understanding Europeans
Watch It Made in the U.S.A. • The Way of the Traveler
Work Worldwide • The World Awaits
The Top Retirement Havens • Yoga Vacations

SERIES

Adventures in Nature
The Dog Lover's Companion
Kidding Around
Live Well

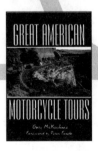

MOON HANDBOOKS provide

comprehensive coverage of a region's arts, history, land, people, and social issues in addition to detailed practical listings for accommodations, food, outdoor recreation, and entertainment. Moon Handbooks allow complete immersion in a region's culture—ideal for travelers who want to combine sightseeing with insight for an extraordinary travel experience.

USA

Alaska-Yukon • Arizona • Big Island of Hawaii • Boston • Coastal California • Colorado Connecticut • Georgia • Grand Canyon • Hawaii Honolulu-Waikiki • Idaho • Kauai • Los Angeles Maine • Massachusetts • Maui • Michigan Montana • Nevada • New Hampshire New Mexico • New York City • New York State North Carolina • Northern California • Ohio Oregon • Pennsylvania • San Francisco Santa Fe-Taos • Silicon Valley • South Carolina Southern California • Tahoe • Tennessee • Texas • Utah • Virginia Washington • Wisconsin • Wyoming • Yellowstone-Grand Teton

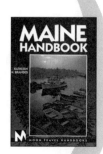

INTERNATIONAL

Alberta and the Northwest Territories Archaeological Mexico • Atlantic Canada • Australia Baja • Bangkok • Bali • Belize • British Columbia • Cabo • Canadian Rockies • Cancún Caribbean Vacations • Colonial Mexico • Costa Rica Cuba • Dominican Republic • Ecuador • Fiji Havana • Honduras • Hong Kong • Indonesia Jamaica • Mexico City • Mexico • Micronesia The Moon • Nepal • New Zealand Northern Mexico • Oaxaca • Pacific Mexico Pakistan • Philippines • Puerto Vallarta • Singapore • South Korea South Pacific • Southeast Asia • Tahiti • Thailand Tonga-Samoa • Vancouver Vietnam, Cambodia and Laos • Virgin Islands Yucatán Peninsula

www.moon.com

Rick Steves shows you where to travel and how to travel—all while getting the most value for your dollar. His Back Door travel philosophy is about making friends, having fun, and avoiding tourist rip-offs.

Rick's been traveling to Europe for more than 25 years and is the author of 20 guidebooks, which have sold more than a million copies. He also hosts the award-winning public television series *Travels in Europe with Rick Steves.*

RICK STEVES' COUNTRY & CITY GUIDES
Best of Europe
France, Belgium & the Netherlands
Germany, Austria & Switzerland
Great Britain & Ireland
Italy • London • Paris • Rome
Scandinavia • Spain & Portugal

RICK STEVES' PHRASE BOOKS
French • German • Italian • French, Italian & German
Spanish & Portuguese

MORE EUROPE FROM RICK STEVES
Europe 101
Europe Through the Back Door
Mona Winks
Postcards from Europe

WWW.RICKSTEVES.COM

ROAD TRIP USA

Getting there is half the fun, and Road Trip USA guides are your ticket to driving adventure. Taking you off the interstates and onto less-traveled, two-lane highways, each guide is filled with fascinating trivia, historical information, photographs, facts about regional writers, and details on where to sleep and eat—all contributing to your exploration of the American road.

"Books so full of the pleasures of the American road, you can smell the upholstery."
~ BBC radio

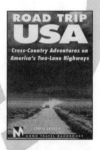

THE ORIGINAL CLASSIC GUIDE
Road Trip USA

ROAD TRIP USA REGIONAL GUIDE
Road Trip USA: California and the Southwest

ROAD TRIP USA GETAWAYS
Road Trip USA Getaways: Chicago
Road Trip USA Getaways: New Orleans
Road Trip USA Getaways: San Francisco
Road Trip USA Getaways: Seattle

www.roadtripusa.com

TRAVEL ★ SMART®

guidebooks are accessible, route-based driving guides. Special
interest tours provide the most practical routes for family fun,
outdoor activities, or regional history for a trip of anywhere
from two to 22 days. Travel Smarts take the guesswork out of
planning a trip by recommending only the most interesting
places to eat, stay, and visit.

*"One of the few travel series that rates sightseeing
attractions. That's a handy feature. It helps to have
some guidance so that every minute counts."*
~ San Diego Union-Tribune

TRAVEL SMART REGIONS

Alaska
American
Southwest
Arizona
Carolinas
Colorado
Deep South
Eastern
Canada
Florida Gulf
Coast
Florida
Georgia
Hawaii
Illinois/Indiana
Iowa/Nebraska
Kentucky/Tennessee
Maryland/Delaware
Michigan
Minnesota/Wisconsin
Montana/Wyoming/Idaho
Nevada

New England
New Mexico
New York State
Northern California
Ohio
Oregon
Pacific Northwest
Pennsylvania/New Jersey
South Florida and the Keys
Southern California
Texas
Utah
Virginias
Western Canada

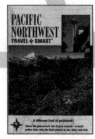

Foghorn Outdoors

guides are for campers, hikers, boaters, anglers, bikers, andgolfers of all levels of daring and skill. Each guide contains site descriptions and ratings, driving directions, facilities and fees information, and easy-to-read maps that leave only the task of deciding where to go.

"Foghorn Outdoors has established an ecological conservation standard unmatched by any other publisher."
~ Sierra Club

CAMPING Arizona and New Mexico Camping
Baja Camping • California Camping
Camper's Companion • Colorado Camping
Easy Camping in Northern California
Easy Camping in Southern California
Florida Camping • New England Camping
Pacific Northwest Camping
Utah and Nevada Camping

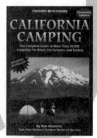

HIKING 101 Great Hikes of the San Francisco Bay Area
California Hiking • Day-Hiking California's National Parks
Easy Hiking in Northern California
Easy Hiking in Southern California
New England Hiking • Pacific Northwest Hiking • Utah Hiking

FISHING Alaska Fishing • California Fishing
Washington Fishing

BOATING
California Recreational Lakes and Rivers
Washington Boating and Water Sports

OTHER OUTDOOR RECREATION
California Beaches • California Golf
California Waterfalls • California Wildlife
Easy Biking in Northern California
Florida Beaches
The Outdoor Getaway Guide For Southern California
Tom Stienstra's Outdoor Getaway Guide: Northern California

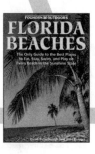

WWW.FOGHORN.COM

CiTY·SMaRT™

The best way to enjoy a city is to get advice from someone who lives there—and that's exactly what City Smart guidebooks offer. City Smarts are written by local authors with hometown perspectives who have personally selected the best places to eat, shop, sightsee, and simply hang out. The honest, lively, and opinionated advice is perfect for business travelers looking to relax with the locals or for longtime residents looking for something new to do Saturday night.

*A portion of sales from each title
benefits a non-profit literacy organization in that city.*

CITY SMART CITIES

Albuquerque	Anchorage
Austin	Baltimore
Berkeley/Oakland	Boston
Calgary	Charlotte
Chicago	Cincinnati
Cleveland	Dallas/Ft. Worth
Denver	Indianapolis
Kansas City	Memphis
Milwaukee	Minneapolis/St. Paul
Nashville	Pittsburgh
Portland	Richmond
San Francisco	Sacramento
St. Louis	Salt Lake City
San Antonio	San Diego
Tampa/St. Petersburg	Toronto
Tucson	Vancouver

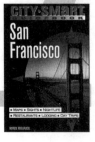

www.travelmatters.com

User-friendly, informative, and fun:
Because travel *matters.*

Visit our newly launched web site and explore the variety of titles and travel information available online, featuring an interactive *Road Trip USA* exhibit.

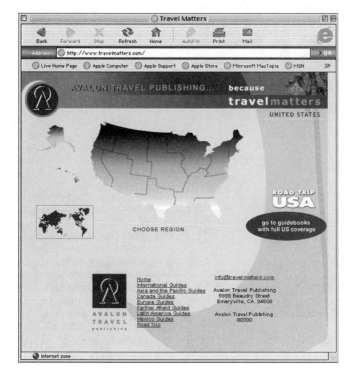

www.ricksteves.com

The Rick Steves web site is bursting with information to boost your travel I.Q. and liven up your European adventure. Including:
- The latest from Rick on what's hot in Europe
- Excerpts from Rick's books
- Rick's comprehensive Guide to European Railpasses

www.foghorn.com

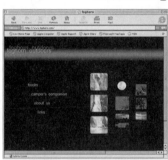

Foghorn Outdoors guides are the premier source for United States outdoor recreation information. Visit the Foghorn Outdoors web site for more information on these activity-based travel guides, including the complete text of the handy Foghorn Outdoors: Camper's Companion.

www.moon.com

Moon Handbooks' goal is to give travelers all the background and practical information they'll need for an extraordinary travel experience. Visit the Moon Handbooks web site for interesting information and practical advice, including Q&A with the author of The Practical Nomad, Edward Hasbrouck.

Rick Steves' Postcards from Europe
25 Years of Travel Tales from America's Favorite Guidebook Writer

1978

1998

TRAVEL GURU RICK STEVES has been exploring Europe through the Back Door for 25 years, sharing his tricks and discoveries in guidebooks and on TV. Now, in his autobiographical book, *Rick Steves' Postcards from Europe*, Rick shares stories—ranging from goofy to inspirational—of his favorite moments and his off-beat European friends.

Postcards takes you on the fantasy trip of a lifetime, and it gives you a close-up look at contemporary Europeans.

You'll meet Marie-Alice, the Parisian restaurateur who sniffs a whiff of moldy cheese and says, "It smells like zee feet of angels." In an Alpine village, meet Olle, the schoolteacher who lets Rick pet his edelweiss, and Walter, who schemes with Rick to create a fake Swiss tradition. In Italy, cruise with Piero through his "alternative Venice" and learn why all Venetian men are mama's boys.

Postcards also tracks Rick's passion for wandering—from his first "Europe-through-the-gutter" trips, through his rocky early tours, to his career as a travel writer and host of a public television series.

These 240 pages of travel tales are told in that funny, down-to-earth style that makes Rick his Mom's favorite guidebook writer.

AVALON TRAVEL publishing

Rick Steves' books are available at your local bookstore. To get Rick's free newsletter and learn more about Europe Through the Back Door call (425) 771-8303 or visit www.ricksteves.com.

For more information about Avalon Travel Publishing, visit www.travelmatters.com

FREE-SPIRITED TOURS FROM

Rick Steves

Great Guides

Big Buses

Small Groups

No Grumps

Best of Europe ■ Best of Europe II ■ Eastern Europe ■ Turkey ■ Italy ■ Britain Spain/Portugal ■ Ireland ■ Eastern France ■ Western France ■ Village France Scandinavia ■ Germany/Austria/Switzerland ■ London ■ Paris ■ Rome

Looking for a one, two, or three-week tour that's run in the Rick Steves style? Check out Rick Steves' educational, experiential tours of Europe. Rather than seeing Europe as a spectator from a bus window, you'll be encouraged to dive into daily life. You'll have opportunities to meet the locals, see how local transportation and services work, and get comfortable wandering off on your own. By the end of the tour, you'll have the knowledge and confidence it takes to travel through Europe independently—which is what many of our tour members do before they return home.

Rick Steves' tours include much more in the "sticker price" than mainstream tours. Here's what you'll get with a Europe or regional Rick Steves tour...

Group size: Your tour group will be no larger than 26. **Guides:** You'll have two guides traveling and dining with you on your fully guided Rick Steves tour. **Bus:** You'll travel in a full-size 48-to-52-seat bus, with plenty of empty seats for you to spread out and read, snooze, enjoy the passing scenery, get away from your spouse, or whatever. **Sightseeing:** Your tour price includes all group sightseeing. There are no hidden extra charges. **Hotels:** You'll stay in small, characteristic, locally-run hotels in the center of each city, within walking distance of the sights you came to see. **Price and insurance:** Your tour price is guaranteed for 2001. Single travelers do not pay an extra supplement (we have them room with other singles). ETBD includes prorated tour cancellation/ interruption protection coverage at no extra cost. **Tips and kickbacks:** All guide and driver tips are included in your tour price. Because your driver and guides are paid salaries by ETBD, they can focus on giving you the best European travel experience possible.

Interested? Call (425) 771-8303 or visit www.ricksteves.com for a free copy of Rick Steves' 2001 Tours booklet!

Rick Steves' Europe Through the Back Door

130 Fourth Avenue North, PO Box 2009, Edmonds, WA 98020 USA
Phone: (425) 771-8303 ■ Fax: (425) 771-0833 ■ www.ricksteves.com

FREE TRAVEL GOODIES FROM

Rick Steves

EUROPEAN TRAVEL NEWSLETTER

My *Europe Through the Back Door* travel company will help you travel better *because* you're on a budget—not in spite of it. To see how, ask for my 64-page *travel newsletter* packed full of savvy travel tips, readers' discoveries, and your best bets for railpasses, guidebooks, videos, travel accessories and free-spirited tours.

2001 GUIDE TO EUROPEAN RAILPASSES

With hundreds of railpasses to choose from in 2001, finding the right pass for your trip has never been more confusing. To cut through the complexity, ask for my 64-page *2001 Guide to European Railpasses*. Once you've narrowed down your choices, we give you unbeatable prices, including important extras with every Eurailpass, *free:* my hour-long "How to get the most out of your railpass" video; your choice of one of my 16 country guidebooks and phrasebooks; and written advice on your one-page trip itinerary.

RICK STEVES' 2001 TOURS

We offer 16 different one, two, and three-week tours (160 departures in 2001) for those who want to experience Europe in Rick Steves' Back Door style, but without the transportation and hotel hassles. If a tour with a small group, modest family-run hotels, lots of exercise, great guides, and no tips or hidden charges sounds like your idea of fun, ask for my 48-page 2001 Tours booklet.

YEAR-ROUND GUIDEBOOK UPDATES

Even though the information in my guidebooks is the freshest around, things do change in Europe between book printings. I've set aside a special section at my website (www.ricksteves.com/update) listing *up-to-the-minute changes* for every Rick Steves guidebook.

Call, fax, or visit www.ricksteves.com to get your...

☑ **FREE EUROPEAN TRAVEL NEWSLETTER**
☑ **FREE 2001 GUIDE TO EUROPEAN RAILPASSES**
☑ **FREE RICK STEVES' 2001 TOURS BOOKLET**

Rick Steves' Europe Through the Back Door
130 Fourth Avenue North, PO Box 2009, Edmonds, WA 98020 USA
Phone: (425) 771-8303 ■ Fax: (425) 771-0833 ■ www.ricksteves.com

Rick Steves' Phrase Books

Unlike other phrase books and dictionaries on the market, my well-tested phrases and key words cover every situation a traveler is likely to encounter. With these books you'll laugh with your cabby, disarm street thieves with insults, and charm new European friends.

Each book in the series is 4" x 6", with maps.

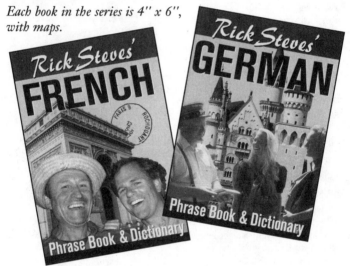

RICK STEVES' FRENCH PHRASE BOOK & DICTIONARY
U.S. $6.95/Canada $10.95

RICK STEVES' GERMAN PHRASE BOOK & DICTIONARY
U.S. $6.95/Canada $10.95

RICK STEVES' ITALIAN PHRASE BOOK & DICTIONARY
U.S. $6.95/Canada $10.95

RICK STEVES' SPANISH & PORTUGUESE PHRASE BOOK & DICTIONARY
U.S. $8.95/Canada $13.95

RICK STEVES' FRENCH, ITALIAN & GERMAN PHRASE BOOK & DICTIONARY
U.S. $8.95/Canada $13.95